THE
AUSTRALIAN
WILDLIFE
YEAR

THE AUSTRALIAN WILDLIFE YEAR

A month-by-month guide to nature

READER'S DIGEST   SYDNEY

FOREWORD

The Australian Wildlife Year is the most wide-ranging survey yet published of animal seasonality in this country. To be dogmatic about the exact timing of events in a land as climatically variable and dauntingly vast as Australia would be absurd. Decisions as to which wildlife events to feature in which months may sometimes appear arbitrary — but they were made on the basis of what seemed most typical. Some readers may therefore find the timing differs from their local experience. What else they come upon in these pages should more than compensate for that shortcoming.

The author makes no pretence to having originated all that is here. Life is probably too short for any one person to see everything we describe. Nor does David Underhill claim to have the technical training necessary to discover much that is hidden to the layman's eye. His observations complement the findings of countless professionally specialised zoologists and gifted amateur naturalists, past and present. In drawing together the diverse strands of their work, he has imparted a journalist's sense of immediacy and vigour without, we believe, diminishing the scientific value of their knowledge.

A seasonal approach was bound to focus attention on the interdependence of many kinds of animals and plants, and their subjection to the vagaries of weather and food availability. It places a less pleasant but unavoidable emphasis on conflict. Things kill things, usually in order to eat them. Interwoven in the fabric that unfolds month by month are patterns of savagery, suffering and waste. The annual cycles of nature are dances of death for many creatures. But there is also — or there should be — renewal.

People are part of the fabric of nature, while at the same time holding it in their hands. We are the only creatures capable of totally destroying it. No effort was made to labour the point, but time and again examples crop up of animals at risk from human actions. It is hoped that *The Australian Wildlife Year*, in helping to widen understanding of the creatures whose homeland we share, will stiffen public resolve to preserve them.

THE EDITORS

Text by David Underhill

Scientific consultants
Arthur Woods
The staff of the Australian Museum

Special feature consultant
Daniel Bickel

Commissioning editor Margaret Fraser
Project editor Richard Williams
Research editor Vere Dodds
Editorial assistants Kay Meades, Karen Wain
Project coordinator Robyn Hudson
Production controller Louise Mitchell

Designed and illustrated by Anita Rowney

FIRST EDITION
Published by Reader's Digest (Australia) Pty Limited
(Inc. in NSW)
26–32 Waterloo Street, Surry Hills, NSW 2010

Main cover photograph: *pelicans in Kakadu National Park*
Front inset: *western pygmy-possum*
Endpapers: *blue-tongued lizard tracks*
Half-title page: *koala climbing a eucalypt*
Title page: *eastern grey kangaroos*
Pages 4–5: *Martens' water monitor*

National Library of Australia cataloguing-in-publication data:

The Australian wildlife year.

   Includes index.
   ISBN 0 86438 071 2.

   1. Zoology – Australia. 2. Zoology – Australia
   – Pictorial works. 3. Botany – Australia.
   4. Botany – Australia – Pictorial works.
   I. Underhill, David, 1937–   . II. Reader's
   Digest Services.

574.994

CONTENTS

Storm clouds gather near Darwin and magpie geese head for breeding grounds.

Part One
THE SCIENCE of SEASONS

Warmth and moisture are the regulators of all natural life. In this country of so many climates, seasonal changes present animals with a fascinating diversity of habitats, opportunities and hardships

A place in the sun

Much of Australia receives over 3500 hours of sunshine a year, more than enough to earn its reputation as a sunburnt, arid country

Life anywhere on earth relies on energy from the sun, radiated across some 150 million kilometres of space. Solar energy is more than our source of warmth and light. It also generates air movement and drives the never-ending cycle of evaporation and precipitation that doles out moisture to sustain plants and animals. But as any Australian knows, the sharing is far from equal.

Latitude — distance from the Equator — is the first factor in climate. It governs the yearly ration of solar radiation that any area can receive. Just as importantly, in Australia's case, latitude determines a region's relationship to globe-girdling belts of atmospheric pressure.

Air must circulate between these bands, which lie more than 3000 kilometres apart. The movement sets up prevailing wind patterns. Some regions are fortunate to receive most of their winds off the oceans, laden with evaporated water. Others lie in the path of hot dry overland winds.

Global pressure belts also have direct climatic effects on the surfaces beneath them. Dry air, descending in a high-pressure zone and spreading out from it, creates conditions of maximum sunniness. Moist air rising from a low-pressure zone produces frequent cloud cover and rain.

Australia is aptly called a sunburnt country. The broadest part of the mainland lies for much of the year under the principal southern hemisphere belt of high pressure. From the midwestern shoulder of the continent to inland southern Queensland and New South Wales, the sun beats down for more than 3500 hours a year. It is the biggest land area in the world to receive such a baking.

These effects of geographical position are enough in themselves to make Australia the driest inhabited continent. Our situation is made worse by the lie of the land. Its average elevation is a mere 300 metres above sea level. There are only a few areas where flows of air are forced to great heights and cooled. So Australia overall is hotter than any other country at

Winter's gentle sunshine invigorates a jacky lizard Amphibolurus muricatus

Sunset over the Olgas brings relief after another blistering day in central Australia

comparable latitudes —and rates of evaporation are greater.

Worse still for our plants and animals, water vapour does not condense in air that is not cooled. Clouds and rain droplets do not form. Air masses can flow for thousands of kilometres across the continent without shedding moisture. Only where humid prevailing winds are blocked and pushed up by sharply rising land is there much chance of reliable rainfall.

Although the high-pressure influence is enormously wide-spread, Australia is vast enough to come under the influence of other systems to the north and south. And the belt itself is not permanently positioned. It wavers all the time and it shifts seasonally — though never with precise timing — to follow the sun. Centred around the Queensland-New South Wales border in late winter and spring, it spans Bass Strait by late summer.

Nor is the high-pressure belt continuous, as any national weather map shows. It consists of a chain of separate, mobile cells as much as 4000 kilometres wide. Air

at the centre of each of these 'highs' — more properly called anticyclones — is dry, warm and calm. Towards the anticyclone's edges, winds rotate gently in an anticlockwise direction.

The size and shape of anticyclones and their direction and rate of travel are dictated by interaction with neighbouring systems. Movement is generally eastward, the cells taking about five days to cross the continent. Only towards the end of that journey, when the winds on their leading edges swing out over the Tasman Sea and back, do they gain moisture and bring any hope of rain.

Unreliable and unpredictable rain

Troughs of lower pressure separate the anticyclones. These produce cool changes and cloud, but seldom much inland rain. Sometimes a cold front — the forward edge of a mass of much cooler air from the south — intrudes on an anticyclone. One or other body of air is forced up and the disturbance may generate a storm.

The high-pressure chain is bordered

and occasionally interrupted by a few 'lows', or depressions. These are tighter formations, rotating more strongly and in a clockwise direction. 'Lows' develop from clashes of contrasting air masses, or from extreme heating of local surfaces. They are dry if they form inland, but over or near the sea the air rushing into and rising from them is moist.

Physical laws demand the elimination of 'lows' by an equalising of pressure. But because of the opposite rotation of contrasting cells, there is no direct flow of air from high to low. Winds spin outwards from an anticyclone and are drawn into a depression, spiralling towards its centre with mounting strength.

Which way such winds blow over any particular place, and whether they bring rain, are influenced by land configuration but are largely matters of chance. Sites where storms yield rain or hail are just as unpredictable. So are the upperatmosphere disturbances that may interfere with surface air. These are factors of weather — not climate. They change from

---

A WORLD OF DIFFERENCE

If the earth were spinning on a vertical axis in its orbit around the sun, we would have no seasons. Days of heating and nights of cooling would be of equal length throughout the year, in every place, and the level of solar radiation would remain constant, depending only on latitude

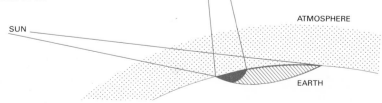

Summer in Northern Hemisphere

SUN

Winter in Southern Hemisphere

Winter in Northern Hemisphere

Summer in Southern Hemisphere

To an astronomer, midsummer and midwinter occur when the sun is directly over one of the tropics. These occasions, called solstices, are around 22 December and 22 June. Mid-spring and mid-autumn — called equinoxes because day and night are of equal duration — fall around 22 September and 21 March. It could be argued that a season must start six weeks before its mid-point. But there is a delay in the effects of varying sunlight, mainly because the oceans are slow to respond. That is why it is conventional in Australia to regard spring as starting on 1 September, summer on 1 December and so on

But our planet is tilted, so it presents more of its northern half to the sun for half of the year, and more of the southern half for the rest of the time. Days are longer than nights, and radiation is increased, during the months in which one or other hemisphere is favoured.

Seasonal contrasts in daylight hours and heating are negligible at the Equator and greatest at the poles. Australia's span of latitude makes the differences plainly noticeable. Cape York has eleven and a half hours of light a day in midwinter and about twelve and three-quarters in midsummer. Southern Tasmania's range at the same time is about nine to fifteen and a half hours.

In theory — disregarding the screening effect of clouds — the sun's rays are strongest where they are most concentrated and where they have the shortest distance to travel through the atmosphere. In other words, radiation is greatest when the sun is directly overhead.

Sunlight beams down vertically at varying latitudes through the year — but only between the lines of the tropics. Their latitude, at 23°27′, matches the earth's angle of tilting. Places outside the tropics must always receive their light more or less obliquely. So while all regions record the same annual total of daylight hours, those farthest from the Equator are the least exposed to radiation.

But general patterns of cloudiness cannot be ignored. Cloud is frequent in a wide band around the Equator because moist, heated air is rising. In practice the areas of greatest insolation — the strength of radiation actually reaching the surface over a whole year — lie just outside the tropics at about 30°. And Australia at that latitude is more than 3500 kilometres wide.

SUN

Radiation is strongest when the sun is highest in the sky. If the rays come obliquely their energy is dispersed over a wider area of ground. And they have farther to travel through the atmosphere, where some of the energy is absorbed by cloud, dust and gases

SUN

ATMOSPHERE

EARTH

PATTERNS OF SEASONAL RAINFALL

Darwin
MONSOON

Broome

TROPICAL WITH PREVAILING SUMMER RAINS

Townsville

ARID

Carnarvon

Brisbane

SUBTROPICAL

PREVAILING
SUMMER RAINS
(over 35% of
annual total)

WITH
Kalgoorlie

Perth
DRY SUMMER

Canberra
Sydney

Adelaide

Melbourne

WINTER
RAINS

UNIFORM RAINS

Hobart

HOT WEATHER RAINFALL

CUMULUS
CUMULONIMBUS

condensation level

rising hot air   thunder showers

heated   land surface

Cumulonimbus, dark at its base and plumed above. Thunder and lightning are associated with this kind of cloud, and also moderate to heavy rain

HOW THE AIR IS HEATED

Sunshine imparts very little warmth to the air through which it passes. Instead it heats the surfaces that it strikes. Soon they discharge some of the heat, warming the air in contact with them

Heated air rises and has to be replaced by incoming cooler air, which in turn takes warmth from the ground. A cycle of convective heating is set up, raising the general temperature of the bottommost layer of the atmosphere. Winds hasten the process.

How much of this type of heating occurs in any particular place depends not only on the local strength of solar radiation but also on the nature of the surface. Part of the sun's energy is always reflected back into space, without producing any warmth.

Proportions of reflected radiation vary widely, from about four per cent off oceans when the sun is overhead, to fifteen per cent off eucalypt forests, thirty per cent off deserts and up to ninety-five per cent off snow and ice. (Snow appears dazzling white to our eyes because most of the solar energy is returning to space, still in the form of light.)

Fluffy cumulus clouds, drifting across the sky in fine weather, let through more than seventy per cent of the sun's energy. But dark, high-piling cumulonimbus can cut out all but ten per cent. Clouds have an average reflectivity of about forty-five per cent.

The impact of ground heating is shallow. Fluctuations between the peaks of daytime heating and nighttime cooling penetrate to only about fifty centimetres below the surface — a fact of great importance to burrowing animals in extreme climates. More gradual seasonal fluctuations reach to depths of about ten metres.

Ground surface temperatures vary between afternoon and dawn by five to fifteen degrees Celsius in most places, but by as much as thirty degrees under clear skies at high altitude. Bodies of water show much less change because the heat travels easily to greater depths and may be carried away in currents. Daily surface temperatures on a lake seldom vary by more than three degrees. On an ocean, the daily range is less than one degree.

Apart from the sun's effects, the lower atmosphere is warmed to a less important extent by outward transmission of the earth's own heat. While shortwave solar radiation enters and escapes fairly freely, longwave terrestrial radiation is mostly trapped by water vapour, carbon dioxide and some other gas particles. These emit the energy in all directions – some of it back to earth.

The greenhouse effect, as it is called, is increased by low-based cloud cover. That is why equatorial regions, though they are often screened by clouds and deprived of much of their share of solar radiation, maintain sweltering temperatures.

HOW LAND ABSORBS SOLAR RADIATION

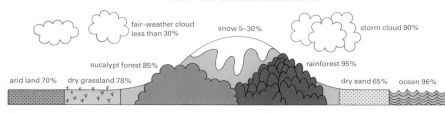

fair-weather cloud less than 30%

snow 5–30%

storm cloud 90%

eucalypt forest 85%

rainforest 95%

arid land 70%   dry grassland 78%

dry sand 65%   ocean 96%

Water, damp soil and dense vegetation have the highest rates of radiation absorption, reflecting little of the sun's energy back into space. They have the most heat to discharge into the air, with the greatest chance of clouds forming above them. Moist or dry conditions tend to be self-perpetuating — though local winds and clashes of weather systems can upset the pattern

summer monsoon and rare before October or after March. But along the south coast, summers are generally dry. Most rain comes with the winter westerly flow and the southwesterly storms that are generated by its depressions. Falls are most lavish where there are scarps and mountain ranges — from Perth to Albany in the southwest, near Adelaide, and from the South Australia-Victoria border to the southeastern highlands.

Sunbaked western and central regions experience seasonal changes in general wind direction. But the air masses flowing over them are usually dry and simply become hotter, whatever the time of year. Lifesaving rain, occurring in unpredictable localities, derives from the rare intrusion of storms. In the northern sector of the arid zone these may come between December and March, as an aftermath of decaying tropical cyclones. Farther south the greatest hope of rain rests in the arrival of cold fronts in May or June.

Hottest and coldest months

Summer-winter contrasts in temperature are slight in the tropical zone and seldom drastic even in the far south, because of the modifying effects of the surrounding oceans. Although frigid polar air penetrates in winter, few areas are high enough to suffer prolonged freeze-ups. Snow lies for significant periods only above 1500 metres in the southeast and 1200 metres in Tasmania.

A sharper demand on animals is made by day-and-night contrasts in higher parts of the arid inland. Without a blanketing of clouds there is strong heating by day, even in winter, and an unlimited escape of heat at night. Alice Springs, at 550 metres above sea level, records more frosts than any southern capital except Canberra.

Cumulus over Bald Rock, Queensland

---

day to day and year to year, adding to the uncertainties of animal survival across most of middle Australia.

To the north of the pressurised belt is a wide band in which winds blow most often from the southeast, off the Pacific. Reliably helpful to sailing ships, they were called trade winds. To the south, in the 'Roaring Forties', air flows strongly from the west, off the Southern Ocean. Both systems bring rain where they are met near coasts by elevated land.

Beyond the bands of prevailing winds are belts where global atmospheric pressure is generally lowest. One, sometimes called the equatorial trough or weather equator, is centred well to the north of the geographical Equator for most of the year. But it curves across the line during our summer, settling over the far north.

Inland, on the southern side of the trough, there is normally no relief from fierce summer heat and aridity. The trough merges with a chain of dry, hot 'thermal lows' that is virtually permanent in the region. But on the northern side a flow of saturated air — the monsoon — is drawn towards the trough. Its penetration is shallow and intermittent, but storms are frequent around northern coasts. And each summer a few depressions, forming over heated waters, become tropical cyclones that may carry rain far inland.

Another low-pressure belt girdles the sub-Antarctic at an average latitude of about 60°S. It injects a series of depressions into the westerly air-flow much closer to Australia. Shifting north in winter, these depressions dominate the climate of Tasmania and the southern mainland. They bring chilling air and a high likelihood of storms.

As the sun pulls the pressure belts to and fro, it is what happens to rainfall patterns that has the most significant impact on Australian wildlife. Animals responding to rising warmth in spring will fare poorly unless there is also ample soil moisture. Whatever they eat, plants are the basis of their food chain.

Of the wetter parts of Australia, only the eastern seaboard and Tasmania enjoy anything like a uniform distribution of rainfall throughout the year. Western Tasmania's is the most consistent, because elevated land is always in or near the path of the Southern Ocean's westerly airflow and the depressions that ride in it.

In summer the mainland east coast receives moist southeasterly prevailing winds as far north as Cape York and as far south as Cape Howe. The upthrust of the Great Dividing Range ensures that rain is extracted from these, and from other variable winds at any time. Average readings are markedly higher in summer in the northeast, however, and slightly greater in winter in the southeast.

Elsewhere, rainfall is strongly seasonal. In the far north it is copious during the

July is the coldest month all over Australia. But the times of greatest average heat, under the influence of air-flow patterns, cloud cover, offshore currents and altitude, differ bewilderingly. It is a measure of the country's vastness and its complexity of climates that 'high summer' in this sense can arrive months later in one region than in another.

Along the far northern coast, including the western side of Cape York Peninsula, the hottest month is November — before the heavy buildup of cloud that heralds the monsoon. After that, sunshine in Darwin dwindles from a spring average of nine hours a day to a summer average of little more than five.

Away from the coast over most of the northern half of the mainland, December is hottest. But on the northwest coast, early summer heating is tempered by an upwelling of cool waters in spring. A spread of very warm waters towards the end of summer brings maximum heat in March. And Darwin, lapped by similar waters under clearing autumn skies, experiences a second peak of heat a month later, in April.

All of eastern coastal Queensland and most of the subtropical mainland are hottest in January — or perhaps February

Snow and ice feed the Meander River in northern Tasmania. Nearby are the only Australian landscapes that were shaped by glaciers

in mountainous country. Nearly all along the west coast, even into the tropics at Northwest Cape, the peak of heating is delayed until February by a cool northward surface flow on the Indian Ocean.

Southern coastal areas and low-lying regions of Tasmania are also warmest in February. The alpine region of the southeastern mainland and Tasmania's highlands often do not record their greatest average temperatures until March, five months after the far north. □

Christmas tidings from El Niño

Every Christmas, Peruvian fishermen witness a strange event. Off their coast, a powerful northward current of cold water is reversed. Warm equatorial water flows south for a time. They call the phenomenon El Niño — Spanish for the Little One. It is their term for the infant Christ.

In most years El Niño causes a brief upset to local fishing — nothing more. But now and again the heating is greater, more extensive and more prolonged. A low-pressure zone is established,

The non-arrival of long-awaited rains, year after year, turns farm soils to dust. Early warning of major Australian droughts may come from events in South America

bringing heavy rain to perennially parched coasts. And for Australia, that probably means bad news.

Meteorologists recognise — though they cannot fully explain — a periodic see-sawing of atmospheric pressure across the Pacific, just south of the Equator. For most of the time pressure is low over Indonesia and high off Peru. Winds blow westward between the two, driving a strong ocean current that grows steadily warmer. But occasionally the pressure imbalance is switched.

If that occurs during our summer, trade wind patterns are disrupted and the far north is deprived of its blanketing of cloud and its rain-bearing monsoon. More subtle effects modify weather over most of the country. If the pressure change persists, we are soon in the grip of widespread drought.

A useful early warning signal
Scientists investigating the so-called Southern Oscillation, and its possible relationship to global weather patterns, realised only recently the significance of El Niño events. They represent a reversal of part of the equatorial current, accompanying a fluctuation in pressure. And in their years of greatest strength, they have coincided with major climatic disturbances all over the world.

Now we know that a welcome, rain-sodden Christmas in coastal Peru may well be the first signal of trouble to come in other regions. Hopes are rising that Australia could receive early warnings of its most severe droughts. The advantages to agricultural, economic and nature conservation planning would be colossal. □

Sea surface temperatures change hardly at all between day and night, and seldom more than ten degrees between summer and winter in any one place. Consequently the exchange of air between land and sea has a moderating influence, not only on coasts but also for considerable distances inland. Daily and seasonal temperature ranges are reduced.

The southern hemisphere has a water area one-third greater than that of the northern hemisphere. So the tempering effect is more pronounced. No region in our hemisphere experiences annual extremes as wide as those suffered in Europe, Asia or North America. Southern plants and animals have a much easier time — as long as moisture is adequate.

How much moisture is actually gained from the oceans in the form of rain depends on many factors of wind direction, land conformation and local weather. But it is fundamentally related to the surface temperature of the water and its rate of evaporation.

All of the populated continents have warm currents flowing away from the Equator along their eastern coasts, and colder water travelling in the other direction on their western side. In Africa and South America the difference is reflected in a drastic imbalance of rainfall, with the eastern side favoured over the west.

That contrast is also evident in Australia, but it is softened to some extent by the seasonal change of wind patterns. While the Indian Ocean shifts enormous masses of cold water northward along the coast of Western Australia all year round, its nearshore surface currents consist of warmer water, forced from the Timor Sea

Upwellings of cool water promote the flowering of marine algae (right), creating the 'red tide' seen below

Solace from the sea

Oceans are climatic equalisers — the world's great air conditioners. Absorbing the sun's energy into their depths, they circulate in vast gyrations that carry equatorial heat towards the poles and bring colder water back to the tropics

in winter and from the Bight in summer. In fact the surface flow reverses its direction twice a year.

Northern waters, buffered by big islands, take little part in oceanic circulation. They too have a reversing flow — eastward in summer when they are pushed by monsoon winds, and westward for the rest of the year. These waters are always warm and sometimes, particularly where they are shallow, very hot.

Southern Ocean movement is constantly eastward, but surface currents are variable. They are generally cold except in late summer. It is the injection of fronts

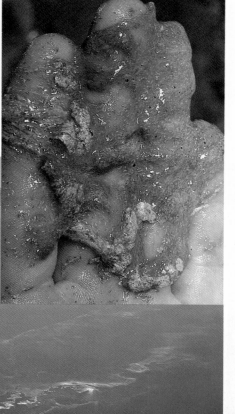

Sea birds enjoy their richest feasts of fish at the boundaries between bodies of water of different temperature. Concentrations of nutrient chemicals are highest along such borders, encouraging the growth of tiny organisms that start the marine food chain

and depressions into the region's westerly air-flow, rather than much evaporation from the sea, that brings rain in the south.

Ocean temperature variations of the greatest significance occur off the east coast. The so-called East Australian Current — really a series of huge eddies — loops southward through the Coral Sea and then east towards New Zealand. In summer, warm water and some of the creatures that belong in it, such as tropical fish in their larval stages, are carried as far south as Tasmania, driven by northern monsoon winds and cyclones.

These eddying currents are slow to mix with neighbouring masses of water. In mid-latitudes, between central Queensland and central New South Wales, they are often as much as three degrees warmer. Their impact on coastal climates and the distribution of marine life is substantial, even though sometimes they are a mere thirty kilometres wide, and their positions are changeable.

When warm currents turn away from a coast, or warm surface waters are forced offshore by winds, cold water wells up to take their place. Upwellings can occur anywhere, but they happen on their grandest scale off the northwest coast in early spring and off the central east coast between July and December.

In major upwellings, nitrates and phosphates brought from the sea bed foster an explosion of organic growth on or near the surface. The sea turns greenish with a profusion of microscopic plants — or even red with the blooming of algae — and marine animals of all kinds thrive on a sudden abundance of food. □

Where aridity is a normal condition, many kinds of animals have been able to adapt. Life can be far more harsh in regions where average rainfall seems, on paper, to be moderately generous. Over the good years there is ample food and shelter in open forests and woodlands. But for long periods, the rains fail.

Australia's climate is notoriously fickle. One district's average of, say, 500 mm of rainfall a year may be made up of readings higher than 800 mm and lower than 200 mm. In a huge part of Queensland, 250 000 square kilometres in area, 1950 was the wettest year on record. It was immediately followed by the driest year on record. Unseasonal droughts are common and widespread anywhere outside the rainforest belt of the east.

The hunger and thirst that such droughts inflict are dangerous enough to wildlife populations. All too often, in wooded country, they lead to something worse. Lack of moisture halts the rotting of tree litter. Dry leaves, discarded bark and fallen branches pile up into organic time bombs. Given a spark — a lightning strike, if not some act of human carelessness — bushfires will rage. The effects on animals are calamitous.

Fire has been a fact of life and death in much of Australia for so long that whole families of trees and shrubs have evolved to cope with it. Thickened bark protects their trunks. Their seeds are enclosed not in soft fruits but in woody, flame-resistant cases. Latent buds, in trunks or underground tubers, enable damaged trees to recover quickly.

Some plants have even adapted to exploit fire, so that they can take advantage of a sudden increase in soil nutrients. Grasstrees do not flower unless their leaves are burnt. The seed cases of eucalypts, banksias, acacias and hakeas are

The tyranny of fire

Many of our plants, including eucalypts, have adapted to fire; some actually require burning to regenerate. But to most animals, fire is a disaster even worse than drought

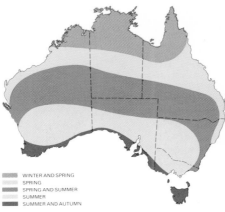

WINTER AND SPRING
SPRING
SPRING AND SUMMER
SUMMER
SUMMER AND AUTUMN

TIMETABLE OF TERROR
In eucalypt-dominated woodlands, bushfire outbreaks are related to lack of rainfall. This chart shows the areas of most frequent bushfire occurrence moving south with the seasons

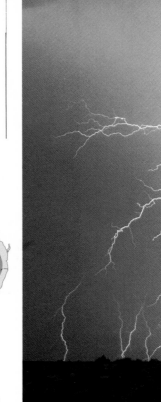

stimulated to open by their sharp loss of moisture during a fire. Forest eucalypts *need* burning, at least once in their seed-bearing lives, to set up the conditions for their reproduction.

Eucalypt seedlings cannot thrive without strong sunlight. Overshadowed in

dense undergrowth, they are attacked by fungi. So the seed capsules are held where they form, high in the trees. They accumulate year after year unless they are brought down in storms.

When fire comes at last, destruction of the leaf canopy causes a shower of capsules. They spring open and the seeds germinate in warm ash, holding nearly all the nutrients that were in the burnt material. Seedlings shoot up and the successful saplings grow with amazing speed, some gaining five metres in a year. No rival tree families have a chance of taking over from burnt eucalypts.

To carry flames from the ground litter to their leafy canopies, the eucalypts proffer strips of peeling bark that act like fuses. And their leaves contain oils that evaporate in hot weather, producing highly inflammable gases. In a fire, even if it is not forced by winds, flames leap explosively from treetop to treetop.

A fast-travelling fire, burning at ground canopy levels but starved of oxygen in between, is just what the trees want. The flames quickly exhaust their fuel and move on, with little time for heartwood destruction. But the very pace of such ideal fires makes them disastrous for wildlife.

Banksias are among many native plants needing fire to open their seed cases

Lightning is the main natural cause of bushfires. Peeling bark makes fuses to carry flames from ignited forest litter up to the tree canopies

Kites swoop on insects forced aloft by the updraft from a bushfire (below)

Dingoes, emus, many marsupials and the bigger goannas are capable of running out of a bushfire's path if they chance on the right direction. Most are killed. Koalas, possums and other climbers scramble higher, to meet almost certain death from asphyxiation or burning. Tree and surface-dwelling reptiles, insects and spiders are wiped out, along with stupefied bats, birds, nestlings and eggs.

Birds can beat the flames
Birds capable of strong and sustained flight — provided they can overcome the torpor induced by heat and smoke — have the best chance of surviving. Some birds are even attracted to bushfires. The migratory fork-tailed swift, for example, heads straight for any smoke columns that it sees. Feasts of helpless flying insects await it in hot updrafts of air.

Burrowing animals such as wombats, lizards, nursing echidnas, ants and insect larvae are likely to live through a blaze. So are small mammals and snakes that in hot weather spend most of their days resting under rocks or in ground crevices. But any survivor that cannot travel far, and relies on surface feeding, may be doomed to die from starvation.

Damaged trees can recover very

quickly after a fire. The undergrowth on which many animals rely may be slower to reappear. Heavy rains may wash away the fertile layer of ash and cause soil erosion. Even if the relieving moisture arrives more gently, the character of the ground cover will be different at first.

One nutrient element, nitrogen, is lost in fires. It turns into a gas and literally goes up in smoke. So the first of the smaller plants to prosper are peas and other legumes that can 'fix' nitrogen. The job is done by bacteria living in their roots. They take nitrogen from the air and convert it into a form that the plants can use, then pass into the soil when they die.

If a full range of animals has been spared in damp gullies or other untouched patches, a burnt area will be recolonised fairly soon. But because of changes in the suitability of food and sheltering places, there is always a change in the makeup of the population. Different animals come into prominence. Among mammals and reptiles, the most mobile predators and scavengers fare best at first. Some insect populations explode, taking advantage of tender new plant growth and the absence of many birds.

Later the seed-eaters, including small marsupials and native and introduced rodents as well as birds, will become

A BOOM TIME FOR BUSH MICE

In the aftermath of bushfires, native-mice thrive on young regrowth

Most of our mice are rarely-seen burrowers that forage at night among mature vegetation. Normally they struggle on patchy diets, often showing low rates of breeding fertility. But one to three years after heath or woodland fires, the little creatures come into their own.

They feast from the various podbearing legumes that dominate burnt areas in the early stages of regeneration, gaining a rich and sometimes year-round supply of seeds. Females of species that normally have a short season become continuous breeders, producing litter after litter. The population in one area increased sixfold within eighteen months of a fire.

Later, as regeneration progresses and other plants and animals take over, the mice fall once more on hard times. Populations scatter and dwindle — until a new area of regrowth is discovered and invaded. To these little-known animals, the greatest threat to continued existence is successful fire prevention.

Eastern chestnut mouse Pseudomys gracilicaudatus   *Darling pea* Swainsonia

Flowering spikes of grass trees appear only after the plants have been burnt. Other natives (right) regenerate from latent buds

dominant. Meanwhile the visits of grazing and browsing marsupials, nibbling persistently at the returning growth, may thin out the forest edges. Shrubby understoreys may be replaced by heaths and grasses. It could be years before old balances are restored — if ever.

Wildlife pays the price

Some bushfires are inevitable. In the national parks, nature reserves and state forests of the southeast alone, about 1500 break out each year. In normal seasons about four per cent of the forested area is burnt. More extensive destruction coincides with prolonged droughts.

Forests are capable of virtually complete regeneration. But immense suffering is visited on wildlife — including some animals whose future is doubtful at the best of times because forest clearances have reduced and broken up their habitats. Controlled burn-offs, when humidity is high and temperatures are low, can forestall some of the worst disasters. But even a managed fire has to take its toll.

Beyond giving support to enlightened wildlife conservation measures and the most effective firefighting methods — which are enormously costly — the public can do little for animals in dry bushland. Nature will have its way, with relentless force. At the very least, though, we can ensure that no action of our own ever causes an unnecessary fire. □

When the time is right

Animals cannot assess the best time of year — let alone predict the availability of food and shelter. The physical changes that ready them for mating and breeding are the result of hormonal activity. It is triggered automatically, by natural stimuli that vary according to the needs of different creatures.

By evolutionary processes of natural selection, the species that do best are those whose biological triggers are fired at the most opportune times. Luck may not come their way every year. Famines cause breeding failures and sharp slumps in population. But while suitable habitats remain, the system works often enough or widely enough to secure the general survival of the species.

In Australia the conditions of climate and food availability vary markedly between the wet tropical zone, the arid regions and the fertile temperate areas. In terms of their seasonal breeding responses, Australian animals live in three different countries.

In the parts of the tropical north that are drenched in summer but have a long dry season, fluctuations in humidity provide the main stimuli. The 'Top End' is often said to have only the two seasons. But its animals react with much greater subtlety, each kind finding its own time

Personal survival is only a secondary goal in the existence of wild animals. Reproduction takes priority. So the most important seasonal responses are those that are geared to breeding. The drive to mate must come in advance of the greatest abundance of food to nourish the next generation

during a year that can be divided into at least six breeding seasons.

Not every tropical animal is programmed to exploit the profusion of growth that comes with the Wet. Birds of prey, for example, breed late in the Dry when grasses are parched and shrivelled. Then the small mammals and reptiles that they hunt are easiest to see on the ground.

Throughout the continent's vast arid zone, the breeding stimulus is rain — either through its direct wetting effect or by an increase in soil moisture. Because

A spring breeder, the banded lapwing Vanellus tricolor *will nest again in autumn in response to summer rains*

animals must quickly take advantage of a flush of food that will probably be brief, the response is often dramatic. Zebra finches, permanently mated, may start building nests the day after a storm.

The triggering systems take some convincing, however. Fleeting showers, insufficient to promote plant growth, provoke no animal response. In higher parts of the arid zone that are subject to frosts, plant and animal reactions to winter rains may be suppressed by low temperatures.

To the millions of nomadic ducks and other waterfowl roaming inland Australia, even heavy and prolonged rains are no use unless the water collects and remains in suitable places. They need swamp plants as food and shelter for weeks to come, and a full development of insect populations to supplement their diets. So these birds are not stimulated directly by rainfall, but by the sensation of water rising around them as they stand in chosen places.

Outside the tropics, in regions of moderate to liberal rainfall, the seasons are distinguished and plant growth is influenced by rising or falling average temperatures. But the vagaries of local weather defy average trends. A sunny spell in June can be warmer than any day in August.

Such aberrations do not matter to life in rivers, deep lakes or the sea. Water temperatures are slow to change, and their reaching a certain point is a stimulus for aquatic and marine animals to breed.

For creatures at home in or on the ground or in trees, however, a reliance on temperature alone could be disastrous.

As long as plagues of mice or insects last, the Australian kestrel Falco cenchroides *raises brood after brood of chicks*

19

WAITING FOR THE LONGEST DAY

Female tammar wallabies on Kangaroo Island, South Australia, show an unusually keen sensitivity to the time of year. Like many other bigger marsupials in arid or drought-prone regions, they have delayed pregnancies. Embryos remain undeveloped while a previous joey is still suckling.

Joeys normally leave their pouches in spring. But in some older tammars, and in all the young females that have mated for the first time, the quiescence of new embryos continues until midsummer. Just after 22 December — as soon as days start to shorten — all the embryos are activated. A flurry of births comes about twenty-five days later.

Tammar wallabies are also remarkable for their ability to survive on plants that contain very little moisture or are salty, such as the succulents that thrive on islands off southern and southwestern coasts

Locust plagues are caused by synchronised

Most such animals are equipped to make an unconscious judgment of the time of year — by seeing the light. Their brains register a comparison of the hours of daylight and darkness. When the ratio best suits the species, hormonal secretions activate sexual developments and breeding instincts are aroused.

Photoperiodicity, as this response to day lengths is called, has been demonstrated in many kinds of animals. It awakes larval insects from winter dormancy — even those that are encased in thick cocoons. It triggers the growth of the distinctively coloured breeding plumage that helps many birds to attract mates, as well as the regular moults that birds undergo at other times of the year.

Some northern hemisphere mammals, whose dark coats go snowy white in winter to deceive predators, are responding entirely to light — not temperature. A snowshoe hare, kept in a heated laboratory but exposed to only nine hours of light a day, stayed white all year long.

Secretions that regularly allow snakes to slough off worn skins may be activated

To save energy the paucident planigale Planigale gilesi *lapses into torpor*

Seasons in the Top End

Southerners speak of only two seasons in the Top End, the Wet (October to April) and the Dry (May to September). Locals refer also to a buildup (to the Wet) from October to December, and a build-down in April. Northern Aboriginals recognise many more changes and have named at least six periods for the weather that can be expected and for the plant and animal responses

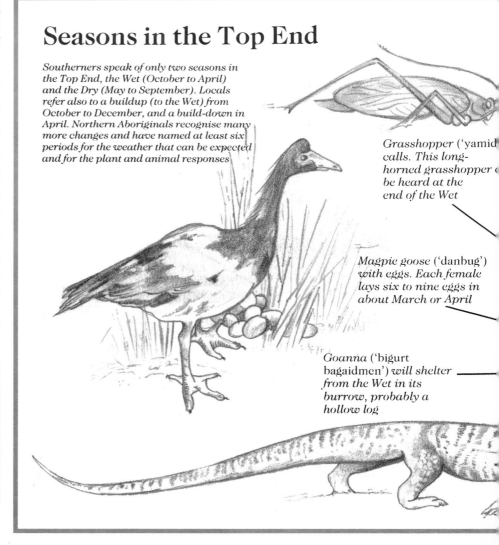

Grasshopper ('yamid calls. This long-horned grasshopper be heard at the end of the Wet*

Magpie goose ('danbug') with eggs. Each female lays six to nine eggs in about March or April

Goanna ('bigurt bagaidmen') will shelter from the Wet in its burrow, probably a hollow log

hatching and forced migration

by periodicity. The darkening of winter-time skins, to absorb more heat, is almost certainly induced by dwindling daylight rather than falling temperatures. Long-living domestic cockroaches, though they may lurk in houses where constant temperatures are maintained, go darker as their night-time forays grow longer.

Precise photoperiodicity helps some species that are out of their element and most vulnerable when they are breeding — seals, for example, and many sea birds. They can synchronise their breeding and practise communal care of the young. A similarly shared sense of timing seems to govern the flocking of migratory birds.

On the whole, exactness in the time of breeding is not as important in temperate Australia as it is in corresponding latitudes of the northern hemisphere.

The plants themselves are of very different character. Ours have generally longer and more varied flowering and fruiting seasons. The predominance of evergreen trees evens out the seasonal highs and lows of soil and river fertility. Because we have no pronounced peak of leafdropping in autumn, there is less emphasis on a surge of organic nutrients in spring. As a consequence of all this, breeding seasons for similar kinds of animals are longer and less rigid in Australia.

Food abundance in itself is not a stimulus to animal breeding, except in those microscopic forms that start the food chain. But good feeding improves the breeding performance of higher animals. In some species a continued supply will prolong the breeding season indefinitely.

When breeding is not the motive

Apart from the annual migrations that many birds undertake, seasonal gluts and shortages of food often dictate major changes in the distribution of other highly mobile animals. Partial or total nomadism is common among some marsupials, and among birds that do not migrate. Snakes converge on seasonal waterways and swamps to feast on frogs. Many insects — most notoriously the voracious grasshoppers that we call plague locusts — travel vast distances.

Extremes of heat and cold force some animals to change their habitats or alter their behaviour. Many birds that are fairly sedentary move some distance north in winter. In the southeast, among highland species, the movement may be simply to lower ground.

Migratory fishes and marine mammals follow currents with temperatures to their liking. Other fishes and mobile marine creatures may stay more or less in the one spot, but move vertically to seek warmer or cooler water.

Land mammals, predominantly night or dusk-and-dawn feeders for most of the year, frequently come out by day in winter. Hunger may embolden some of them to invade urban areas. Snakes, mostly nocturnal hunters in the warmer months, take to feeding by day and basking in sunshine.

The true dormancy of hibernation is very rare among Australian animals. But many, including bats, snakes, lizards and the smallest marsupials, find secure shelters and lapse into a winter torpor. They eat little or nothing and save energy by lowering their rates of metabolism. Meanwhile countless insects in their larval stages wait out the winter in a quiescent state of arrested development.

Aestivation — a similar phase of inactivity at the height of summer — is common among animals that cannot retreat to higher altitudes and would be in danger of overheating or desiccation. Snakes are especially vulnerable, because excessive heat alters their body chemistry. They have to hide in deep crevices or the burrows of other animals. □

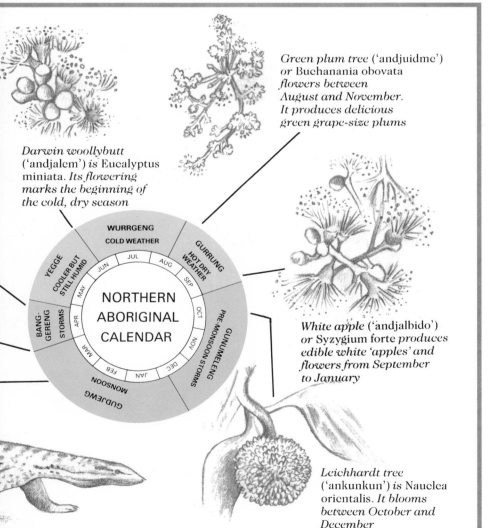

Green plum tree ('andjuidme') *or* Buchanania obovata *flowers between August and November. It produces delicious green grape-size plums*

Darwin woollybutt ('andjalem') *is* Eucalyptus miniata. *Its flowering marks the beginning of the cold, dry season*

NORTHERN ABORIGINAL CALENDAR

WURRGENG
COLD WEATHER

YEGGE
COOLER BUT STILL HUMID

GURRUNG
HOT DRY WEATHER

BANG-GERENG
STORMS

GUNUMELENG
PRE-MONSOON STORMS

GUDJEWG
MONSOON

JUN JUL AUG SEP OCT NOV DEC JAN FEB MAR APR MAY

White apple ('andjalbido') *or* Syzygium forte *produces edible white 'apples' and flowers from September to January*

Leichhardt tree ('ankunkun') *is* Nauclea orientalis. *It blooms between October and December*

Part Two
ANIMAL OPPORTUNISTS

Seasons count for little in the arid zone where haphazard rains trigger exuberant but short-lived plant growth and wildlife population explosions. Mastery over this harsh environment is gained through adaptation to a waiting game

Nomadic flock bronzewings Phaps histrionica *discover a field of seeding grasses*

Cycles of boom and bust

In arid regions, both native and exotic mammals flourish and falter, not according to time of year, but in response to erratic weather conditions

Rats in millions ... from the air they look like a tide washing across outback plains, tingeing the red or black soils a silvery grey. On the ground they form a squabbling, squealing army, extending to every horizon and advancing at speeds of up to twenty kilometres a day.

The weather has been freakishly kind in their arid home district. Good rains have fallen, perhaps three years in succession. Native long-haired rats — the most explosive breeders of all Australian mammals — have responded to an unaccustomed abundance of nourishing plants. Where once there may have been a few hundred rats, their numbers have multiplied many thousandfold. Now, having eaten themselves out of their domicile, they are on the move.

Not even rivers stop them as they spread in search of fresh grass seed. And nothing else that is edible is spared their ravenous attentions. The ground is bared of fresh plant cover — even roots are destroyed.

Farm outbuildings are raided and fodder stocks gobbled up. The hooves of sleeping livestock are gnawed and their feet left bleeding. Flimsy flywire screens are torn apart, allowing the rats access to household foodstuffs and then fabrics, paper, shoes — even soap.

Thousands of the invaders may be shot — a waste of ammunition, for all the difference it makes. The ordeal of people living on the fringes of the arid zone may last for weeks as the rats pass through in waves, each generation hungrier than the one before. If the travelling armies reach good grazing country, their descendants

Plains rat Pseudomys australis

can keep on going for years.

More often, fortunately, the hordes are overtaken by a return of drought and high evaporation. Food and water quickly run out. Turning on one another, many rats die from cannibalism or the stress of fighting. Most others starve to death.

Close to scanty water supplies, tiny

numbers survive to found new colonies. They resume a sedentary existence of burrowing and nocturnal foraging. In all likelihood they will live and die without being seen by humans again.

The stripping and uprooting of vegetation during rat plagues is disastrous for competing animals, such as the grazing and browsing marsupials. Predators, on the other hand, enjoy a bonanza. Inland kites and owls, dingoes, feral cats and big snakes all increase their populations.

Plagues at about ten-year intervals

Burke and Wills, exploring the Channel Country in 1860, were the first Europeans to report an onslaught by migrating rats. Reaching Cooper Creek after a desert trek of more than three weeks, they lost much of their gear on the first night and were forced to shift their camp.

Major plagues have since been recorded at highly irregular intervals, averaging about ten years. The most economically destructive have been in far western Queensland. In one of the more recent plagues, lasting for three years from 1966, a bush pilot reported rats moving southwest across the Birdsville Track stock route. By his estimate, the swarm was 240 kilometres long and eighty kilometres wide.

The long-haired *Rattus villosissimus* is one of several 'new endemic' rodent species that came to Australia from the north within the last million years. Its range is vast — from the Kimberley in Western Australia to northwestern New South Wales. But it has not evolved as a true arid-lands specialist. Though its reproductive capacity is astonishing, it cannot live without some water to drink. That is why its populations go through cycles of spectacular boom and bust.

To the south the smaller plains rat *Pseudomys australis* provides an interesting contrast. Its home range is the most barren of all: the gibber plains and salt pans of the Lake Eyre basin. But this

Long-haired or plague rat Rattus villosissimus

Shade in summer is vital to a travelling mob of red kangaroos Macropus rufus

species has been around much longer and is fully conditioned to arid living. Between the rains that bring on breeding it can eke out an existence on dry seeds, gaining moisture by converting their starches.

Plains rats dig shallow, complex burrows connected by surface runways, used only at night. Communities may extend over enormous areas. Investigators gave up tracing one system after they had

covered fifty square kilometres. Populations soar and crash with food availability, but forced migrations do not occur.

Also well able to survive without water are various species of hopping-mice, *Notomys*. They spend their days in deep horizontal burrows, with a choice of many vertical shafts leading to 'pop holes' around which they feed on plant material and insects. In this way the most prominent, the spinifex hopping-mouse *Notomys alexis*, maintains itself in sand dunes and is ready to exploit the occasional blessing of rain with a burst of reproductive activity.

Hopping-mice are placental mammals, like the rats. But their general physique and their bouncing, two-legged gait — ideal in parched habitats where energy and body fluids must be saved — suggest the same environmental influences that selected our most successful inland marsupial species — the kangaroo family.

Marsupials, the survival experts
Kangaroos, wallaroos and wallabies of the arid zone do need to drink sometimes. But they conserve what water they get, and survive long wanderings in search of it. They have kidney modifications — not found in their forest-dwelling relatives — that concentrate their urine. And their

Western greys Macropus fuliginosus

rates of body metabolism are lower than those of placental mammals, which means that less external heat is generated. The marsupials need less moisture, in the form of saliva or sweat, for evaporative cooling. A low metabolic rate also reduces protein requirements. Food of poorer quality can be eaten.

Like sheep and cattle, members of the kangaroo family have fore-stomachs which allow bacterial fermentation to break down cellulose-rich roughage before it goes to the stomach proper.

Amazingly efficient and exploitative with their reproductive responses are the red kangaroo and the euro. Their range is almost identical, from the midwestern coast to central Queensland and New South Wales. But they favour different habitats. The red travels in semi-nomadic mobs through open country with scattered trees for shade. The euro, a type of wallaroo, is usually solitary and stays close to rocky formations where overhangs or caves offer shelter from the blistering, desiccating sun.

A marsupial mole Notoryctes typhlops *making a meal of a gecko*

SWIMMER IN THE SAND

Rain in the very driest parts of Australia — the sandy deserts — sometimes brings to light our most mystifying animal. The marsupial mole emerges, for reasons known only to itself, to sample the open air

Nearly all of the life of *Notoryctes typhlops* is spent buried in sand. It does not make burrows but simply claws its way through the shifting grains like a swimmer through water. Proceeding blindly — its vestigial eyes are covered by skin — it feeds mainly on insect larvae. Scientists know little more of its behaviour or life cycle.

Densely coated with short creamy or ginger fur, the marsupial mole is small enough to be enclosed in a man's hands. Its shape is something like a platypus. Toes and teeth suggest a link with quolls and the Tasmanian devil. Genetic studies put it closer to the possums. But in practical terms it is like nothing else at all.

Euro Macropus robustus

The bilby Macrotis lagotis *is now rare*

The fat-tailed dunnart Sminthopsis crassicaudata *has a built-in energy reserve*

Both species are totally non-seasonal, however. Given favourable conditions, they breed at any time of year. 'Blue fliers', the females of the red kangaroo *Macropus rufus*, come into breeding condition every thirty-five days. Female euros *Macropus robustus erubescens* are thought to have a forty-five-day cycle.

In either case, severe drought suspends the process. Young females reaching sexual maturity do not even start their cycles of ovulation. They may spend two or three of their prime years without mating at all. But soon after good rains and a flush of food, they are ready.

Both of these species also exhibit the widespread marsupial capacity for embryonic diapause. The females mate again soon after giving birth. But the fertilised egg reaches only the first stage of cell development. Nothing more happens until the earlier joey leaves the pouch, months later, or unless it is prematurely lost.

The third big kangaroo of the arid zone, the western grey *Macropus fuliginosus*, ranges to the south of the other two. It too can breed year-round, but it is incapable of embryonic diapause. Births peak in summer and most joeys leave the pouch in winter, when rain is most likely to fall.

Fluctuations due to unnatural causes

Populations of any of these species collapse drastically when emerging joeys are starved and prolonged food shortages suppress breeding cycles. In natural circumstances, free of human interference, numbers rebound strongly when times are better. Districts may see annual increases as high as twenty per cent, compounding year after year while pasture growth continues. Fluctuations of that order are central — and confusing — to arguments over the culling of kangaroos and wallaroos in marginal farming areas.

Inland species of *Petrogale*, called rock-wallabies, are just as specialised for arid living conditions as kangaroos and euros. But in recent times they have not been such great survivors. They rely on rocky refuges and cannot safely move between them without the cover of tall vegetation. Agricultural clearances have made them easy targets for eagles and dingoes, as well as foxes and feral cats.

The attractiveness of rock-wallabies added to their survival problems. Most species have brightly coloured coats and well defined markings, prized by furriers. Before legal protection, they were hunted extensively by trappers and shooters.

Hare-wallabies, about the size of cats, once were plentiful in the arid zone. Exotic predators and the burning of sheltering spinifex have wiped out virtually all but the spectacled hare-wallaby *Lagorchestes conspicillatus*, which holds on in tropical grasslands. It spends the hot days tunnelled into the biggest tussocks.

Other native mammals of arid Australia are all small marsupials that live in burrows and are little known except to scientists. The oddest are the mouse-like dunnarts, which feed at night on insects and spiders. Far from having a lowered metabolic rate like other marsupials, their normal rate is about two-thirds higher — even well above that of placental mammals. But dunnarts get enough fluids from their prey to need no drinking water, and save energy by falling into torpor at any time food is short. The fat-tailed dunnart *Sminthopsis crassicaudata* stores a reserve supply of energy in its swollen tail, which shrinks in winter.

A desert member of the bandicoot family, the bilby *Macrotis lagotis*, was common over a vast range until the end of last century. Now its colonies are rare and scattered. One of the triumphs of modern wildlife conservation has been the assisted re-establishment of the bilby in the Northern Territory's Tanami Desert sanctuary, where it appears to be secure. □

Yellow-footed rock-wallabies Petrogale xanthopus

Camels find their ideal home

The most obviously contented, least-stressed animal in the parched heartlands of Australia is a relative newcomer — the one-humped camel, or dromedary. It has flourished with a freedom that its kind had not known since domestication began more than 5000 years ago

Camels were imported from northern India as beasts of burden, mainly between 1860 and 1900. The workforce numbered about 20 000 in the 1920s. Soon after, when they were made redundant by trucks and trains, those that were not shot were turned loose to fend for themselves.

Recent aerial surveys suggest that the population has more than doubled, to at least 43 000. These are the only wild dromedaries in the world, and they suffer none of the diseases that beset their domesticated relatives overseas.

Herds of dozens or hundreds — each led by a dominant female — roam sand-ridge country from the western Nullarbor Plain to the Northern Territory and out into the central-western deserts. The range covers nearly a million square kilometres. Browsing trees and shrubs, the camels thrive on tough and bitter material that most other animals would reject. They mate whenever food is especially plentiful.

Their ability to travel long distances without drinking is well established. But it is not true that camels draw on water stored in their humps. The hump contains surplus fat — a food reserve.

The camel excels even our arid-adapted marsupials in conserving what moisture it can gain. Most warm-blooded animals need to keep their body temperature stable, and have to sweat to combat overheating. But a camel's body temperature can fluctuate widely, especially if it is thirsty. It may start as low as thirty-five degrees Celsius in the morning. Then if necessary it will rise to match the air temperature, going to forty degrees or more before the animal starts sweating.

Water loss must occur, of course, if camels are forced to travel in very high temperatures. But they also have an extraordinary tolerance of dehydration. If humans lose more than ten per cent of their body weight in water, they start to die. A camel can lose more than twenty-five per cent without even weakening.

Aliens at home in the deserts

Other introduced mammals run wild in the arid zone. Brumbies — feral horses — do fairly well where they can find flushes of grass and ephemeral plants. Donkeys, of North African ancestry, fare even better. So do goats. Feral pigs are a serious nuisance in marginal farming areas. Rabbits thrive, beyond the reach of the myxomatosis virus that cleared them out of more fertile regions. When short of water and ground-level food, they scramble up tall trees to get at juicy leaves.

Feral cats prey on the rabbits, and also take reptiles, birds and smaller marsupials. They have become the most formidable four-footed killers in the country. And they are at their best in arid environments, where only the strongest win hunting territories and breeding opportunities.

Natural selection among the ginger toms of the Simpson and Gibson deserts has improved the

One-humped camels Camelus dromedarius *wandering in the Northern Territory*

A feral cat Felis catus *is likely to breed twice between spring and autumn, bearing about ten kittens a year* breed so much that some reach a metre in head-and-body length, stand twice as tall as domestic cats and weigh up to twenty kilos. They need no water, getting enough fluids from their kill. Rabbits are the favoured prey — but giants like these can bring down small wallabies. □

Budgerigars Melopsittacus undulatus *roam in search of seeding grasses, breeding when they are best fed*

Nomads of the air

Some animals live permanently in very dry conditions; others, especially birds, travel in search of food and can time their breeding to exploit an environment temporarily lush after good rains

Affectionate, talkative pet budgies, often decked in colours wild budgies would never recognise, are the most widely known of Australian birds. But few people see budgerigars in their natural state — especially when massed in the joyous sundown flights with which they celebrate each day's survival in the wild.

In hundreds and sometimes thousands, these tiny grass parrots fly up from their feeding grounds and form a whirling, loudly chirping cloud of bright green. On some signal the direction is reversed, trailing birds becoming leaders in an instant. Back and forth they wheel, until just as suddenly the aerobatics are over. Agreed on a roosting site, all the birds swoop into the same stand of trees, lending bare branches a dense, vibrant foliage.

Different trees are selected almost every night. Even so the flocks share their resting spaces amicably and are soon ready for sleep. Energy cannot be wasted on squabbling. If food is running out, an exhausting journey may lie ahead. The budgerigar *Melopsittacus undulatus* is a complete nomad, pursuing the patchy rains of the hinterland in search of seeding plants. Where it can find a supply lasting a few months, it reproduces.

Travelling parties generally number only a few dozen birds. But in any feeding area they will be joined by other flocks. Naturalists have claimed to see millions

gathering throughout a day. Budgerigars socialise gladly. When collected in huge numbers, they are mutually understanding and tolerant. Crowding is accepted without stress, even when the birds are breeding. Holes and hollows in one tree branch may accommodate nesting pairs less than a metre apart.

Budgerigars can eat a wide range of seeds, including saltbush and bluebush as well as grasses, and seldom need water. But extremely high temperatures force them to drink — and this can be their undoing. Flocking to unshaded water in the middle of the day, they may be stricken by heat. Stories abound of farmers finding dams choked with tens of thousands of dead birds.

In spite of such disasters, the mobility of the species ensures its survival. Budgerigars are prolific breeders in favourable conditions. Eggs are laid in clutches averaging five or six, and the parents breed repeatedly while food lasts.

Other grass parrots of the arid zone are similarly nomadic. They do not assemble in such great numbers and may go unseen for years — but that does not mean they are rare. The scarlet-chested parrot *Neophema splendida*, only slightly bigger than a budgie, seems to survive without any obvious source of water, perhaps

Cockatiels Leptolophus hollandicus

getting enough moisture from dew or by chewing water-holding plants.

Cockatoos need water every day, and most lead sedentary lives near permanent supplies. One exception is the cockatiel *Leptolophus hollandicus*, which is nomadic in the northern part of its inland range. Its narrow wings and tail — more like a parrot's — suit it for long flights.

The pink cockatoo or Major Mitchell, *Cacatua leadbeateri*, is also nomadic where water is unreliable. It particularly likes to eat the seeds of cypress pine and mulga. Illegal trapping for the cage-bird trade and the increasing scarcity of their preferred native food plants because of spreading agriculture have caused a decline in the numbers of pink cockatoos, which used to be as common as galahs.

Kites, eagles, falcons and many other birds of prey roam through the interior, though not all are fully at home there. The wedge-tailed eagle, for example, suspends breeding through a drought even when it lasts for years. Opportunists, breeding whenever food is most abundant, include the black and whistling kites, the spotted harrier and the brown and black falcons.

Fortunes of the Channel Country's letter-winged kite *Elanus scriptus* are tightly interlocked with those of the long-haired or 'plague' rat — virtually its only food. Their populations boom and crash together. The kites breed continuously while the rats are spreading. Their young become sexually mature at three or four months. As the rats die out so do most of the birds, though a few disperse to coastal districts. Inland populations of the grass owl *Tyto capensis* also fluctuate wildly for the same reason.

Among the most colourful of desert nomads — when the males are in breeding plumage — are the crimson and orange chats *Epthianura tricolor* and *aurifrons*. Both species range over shrublands and saltbush plains, and sometimes forage together. The orange chat eats only

Orange chat Epthianura aurifrons

insects, but the crimson occasionally takes nectar from ground-level flowers. All chats have brush-tipped tongues, a clue that they descend from honeyeaters.

Conversely, those honeyeaters that cope with aridity are willing to supplement their diet with insects. They attempt to follow the erratic flowerings of trees and shrubs — especially the various eremophilas that are commonly called emu bush, poverty bush and desert fuchsia. Most prominent of the nomadic honeyeaters, massing and breeding where food is plentiful after rain, are black and pied species of *Certhionyx*.

An easy target for shooters

Native grasses on the inland plains used to support millions of flock bronzewings *Phaps histrionica*. Sheep and rabbits starved these nomadic pigeons out of the southern part of their range. Fair numbers make unpredictable appearances in cattle country farther north. More commonly seen is the smallest of pigeons, the diamond dove *Geopelia cuneata*, which follows rains to harvest the seeds of ephemeral plants.

Kori bustard Ardeotis kori

Dry, deserted areas of the north are the last strongholds of the so-called plains turkey, the kori bustard *Ardeotis kori*. Omnivorous — eating grasses, native fruits and seeds, insects galore, and even small mammals and reptiles — this big and stately bird was once common in any open country. But it is good eating, and made an absurdly easy target for shooters. When disturbed it 'freezes', then prefers to walk rather than fly.

The plains wanderer *Pedionomus torquatus*, on the other hand, maintains its range in the arid zone and beyond, in agricultural districts. Resembling a quail, it owes its survival to cryptic plumage and secretive, nocturnal habits. Surprisingly, the plains wanderer, so well adapted to parched grassland, is now known to be descended from wading birds.

SEEDS THAT BIDE THEIR TIME
Drenching rains briefly provide a plentiful food source for inland animals

After rains in the desert, the first new food for animals is available within hours. From apparently barren soils come the shoots of ephemeral plants — mostly members of the pea and daisy families —whose seeds may have lain through years of drought. They flower within a few days and quickly die, leaving another scattering of seeds.

The response is a complicated one. It is not triggered by inadequate passing showers, or even by soaking rains if they come at times when the shoots could be endangered by frost or excessive heat. The stimulus is a combination of soil moisture, temperature and light intensity, all within ranges that most favour the plants.

In western New South Wales, arid plains burst into a brief spell of colour

Pink-eared ducks Malacorhynchus membranaceus

Water birds of many kinds wander far inland when flooding occurs. Many of our dry-country birds that feed on, above or under the water surface must live as nomads, and so must wading birds that probe for food or graze for it at the water's edge. These birds react to water level rather than to season or length of day to start breeding. How they find and follow the water is not yet understood. Perhaps they see clouds over great distances, or can register barometric pressure changes. Nomadism and opportunistic breeding are common among dotterels, plovers and lapwings. Seasonal swamps are thronged by native hens, and salt lakes by avocets and pelicans. The Pacific heron *Ardea pacifica* is rarely seen on the coast, but prefers to roam temporary waterways.

Among many nomadic species of waterfowl, the most dedicated wanderers are the grey teal *Anas gibberifrons* and the pink-eared duck *Malacorhynchus membranaceus*. Pink-ears make for stagnant shallows remaining after floods, and by cruising with their bill completely immersed, filter-feed on microscopic organisms. Zoologists believe that this duck, which shows little relationship to any other, represents a very ancient, isolated evolutionary response to the drying-out of inland Australia. □

Camouflaged king of the saltbush country

Inland dotterels and other permanent residents of the dry inland have developed sombre plumage and abstemious drinking habits

Sparse clumps of saltbush and bluebush dot the sunbaked gibber plains and claypans that are home to the inland dotterel. Although it is a type of plover, which generally relies on ample water, the inland dotterel has completely adapted to the harsh conditions of the arid interior. It wanders over its range to find the most abundant food, but it does little or no drinking.

By day, small flocks spend most of their time standing in the shade of low shrubs, browsing now and then on the salty but succulent leaves. They obtain most of their moisture this way, excreting the salt through nostril glands. If rains bring up ephemeral daisies, the flower heads are also eaten. At night the birds disperse to forage for insects.

In the art of camouflage, *Peltohyas australis* rivals any ground-dwelling bird in the world. Caught out in the open, it crouches with its buff, dark-flecked back towards the intruder. Among shrubbery it stands facing the threat, the breast markings of its breeding plumage looking like plant stems. The bird's knack for concealment extends to protection of its eggs, which are laid in a scrape on open ground. The lining material of loose soil, sand, pebbles or twigs is kicked over the eggs whenever an incubating parent has to leave the nest.

Another bird totally adapted to desert conditions is the gibberbird, a permanent resident of the parched, stony plains of the Lake Eyre basin.

Black bands on the inland dotterel Peltohyas australis *are seen only when it is breeding and has to stay close to its nest*

Scientists have yet to fathom how *Ashbyia lovensis*, feeding exclusively on insects and spiders, gets enough moisture. All of its relatives in the chat family need to drink frequently.

Tree-nesting chats, in more fertile country, will flop to the ground and feign injury to distract an intruder's attention from the nest. Without a tree in sight, the ground-dwelling gibberbird retains its version of this behaviour. It pretends to struggle away from the nest, staggering with outspread, drooping wings and tripping over pebbles.

Birds with discreet colours and habits
Among the most handsome birds living permanently in the arid zone is the spinifex pigeon *Geophaps plumifera*. Its existence is precarious because it must have water. For food it relies on unpredictable, rain-induced flushes of plant growth. If they fail it has to survive on the erratic seedings of spinifex hummocks.

Most other sedentary birds of the hinterland are small, discreetly coloured and furtive. They include the sparrow-like spinifexbird *Eremiornis carteri*, the chestnut-rumped thornbill *Acanthiza uropygialis*, species of wedgebills *Psophodes*, grasswrens *Amytornis*, quail-thrushes *Cinclosoma*, scrub-wrens *Sericornis* and babblers *Pomatostomus*.

By contrast, the two arid zone finches are unusually eye-catching. Both the painted firetail *Emblema picta* and the zebra finch *Taeniopygia guttata* are seed-eaters and have to drink every hour or two, so during droughts many of them die. But when numbers are rising after good rains and successful breeding, exuberant flocks produce spectacular displays of colour. □

Crested bellbird Oreoica gutturalis

LIVING ORNAMENTS
Nests with that individual touch
Crested bellbirds, common in arid scrublands, decorate their nests with live prey. From the time their eggs are laid, they start bringing home hairy caterpillars. The victims are partly crippled by pecks along their backs, then distributed round the rim of the cup nest. This unique habit of *Oreoica gutturalis* seems to be purely ornamental: nestlings do not eat the wriggling captives and the adults have no need to store food.

Spinifex pigeons Geophaps plumifera *(above) forage for seeds in groups of about a dozen. They sleep in ground depressions, huddled together in order to conserve energy*

Painted firetails Emblema picta *(below) always feed out in the open, but rest in low shrubs or under hummocks of spinifex*

Science gave the thorny devil a terrible name, belying its amiable nature. The first zoologist to study it, around 1840, thought it looked so grotesque, even monstrous that he called it *Moloch* (after an ancient god for whom children were burnt in sacrifice) *horridus*.

In fact this plump little lizard, no more than fifteen centimetres long including the tail, is the most placid of reptiles. Extremely slow-moving, it can be touched and even picked up without any sign of fear or ill-temper. And it is completely

The secret drinker

Devils, dragons and other lizards with a talent for desert living

Spikes of the thorny devil Moloch horridus *have a dual purpose*

harmless, except to those small black ants that move in trails. It ambles about by day among sand dunes until it finds a file of ants. Then it licks up as many as 1500 of them in a meal — one at a time.

Grotesque scale formation is not uncommon among lizards. Spines, mock horns and neck ruffs usually work as a defence, or at least a bluff, against predators. Familiar examples are the frilled lizard and bearded dragon.

No doubt the thorny devil's very sharp spikes deter birds of prey and big snakes. No snake could swallow one without severely damaging its insides. But the spikes serve another life-preserving purpose, which gives this creature a unique advantage in the desert. They enable it to drink, without conscious effort, whenever chilly nights bring dew.

Fine grooves radiating from the point of each scale are linked in a network covering the whole body. Dew picked up on the spikes is drawn along the grooves by capillary action. Eventually moisture is channelled to the animal's lips.

The thorny devil has no close relatives, but is classified among a family of rough-skinned, mostly insect-eating lizards commonly called dragons. Many are specialised to survive in a dry climate — though few face conditions as tough as those enjoyed by the Lake Eyre dragon *Ctenophorus maculosus*. Though active by day like all the dragon family, it avoids extreme heat by burrowing into the sand beneath the crusts of dry salt lakes. It too feeds exclusively on ants, which in a barren environment receive their only sustenance from windblown plant debris.

Goannas, skinks and geckoes

Rocky outcrops in the arid zone shelter the biggest of all Australian lizards, and the second-biggest in the world. The perentie *Varanus giganteus* averages more than one and a half metres in length and sometimes exceeds two metres. Only the rare Komodo dragon of Indonesia — a fellow-member of the monitor family — grows to a greater size.

Perenties hunt early in the morning, seizing other reptiles, small mammals, birds or insects. But much of their time is spent in deep crevices or burrows. More commonly seen, and nearly as big, is the sand monitor. This is a desert subspecies of *Varanus gouldii*, which in its forest and woodlands form most people know as Gould's goanna.

The skink family, some members of which are common around the coast and in urban gardens, has dozens of inland species. Often heavily dependent on spinifex hummocks to provide living quarters and refuge, skinks come in all shapes and sizes. Most recognisable are arid-living species of blue-tongued lizards

Tiliqua and the shingleback *Trachydosaurus*.

Two unusual species of desert skinks are sand swimmers *Eremiascincus*. Unlike most skinks they are active at night, and shelter by day in shallow burrows. If disturbed they do not run but try to slip away beneath the surface, hitching themselves forward like snakes. Even more snakelike — or wormlike in the case of the smaller ones — are the burrowing legless lizards. Although plentiful in dry country, they are seldom seen.

Many kinds of geckoes live in the harsh

A legless lizard Pygopus (above) is easily mistaken at first glance for a small snake

Sand swimmer Eremiascincus (above left)

Our biggest lizard, the perentie Varanus giganteus (left and below), shows its richest patterns when it is young

conditions, in spite of their tender skins. Strictly nocturnal feeders, most spend their daytime in or under grass tussocks. *Gehyra pilbara*, an orange to reddish-brown denizen of the northwestern deserts, retreats deep into the galleries of termite mounds. The desert cave gecko *Heteronotia spelea* favours underground cavities, taking happily to mine shafts.

Fattened tails that function as food stores help some inland geckoes through prolonged drought. In some species of *Diplodactylus*, Australia's largest genus of geckoes, the tail is also a defensive weapon. It contains glands that squirt a sticky fluid at attackers. □

One of the squirting geckoes Diplodactylus taeniatus

A not-so-fierce rat-hunter and other desert-dwelling snakes

The fierce snake Oxyuranus microlepidotus *can reach a length of 2.5 metres. Females lay up to twenty eggs*

A blind snake Ramphotyphlops *eats only ants and termites*

Most snakes cope with the inland's high daytime temperatures by hiding in rock crevices or burrows, and hunting at night

Desolate plains of the Channel Country, where ephemeral watercourses run from Queensland into South Australia, are the known territory of the fierce snake *Oxyuranus microlepidotus*. Its range may be much wider, but the snake's underground habits make an encounter with it most unlikely. And that is just as well, because it has the most toxic venom in the world.

The fierce snake (so-called last century, though it seems to have a placid temperament) lives on long-haired 'plague' rats. One kill lasts it for weeks. But some quirk of chemistry gives it a venom so potent that it could dispatch thousands of rats at a time. Even so, the fierce snake is not such a danger to people as the related taipan, mainly because its fangs are only about half as long and give out only a third as much venom.

Though active by day the fierce snake cannot tolerate extreme heat, and has to conserve moisture during long droughts. It retreats into deep cracks. If rats are scarce and a snake is fasting, it may occupy the empty burrow of one of its prey.

Little chance of a daytime encounter

Snakes are common enough in the arid zone, but are not generally conspicuous because most move about by night and seek shelter by day. The common death adder has a reddish (to match the soil) desert relative, but no other important venomous type shows a specialised adaptation to arid living. Various brown snakes *Pseudonaja* and the mulga snake *Pseudechis* differ from their bushland counterparts only in their hunting hours and choice of shelter.

Specialised burrowers of the hinterland include banded snakes *Simoselaps* and wormlike blind snakes *Ramphotyphlops*. One python, the woma *Aspidites ramsayi*, lives only in the arid zone, and is found even in sandhills. Children's python *Bothrochilus childreni* and one or two of its relatives, though more at home in woodlands, are sometimes found living in termite mounds. □

Some long-living animals that depend on ephemeral water have perfected techniques to escape from desiccating heat and conserve their body moisture. Others, destined to breed only the once, reach a hardened stage of early development — like the seeds of plants — and pause there until conditions are right. Both types breed overabundantly when they get the chance, producing food for a host of other opportunistic creatures.

Frogs are gifted drought-dodgers. They bury themselves in soil or under litter in any region where rainfall is unreliable or markedly seasonal. In the arid zone, where the waiting period may be years, frogs have to be even more resourceful.

On the rare occasions when the deep-burrowing frogs of central Australia are seen above ground, they have a swollen, globular body shape. This is because they absorb extraordinary amounts of moisture while the going is good. They store it in their bladders. In the desert spadefoot 'toad' *Notaden nichollsi*, eighty per cent of the bodyweight can be water.

Before the last moisture disappears from the claypans and puddles where they breed, burrowing frogs start a backwards descent into the ground. Shuffling and scraping with wide-toed hind feet, and with sand or clay falling in on top of them, they dig to depths as great as one metre.

Experts at seizing the moment

Water-breeding animals of many kinds survive in deserts by playing a waiting game. Life is long periods of suspended animation during droughts, followed by bursts of accelerated activity when useful rain collects. Reproduction must be completed before the water soaks away or evaporates

Water-holding frog Cyclorana platycephalus *in its sheath*

There they make chambers, which some seal by pressing a mucous skin secretion against the walls.

Water-holding frogs in a group called *Cyclorana* are the supreme conservators. They secrete airtight cocoons. The most widespread and thoroughly studied species, *Cyclorana platycephalus*, may burrow no deeper than thirty centimetres below a sunbaked surface. But it can survive there for at least two years.

This frog compacts the walls of a spherical chamber about twice its own

Ephemeral puddles, soon to shrink

The trilling frog Neobatrachus centralis *(left) is the only frog to be found in the Simpson Desert*

Cyclorana novaehollandiae *(right) is among the biggest of the water-holding burrowing frogs, reaching ten centimetres in length. It occurs throughout almost all of Queensland*

size. As soon as that task is completed it subsides into dormancy — its usual state for most of its life. Heart and breathing rates are slowed to a minimum. The head is lowered against the chest and the legs are tucked tightly under the body.

After about two weeks, close-packed layers of skin cells start to form a membrane that separates from the underlying skin. Within a month the animal is entirely covered by a loose envelope, except for tiny tubes from its nostrils. Laboratory studies, comparing similar frogs with and without cocoons, have shown reductions of ninety-five to ninety-eight per cent in the rate of water loss.

When soaking rains occur, the rise in soil moisture triggers an end to the dormancy of burrowing frogs. They hurry to the surface for a hectic session of feasting and spawning. Temporary ponds resound

to a hubbub of mating calls — snoring sounds from *Cyclorana*, plonkings from *Notaden*, high-pitched tremeloes from the trilling frog *Neobatrachus centralis*, another specialist of the arid zone. Eggs hatch and tadpoles develop with amazing speed. After just a few days, little *Cyclorana* frogs, bulging with water, are ready to go underground for the first of the timeless pauses that will dominate their existence and ensure the survival of their species.

During their brief flings in water and the open air, the tadpoles feed on microscopic organisms and the frogs mainly on insects, all programmed to be there at the same time. Everything in the food chain of ephemeral waters, including the algae and other aquatic plants that start it, appears with good rains and disappears with drought. But life goes on in various hidden ways. Water does not lie long in the arid zone without the emergence of swarms of small flies — especially midges — from drought-resistant larvae stranded when the last rains evaporated. Where there are trees or shrubs, moths soon fill the night air; their larvae were lodged inside the stems or among the roots.

Mosquito larvae wait for years

Mosquitoes seem to come from nowhere. In fact females of some *Anopheles* and *Culex* species can lurk in cool crevices and mammal burrows for months, their eggs fully developed, while they wait for water in which to lay them. Inland *Aedes* mosquitoes do even better. Their eggs were inserted in the drying mud of previous pools. Only a day or two's humidity was needed for the larvae to form, still inside impervious shells. Since then they may have lain dormant for years.

Tiny crustaceans such as waterfleas burst into prolific life in temporary pools. So do many kinds of shrimps, some big enough to be easily noticeable as they flit about in search of plant food and mates.

Wood moth Xyleutes *larva*

WHICH WITCHETTY?

Tasty morsels in a spartan diet

Many edible insect larvae dug from around the roots of dry-country trees could loosely be called witchetty grubs. Witchetty was a word originally used by only one Aboriginal language group. But every hinterland tribe ate the larvae of various moths and beetles, using their own words for them. Entomologists of the Commonwealth Scientific and Industrial Research Organization (CSIRO), however, confidently assert that the only 'true' witchetty are the larvae of a small wood moth, *Xyleutes leucomochla*. In inland South Australia the grubs spend years feeding on the roots of a shrubby acacia called small cooba.

Shield shrimps Triops *complete their life cycles in a few days*

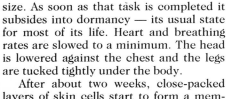

Desert crab Holthuisana transversa

A hinged plug of sunbaked mud caps a trapdoor spider's burrow

STOPGAP MEASURES

Defending against rain, dust and predators

Burrowing to dodge drought carries an ironical hazard for desert spiders — they could drown in floods. Hinged, tight-fitting 'bathplugs' of baked mud are a common form of defence. They also prevent burrows from filling with windblown sand or dust, and keep out predatory scorpions.

Other anti-flooding devices include collapsible silk collars inside burrow entrances, and external towers or parapets of silkbound soil to divert flows of water. A few species strengthen their levees with stones. Species of *Lycosa* in Western Australia cover their burrow entrances with pebbles, one of which is movable and is re-sealed from below with silk.

Often blown in the wind, their eggs can withstand many years out of water. A thorough drying may be essential to their proper development.

Inland Australia even boasts an arid-adapted freshwater crab, *Holthuisana transversa*. It shuns permanent water, preferring to live most of its life in a clay burrow near a site of occasional flooding. When it takes to water — to moult, breed and build up food reserves of fat — it breathes through gills. In its burrow it uses lungs, in a way of its own that is not known in any land crabs.

Protracted waiting in permanent burrows is also an inevitable part of life for most inland spiders. They emerge from their humid underground micro-climates only after rain has moistened the ground.

Natural trapdoor types are the most successful: because they live for many years, it does not matter if they fail to breed for a year or two. Wolf spiders and huntsmen — surface-dwellers in forests and woodlands — take to burrows in deserts. And they live at least twice as long as their more favoured relatives, most of which breed only once.

Other vagrant hunting spiders depend heavily on the shelter of spinifex. Orb-web weavers lead a hazardous existence, but the wind-blown dispersal of their young helps them to take advantage of erratic rains and flushes of insects. Desert species of two groups of trapdoor spiders, *Conothele* and *Missulena*, also disperse on gossamer — behaviour unheard-of in the rest of their kind. □

Keeping it in the family

A sweet harvest for the honeypot ants

Far from shunning the full blaze of the sun, as desert creatures generally do, *Melophorus* ants revel in it. Busily foraging in the middle of the day while other ants are sheltering, they are the centre's most abundantly visible animals. Out of sight, some of them also engage in a curious activity.

Melophorus bagoti is aptly called the honeypot ant. It provides for hard times by laying up stores of sugary food. Containers are convenient and easy to come by — in the living bodies of a specially-bred caste of passive workers.

After rains, when plants are putting out leaves and flowers, the real workers gather nectar and the 'honeydew' secreted by sapsucking aphids and psyllids (plant lice). There is more than the community can use immediately. Deep inside the nest, a metre or two underground, excess supplies are forcefed to the storage caste, which exists solely for this role in life.

Long and slender at first, the abdomens of the honeypots soon swell to the size of peas. Their casings are so stretched that they are transparent. Unable to walk, the overstuffed ants are hung by their forelegs from the ceilings of nest galleries.

Fed to bursting point, this honeypot ant Melophorus bagoti *is ready for hanging. Life offers nothing else for its caste*

When surface harvests dwindle because of drought, the community draws on its savings. Starving workers queue up to reclaim their investments of months before. Stroked zealously, the abdomens of the helpless honeypots yield drop after drop of high-energy food. □

Sanctuary in spinifex

Unique plants that shelter desert animals

Throughout the most sunstricken parts of Australia, parched landscapes are dotted with spiky hummocks. These are grasses like no others in the world, with hard, folded blades. We call them spinifex — though the name really belongs to a seashore plant. On sandy and stony soils in the tropical arid zone, species of *Triodia* and *Pletrachne* provide an average thirty per cent of ground cover. Persistence of these plants is crucial to desert wildlife. Animals of many kinds gain shade, a defensive shield and an erratic supply of food. Hummocks can grow one metre tall and two metres across, developing hollow centres as they age. Foliage lost to drought, burning or grazing is regenerated from underground stems. Flowering stalks may shoot up in response to a soaking at any time. Seeds, which normally set only after good summer rains, remain viable for at least fifteen years.

The Great Victoria Desert, dotted with old and new Triodia *clumps*

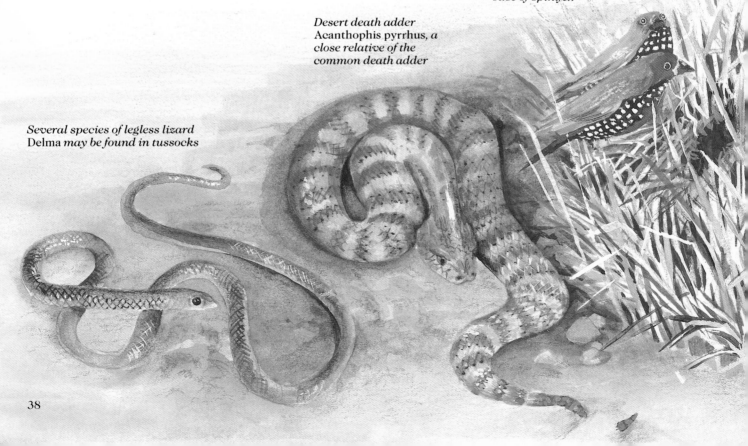

Painted firetail finches Emblema picta *build their domed nests near the base of spinifex*

Desert death adder Acanthophis pyrrhus, *a close relative of the common death adder*

Several species of legless lizard Delma *may be found in tussocks*

38

Spinifexbirds
Eremiornis carteri *live
and nest deep within
old, well-established
hummocks. The male
defends his nest by
singing from a grass-
stem perch above
the tussock*

Crested grasshopper
Alectoria superba *lives
only in the arid inland*

Dragonflies are mainly
aquatic insects, but
nomadic desert species
follow ephemeral pools
and are often found in
spinifex country

One of many hopping-
mice, the spinifex
mouse Notomys alexis
spends the day
underground beneath a
grass tussock to avoid
the heat

Pie-dish beetles Helaeus
brevicostatus *live in the
driest parts of inland
Western Australia and
Queensland*

39

Where the living is easy

Not only in arid zones are seasons fairly meaningless. Many animals in other regions can afford to ignore the seasons. They feed and breed according to inclination rather than conditions dictated by weather and food supplies

A sea-lion cow Neophoca cinerea *cares for her pup for more than a year*

Australian sea-lions — the only seals peculiar to this country — show an utter disregard for the seasons. Other seal species synchronise their breeding during a few weeks late in spring. But in spite of the bleakness of rocky Southern Ocean shores, pups of *Neophoca cinerea* may be born at almost any time.

Where peaks in the birthrate have been noticed they indicate an eighteen-month cycle — many animals breeding in winter one year and in summer the year after. Such an unusual pattern may be connected with the length of time that mothers devote to rearing and training their pups. Nursing lasts for over a year, and strong associations continue long after weaning. A mammal born and raised on land has much to learn if it is to survive in a marine environment.

A sea-lion pup takes its first swimming lesson at about nine months, nuzzled and encouraged by a fiercely protective mother. Soon the two cavort together, exchanging hoots of delight. But they are on serious business. The pup has to copy all of its mother's aquatic skills — not only in locating and diving for shoaling fish, but also in avoiding the arch-enemy of all

seals, the insatiable white pointer shark.

Males take five years to reach sexual maturity, and may have to stay out of trouble a lot longer before they can challenge successfully for the right to mate. Older bulls are generally easy-going, but ferociously jealous of their breeding territories and their harems of cows. Often exceeding two metres in length and weighing over three hundred kilos, they are surprisingly nimble on land. Cows are smaller and very much lighter.

Australian sea-lions are sometimes called white-naped hair seals. Bulls grow a creamy or yellow mane. 'Hair' seal was a commercial term applied to species lacking the fine undercoat of fur seals. But juvenile sea-lions do have fur, and that made them a target of sealing gangs early in the nineteenth century. Populations on

the Bass Strait islands were all wiped out.

A few thousand sea-lions remain, seemingly secure, on islands off the south-western and southern coasts. One community is accessible to the public at Seal Bay, on Kangaroo Island, South Australia. The only mainland breeding ground is to the northwest at remote Point Labatt, on Eyre Peninsula.

A world of warmth and plenty

The sea-lion's indifference to seasons is a product of a steady supply of food and an unusual tolerance of temperature fluctuations. On land, an easier world of perpetual warmth and plenty is found in tropical rainforests. Soils that are always shaded and moist support the continuous growth of trees, vines and fungi and receive continuous enrichment from recycled litter.

These are the conditions which nurtured the first animal life on land. Scorpions, burrowing spiders, millipedes and primitive insects, still in their ancestral form, lead busy lives on the forest floor. More recently evolved invertebrates crawl and hop and scurry and fly above. Flowers bloom and fruits ripen in random abundance. Vertebrate animals, at the end of the food chain, need only be on hand to reap the benefit.

Rainforest marsupials of far northern Queensland, apparently capable of breeding at any time, show affinities with the fauna of New Guinea rather than the rest of Australia. Most remarkable of them are two species of tree-kangaroos *Dendrolagus*, found in limited areas between Cairns and Cooktown.

Tree-kangaroos, slightly smaller than most wallabies, feed at night on leaves and fruits, and find high roosts for sleeping by

---

White-rumped swiftlet Aerodramus spodiopygius

FLYING BLIND
Little birds that go click in the night

Swooping into a pitch-dark cave to roost or nest among hundreds of other birds, the white-rumped swiftlet *Aerodramus spodiopygius* uses the skill of a bat. It avoids collisions by echo-location, making clicking sounds that bounce around the walls.

By day this bird is a far-ranging wanderer, gliding over the canopies of Queensland rainforests and snatching flying insects. At night, back in the security of its cave, it accepts conditions of confinement and overcrowding that seem scarcely tolerable.

Nests are cups of moss, grass and feathers, bound with saliva and usually fixed to the cave walls. Shortage of nesting space is partly overcome by random breeding, any time from July to February. Still, the walls become so densely covered that some birds have to join their nests to those already there.

day. They are the only members of the macropod family that can move each hind leg independently of the other. Strong forelegs, nearly as long as the hind pair, and short paws with curved claws enable them to climb. But tree-kangaroos are ungainly, and it is surprising that they have held their territories against the more agile possums.

Occasionally seen peering from forest edges near Cape York is the spotted cuscus *Phalanger maculatus*. Its round face and handlike paws prompted early settlers' stories of monkeys in the region. It rests by day in relatively open positions — unlike the grey cuscus *Phalanger orientalis* which hides in a den. Fruits, flowers and leaves are their main food, but both species have long canine teeth. In captivity they enjoy meat.

Another kind of possum possesses a most intriguing trademark. The striped possum *Dactylopsila trivirgata* has bold black-and-white markings very like those of a skunk — and for no understandable reason its skin emits a pungent, clinging stink. A shy, slender night-feeder, the striped possum is sparsely distributed in forests north of Townsville.

In spite of the region's drastic division of wet and dry climates, the northern brushtail possum *Trichosurus arnhemensis* breeds year-round in woodlands and open forests from North West Cape to the Gulf of Carpentaria. Sometimes, like the all-too-familiar southern brushtail, it takes up residence in houses.

The brushtail shares its range in the Kimberley and Arnhem Land with the rock ringtail *Pseudocheirus dahli*. This is a specialist of rough, broken country,

Spotted cuscus Phalanger maculatus

Noolbenger Tarsipes rostratus *feeding on banksia blossom*

sheltering among boulders and in crevices and climbing trees only to feed at night.

Among the mountain ash (eucalyptus) forests of Victoria's central highlands, and apparently nowhere else, Leadbeater's possum not only braves bitter winter conditions but is also able to breed year-round. The key to the success of *Gymnobelideus leadbeateri*, and the reason for its limited range, is its reliance on a continuous supply of big tree-crickets. When other insects are available, they are eaten too, along with the secretions of sap-suckers, the sugary solutions produced by damaged eucalypts, and the gums exuding from acacias.

Far away on the southwestern sandplains, the noolbenger or honey possum is another continuous breeder. *Tarsipes rostratus*, the size of a mouse, feeds only from the blossoms of heathland shrubs such as banksias. A long, brush-tipped tongue — like that of a honeyeater bird — extracts nectar and pollen. Not a possum at all, the noolbenger has toes rather than claws, and rudimentary teeth unsuited to chewing. It is the only known survivor of an extinct marsupial group.

Hard times for the rat kangaroos

Bettongs and potoroos, nest-building scaled-down members of the kangaroo family, are capable of breeding at any time. Before European settlement they were among the most widespread and abundant of marsupials. But they suffered heavily from woodland clearances, competition from livestock and the depredations of cats and foxes.

Bettongia gaimardi, formerly common on the southeastern mainland, is now restricted to Tasmania and called the Tasmanian bettong. Probably the most secure of its kind, it lives in grassy open forests and feeds mainly on fungi, seeds and roots. The rufous bettong *Aepyprymnus rufescens* is still reasonably common on the eastern mainland, though its range has been broken up by clearances. The brush-tailed bettong or woylie *Bettongia penicillata*, once distributed from the west coast to central New South Wales and parts of Queensland, survives only in three forest pockets in the southwest and two in the northeast.

Tasmania is also the last stronghold of potoroos. The long-nosed *Potorous tridactylus* is common in the north and east of the island. Mainland populations are scattered from western Victoria to southeastern Queensland. West Australian specimens have not been found since last century.

Among birds that may breed at any time are two of the most imposing — the black swan and the pelican. In the black

Tree kangaroo Dendrolagus lumholtzi

swan *Cygnus atratus*, readiness to breed is marked by a reddening of the male's eyes, which are white at other times. Courtship begins with a show of male aggression towards an intruder, incited by the female. Then paired birds face each other in prolonged greeting displays.

Swans breeding for the first time, as young as eighteen months, are often promiscuous. Whichever partner is not incubating eggs may go off to mate again. Older birds usually form permanent pairs. Three or four clutches of eggs are commonly laid during a breeding period, after which the birds moult and are unable to fly for a few weeks. That is when they are seen gathered on lakes, quietly feeding on aquatic plants.

Colourful courtship signals

Flocks of the Australian pelican *Pelecanus conspicillatus* gather in dense nesting colonies wherever islets are surrounded by sufficient water. Whether it is fresh or salt, still or running, does not matter as long as fish are plentiful. Birds team up to feed, swimming in formation to drive their prey into shallow water.

Sexual maturity is reached at four years. Pelicans ready to breed show courtship colours. In both sexes the pouch under the bill turns scarlet; the end of the bill itself and the skin around the eyes turn orange. After pairing — a simple matter of a female allowing a male to follow her and then engaging in a short flight with him — these colours quickly fade.

In the heron family, readiness to mate is signalled by the raising of nuptial

Long known from Indonesia and New Guinea — where it is hunted — the shy grey cuscus Phalanger orientalis *went undiscovered near Cape York until 1938*

Black swans Cygnus atratus *and grey cygnets (below) may gather in thousands during the adults' annual moult, when all are flightless*

plumes — in some cases specially grown for the breeding period. Australia's most commonly seen species, the nomadic white-faced heron *Ardea novaehollandiae*, breeds when and where food is most abundant. So do the great-billed heron *Ardea sumatrana* and some egrets.

Year-round breeding, or at least for as long as grasses and herbs are seeding, is common among finches. Grasslands pigeons such as the squatter pigeon *Geophaps scripta* and the crested pigeon *Geophaps lophotes* are similarly attuned to long seasons of good eating.

Considering the ease of life in tropical rainforests, evidenced by the year-round breeding of marsupials and many insects, it is surprising that few birds have extended seasons. A tiny but eye-catching exception is the lovely fairy-wren *Malurus amabilis*. Family parties hop about jauntily in shrubs and saplings, foraging for insects. Courtship occurs at any time of year, and begins charmingly with a male picking a flower petal — always yellow — and displaying it to his intended mate. □

Pelican chicks Pelecanus conspicillatus *are cared for in creches*

FLEETING GLORY

Depending on the species and the climate, butterflies can live from as little as two or three weeks to as long as two years

Tropical butterflies lead adult lives as short as two weeks. But the growth of their larvae is accelerated and rainforest conditions make breeding possible at any time. Some of the biggest and most brilliantly coloured species can be seen year-round. The place to look for them is not deep in the rainforest itself, but along tracks, on forest edges and in clearings, wherever flowers can blossom. Rainforest butterflies flock to lantana when it is in bloom.

Ulysses Papilio ulysses

Birdwing Ornithoptera priamus

Cruiser Vindula arsinoe

Common oakblues Arhopala micale

A little help from their friends

European settlement has helped make life easier for some animals

Sunbirds, arriving at any time of year to prepare for breeding, are among the chief delights of living on the tropical Queensland coast. Suburban gardens are filled with chirping and singing as tiny blobs of brilliant colour flit about, sipping nectar from flowers and plucking spiders from their webs.

Its small size and fluttering habits make the yellow-bellied sunbird *Nectarinia jugularis* Australia's nearest equivalent to a humming-bird. Rainforest edges and mangrove stands are its natural habitats, but it has adapted enthusiastically to human settlement. Spindle-shaped nests, with cowled entrances at the side, are hung under roof eaves and verandahs, from the ceilings of open sheds, and from clotheslines or power cables.

Though sunbirds are nomadic when not breeding, pairs return to the same nesting territories for as long as fifteen years. Nests still hanging from previous seasons are spruced up with new plant material and bound with spider webs and cocoons. Up to three broods of chicks may be reared before the visit ends.

Few associations between people and wildlife are so mutually enjoyable. Some frogs have benefited in a similar way, not only from the establishment of gardens but also from gutters, roadside ditches and so on. The commonest species in settled areas, from southern Queensland to South Australia and Tasmania, is the eastern froglet *Ranidella signifera*. It breeds year-round and is one of the few frogs to be heard calling in winter.

Spiders exploiting the shelter and consistent warmth of houses are generally less welcome guests. Most remain summer breeders but the grey house-spider *Achaearanea tepidariorum*, a worldwide species, is so thoroughly adapted that it mates and lays eggs at any time.

Native rats thrive on introduced crops

Sugarcane planting brought an unnatural abundance of food for native rodents and allowed them to breed continuously. Among those most cursed as pests now are the canefield rat *Rattus sordidus* and the grassland melomys or banana rat *Melomys burtoni*. It need hardly be added that introduced rats and mice breed year-round. So, to the chagrin of farmers, do rabbits, hares and feral pigs. Introduced birds that ignore the seasons include the house sparrow, the feral pigeon, the nutmeg mannikin and the mute or white swan. □

A female sunbird Nectarinia jugularis *feeds her chick. The male has a vivid blue throat*

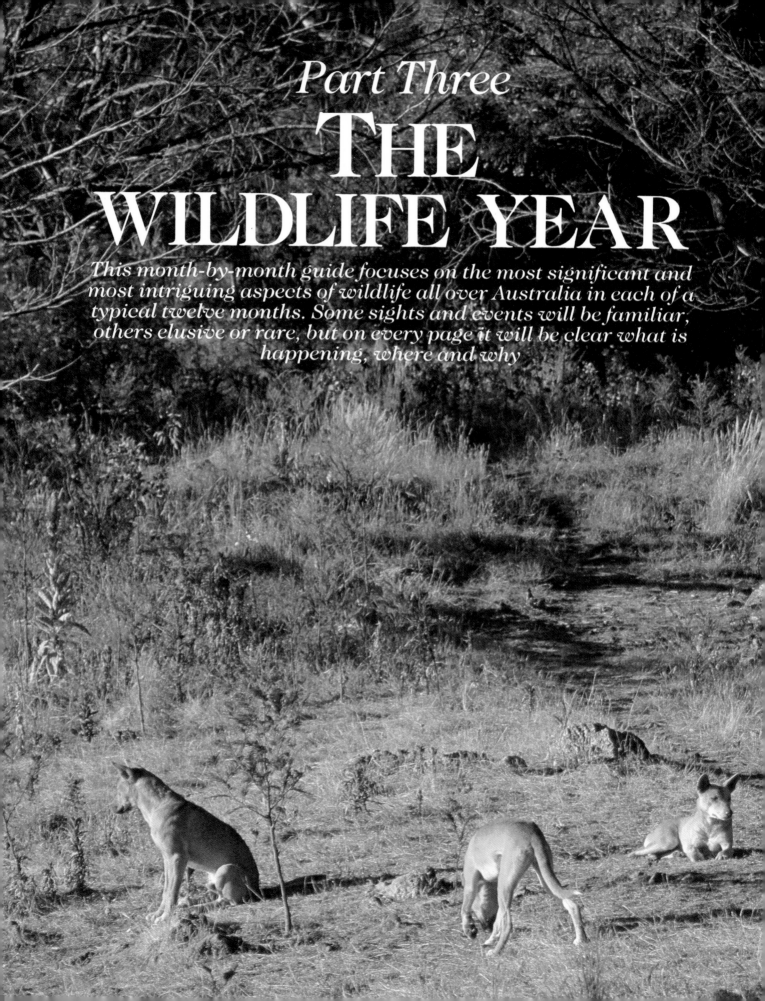

Part Three
THE WILDLIFE YEAR

This month-by-month guide focuses on the most significant and most intriguing aspects of wildlife all over Australia in each of a typical twelve months. Some sights and events will be familiar, others elusive or rare, but on every page it will be clear what is happening, where and why

A family group of dingoes relaxes in the evening sun near Bega, New South Wales

A damselfly in a Queensland stream at rest on the head of a freshwater snake

JANUARY

THIS MONTH'S WEATHER

Monsoonal northwesterlies dump drenching rain on the Kimberley, the Top End and Cape York. The Queensland coast enters its period of heaviest rainfall, with tropical cyclones sometimes adding to the effects of prevailing moist southeasterlies. Heating of the southern mainland, under generally clear skies, can be fierce. Dry spells intensify in South Australia and the southwest, and Tasmania's driest season begins. Summer storms increase rainfall in coastal New South Wales.

AROUND THE COUNTRY	RAIN (mm)	MAX. (°C)	MIN. (°C)	SUN hrs/day
Adelaide	22	29	17	10.0
Alice Springs	38	36	21	10.2
Brisbane	174	29	21	8.1
Canberra	60	28	13	9.7
Darwin	409	32	25	5.6
Hobart	48	22	12	8.1
Melbourne	48	26	14	8.7
Perth	9	30	19	10.8
Port Hedland	59	36	25	10.5
Sydney	102	26	18	7.1
Townsville	297	31	24	7.5
Weipa	451	32	24	5.2

Rocky heights backing the floodplains of the far north are lashed by rain on most days now. Run-off rivulets swell into boisterous surges, churning up a soup of mud, leaves and twigs. The flows follow time-worn pathways between drought-isolated pools, linking them once more into creeks. Riding these sudden tides, literally body-surfing on the crests, are tiny fish.

For every swimmer that a sharp eye can spot, thousands of smaller creatures are carried along unseen. Insects, molluscs, crustaceans and myriad micro-organisms, along with all the plant debris, will found the food web of a new wetland territory.

Behind at a more sedate pace will come bigger fish, snakes, water monitors, turtles, crocodiles. All across the monsoonal north, from the Kimberley to Cape York Peninsula, aquatic animals are breaking free of a long confinement in stagnant, oxygen-depleted billabongs.

As the streams settle into steady flows their meanders fill lily-covered paperbark swamps. The air is soon abuzz with insects. Frogs appear seemingly from nowhere. During the Dry, they were holed up in tree hollows, rock crevices or burrows. Now the waters seethe with their rapidly bloating bodies. Clamorous breeding choruses assemble.

A black-necked stork or jabiru in hot pursuit of a flying long tom fish; birds need to

The file snake is non-venomous and is found in northern Australia

Surfers on once-a-year breakers

Pent-up life explodes out of back country billabongs. Reborn, the downstream wetlands make a paradise for tropical birds

Little gobies and gudgeons that were virtually colourless, to avoid the attentions of predators, signal their readiness to spawn by displaying vivid body and fin markings. In some cases, the change lasts only a few minutes. Fertilised eggs are strung on water plants or clustered in nest holes, often guarded by the male parent and fanned with his tail and pectoral fins.

In preparation for spawning, male eel-tailed catfish *Neosilurus* collect creekbed pebbles and heap them in nesting mounds up to two metres in diameter. Tens of thousands of eggs are laid in each and guarded by the female. Male fork-tailed catfish *Arius*, on the other hand, brood smaller numbers of eggs in their mouths. Most mouth-brooded eggs hatch very quickly, but the male cardinal fish *Glossamia aprion* has to go without food for two weeks until his progeny swim out.

Nursery fish *Kurtus gulliveri* have a highly unusual, trouble-free strategy for protecting their eggs. The male has a hook-like appendage growing from his forehead. The female strings her fertilised ova on a filament and fixes it to the hook, so that he carries the eggs with him wherever he goes.

Water snakes are active mainly at night. *Acrochordus arafurae*, called a file snake because of the exceptional roughness of its skin, can exceed two metres in length. It is a specialist hunter of fish. Most other freshwater snakes, also land snakes that take readily to water, prefer frogs. The water python *Liasis fuscus*, sometimes measuring three metres, kills and eats a wide variety of vertebrates including rats and birds.

Snakes of monsoonal swamps and creeks are generally very timid. An exception is the slaty-grey snake *Stegonotus cucullatus*, which boldly frequents settlements and may climb into water tanks. Growing more than a metre long, it is highly aggressive if aroused and bites furiously, but it is not venomous.

Carnivorous freshwater turtles feed richly now. Most commonly seen along

feed well before breeding

billabong chains and in swamps is the northern snake-necked turtle *Chelodina rugosa*. It swims with a broad, flat head thrust out on a slender neck from which it gets its name. Its neck can stretch more than forty centimetres, more than the length of its dark, blotched shell.

Pitted-shelled or pig-nosed turtles foil predators with delaying tactics

Hiding among pandanus roots or beneath undercut banks is a much bigger turtle that few people see. The pitted-shelled or pig-nosed turtle *Carettochelys insculpta* reaches seventy centimetres in length and can weigh over twenty kilos. It has a distinctive, fleshy proboscis and a covering of soft skin over its bony carapace. Paddle-shaped limbs resemble those of sea turtles. Zoologists used to regard it as a link between marine and freshwater species; now they simply put it in a category all of its own.

Though depicted in Aboriginal rock paintings and told about in legend, the pitted-shelled turtle was known to scientists only from New Guinea specimens until 1970. Its breeding pattern in northern Australia was not studied until the mid-1980s, and produced a surprise. The eggs have a delay mechanism.

Between late August and the middle of November, females crawl from billabongs or depleted rivers. They excavate holes in sandy banks well above the waterline and deposit hard-shelled, spherical eggs that look like table tennis balls. Clutch sizes average twelve to fifteen and as many as three clutches may be laid in a season.

Covered in sand that is intensely heated by the fierce sun of the late dry season, the eggs incubate in about seventy days. But unless the sand is water-saturated by then, the young do not break out. They lapse into torpor, needing no nutrition and hardly any oxygen. Heavy rain or flooding revives them and they slip into turbid waters where they easily escape notice. If their home is an overflowing billabong, many predators will have already dispersed.

As the rains continue, streams of excess water from lowland billabong systems and swamps join up with already-rising permanent rivers. During the Dry these meandered sluggishly at low levels, framed by vast, silvery-grey mudbanks. Ocean tides pushed far inland, making their waters brackish. Quickly now the rivers freshen and swell, soon topping their banks.

A gentle inundation

Even in flood, most rivers flowing to the north coast do not rush destructively. The waters spread over broad plains, formed through millennia of annual inundations and deposits of silt. Billabongs, creeks, swamps and the river courses themselves disappear under vast but shallow sheets of gently moving, muddy fresh water. Rock outcrops and higher hills stand out as rare islets, often giving refuge to land-loving mammals and lizards.

Spiky rushes and other sedges shoot up from what were dusty red soils before Christmas. Waterlilies spread among stands of paperbark and pandanus. Around the margins of the flood, annual grasses and wild rice sprout. Where dense growths are plucked at by swirling water, they sometimes break free of their anchorages and form drifting islands.

By late January in a good season this transformation has created the most extensive wild tropical wetlands in the world. And everywhere now there are birds. Especially at the Top End and around the Gulf of Carpentaria, enormous populations of waterfowl depend on a yearly inundation to provide food, nesting materials and breeding space.

Birds get ready to breed

The birds too have suffered many months of confinement. In fact their vast numbers were easier to assess back in the Dry when flocks were concentrated on dams, billabongs and permanent water-courses. Now they are scattered far and wide on the marshy plains. But to an observer, what may be lost in mass impact is made up for in animation.

Noisiest of the wetland birds, and usually the most numerous, is the magpie goose *Anseranas semipalmata*. The high-pitched honk of a male, in flight or on the ground, is invariably answered by deeper-voiced females from all around. Other males are provoked into calling and a deafening chorus ensues.

Flocks have been settled in since October or November, when early storms began to fill swampy areas. Until now the birds have walked about in big, closely packed groups, tweaking up new shoots of grass and rice. As waters rise, lifetime breeding partnerships — often two females to each male — form and withdraw to stands of rushes.

A gander bends and tramples a chosen clump until the stems break and the whole mass bobs to the surface. Day after day, all the members of a breeding trio weave more stems into the floating clump, building a sturdy platform that may be one and a half metres wide. It serves first for resting, and as a stage for courtship displays and preening.

Egg-laying starts when all swamp plants are flourishing and the water is not less than twenty-five centimetres deep. Availability of eggs in the Alligator Rivers region of what is now Kakadu National Park was so important in the food-gathering timetable of the Gagadju people that they named the season's opening *danbug,* after the magpie goose.

Fresh rushes are heaped on the platform before the first egg is laid. Then a thick-walled nest is erected round it, the birds continuing to add stems until a cup stands about fifty centimetres above the water. Each of the two females lays six to nine eggs into the same nest.

Attendance during the twenty-five days of incubation is shared by all three parents. During sunny breaks, they stand over the clutch to shade it. Hatchlings remain in the nest for no more than a day before they are led to grassy swamp margins. The parents help them to feed on the seeds by treading down the stems.

Magpie geese can fly at eleven weeks. Around this time their parents are moulting, but wing feathers are shed so gradually that they are still able to escort the young to flock roosting sites. This is almost certainly the only waterfowl species in the world not to undergo a vulnerable flightless period.

Young magpie geese get plenty of care
Juveniles stay with their parents until the following summer and in family groups after that. During the Dry, flocks may have to wander but they will feed fairly well, jabbing their bills into hardened mud to expose rhizomes of the same kind of rushes that they took to build their nests.

Sustained parental and group support given to young magpie geese results in generally high survival rates in the first year, after which they could well live for twenty more. This is a highly successful

species, with a natural range that used to take it into marshlands and seasonally flood-prone areas far beyond the tropical zone. But the feeding habits of the birds clashed catastrophically with European pastoral agriculture and cereal cropping. Where breeding swamps were not drained, or degraded by trampling livestock, flocks were poisoned or shot.

The former range of magpie geese is indicated by the wide scope that the plumed whistling-duck *Dendrocygna eytoni* enjoys. Flocks are preparing to breed now on the grassy margins of the tropical wetlands. Many others are deep in the hinterland, taking advantage of local rains. Some are spread down the east coast as far south as Victoria.

Whistling-ducks are so called not only because of their constant piping and twittering to one another but also because of the shrill sound of their wingbeats. The plumed species, though it always alights on water, is essentially a land bird. It feeds and rests on the ground, and nests in a grass-lined hollow screened by a shrub.

Groups make their camps near water, but a farm dam serves just as well as a

billabong or a lagoon. In providing supplementary water and short-bladed pasture grasses, agriculture has worked to the benefit of this species. Grazing flocks are seldom so numerous that they provoke persecution and in any case they always feed at night.

Wandering whistling-ducks *Dendrocygna arcuata* make similar ground nests and communal camps. But they are water feeders, favouring deep lagoons. Aquatic plants or flooded swamp vegetation make up nearly all of their diet, though some insects are taken. These ducks feed by day. Dense groups move purposefully across the water surface in rotation, with always some trailing birds flying ahead to land in the lead.

Shelducks travel in pairs
Radjah shelducks *Tadorna radjah* fly in every afternoon to patrol feeding territories at the swamp edges. Always in isolated pairs at this time of year, they stamp through the mud to force up worms, and swing their bills in it to sift out insects and snails. These birds are visitors, usually more at home around brack-

Wandering whistling-ducks form a strong pair-bond; together they choose a nesting-site, incubate and care for their young

The comb-crested jacana dives underwater if threatened by a predator, using its enormous feet for propulsion; it is an awkward flier

ish estuaries or coastal mangroves. They will breed in late autumn when the floodplain swamps are drying.

Cruising among waterlilies, again always in pairs, are little green pygmy-geese *Nettapus pulchellus*. Lily buds and seeds are their favourite food, and the broad pads will provide cover for their young. Frightened chicks dive under and stay motionless until called out by a parent. Though called geese, because of their short, goose-like bills, *Nettapus* species are perching ducks. They nest among sedges or on the ground if they have to, but much prefer hollows in trees that stand in the water.

No bird of the wetlands is more endearing than the comb-crested jacana or lotus bird *Irediparra gallinacea*, scampering perkily over lily pads or lounging on one — absurdly stretched out on its side — to sunbathe. Toes of freakish length spread the weight of this dainty bird over an area of 200 square centimetres, enabling it to use floating leaves as feeding platforms and earning it the alternative names of lily-trotter and christbird.

Lotus birds limp and brolgas dance

Jacanas occupy their swampy territories permanently, relying on the year-round growth of lilies. Nests are rafts of sedges or grasses propped on living water plants. If the water level should change dangerously, adult birds carry eggs or chicks to safety under their wings. Disturbed while brooding their young, they sometimes flap about, feigning a broken wing, to distract attention from the nest. At such moments of great excitement, blood drains from a jacana's comb and it turns from red to yellow.

January is the start of the jacana's breeding season on tropical wetlands, and mated pairs defend the nesting territories energetically. In southern Queensland and New South Wales, almost to Sydney, breeding begins in September. A similar contrast between northern and southern breeding patterns is seen in the brolga *Grus rubicundus*.

Northern brolgas flocked in as swamps were filling before Christmas. They are starting to pair off now, so the chances of seeing one of their celebrated massed dancing displays, said to be the model for important passages in Aboriginal corroborees, is receding.

Though they may play a part in courtship or in reinforcing pair-bonds, brolga ceremonies are more frequent among close-knit family groups outside the breeding season. Then, while they seem to be performed for sheer social enjoyment, they probably emphasise the dominance of one bird, who leads and protects his group during dry-season wanderings. Immature birds take part after the synchronised movements have been carefully demonstrated to them.

As many as forty of the tall, stately birds line up in facing rows. Bobbing their heads and shaking half-open wings, they advance and retreat. On a trumpeted signal from one bird, all may spring a metre into the air, opening their wings fully so that they glide down gently. Twigs or grass stems are snatched from the ground and flung wildly into the air. Then the to-and-fro dancing resumes until the next trumpet call. Sequences may continue for several minutes.

The black-necked stork or jabiru *Ephippiorhynchus asiaticus*, usually seen solitary and immobile as it watches for fish, occasionally surprises with a paired dancing display. Two birds goose-step jerkily, wings spread, necks stretched back and open bills pointed to the sky. At intervals the pace quickens and they prance, stepping high. And by shaking their bills up and down they produce a noise like sticks snapping, the only sound that these voiceless birds ever make.

The jabiru is Australia's only stork

On top of tall trees around northern swamps and billabongs, their bulky nests stand out at any time of the year. Platforms of criss-crossed sticks, nearly two metres across and a metre deep, are used from season to season, with both sexes carrying out repairs before egg-laying starts in February.

The young learn their bill-clattering early, as a defence while their parents are away foraging. For nearly four months until they are fledged they will eat only regurgitated food: frogs and reptiles as well as fish. When the monsoon clouds have rolled back and parching southeasterlies return, the chicks, still in shadeless treetops, may also have to be given regurgitated water.

Adding to the profusion of birds now breeding or about to breed in tropical wetlands are many species found almost everywhere in Australia: the pelican, the Pacific black duck and many types of herons. One attractive and abundant little heron is peculiar to the floodplains and coastal swamps of the far north, however.

Plumage of vividly contrasting blue-black and white distinguishes the pied heron *Ardea picata*. It is a busy forager for small aquatic animals, nearly always on the move rather than standing and peering as most herons do. Nesting platforms of sticks are built at a moderate height in trees, often in company with egrets and cormorants. □

This Top End brolga is dancing to impress his newly chosen mate

Holding a place in high society

How insects stay put in fast-flowing alpine streams

Turbulent torrents of icy water, fed by melting snow, seem unlikely places for insects to breed. But many are specialised to such habitats, with organs adapted for clinging to rocks. The larvae of net-veined midges and stoneflies have suckers. Blackfly larvae spin lifelines of silk. Various caddisfly larvae construct portable cases of sand, pebbles or plant material that weigh them down and divert the flow of water. Many such insects, providing the food supply of native galaxias, introduced trout, and freshwater crayfish and shrimps, are unknown at lower altitudes. The streams commonly fill bogs of sphagnum moss which store moisture for frogs and worms, and support many other plants including insect-catching sundews.

An alpine stream in Kosciusko National Park

Stoneflies spend a year on riverbeds as nymphs (below) before emerging in adult form (above)

The caddisfly as an adult; many caddisfly larvae live and pupate underwater, in silken cases of various designs (below)

Verreaux's alpine tree frog as tadpole

Male dance-flies offer silken balloons containing prey to the females as a courtship ritual

The blackfly has short larval and pupal stages in flowing water before transforming into an adult

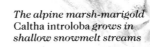

The alpine marsh-marigold Caltha introloba *grows in shallow snowmelt streams*

The pupal (above left) and larval (above centre and right) forms of the net-veined midge (top)

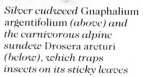

Silver cudweed Gnaphalium argentifolium *(above) and the carnivorous alpine sundew* Drosera arcturi *(below), which traps insects on its sticky leaves*

The common and colourful Gunn's willowherb (above)

Sphagnum bog (top) is the habitat of the corroboree frog Pseudophryne corroboree *(above)*

A lush sphagnum bog of northeast Victoria

Instant frogs — just add water

Amphibian breeding strategies vary with habitats

From bogs of sphagnum moss on high plateaus around Mount Kosciusko, garishly striped miniature frogs creep out to prey on summer's swarms of alpine insects. Smaller than your little fingernail, they are juvenile corroboree frogs *Pseudophryne corroboree*, born from eggs without an intervening larval feeding stage. Up here, the season of mild temperatures and good growth is too short to breed tadpoles.

Parent frogs may have spawned as long ago as November. In burrows deep in the moss, each female deposited a few large eggs containing enough yolk nutrient to sustain the entire development of the embryos. Water held in the sphagnum maintained a humid atmosphere. But if the matured eggs were not thoroughly soaked at the time they were ready to hatch, the final stage of metamorphosis from the larval form into frogs was suspended. It happens only when the bog is flooded by snowmelt or rain.

Direct development from eggs laid on land is prevalent among summer-breeding frogs in high country from Tasmania to southern Queensland. They are other *Pseudophryne* species, seldom more than three centimetres long and generally called toadlets, or equally small species of *Philoria*, including the Baw Baw and sphagnum frogs. All make nesting burrows in moss or damp soil.

The phenomenon also occurs at the other end of the Great Dividing Range, on high peaks and rainforest slopes in far northern Queensland. Species of *Cophixalus* and *Sphenophryne* exploit deep, damp layers of forest litter. In that climate, seasonal urgency cannot be their motive. It is more likely avoidance of the violent torrents of steep streams in Australia's region of highest rainfall.

Far more frogs have to develop from submerged,

Most cold-blooded animals cannot survive in alpine areas, but the corroboree frog (above) controls its temperature by living in the sphagnum moss

The white-spotted frog Heleioporus albopunctatus *(below) spawns underground, trusting to floods to release the tadpoles from its burrow*

gill-breeding tadpoles. Most also need to mate in loose water, through which the male sperms swim to fertilise the eggs. Males usually clutch the females in mating but it is merely a stimulus to close spawning. There is no copulation.

A tadpole phase relieves a mother of any need to furnish nourishment for the egg cells. So she can produce many eggs — thousands in a season in some cases. Permanent swamps and gently flowing streams are thickly sown in summertime with clusters, rafts and strings of fertilised eggs fixed to vegetation or lodged among stones.

Frogs that take no chances with their young

The great drawback of aquatic development is heavy predation of eggs and tadpoles by countless other creatures. This is allowed for in overabundant spawning. But two types of Australian frogs give unusual personal protection to limited numbers of their young.

High ranges flanking the Tweed Valley, on the eastern Queensland–New South Wales border, are the only known home of the marsupial frog *Assa darlingtoni*. It spawns in streams intersecting Australia's northernmost Antarctic beech rainforests. Males have a broad pouch on each flank. They squirm into masses of hatching eggs and some of the emerging tadpoles wriggle into the pouches, staying and feeding there until they metamorphose.

A more surprising method, unknown anywhere in the world until 1972, is employed by gastric-brooding frogs. Females take eggs into their stomachs — somehow stopping the flow of digestive juices — and carry the hatchlings through their tadpole stage.

The first *Rheobatrachus* species was discovered in ranges backing Queensland's Sunshine Coast, another far to the north in Eungella National Park, west of Mackay. Whether or not the gastric-brooders are extremely rare, they are certainly obscure. Hiding under river stones by day and clinging to them at night, still partly submerged, they are rivalled by only one African group as the world's most thoroughly aquatic frogs.

Queensland mountain streams are also nurseries and refuges for summer-breeding torrent frogs *Taudactylus* and the torrent tree frog *Litoria nannotis*. Adults leap into cascades and rapids when alarmed, using extended toe pads to clamber among rocks. And their tadpoles have oral sucker discs to hold them in place in swift currents.

Outside the northern and eastern belts of assured midsummer rainfall or snowmelt, frogs breeding now have to be opportunistic. Most swarm from the shelter of plants and burrows to exploit temporary water, spawning fast-developing young. A few have eggs that are capable of dormancy for a while. Spawned after one downpour, they may be washed into a stream by a bigger one.

Some burrowing frogs emerge in response to heavy rain, gorge on insects and then retreat to spawn underground. They trust that their burrows will flood. The southeast's giant burrowing frog *Heleioporus australiacus*, nearly ten centimetres long, tunnels into sandy creek banks and breeds there, relying on the water level to rise. □

A dragonfly devours its insect prey

HAWKS OF THE INSECT WORLD
Dragonflies always take their prey on the wing

Big, gaudily coloured dragonflies are at their most numerous now, breeding in southern streams as well as in freshened tropical swamps and billabongs. In their aquatic larval form, sheltering on the bottom among stones, they are voracious predators on other larvae. As flying adults they can overpower any other insect apart from giant robber flies.

Dragonflies and the daintier forms that are called damselflies mate and hunt in flight. Their legs, unsuited for walking and crawling, trap flying prey and carry it to the mouthparts. Hunting is done by extremely acute sight, in patrols over set areas. The swooping style of bigger species is aptly known as hawking.

The analogy with birds can be carried further, for the males of many types are fiercely territorial, driving off their own and other species. Visual courtship displays seem to be involved in mating. Both sexes mate several times in the one day, which occurs in areas most suited to the larval development of each species.

A turtle's turn to take a walk
Southern swamp-dwellers may be evicted by drought

While monsoon rains bring ideal conditions for tropical freshwater turtles, many of their southern cousins are suffering. They can withstand midsummer heat by burying themselves in mud, but drought cannot be endured. Turtles that live in drying swamps, streams or lakes are forced to migrate overland to permanent rivers.

They walk slowly but strongly on jointed limbs and clawed feet (sea turtles have flippers). Surprising distances may be covered, after sundown over bare country, but also by day if long grass or other dense vegetation gives protection. The frequency with which they were seen on land in southern Australia led to their being commonly called tortoises, a term reserved in other countries for truly land-based types.

The eastern snake-necked turtle Chelodina longicollis *lives in fresh water in eastern coastal areas. It is also known as the long-necked tortoise because it has been mistaken for the land animal on its lengthy overland treks in search of water. It lives for up to twenty years*

Species well known for their summer migrations are the oblong turtle *Chelodina oblonga* of the southwest and the eastern snake-necked turtle *Chelodina longicollis*, which is found from mid-Queensland to Bass Strait and eastern South Australia. The western type reaches forty centimetres in shell length, the eastern only twenty-five.

These two belong to a family distinguished by exceptionally lengthy necks, which when extended may be at least as long as the shell. If overturned, they easily right themselves by using their necks as levers. And they possess a defence that dissuades most other animals from bothering them — glands on their legs ooze a foul-smelling, sticky fluid.

Most lay their eggs in summer
Though toothless, all southern freshwater turtles are largely carnivorous. They grind their food with hard plates along their jaws, preying on molluscs, crustaceans, tadpoles, aquatic insects and, to a lesser extent, fish. Breeding patterns are broadly similar in all species, the females laying a dozen or so eggs in holes dug in the banks of swamps and watercourses. Most lay in summer but incubation periods vary widely.

Biggest of the non-tropical species, reaching a shell length of fifty centimetres, is the broad-shelled river turtle *Chelodina expansa*. It is said to breed in autumn, the eggs not hatching until spring. Its stronghold is the Murray-Darling river system, which it shares with the more common Murray turtle *Emydura macquarii*.

Western Australia has two small, drought-adapted species. The flat-shelled turtle *Chelodina steindachneri* lives in the waterholes of seasonally flowing rivers of the northwest. It stores water in its bladder and burrows deep in muddy beds. At Bullsbrook, on the Swan coastal plain near Perth, the western swamp turtle *Pseudemydura umbrina* was rediscovered in the 1950s. Restricted to a few swamps that dry up for half the year, it is Australia's rarest and most endangered reptile. □

Platypus days

This native Australian is a complex beast. January brings a new crop of young oddities to baffle the scientists

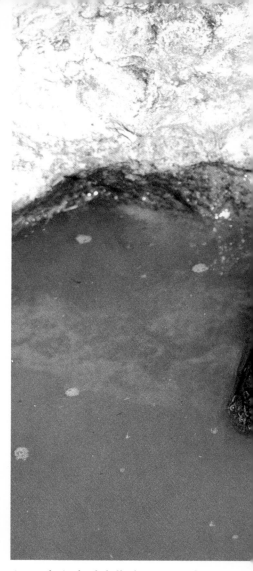

Fourteen weeks after hatching in the farthest recess of a long burrow, a lean young platypus emerges on a riverbank. It is seeing daylight — or more likely moonlight — for the first time. Almost immediately it plunges into a new darkness, tightly shutting its eyes and planing down to the river bed. It must quickly start finding food to replace its mother's dwindling milk supply.

Diving for a minute or so at a time, with ears and nostrils also sealed, the youngster thrusts its soft muzzle into thick mud or under stones. After a little experience its cheek pouches are stuffed with crustaceans, worms or insect larvae each time it surfaces.

Until 1985 baffled scientists could only suppose that the platypus had an exceptionally delicate sense of touch concentrated in the muzzle. Now, thanks to joint Australian and West German research, we understand that it hunts by electricity. The muzzle contains nerve receptors of a type previously known only in tadpoles and some fishes. They detect the small, weak electrical fields that are set up by discharges from the muscles of tiny prey animals.

The capacity of *Ornithorhynchus anatinus* to confound zoologists seems never-ending. It was astounding enough to late eighteenth century observers — it still is — that any furry animal should have feet with webs as well as claws, and take its food with a toothless apparatus looking like the bill of a duck. But the proof that emerged in the 1880s that such a creature laid eggs, even though it suckled its young, shattered all precedent.

In spite of having some reptilian anatomical features, the platypus, like all true mammals, controls its body temperature. But it tends to make nonsense of our term 'warm-blooded' for mammals. Its constant temperature is five degrees Celsius below that of a healthy human, and as much as ten degrees lower than those of some other mammals.

Unusually adaptable body chemistry, aided by the climate-tempering effects of aquatic and burrowing habits, allows the platypus a remarkable range from north to south. It can be found throughout almost the entire longitudinal span of eastern Australia, wherever there are permanent and relatively undisturbed waterways. Rarely is a single animal species capable of year-round activity in conditions as different as a Tasmanian highlands winter and a Daintree rainforest summer.

The only physical variation between platypuses at the two extremes of the range seems to be greater size in the southerners. They attain average lengths of about fifty centimetres for males and a little over forty for females, with males nearly twice as heavy at about 1.7 kilos. The biggest platypus on record was a male sixty centimetres long, weighing 2.4 kilos.

The dog-paddling duck-bill

All other amphibious mammals swim by kicking their hind legs. But a platypus 'dog paddles', alternating its fully webbed forefeet. The hind feet, only partly webbed, are used for steering and as brakes to pull out of a dive. If a platypus is burrowing or walking the forefoot webbing folds back, exposing strong nails.

Young platypuses begin to appear in January in Queensland but not until March in Tasmania. Growth in the nesting burrow has been very rapid: hatchlings only fifteen millimetres long have now reached about four-fifths of the adult length, though only half the weight.

Two young — occasionally one or three — are raised. Until they are weaned, within a fortnight of emerging from the burrow, they spend some of their time splashing about playfully on the surface. Tadpoles may be gobbled up and cicadas or moths snatched from the air. At this stage a platypus has teeth — which will soon be replaced by horny grinding pads.

The best opportunities to observe platypuses in numbers come during this weaning period, especially in warmer regions where it occurs early in the year. The young are feeding greedily and so are the mothers, having lost condition during their long lactation. And while they are primarily nocturnal feeders, the shortness of summer nights means that they will probably be active at dusk and dawn.

Juveniles on becoming independent apparently forage fairly widely, occupying various simple resting burrows. Competition for food and burrowing sites must force the dispersal of many juveniles;

Australia's duck-bill platypus is the most

unusual mammal in the world — it is found in fresh water from Queensland down the east coast to Tasmania

their mortality is probably high. Those reaching breeding age, in their third year, seem to have a good rate of survival and may live for about fifteen years.

Nesting burrows of some complexity

Mating occurs in the water as it gains springtime warmth, between August and October, depending on latitude and altitude. First comes a seasonal enlargement of the reproductive organs of both sexes, and a remarkable development of the female's two mammary glands. Outside the breeding season these are only about a centimetre long. Before the time of mating they enlarge by cell division, fanning out under the skin until they take up most of the belly area.

Nothing is reliably known of mating behaviour in the wild. If observations of captive animals are anything to go by, the female starts a courtship with display manoeuvres near the water surface and the male responds by grasping her tail in his muzzle before seizing her body between his legs.

Adult females have extensive and elaborate nesting burrows. A tunnel usually about eight metres long — but sometimes more than thirty — leads up from just above the normal waterline to a dry level, following the slope of the bank. Often it winds among tree roots that help stabilise the soil. The burrow may have more than one entrance, and usually has several chambers and dead-end branches.

A mated female pads her chosen nesting chamber with sodden leaves or grass, dragged in with a curled-up tail. The warming of this material probably helps keep humidity in the chamber at a desirable level. About a month after mating, the mother-to-be seals off the tunnel at one or more points, using her tail to tamp plugs of earth into place.

Glossy white eggs, smaller than a pigeon's, are laid onto the mother's belly so that she can curl her tail round them in a normal sleeping position. Incubation probably takes a week to ten days. After the eggs have hatched, milk starts seeping from the enlarged mammary glands into ducts that converge at two patches of fur-covered skin. There are no teats. Prodding by the young squirts milk out into the fur, from which they suck.

During the nursing period the mother departs often to feed. On each journey in and out she destroys and replaces her defensive plugs. When her flow of milk declines she leaves the tunnel open and the young find their way to the water.

Eels, snakes and rats may prey on platypuses. Crocodiles certainly do, in the northern part of their range. Burrow destruction by violent floods is also a natural hazard. All are outweighed by the potential dangers presented by human interference through water engineering works, pollution, fish traps and even some hunting, in spite of full legal protection.

Where they can, platypuses seem to go from strength to strength. They are abundant in suitable rivers, though few people see them. Should they ever be denied such habitats, however, a unique life form will be lost to the world. People have tried for a century to breed platypuses in captivity. But only one man, the celebrated wildlife curator David Fleay, was ever successful. □

An eastern grey joey suckles at its mother's pouch — inside a baby sucks on another teat, which gives a different milk

A joey's first journey

Giving birth is so easy. But motherhood for a kangaroo means a never-ending procession of hungry mouths to feed

Lolling in the shady woodlands that border their feeding grounds, eastern grey kangaroos wait for sundown. Most of the mob, scattered now, are dozing. Here and there an ear is flicked to ward off a fly, or a paw is raised indolently to scratch. But one female stirs as if she has heard a secret alarm.

She energetically licks her pouch, thrusting her muzzle deep inside. Then she stands up and rocks back on her heels, toes in the air and abdominal muscles tensed. Very soon she resumes her resting position. As simply as that she has expelled an offspring from her uterus and for want of a better term, given birth.

This is no great feat, for all the kangaroo has produced is a part-developed embryo — more wormlike than anything else — about the size of a string bean. In the manner of all marsupials, it requires a long period of nurturing in the pouch before it will take on a recognisable form.

The mother seems oblivious as this creature wriggles from her cloaca, the single opening shared by her reproductive and excretory tracts. The newcomer is blind and its hind legs are only just budding, but it has tiny forepaws and uses these to drag itself through the parent's dense belly fur. In three or four minutes, probably following traces of milky saliva, it has found the pouch entrance. Quickly it fastens its mouth to one of the four teats inside.

Unless the mother has mated for the first time, approaching two years of age, or unless she has lost her previous joey, one of the other teats will be swollen and stretched. The newborn's brother or sister, now a year old, still has a claim to it.

Though the senior joey is sleeping out now and grazing at the mother's heels, it will suckle occasionally for six more months, thrusting its head into the pouch. Remarkably, the fatty milk that it receives

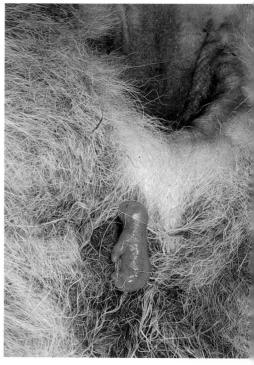

A newborn and only partially formed wallaby climbs towards the pouch

HARD TO HOLD

Few fences can keep them out ... or in

In their bounding runs big kangaroos do not normally jump higher than about 1.5 metres from the ground. But to clear obstacles when fleeing from danger, they can jump twice that height. A 'boomer' pursued by dogs is said to have cleared a wood-pile more than four metres high.

The daunting cost of fencing is one of the major drawbacks to notions of farming kangaroos for meat and hides. Kilo for kilo in bodyweight, they need less food than sheep, are more drought-tolerant, and convert grass into meat with far greater efficiency. A kangaroo is more than half meat — a sheep about one quarter.

A red kangaroo at speed

is different in composition from the supply delivered to the pouch occupant.

It was the older joey's vacating of the pouch, around eleven months of age, that brought the mother into breeding condition. She was mated five weeks before by one of the biggest males, probably after he had asserted his dominance over rivals in a series of boxing matches.

The 'old man' or 'boomer', as a dominant male is sometimes called, makes daily checks on the females under his control, sniffing their lower parts. Finding one that is approaching readiness, he courts her by pawing gently at her head and grasping the base of her tail. For some days his attempts to mount her fail. Finally, the successful copulation may last as long as three-quarters of an hour.

Delayed implantation

Four months or more after giving birth, and while still allowing milk to the young at foot and nursing the pouch offspring, a well-nourished eastern grey may mate again. This time the fertilised egg — very rarely is there twinning among kangaroos

— develops into a globular sac no wider than a pinpoint, then becomes quiescent.

The blastocyst, as biologists call this sac, will not be implanted on the uterus wall and develop further until the pouch is unoccupied. Normally that will occur eleven months after the previous birth. But if the pouch young dies or is lost through some mishap — it starts venturing out briefly at nine months — it is replaced in a month without mating.

A midsummer breeding peak

The eastern grey *Macropus giganteus* is the most strongly seasonal of kangaroos because it has the most reliable food supply. Though breeding can occur at any time there is a pronounced midsummer peak. Relatively little use need be made of embryonic diapause, the technical term for delayed implantation.

In contrast, the red kangaroo of more arid country (see page 26) employs diapause as a matter of course. A 'blue flier', as the female is often called, remates immediately after giving birth and holds the blastocyst until good rains bring a flush of grasses.

Diapause is also common among wallaroos and wallabies, but strangely does not seem to occur at all in the western grey kangaroo. Yet the western is the closest relative of the eastern grey. Populations mingle in South Australia and far western Victoria and New South Wales; in captivity, the two species have interbred.

Male eastern greys can grow to 2.3 metres in head-to-tail length and weigh more than sixty kilos. Females seldom exceed 1.8 metres and are slender, weighing only about half as much as their mates. Fur colours vary from silvery to golden grey on the mainland while a subspecies in Tasmania, known as the forester kangaroo, is dark grey.

The mainland population of eastern greys fluctuates with major changes in food and water availability. But at the worst of times it is numbered in millions. Like all grasslands kangaroos the species has benefited from forest clearance, the development of pastoral agriculture and the extermination of dingoes. In spite of heavy culling in most years, it is more numerous now than before European settlement. Tasmania's forester type is at some risk, however; stocks are conserved in offshore island reserves. □

The eastern grey kangaroo has a hairy muzzle, unlike other large kangaroos

A kangaroo joey beginning to take shape at about five weeks old

Night shift dodges the heat

Soaring temperatures can spell disaster for land snakes. Many venomous types take to hunting in the dark in summer

Snakes thrive on warmth — but not too much of it. In common with all reptiles they can do little to regulate their body temperatures, which fluctuate in response to surrounding conditions. If a snake's internal temperature climbs into the forties Celsius for more than a few minutes its body chemistry is permanently disrupted and it dies.

Their subjection to the whims of weather makes land-based snakes the most vulnerable of reptiles. They lack the shells of turtles or the thick hides that partly insulate crocodiles and many lizards. They do not even have legs to keep their bodies off scorching ground. They can swim, but few have access to water.

Under the most torrid conditions some land snakes choose to abandon all activity. They retreat, for weeks on end if necessary, into cool, deep shelters. Rock clefts, ground crevices and the burrows of other animals are commonly used.

Aestivation, as this summer resting-up is termed, is not like the torpor of hibernation, which renders an animal helpless. Though inert, an aestivating snake retains its physical powers and will defend itself if disturbed. Its voluntary fast does it no harm; snakes normally go for long periods between good meals.

Species that are usually inclined to feed by day may have to avoid hot ground and direct sunshine at the height of summer. If they do not aestivate, they delay their hunting until after sundown. During the day they rest — sluggish, perhaps, but still able to look after themselves — under rocks, in or under logs, or

The diamond python Morelia spilota is found throughout Australia, but with many local variations in its dramatic markings

·*Black-bellied swamp snakes* Hemiaspis signata *bear live young*

hidden in dense vegetation or leaf litter.

When such snakes adjust their routines to dodge daytime heat, they fall into line with the vast majority of Australian snakes that are nocturnal all year round. Most attention is focussed on the day-to-night minority because of a curious co-incidence: they include nearly all of the dangerously venomous species. And their wanderings in the dark coincide with peak holiday time, when people, especially campers, are likely to cross their paths.

Among the egg-laying snakes (see November, page 267) that convert from diurnal to nocturnal hunting in hot weather are the taipan, the mulga and the various brown snakes. A similar adjustment is made by tiger snakes, the females of which bear their young live.

Live-bearing snakes give birth
January is a peak month for live births, though it may be too early for many southern snakes. Gestation periods vary from less than three months in the tropics to four in cooler climates, and the time of mating is also later in the south.

Snakes do not come into breeding condition until they have fed amply during a period of full activity, which requires a body temperature above 20°C. But the air does not have to be that warm all the time — a snake can gain extra heat by basking in sunshine.

A female snake, reaching sexual maturity in her second spring in tropical conditions but probably a year later in the south, produces an anal gland secretion that leaves a scent trail for males. Courtship consists of a gentle writhing together while both sexes twitch their tails. If two snakes are seen tightly intertwined in a more vigorous struggle, they are likely to be both males, engaged in a mock fight.

To complete the mating the male inserts one of his twin penises into the female's cloaca, pushing down a movable plate that covers the entrance. The cloaca is a tract serving jointly for excretion and reproduction, a feature shared by all reptiles and birds and most fishes. Marsupial mammals and the platypus and echidna also have a single opening.

Snakelets of live-bearing species emerge encased in thin sacs. Some types stay in these for hours, but infant tiger snakes break out immediately. While still wet with the nutrient fluid in which they developed, pencil-sized snakes rear up in mock strikes, darting their heads at pretended prey. They are strengthening their muscles and charging their fangs with venom, which they possess from birth.

Live-bearing and egg-laying elapid snakes differ little otherwise. Neither type gives any care to the young. Live litters tend to be more numerous than egg clutches; tiger snakes average about thirty, with a litter of more than a hundred on record. Live-born snakelets also stand a better chance of survival, provided that they escape cannibalism.

Hunting within about a fortnight of their birth, the successful young of larger species grow two to three millimetres a week. Growth slows after the first year or two, by which time only about ten per cent of snakes are still alive. The rest have succumbed to the attacks of birds of prey, goannas and bigger snakes, or fallen foul of people. Survivors of some species reaching maturity may live for more than ten years. Some recorded specimens, far bigger than the average for their species, may have been as old as thirty.

Stealth not speed catches a meal
Snakes evolved from lizards, developing an exaggerated slimness that enables them to slip through tiny openings in search of prey or shelter. To compensate for their loss of legs they perfected a unique method of locomotion. It is based on an intricate arrangement of muscles and mobile ribs exerting backward pressure on the surface of the ground.

An elapid snake — any of Australia's front-fanged venomous types — has two ways of moving. It can squirm, flexing its body in a series of backward-travelling waves that push against obstacles and thrust the animal forward. But it can also creep ahead in a straight line, so smoothly that it seems to flow. In rapid sequence the wide belly scales are hitched forward, then their trailing edges are forced backwards against the ground.

Even in panic a snake is unlikely to cover more than two metres a second — a brisk walking pace for us — and shortage of oxygen soon slows it down. It can raise the front third of its body off the ground, but it cannot jump. Unable to chase prey, it has to rely on stealth, and then the speed and accuracy of its strike.

All snakes are carnivorous, and few will eat anything but live or freshly-killed animals. The size of their prey is limited to what they can subdue and swallow whole. No snake can chew. But the jaws of snakes are loosely attached at the rear and the connections of other head bones are elastic, allowing a huge gape.

Sizable prey is swallowed head-first so that limbs, feathers or fur are forced back and go in smoothly. A snake's small, backward-pointing teeth draw its head

The brown tree snake Boiga irregularis *grows up to two metres*

A black tiger snake swallowing a fish

over the victim. Meanwhile, to avoid choking, the opening of its windpipe is thrust out of the side of its mouth. The snake's body stretches to accommodate anything that the jaws can engulf.

Prey animals are tracked by their scent trails. A snake's forked tongue, flicking in and out through a notch in its lips, takes samples of chemical particles on the ground and in the air. They are carried to sensory organs in the roof of the mouth. Vision seems important only at killing range, to detect movement by the quarry.

In our terms snakes are deaf. They cannot hear sounds. But they have internal 'ears' that give them a perfect sense of balance and pick up the slightest ground vibrations. That is why, if someone walks near them, they nearly always flee if they can. It is no good shouting or waving your arms at an obstinate snake, but a stamp of the foot usually works.

Fangs designed to kill small prey

If a snake is venomous — and many are not — modified salivary glands produce a toxic mixture that is primarily aimed at paralysing prey. The venom is led through ducts to a pair of fangs, which are teeth adapted to work as injectors, like hypodermic needles. The dental material is curved round a deep groove, forming a tube that has its outlet near the tip. Jaw muscles tightening round the glands cause the venom to squirt out.

A few water snakes and the brown tree snake have open-grooved teeth at the rear of their jaws. They can use them only on small animals already in their mouths. But the elapid land snakes, along with sea snakes, have fangs at the front of the upper jaw. These are mounted on a swivelling bone and can be thrust forward in an attack. Big snakes of this kind are potentially dangerous.

Fangs are delicate, even in the largest snakes. They are easily broken if they strike bone, or wrenched out in struggles with prey. Otherwise they are soon blunted. Worn fangs work loose every few weeks. Each is backed by a renewable battery of replacements. And a snake can bite with a single fang if it has to.

World rankings in venom toxicity among land snakes are headed by Australian species. But our elapid snakes are ill-equipped to attack big targets. With the exception of brown snakes and the rough-scaled snake, they do not really 'bite' but strike with their mouths shut. And only death adders are capable of a significant forward rotation of their fangs. The fangs of other species hit at an acute angle. Often they glance off or do not penetrate far enough for a serious envenomation.

Tiger snakes like river valleys

Even more fortunately for us, the fang length of an elapid is limited by the size of its mouth. It cannot fold back its fangs. Foreign vipers have highly mobile fangs many times longer than those of Australian snakes of comparable head size. A

The Oenpelli python Morelia oenpelliensis *is restricted to a small area of western Arnhem Land, where it lives in sandstone gorges and escarpments*

taipan's fangs, the longest in this country, rarely measure more than twelve millimetres. A brown snake's are less than three millimetres.

In any case no snake is inclined to waste venom on something that is too big to swallow. Snakes strike at people only if they are frightened and have no way of escaping, or if they are touched. Most bites occur when people try to kill or capture snakes, or poke things at them instead of letting them quietly slip away. In a minority of cases unseen snakes are trodden on, or touched by people who unthinkingly reach into their shelter.

Tiger snakes inflict most of the medi-

This common death-adder is hunting, using its tail-tip lure to attract prey

---

FEAST AND FAMINE

A two-month-long bonanza for these tiger snakes

On desolate islands in the Furneaux group, at the eastern end of Bass Strait, juvenile black tiger snakes sustain their rapid growth by eating lizards. But the adults eat only the chicks of short-tailed shearwaters — muttonbirds. Sliding into the close-packed burrows while the parent birds are feeding at sea, the snakes dine richly on helpless prey.

The chicks hatch in late January, and fledge by early March. So the snakes have a feeding season of only two months, fasting for the rest of the year. The regimen is obviously good for them. Averaging 1.8 metres in length and sometimes reaching 2.4 metres, the Chappell Island tiger snake *Notechis ater serventyi* is the biggest tiger snake of all.

Chappell Island tiger snakes bask near muttonbird burrows

---

cally serious bites in this country, not because they are unusually venomous or aggressive, but because they occur near major centres of population and in areas of intensive farming. Like us, they favour river valleys.

Feeding mostly on frogs, the prominently banded eastern tiger snake *Notechis scutatus* breeds prolifically on the southeastern mainland from Adelaide to the ranges near Brisbane. Black tiger snakes *Notechis ater* fill a similar role in Tasmania and the southwest. Subspecies with specialised diets are isolated on islands off South Australia and in Bass Strait. Western Australians know their type as the norne, from an Aboriginal word, while some Tasmanians call theirs a carpet snake.

Tiger snakes are especially troublesome around Melbourne, where they become hungrily active in late spring, and near the great rivers of the southeast. Summer flooding along the Darling-Murray system may force them out of the marshes where they normally hunt frogs. That increases the likelihood that their night-time excursions, on the trail of rats and mice, will take them to buildings.

Death adders hunt the easy way

From spring to autumn in drier areas across most of the mainland except Victoria, death adders seem almost to invite being trodden on. They are the one exception to the rule that snakes will flee if they sense vibrations from human footfalls. Instead they hold their ground, bodies tensed in flat coils, ready to strike fast and low if they are touched.

A death adder is nocturnal throughout the year. By day it partly buries itself in shaded soil or leaf litter. Even at night it is the laziest of snakes. It lies still with most of its tail buried, waiting for small mammals or birds to come its way. A soft, curved spike — a modified scale — on the end of the tail protrudes from the ground. Looking much like a worm, it twitches alluringly.

With broad, angular heads on narrow necks, death adders look like no other Australian snake. Though they are elapids, their appearance led to their being called after the adders of the northern hemisphere, which are members of the viper family. Curiously enough they have another viper-like characteristic. Their fangs are much more mobile than the rest of the elapids, pushing well forward when they strike and entering the target at right-angles.

The species most often encountered, in Western and South Australia, New South Wales and Queensland, is the common death adder *Acanthophis antarcticus*. A reddish species with a dark tail-tip lure, *Acanthophis pyrrhus*, lives and hunts in arid spinifex country (see page 38). *Acanthophis praelongus*, smaller, more slender and predominantly ginger in colour, is limited to the monsoonal north.

Among other live-bearing, venomous land snakes reaching a formidable size are copperheads *Austrelaps*, small-eyed snakes *Cryptophis*, the ornamental snake *Denisonia maculata*, broad-headed snakes *Hoplocephalus*, the myall or curl snake *Suta suta*, the rough-scaled snake *Tropidechis carinatus*, and the red-bellied black snake *Pseudechis porphyriacus*.

The red-belly hunts frogs by day except in the hottest weather, and is the snake most likely to attract attention in forested country around streams and lagoons near the east and southeast coasts. It happily goes into water — lying still, it can be taken for a fire-blackened branch — and sometimes feeds on eels and yabbies. □

High in an ironbark tree a plump lace monitor clings precariously with her hind legs, using the great claws of her forefeet to scratch into the top of a termite nest. Morning after morning, before the sun becomes too hot, she returns to the task until she has hollowed out a bowl. Rivals attempting to climb the tree are warned off with an angry hissing.

Bulging from a fork of the ironbark, the material of her sculpture is fairly soft and flaky, rather like cardboard. It is produced by a termite species that regurgitates chewed wood and binds it with faeces. Now it forms not only the insects' nest but the monitor's as well. Heaving herself into position she spends an hour or more laying six to ten eggs, about the size of a hen's but more elongated. The clutch is lightly covered with a further scratching of the nest material, then abandoned. Care of the eggs can be left safely to the termites.

Reacting instinctively as they would to any damage to their communal home, hundreds of thousands of workers hastily rebuild. New galleries are formed round and over the eggs. Sealed up in the warmth and humidity of a perfect incubator, they will hatch quickly.

Vividly patterned young, a little over twenty centimetres long, chip their way out with a special 'egg tooth' that grows from the snout but is discarded soon after hatching. They are immediately ready to hunt, starting on the insects that live in the tree of their birth.

Juveniles move tentatively at first, wary of the attentions of snakes, hawks, kookaburras and butcherbirds. Growing bigger, they take to foraging confidently on the ground, widening their diet to include snakes and lesser lizards, small mammals and carrion, but they return to trees to rest or if they are frightened, and comb them frequently for their favourite food — nestling birds and eggs. In spite of their bulk — some weigh more than twenty-five kilos — adults can climb saplings and nimbly negotiate slender branches.

Australia — a land of lizards

Taking over termite nests is common among monitor lizards, or goannas as they are generally called in Australia. Ground monitors often dig into softer mounds or subterranean nests. Hollow logs, heaps of litter or holes scratched in the ground also prove satisfactory, but incubation is probably slower and the eggs are less secure from predators.

Tropical water monitors dig nesting burrows in riverbanks and pack them with plant matter, which provides extra heat as it rots. Ground monitors have been

Lace monitors are agile climbers, and regard trees as places of refuge

Lizards with cuckoo-like habits

Midsummer is breeding time for lizards — and big goannas will take whatever help they can get

known to use the nesting mounds of brush turkeys for the same reason. In the far north, some raids by goannas on crocodile nests may not be attempts to take eggs, but rather to lay their own.

Though often called a land of snakes or of birds, Australia could more aptly be called a land of lizards. There are more species, finding niches of their own in every conceivable type of habitat, than there are of breeding birds. And the skink family alone outnumbers all the different kinds of snakes.

In spite of their wide geographical spread and great diversity of form, size and habit, the breeding biology of lizards is fairly uniform. With the exception of a few skinks — blue-tongued lizards, for example — the females all lay eggs. And regardless of regional climates, nearly all reproduction occurs in midsummer.

Lizards differ from snakes in having external ear openings. In most cases they have mobile eyelids and tails longer than their bodies. What may seem a more obvious distinction, the possession of legs, is not entirely reliable. Australia has a big family of legless burrowing lizards and also some legless skinks — prominent at this time of year — that are easily mistaken for snakes. People sometimes victimise them for that reason, though they are far too small to be dangerous even if they were snakes.

All lizards are carnivorous, but none in this country is venomous. And unlike a snake a lizard's lower jaw is fixed to its skull, so it is more limited in the size of

The land mullet lives in rainforest and is the biggest of Australia's skinks

live prey. The carrion of big animals presents no problem for goannas, however. They can use their forefeet in the manner of dogs, pinning down a carcass while they wrench mouthfuls from it.

Goannas may display aggression if disturbed. It is a defensive bluff; none will launch a deliberate attack. Their next inclination is to make for the nearest tree. A frightened goanna may run on its hind legs, presumably to get a better view of possible refuges, although it is faster on all fours. On rare occasions stationary people have been mistaken for trees and suffered deep scratches from a goanna's efforts to scramble up. Certainly no attempt should be made to restrain or pick up a sizable goanna.

Left to themselves, all lizards are harmless to people. Apart from the unfortunate impact of tree-climbing goannas on bird life, they and all their relatives are good to have around. Houses and outbuildings frequented by goannas will be free of rats, mice and snakes, while the small geckoes and skinks that have adapted to human settlements take a heavy toll of insect pests, spiders and centipedes.

In the lace monitor or tree goanna *Varanus varius* Australia has the biggest lizard that most people are ever likely to see. Common from northern Queensland to Victoria, it averages about 1.5 metres in length. Some long-lived specimens exceed two metres. Only our desert-dwelling perentie and the rare Komodo 'dragon' of Indonesia, both of them close relatives, outdo it in size.

Lace monitors in natural bushland settings are furtive. The scrabbling of claws may be heard as an animal flees into a tree but it remains unseen, even if we walk all round the tree. It spirals up the trunk, always keeping on the far side from an intruder. But once accustomed to people — at camp sites and picnic grounds, for example — lace monitors become tame enough to be fed by hand.

Dragons of the bushland

Though they cannot match goannas for size or killing power, lizards of the agamid family are more talked about, especially by visitors from overseas. The grotesque scale formations of many of them, and their displays of ferocity, earn them the common name of dragon lizards. When alarmed they stand their ground to issue a defiant threat before scampering away, some with a comical two-legged gait.

Most celebrated of the agamids is the frilled lizard *Chlamydosaurus kingii*, a tree-dweller that frequently forages on the ground. If confronted it puts on a startling display of aggression that disconcerts any natural enemy. Rearing on its hind legs and rocking from side to side, it opens its mouth to an improbable dimension, hissing loudly. The jaw movement causes a ruff of leathery, mobile neck scales to fan out like an opening umbrella. Suddenly the lizard, never more than fifty centimetres long, looks huge.

Frilled lizards live in open forests and woodlands in Queensland and across the north to the Kimberley. A sombre greyish brown in the eastern part of their range, they tend more to an orange or brick colour in monsoonal areas. There they shelter in tree holes late in the dry season,

The frilled lizard's bark is worse than its bite: it eats mainly insects

reappearing around the end of the year when the cloud cover of the Wet has reduced solar radiation. Though lizards are more tolerant of heat and cold than most snakes, they too have to adjust their activities according to the weather.

Also impressive in their displays of defiance are the bearded dragons *Pogona*. They erect spiky fringes round their bottom jaws and spread their ribs to puff out their bodies. Occasionally they rush towards an intruder.

The most commonly seen bearded dragon, *Pogona barbata*, is also known as the jew lizard. Sometimes more than fifty centimetres long, it is encountered foraging on roadside verges or resting on fence posts. Though basically carnivorous, preying mainly on insects, it also eats flowers and other plants.

An extraordinarily varied diet is enjoyed by the eastern water dragon *Physignathus lesueurii*. Hunting in eastern waterways as well as in trees, it eats insects, frogs, worms, mice, smaller lizards and the fruits of many plants. If surprised while sunning itself on an overhanging branch it will drop immediately into the water, where it can remain submerged for half an hour. A tail two and a half times as long as the body gives some males a total length of ninety centimetres. The tail is keeled, which accounts for the

This Lesueur's velvet gecko Oedura lesueurii is shedding its skin. It is found in coastal areas of New South Wales and southern Queensland

swimming ability of these lizards, and the legs are unusually long.

The jacky lizard *Amphibolurus muricatus* is common among shrubs in forests and coastal heathlands of the east and southeast. Some of its upland habitats overlap those of the mountain dragon *Amphibolurus diemensis* and the two are easily confused. But you can tell them apart by their threat display: the inside of the jacky's mouth is bright yellow, the mountain dragon's blue.

Blue-tongues and other skinks

Skinks form not only our biggest lizard family but also the most varied in size, habits and resistance to extremes of temperature. They range from slender suburbanites such as the garden skink *Lampropholis guichenoti* and the weasel skink *Saproscincus mustelina*, not reaching more than ten centimetres, to bushland heavyweights such as the land mullet *Egernia major* and the eastern blue-tongue *Tiliqua scincoides*, both growing to seventy-five centimetres.

Contrasts are magnified when agility and temperament are considered. The land mullet is as shy and swift-moving as a garden skink. It hides as soon as it senses intrusion in its rainforest habitat. The only sign of its passing may be the crushed shells of eaten snails. Blue-tongues on the other hand are ponderous in their movements, relying on the surprising appearance of their open mouths to scare off enemies. When used to humans they are placid, and sometimes boldly curious.

Striking differences arise even among closely related skinks. For example a well-nourished female eastern blue-tongue, active by day and feeding on a huge variety of insects, snails, spiders, blossoms and

A thick-tailed gecko demonstrates how it copes without eyelids

berries in districts with reliable rainfall, may give birth to a litter of twenty-five young. Some *Tiliqua* species of less favoured regions, restricted in diet and generally nocturnal, are much smaller and produce as few as one or two young.

Creatures of the night

Mainland Australia has an abundance of big-eyed, graceful geckoes. The family includes some of the most prettily marked of all lizards, especially the velvet geckoes *Oedura*, and some with the most bizarre tail formations. But all our geckoes are nocturnal and many are desert specialists, so most types are not widely known.

Lacking movable lids, geckoes lick their eyes clean with their tongues. While ground-hunting species have narrow, birdlike toes, the climbers are equipped like tree frogs, with adhesive pads. In pursuit of insects and spiders they can move vertically or upside-down on the smoothest surfaces, even glass.

Some dtellas, geckoes of the genus *Gehyra*, have domesticated themselves, taking advantage of artificial lights as a lure for flying insects. But the dominant house gecko of the far north is a lizard of Asian origin, *Hemidactylus frenatus*. It seems to be conditioned to a total dependence on humans, because while it has moved into cities such as Darwin and Cairns, it has disappeared from old goldfields and other abandoned settlements. For the cheeriness of its clucking calls, and its zeal in killing tropical pests, this lizard deserves a warm welcome. □

This marbled gecko sacrificed a long tail and grew three short ones instead

MAKING GOOD THE LOSS

Replacing a lost tail can produce a bizarre result

Most lizards' tails have built-in fault lines so that they break easily, allowing the reptiles to escape from the grasp of predators. Many geckoes and smaller skinks can throw off their tails, using them as twitching decoys to confuse their enemies. This voluntary amputation is called autotomy. Lost tail tissue is usually regenerated, sometimes in such abundance that a lizard ends up with more than one tail. A Victorian gecko is on record as having seven. Replacement tails are supported by cartilage rather than bone, and may lack the patterns and sometimes the spines of the original. Often they are shorter, making confusing differences to the appearance of some species.

The burrows of a colony of trapdoor spiders Anidiops *in Mootwingee National Park, New South Wales*

FEBRUARY

THIS MONTH'S WEATHER

The high-pressure belt of travelling anticyclones settles over Bass Strait, maintaining hot, dry conditions in all southern regions. Rainfall continues to increase in New South Wales and Queensland. Central Australia and other regions in the northern half of the arid zone stand their best chance of storms, and rivers run in the Channel Country. Monsoonal rains continue across the far north, with cyclones a strong possibility.

AROUND THE COUNTRY	RAIN (mm)	MAX. (°C)	MIN. (°C)	SUN hrs/day
Adelaide	22	29	17	9.3
Alice Springs	45	35	21	9.9
Brisbane	182	29	21	7.5
Canberra	57	27	13	9.3
Darwin	354	31	25	5.9
Hobart	40	21	12	7.2
Melbourne	48	26	14	8.4
Perth	12	30	18	10.2
Port Hedland	97	36	25	10.3
Sydney	113	26	19	6.6
Townsville	300	31	24	7.0
Weipa	403	31	24	4.9

Pale, blimpish shapes cruise winding courses over a shallow seabed. Some are the size of fishing dinghies. Their front ends nose into marine grasses. The greenery vanishes, roots and all, as if it were being sucked into giant vacuum cleaners. Dugongs are feeding, each snuffling up as much as forty kilos of seagrass a day.

The scene is typical of lonely tropical reefs and estuaries, but these dugongs are moving south along the populated northern coast of New South Wales. Here people catching fleeting glimpses in turbid waters may well mistake them for dolphins.

Dugongs are among the biggest but least numerous of warm-water creatures to travel south at this time of year. They are helped by the east Australian current, which is at its strongest now. Warm, tropical waters can reach to Tasmania, though the dugongs will not go that far.

Curling out from the coast in a series of eddies into the Coral and Tasman seas, the current flows year-round. Its main origin is a great westward oceanic movement across the Pacific, just south of the Equator. The planet's rotational force bends this southward near northern Australia. In winter and spring not all of the flow turns south; some passes westward through Torres Strait. But in summer and autumn, pushed by monsoonal nor-westers, movement through the strait is reversed. Hot water from the shallow Timor and Arafura seas gives added force to the east coast current.

From mid-Queensland to northern New South Wales the current runs at up to four kilometres an hour and can be as much as a hundred kilometres wide. Farther south it is slower and inclined to divide and deviate unpredictably. But masses of water of different temperature take a long time to mix. Parts of the

Seafarers from the tropics

Warm waters push powerfully down the east coast in late summer. Some unusual travellers catch a ride

current retain their tropical heat, generally 3°C higher than surrounding waters, which are themselves at a summer peak.

Such warmth — enough for coral reefs to grow around Lord Howe Island — sustains many life forms far from their tropical origins. Some of the travellers are willy-nilly drifters, such as jellyfishes and countless kinds of marine larvae. Others are determined foragers or predators, taking advantage of a seasonally extended feeding zone.

Growing to three metres long and sometimes more than 400 kilos in weight, the dugong or sea cow *Dugong dugon* is one of the world's last vegetarian marine mammals. A sea cow of cold north Pacific waters was wiped out by sealers and whalers in the eighteenth century. Distantly related manatees, now rare, live in rivers, estuaries and coastal waters on each side of the tropical Atlantic.

Dugongs eat some seaweeds and other algae if they have to, but depend almost entirely on shallow-growing seagrasses. Groups move with the rising tide onto beds of vegetation and reef flats near shore, retreating as the water ebbs. Skirting coastlines in calm conditions, they may travel up to twenty-five kilometres a day in search of new food supplies.

Grasses are not wrenched up in the

The dugong's slow rate of reproduction

teeth but grasped and conveyed to the mouth with a sensitive, protrusive and flexible upper lip — this suggests that the dugong and the elephant may have an ancestor in common. Teeth are developed in the same way as an elephant's. The secondary incisors of aging males even erupt as short tusks, though dugongs are not known to use them aggressively.

Power comes from the tail

Connections with an ancestral life on land are very remote, however. The dugong has no hind limbs, and the forelimbs are short paddles useful only for steering in the water and for holding a feeding or resting position. Swimming thrust comes from slow, up-and-down beats of the horizontally fluked tail, which can propel it at over twenty kilometres an hour.

Nostrils on top of the snout enable a dugong to breathe by raising its head for a second or two, without the rest of its body emerging. Valves seal the nostrils under water. Dugongs can stay down for many

A female dugong with her calf in Shark Bay, Western Australia

makes it a very vulnerable marine species. Man is the greatest threat to this gentle vegetarian

minutes, though while feeding they prefer to take air every minute or so.

The only time a dugong is seen clear of the water is when a female calves. She beaches herself at low tide as a protection against sharks, but remains in the wash of waves. As the tide fills she jostles her calf onto her back and carries it off. Weighing about twenty kilos at birth, the calf rides for the next few weeks, sucking on teats near the flippers while its mother is feeding. Even when it can take grass for itself the two remain bonded, staying together for two years or more.

Dugongs may live as long as seventy years, but their rate of reproduction is very low. Females are at least ten before they bear a calf, and the next will not come for three more years, while it can take as many as eight. Little is known about mating but the gestation period is probably much longer than a year.

In natural circumstances tiger sharks are the leading predators of dugongs. But the greatest enemy of these gentle and

MOST UNLIKELY SIRENS

Though plain and dumpy, dugongs are associated with fantasy figures

People often suggest that dugongs inspired legends of mermaids, and of sirens who lured sailors to destruction with bewitching songs. It takes a wild stretch of the imagination to see any connection. The belief is partly based on early seafarers' claims to have seen female dugongs rising upright, half out of the water, to nurse calves clasped to their breasts.

No such behaviour has been observed in modern times, though it is conceivable that a dugong could surge from the water if a shark were below. As for singing, the only noise-making known among captive dugongs is a birdlike chirping under water. Some old herdmaster bulls make a whistling sound, according to traditional Aboriginal hunters.

defenceless mammals is man. Over the centuries, dugongs have been killed for meat and medicinal oils; more recently many have been accidentally trapped and drowned in fishing nets and the gill nets set for sharks, or denied their food by the engineered alteration or pollution of in-shore sea beds.

Few dugongs are seen now in the southeast because of their virtual elimination from a key grazing and breeding ground, Brisbane's Moreton Bay. Herds of hundreds used to congregate there. They were relentlessly hunted, and port developments destroyed many feeding beds.

Dugongs are protected throughout their range, which reaches to Shark Bay on the west coast. Only Aboriginals and Torres Strait Islanders following a traditional diet are allowed to take them. Populations seem reasonably buoyant around the north coast, and aerial surveys indicate unsuspected numbers in out-of-the-way areas of the Great Barrier Reef. Netting bans and preservation of seagrass beds under marine park laws covering the reef region help to sustain realistic hopes for the dugongs' survival.

Tiger sharks *Galeocerdo cuvieri*, breeding far out in tropical waters but migrating south and inshore with the east Australian current in summer, kill more than dugongs. They are the most indiscriminate feeders, swallowing whatever they can take. Inedible flotsam — cans, bottles, pieces of wood and so forth — is gulped down and later regurgitated.

Young turtles, dolphins and seals and resting sea birds, along with fish, all fall prey to tiger sharks. The hunters feed greedily even when not hungry, because they can store excess food. One caught near Sydney was kept in an aquarium for a month, accepting offerings of horsemeat but always throwing them up. Cut open after it died, it was found to contain two undigested dolphins.

Man-eating tiger sharks
Tiger sharks average about three metres in length but can exceed five metres. They are the biggest of the carcharhinid or requiem sharks — a name they received because of their habit of following ships, supposedly in the hope of receiving the corpses of sailors. Species frequenting cooler bays and estuaries in Australia are generally called whalers. In the old days they were cursed for mutilating captured whales, and they are still a nuisance to fishermen.

Shipwreck reports are mainly responsible for the tiger shark's fearsome reputation as a man-eater. There is little hard evidence of its attacking inshore swimmers or divers. It is hesitant when it sees a target as big as a human, and will usually circle for some time. But its attraction to warm shallows, especially after sundown when it is less easily spotted, makes it unquestionably dangerous.

Tiger sharks have a particular aptitude for which nervous swimmers should be thankful. They are inveterate hunters of sea snakes, most of which face no other regular predators outside tropical waters.

One sea snake, the yellow-bellied *Pelamis platurus*, occurs year-round in temperate as well as tropical waters and may be more abundant in the south. Avoided by sharks and most other predators, it is an ocean surface dweller that seldom enters shallow waters of its own accord. Specimens are occasionally found stranded after being blown in by storms, as far south as Tasmania.

Four inshore sea snake species, breeding in far northern waters, migrate in the east Australian current. They reach southern New South Wales in most years and two of them occasionally turn up off northeastern Tasmania. Stokes' sea snake *Astrotia stokesii*, the bulkiest of these travellers, averages around 1.5 metres in length. The elegant sea snake *Hydrophis elegans*, which sometimes enters the tidal reaches of rivers, is slimmer but longer,

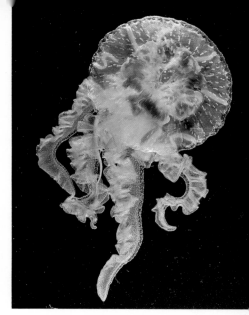

A luminous jellyfish, the little mauve stinger Pelagia noctiluca

averaging 1.7 metres. *Disteira major* and *Hydrophis ornatus* measure a little over a metre.

Sea snakes are air breathers with adaptations that allow them to dive deeply and stay submerged for an hour or more. They have an elongated lung, part of which stores air. Extra oxygen is absorbed through a water-permeable skin, which is renewed as often as every fortnight, not because it wears out so quickly, but because it accumulates marine growths. Swimming is aided by a flattened, oar-shaped tail.

Fish-eating sea snakes are even more venomous than elapid land snakes, to which they are closely related. They need exceptionally powerful paralysing toxins because their prey is elusive and has to be overcome quickly. But fangs are generally small, with the exception of *Astrotia*. Prey is located by detecting chemical traces with the tongue, generally after a snake has poked its head into crevices where fish sleep. Fish are not chased, but struck only if they swim near a snake's head.

Sea kraits, restricted to far northern waters, lay eggs, clambering onto rocks to do so. All other sea snakes bear their young live. Some may slither over wet mudflats but none can move on dry land because they lack suitable belly scales. So storm-beached sea snakes are helpless. But they may survive for a while, so they must be treated with caution.

The deadly chironex and most other box jellyfishes do not leave tropical waters, though one species reaches Brisbane. Stinging jellyfishes of other types are nuisance enough, especially at this time of year. The jelly blubber *Catostylus mosaicus*, reaching forty-five centimetres in diameter, is probably the most commonly seen. It is blue in the ocean but yellow or brown when it feeds in estuaries or lagoons.

The tiger shark (above) can grow to well over five metres and 1500 kilograms in weight. The dark stripes on its back fade with age. One of its favourite prey species is the elegant sea snake Hydrophis elegans *(left), which grows to two metres*

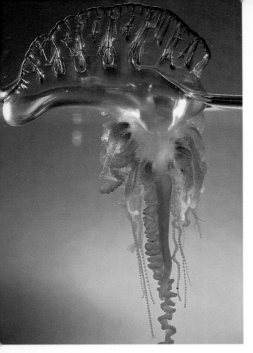

The Portuguese man o'war or bluebottle is a siphonophore, not a jellyfish

More trouble is encountered from swarms of little mauve stingers *Pelagia noctiluca*, which have venomous cells on their warty bodies as well as on their tentacles, and from sea blubbers or hairy stingers *Cyanea capillata*. Either can occur in all Australian waters, including those around Tasmania.

Jellyfishes are related to sea anemones and corals, and share with them a special armament for immobilising their swimming prey. Their tentacles and sometimes other parts of their bodies are coated with cells called nematocysts, each containing either a stinging thread and a supply of venom, or sticky substances that catch the prey and hold it fast.

Predatory jellyfishes
Shrimps, prawns and tiny fish are the intended prey of the types of jellyfish that can cause severe pain to swimmers. The venom is exceptionally potent in order to protect the creature in case it seizes something that is too big to eat. If a bigger fish, for example, is not paralysed quickly its struggles could tear the jellyfish apart.

When a person is stung, thousands of nematocysts are triggered at once. We break away all too easily, often wrenching off tentacles that cling and may have many more stinging threads still to be fired. A drenching in vinegar renders them inactive.

The most notorious late-summer stinger in southern waters is the Portuguese man o'war *Physalia physalis*. In the southeast it is more often called a bluebottle. *Physalia* is not a jellyfish but a siphonophore. It is a colony of hydroids, individual organisms that are born from the one egg but take different forms and carry out specialised functions. One be-

comes a gas-filled float. Others produce eggs and sperm. The rest, forming the main dangling tentacle, are for stinging and feeding.

Because their floats stand up like sails, Portuguese men o'war are driven more by winds than by currents. The float is set so that the direction of travel is at an angle of forty-five degrees to the wind — to the left for about half the members of a swarm, and to the right for the others. So while multitudes may be forced inshore and stranded in a storm, a roughly equal number will have been pushed out to sea.

Sailfish, the world's fastest swimmers, appear now off Moreton Bay and as far south as the central coast of New South Wales. In the west they make a similar but more arduous migration from the tropics, swimming against a warm surface current that flows up the west coast out of the Bight. The westerners will reach the vicinity of Geraldton. A lively fighter capable of more than a hundred kilometres an hour in short bursts, *Istiophorus platypterus* rivals marlin in the regard of game fishermen, though it rarely exceeds sixty kilos in weight.

Schools of sailfish feed cooperatively, encircling shoals of small fishes such as pilchards or mackerel and herding them into tight masses. Then they eat their prisoners, each taking a fair share. Squid and octopus are also favoured foods.

A sailfish's spearlike upper snout extension can be used to stun prey, but it is not an impaling weapon. Its principal purpose is for streamlining, to knife through the water. The immense dorsal fin, spectacularly erected while the fish is at rest on the surface, folds back into a groove along the back to reduce drag when it is hunting. Pectoral and ventral fins are pulled back against the body.

Sailfish spawn in summer, in tropical inshore waters. Two males usually accompany each female, which in the prodigal fashion characteristic of oceanic fishes may lay as many as twenty million eggs. Nearly all the eggs or hatching small fry end up as food for cannibal parents and myriad other marine species. Survivors live for up to ten years.

Black marlin come well down the east coast, rapidly gaining size and weight as they travel. They are joined by blue marlin moving north. But the southwest boasts the best blue marlin: giants of 300 kilos are caught near Perth in February.

Notable light game fishes that migrate from the tropics in late summer, moving down both coasts, are Spanish mackerel *Scomberomorus commerson*, wahoo *Acanthocybium solandri* and dolphin fish *Coryphaena hippurus*. In contrast to marlin and sailfish, these are prized for eating as well as for their speed and fighting qualities.□

The yellow-bellied sea snake is an ocean voyager that seldom comes inshore

REVERSE THRUST
A sea snake that can tie itself in knots

The yellow-bellied sea snake *Pelamis platurus* can swim backwards as well as forwards, simply by making the muscular convulsions of its body travel in the opposite direction. With this ability it kills by ambush, lying on the ocean surface, ready to attack small fish that come too close in any direction.

This vividly coloured species also enjoys near-total rejection by predators. Sharks and sea birds will not touch it. They seem to fear more than the venom: they even refuse pieces of the snake's flesh.

Because *Pelamis* is a permanent surface-dweller it has one problem. It cannot use firm, rough objects to break a skin that needs to be shed. Instead it ties itself in tight knots during the sloughing process, rubbing one section of skin against another to loosen it.

Wallabies feast in the Wet

Tropical marsupials feed by day under overcast skies — among them is a tiny rock-wallaby with a peculiar appetite for hard rations

In the leaden gloom of a drizzly afternoon, lowland margins of flooded northern plains are dotted with grazing wallabies. During the dry season they were never seen in daylight. They sheltered in woodlands or among outcroppings of rock. Now they take advantage of heavy cloud cover to move into the open and extend their feeding hours, fattening on the glut of annual grasses.

Monsoonal Australia has many marsupial species that live nowhere else. Strangest of these is a tiny rock-wallaby, the nabarlek *Peradorcas concinna*. Though barely the size of a domestic cat, it enjoys an extraordinary advantage. To the utter perplexity of zoologists, the nabarlek is the only marsupial with a limitless supply of teeth.

All other members of the group have a finite number of teeth, developing in various ways. In grazing marsupials the molars or grinding teeth are produced in a gradual sequence. Each erupts at the back of the jaw, works its way forward and when it is worn down, falls out. Kangaroos and typical wallabies have a lifetime quota of sixteen molars — four growing in succession on each side of both jaws. In youth they chew with the first one or two of each set, in middle age all four. Towards the end of their lives they are down to the last one or two molars in each series.

But a nabarlek has sets of up to six molars in use at once and replacements keep on coming. Careless of the rate of wear, it can exploit sources of food that would quickly render other animals toothless and doom them to starvation.

Its staple is a species of nardoo, a tough fern with fronds like four-leafed clovers. Nardoo grows at the edges of billabongs and rock pools, dying back if the water dries up and regenerating from rhizomes when it returns. In the sandstone country of Arnhem Land and the Kimberley, where nabarleks live, the solid content of nardoo is about one-quarter silica.

As the wet season advances, nabarleks venture from their rocky hideaways to augment their diet with grasses. The types that they choose are also unusually rich in silica. This persistent intake of abrasive material and cellulose could be likened to living on sandpaper.

The short-eared rock wallaby emerges

Although they have an advantage in preferring such foods, and in an apparent ability to breed all year round, nabarleks are few and not widespread. Their size is against them. At their biggest and plumpest they seldom weigh more than 1.5 kilos. Anywhere outside the shelter of caves, the young and adults make easy prey for eagles and dingoes.

Given rare distinction by having a uranium mine named after it, the nabarlek was thought to be the smallest macropodid ('bigfoot') marsupial. Another rock-wallaby of similar size but weighing even less, the warabi *Petrogale burbidgei*, remained undiscovered until the late 1970s. It is restricted to broken sandstone structures of the west Kimberley district and some nearby islands.

Far more abundant and widespread across the Kimberley, the Top End and the western side of the Gulf of Carpentaria is the short-eared rock-wallaby *Petrogale brachyotis*. It measures about half a metre in head-and-body length — the same size generally as other rock-wallabies found over most of the mainland.

Before Aboriginal fires reduced covering vegetation, the ancestral petrogale probably had a continuous range. Big mobs would have moved between rocky habitats, covering long distances under

The bridled nailtail wallaby is restricted to a small area in Queensland

from its cool crevice shelter to feed in late afternoon or evening

galea unguifera feed alone or in loose groups of four or five at the most, including young at heel at this time of year. They are easily distinguished when they run: their forelegs, thrust downwards and outwards, appear to be describing circles. Hence the old popular name for nailtails: 'organ grinders'.

Nailtails rest during the day in scraped-out hollows hidden by shrubs or long grass. Unusually long and powerful claws on their forefeet aid the excavation work. Their tails end in naked, horny spurs — for no obvious reason.

In grassy eucalypt woodlands farther from the floodplains, the dominant marsupial is the antilopine wallaroo *Macropus antilopinus*. It fills a role equivalent to that of the great kangaroos elsewhere in the country. In fact, many Top Enders call it a red kangaroo. Active at any time of day under cloudy skies, it is the most

screens of long grasses and shrubs. A process of separation and isolation — made permanent by the inroads of European agriculture — produced an array of species and races that biologists have only recently begun to sort out, through genetic studies.

Petrogales adapted for rock-climbing
Most petrogales are noted for their distinctive fur colourings and markings, though the main Queensland species is so plain and sombre that it is called the unadorned rock-wallaby, *Petrogale inornata*. All species have a characteristic foot structure that shows their long adaptation to climbing among rocks. They do not have the extended claws on their hind great toes that kangaroos and other wallabies use to gain purchase on the ground as they bound along. Rock-wallabies get their thrust from friction, which is generated by the grainy skin and fringes of coarse hair on their feet.

Female rock-wallabies are sexually mature in their second year. Their breeding cycles are continuous, with delayed implantation to ensure that lost young are quickly replaced. Unweaned juveniles seldom follow their mothers about after leaving the pouch, as other young macropods would. They are left to await her

return in sheltered positions, close to their home caves or crevices.

Lots of other wallabies graze the floodplain margins in overcast daylight at this time of year. The most abundant is the agile wallaby *Macropus agilis*. Family groups gather into big feeding mobs. They eat swamp sedges as well as grasses, and occasionally browse on the leaves and fruits of trees. In times of drought they may dig out the roots of grasses.

Such versatile feeding habits make the agile wallaby one of the most successful of its type — all too successful from the point of view of farmers. Officially declared as pests in some areas because of crop and pasture damage, populations have been poisoned or shot. But the species remains generally secure over a wide range, extending across the north and down the entire tropical coast of Queensland.

Far from exploiting agriculture, nailtail wallabies *Onychogalea* have succumbed to it. Only in wilderness areas of the monsoonal north can they be said to be safe. A central and southwestern species became extinct during this century. An eastern type survives only in a small district near Dingo, central Queensland, yet just a few decades ago it ranged from near Townsville to northern Victoria.

Northern nailtail wallabies *Onycho-*

Unadorned rock-wallabies tolerate wet habitats, where they climb trees

The antilopine wallaroo gets its name from its supposedly antelope-like fur

Red-necked wallabies are usually solitary, but will gather together to feed

social of wallaroos, though groups of more than half a dozen are uncommon.

A smaller but striking-looking wallaroo is restricted to the western edge of the Arnhem Land plateau, where the abrupt escarpment borders Kakadu National Park. The black wallaroo *Macropus bernardus* is shy and elusive, but occasionally descends to drink at waterholes at the foot of the escarpment. Only the males are black; females are light grey or greyish brown. Pairs with a joey at heel may be seen, but no bigger groups.

In open forests to the east and southeast, wallaby births are reaching a peak now. Joeys have a pouch life of nine to ten months, emerging to feed independently towards the end of the year. Seasonality is most pronounced in Tasmania, where nearly all red-necked wallabies *Macropus rufogriseus* are born in February and March and appear in November or December.

Rednecks, ranging from southeastern Queensland to Bass Strait and throughout Tasmania, are the most abundant and frequently seen wallabies. They come out to graze at forest edges well before darkness. Some are destroyed as pests in agricultural areas.

The redneck's breeding potential on good grassland was demonstrated in New Zealand, where assorted marsupials were taken as curiosities or to found fur industries. Three rednecks were released in a hilly South Island district in the 1870s. Seventy years later, before a control campaign started, their descendants numbered more than a quarter of a million.

Whiptails are daylight feeders

Whiptail wallabies *Macropus parryi* are seen fairly often in and near the open forests of the east. More than any other macropodid species they are active in daylight, feeding from dawn well into the morning and again late in the afternoon. Unmistakable head markings earned them another name, pretty-face wallaby.

Over a similar range in Queensland and New South Wales the black-striped wallaby *Macropus dorsalis* is probably as common as the whiptail but it is seldom seen. It favours denser forests with thick shrub cover, and usually feeds at night.

Wallabies of the southwest, markedly smaller than their eastern counterparts, also display contrasting preferences in feeding hours. The tammar *Macropus eugenii* hides in scrub throughout the day. But the western brush wallaby *Macropus irma* may be seen in ones or twos long after dawn and before sundown.

Typical wallabies used to be classified in a genus of their own, *Wallabia*. Now zoologists see no basic distinction between them and the kangaroos and wallaroos — all are *Macropus*. By one conven-

tion, those that do not exceed twenty kilos are called wallabies. Of the bigger macropods, species inhabiting flat or gently undulating grasslands are kangaroos, and those preferring steep and rocky country are wallaroos or euros.

Rainforests and the densest eucalypt forests of the east shelter pademelons *Thylogale*, which look very much like small wallabies. The most abundant species, the Tasmanian pademelon *Thylogale billardierii*, used to live also in Victoria and the southeastern corner of South Australia. It grazes by night, never far from forest edges. Prolific enough to be a pest in some areas, it is the basis of a lucrative trade in skins and meat.

The red-necked pademelon *Thylogale thetis* of southern Queensland and northern New South Wales also eats grasses at forest edges. By contrast the red-legged pademelon *Thylogale stigmatica*, occupying a similar range but with tropical subspecies distributed as far as Cape York, stays always under cover. It feeds mainly on fallen leaves and fruits.□

Male Tasmanian pademelons grow up to 1.2 metres long, including tail

A marsupial bedtime tail

Rat-kangaroos, bettongs and potoroos employ a rare skill

In February, musky rat-kangaroos living deep in the sodden rainforests of far northern Queensland start to breed. Day after day adult pairs of these stocky, rabbit-sized marsupials repeat a courting ritual, standing face to face and dabbing at each other's head and neck with their forepaws. After they mate the females will bear twins, a feat that is unique in the kangaroo family.

Sunlight never penetrates into the world of *Hypsiprymnodon moschatus*. Again uniquely among kangaroo-like creatures, it is active entirely by day. Early in the morning and late in the afternoon it scrabbles in leaf litter, foraging for fallen fruits, insects and worms. Food is eaten squirrel-fashion, manipulated in the forepaws.

Throughout the night and in the middle of the day the rat-kangaroo sleeps in a cosy bed of leaves and fern fronds, tucked in a tangle of vines or among tree roots. Dry bedding material is sometimes gathered a long way from the nesting site and the problem of transportation is overcome in a unique fashion. First, the material is placed in a pile between the animal's legs. Looping its naked, scaly tail downwards, it rocks onto its forepaws and kicks the litter back. Then, tail tightly crooked round a bundle of fresh bedding, it hops home with a slow, four-legged gait like a bandicoot's.

Potoroos and bettongs use their tails in the same way to carry various nesting materials — grasses, bark and so on. Together with rat-kangaroos they make up a family of marsupials that probably had its heyday before *Macropus* kangaroos and wallabies came into prominence. Fossils show that their ancestors were big animals, but modern species are small, obscure and furtive in their habits. Some have become extinct since European settlement, and all have reduced ranges through

The musky rat-kangaroo is the smallest of the macropods, a large specimen weighing only around 500 grams. It is also the only one to have kept the first digit (the 'big toe') on its hind foot

loss of cover and predation by foxes and cats.

Tasmania, where foxes have never become established, is the stronghold of the two most secure potoroid species, the long-nosed potoroo *Potorous tridactylus* and the Tasmanian bettong *Bettongia gaimardi*. They have similar diets of roots, bulbs, fungi and insects, but do not come into competition. The potoroo, which also occurs on the eastern mainland, lives in dense forest shrub cover, while the bettong favours grassy patches.□

The Tasmanian froglet (above) has a call like the bleat of a lamb; the Tasmanian tree frog Litoria burrowsi (top) has a duck-like call

The freshwater crayfish or 'yabby' Parastacoides tasmanicus insignis (below) is well adapted to life in acidic, almost stagnant water

Mount Field National Park, Tasmania (above)

Etchings of an ice age

Tiny lakes hold fascinating life forms

Craggy bluffs surround the central plateau of northern Tasmania, their flanks chewed away by glaciers 20 000 years ago. Boulders dragged by a creeping sea of ice gouged hollows in the tough, riverless dolerite capping of the plateau. Now glittering waters, abuzz with insects, fill thousands of miniature lakes.

Life in the cold, confined waters of the tarns, as they are called, is limited by a low level of nutrients but is rich in curiosities. Water fleas change their forms seasonally. Plankton commute daily between the surface and the bottom. And preserved here, safe from the trout introduced into streams and bigger lakes, are anaspids — primitive, soft-bodied crustaceans of a type found only in Tasmania and Victoria. Elsewhere in the world they are known only from fossils.

Water-fleas of the family Daphnidae are among the largest in the world, with bodies up to six millimetres

The larvae of some midges are called phantom larvae or glassworms, because they are transparent

Tadpole of the Tasmanian froglet Crinia tasmaniensis, *which is endemic to the island*

The climbing galaxias Galaxias brevipinnis *uses its pelvic and pectoral fins to cling to rocks and ascend steep waterfalls*

Paragalaxias julianus is the largest of the paragalaxias, growing up to ten centimetres

The mountain shrimp Anaspides tasmaniae (left) *is found in fresh water at elevations of 500 metres or more*

79

Sulphur-crested cockatoos gather in large flocks in the south and east; some birds watch for predators while others feed

Sentries guard roaming flocks

Ravens and cockatoos of lowly social position must stay on the edges of feeding flocks, keeping watch and getting less to eat

A raven cowers, head tucked between its shoulders on the bare branch of a eucalypt. Senior members of its flock surround it, cawing angrily. The accused bird was one of their sentries, part of a subordinate group relegated to the fringes of the feeding area. Leaving its post (and thus endangering the flock), this bird committed the crime of attempting to move up the pecking order.

If it is lucky the chorus of abuse may be lesson enough. Perhaps the guilty bird draws extra sentry duty, paying a price in hunger as the others feed. But sometimes the accusers incite one another to such a pitch of rage that the culprit is attacked and killed, or driven into exile.

Foraging flocks of white cockatoos can be similarly vindictive. Their habit of posting sentries — and perhaps the threat of harsh penalties for failure — has made a contribution to underworld parlance. A lookout responsible for spotting police approaching an illegal gambling school is called a cockatoo.

Both groups of birds form their biggest roaming flocks in late summer. To the despair of farmers, from now until next spring, scores or sometimes hundreds will emerge every morning from woodland roosts to forage in open country. Before European settlement they would have made their sorties to natural grasslands. These days the targets are more likely to be crops and pastures.

Ravens, generally called crows, incur most wrath in wool-growing country because they are blamed for killing lambs. Thorough research has shown, however, that the Australian raven *Corvus coronoides* nearly always selects prey that is dead or close to death. In cleaning up carrion it helps farmers by eliminating blowfly breeding sites. At this time of year its main diet is insects, including such serious crop pests as grasshoppers and army worms. Grains taken are mostly those spilt during harvesting.

Breeding is always in spring, regardless of the locality. Wool and fur from animal carcasses are matted together with pieces of bark to line stick baskets built in high tree forks. Building a nest can take up to three weeks. But the same nests, refurbished, are used year after year by the same pairs — ravens mate for life. Females are liberally fed by their mates as they incubate four or five green, dark-blotched eggs. These hatch in three weeks and chicks are fledged after a further six.

In late summer, at about five months of age, surviving members of the new generation join passing flocks. These are composed of all birds yet to breed, some of them more than three years old. Once they mate they become sedentary, pairs permanently occupying territories of about a hundred hectares each.

Little ravens *Corvus mellori* of the southern and southeastern mainland remain sociable throughout their lives. The flocks that travel farthest are generally made up of non-breeders, but paired birds also forage and breed in groups. In spite of its common name the species is not noticeably smaller than the Australian raven. It is most easily distinguished by a deeper voice. Little ravens are heavily reliant on insects in their diet; their slender bills are not suited to opening up the carcasses of big animals.

An even deeper, bass-baritone call distinguishes the forest raven *Corvus tasmanicus*. Of greater average size than any others, it is the only raven or crow likely to be seen feeding under a dense canopy of tree foliage. It is also the only one found in Tasmania.

In most of the drier parts of the mainland the dominant corvid is the highly nomadic little crow *Corvus bennetti*. Western populations migrate to the coastal plain of the Swan River in midsummer. The species breeds in spring if conditions are suitable but can wait for rain. Because nests include a layer of mud, they are always built near water.

In the far north, Torresian crows *Corvus orru* are still nesting. More southerly populations — overlapping and competing vigorously in the east with the Australian raven — breed in spring. Sparsely lined twig nests are built in shady tree canopies. Only the non-breeding birds form flocks.

Ravens and crows of Australia evolved from a common ancestor so recently that there is little to distinguish them in appearance. All are white-eyed — like no other corvids in the world apart from Torresian crow populations in New Guinea and on some nearby islands. The crows have white feather bases; those birds that scientists call ravens do not. Ravens hold to a level course during long flights, but flocking crows may adopt a pattern of steep soaring and swooping.

Crop-busting cockatoos

Cockatoos are now mounting a threat to crops, but the most abundant is the sulphur-crested cockatoo *Cacatua galerita*. Only in the south and east, where a long breeding season has just ended, do these birds form flocks.

Screeching mobs choose a feeding ground and sally out every morning until the area is stripped of seeds, fruits, bulbs and leaf buds. Some insects and their larvae are also taken. At the hottest time of day birds retreat to trees but remain active, gnawing bark and eating leaves.

Foraging flights grow longer and longer as new grounds have to be found. But a flock always returns in late afternoon to the same roosting site. Swirling and darting aerobatics precede their settling, and games and noisy disputes over sleeping positions go on well after dark.

In spring and early summer, sulphur-crested cockatoos nest in hollows high up in eucalypts, except for some along the lower Murray River that prefer holes in cliff faces. Parents share the incubation of two or three white eggs, taking about a month. Chicks are fledged at six weeks.

In confined areas of the south and southwest, the greatest crop damage may be done by huge flocks of long-billed corellas *Cacatua tenuirostris* or little corellas *Cacatua pastinator*. Though smaller than the sulphur-crested cockatoo, they are closely related — as is the galah — and very similar in habit.

February in the far north is a peak breeding month for finches. Fattening on the wet season glut of insects as well as on grasses that are starting to seed, they include some of the most boldly coloured species in Australia. Sadly their ranges and populations are shrinking, partly because of trapping for the cage-bird trade.

Among the tropical finches that are commonly seen, the most eye-catching is the male crimson finch *Neochmia phaeton*. The species occupies year-round territories along streams bordered by pandanus palms and wet grasslands, often near settlements. Pairs may roost and nest close together but neighbours bicker constantly and do not form flocks. When feeding they clamber and hop among grass stems, seldom alighting on the ground.

A flight display by the less brightly plumed female initiates courtship but the male chooses the nest site and gathers material. Together they build a dome of grass, leaves and bark, lined with feathers. Usually it is in a pandanus palm, but these birds take readily to the shelter of eaves and holes in buildings. Small white eggs hatch in two weeks, and chicks develop rapidly, fledging in three more weeks.

Smaller star finches *Neochmia ruficauda* are found in similar habitats, feeding and roosting in compact flocks. Their range used to extend across the north and through the east all the way to New South Wales. The related red-browed finch or waxbill *Neochmia temporalis* remains common from Cape York to South Australia, breeding in spring and early summer in the southern part of the range. It shows the crimson markings of its group only on the brows, bill and rump.

Confusing finches

Patchwork-coloured gouldian or rainbow finches *Erythrura gouldiae* used to form flocks of thousands all across the north. They are seen now only in small numbers, mostly in Arnhem Land and the Kimberley. Their two colour forms can confuse observers: most birds of both sexes have a jet black face, but in about a quarter of the population it is crimson.

At breeding time gouldian finches switch from grass seeds to a diet of insects, catching mating swarms of termites and ants in midflight. Little or no effort is made to prepare a nest. Uniquely among Australian finches, these birds, like cockatoos and parrots, exploit tree hollows and holes in termite mounds. They are remarkably sociable, several pairs sharing the same tree or even hollow. Two or three broods may be reared from midsummer to autumn.□

Little ravens tidy up another animal's lunch — note the 'lookout' on the branch

For their eyes only

Butterfly wing patterns contain a secret code

A butterfly's wings are coated with as many as a million and a half scales, overlapping like roof tiles. Some are pigmented, others transparent but structured to split up light into brilliant iridescence. Much as we may enjoy a butterfly's beauty, we see only those rainbow colours of the spectrum visible to simple human eyes.

A butterfly's huge compound eyes, with thousands of facets, also detect infra-red and ultra-violet light. They reveal wing patterns that uniquely identify each species. Recognition is vital to breeding success, because the two sexes of a species often do not mature in the same locality or at the same time. Males may have to search long and hard for mates, relying heavily on vision.

Many males show small additional markings, usually dark, in bold contrast to a background colour. These sex-brands, as they are called, not only form part of the identification pattern, they also give off a scent which stimulates the responses of an appropriate female.

A butterfly's large compound eyes (above) see more than we do of the beauty of Macleay's swallowtail (below)

The butterflies that are emerging and breeding now, in the southeastern and Tasmanian highlands where summer comes latest, have probably spent two years as caterpillars and pupae. They will continue to live a relatively long time as adults. Development is slowed by low temperatures — ceasing altogether during a winter diapause — but lifespans are lengthened. A tropical butterfly, on the other hand, may go through its whole cycle in a couple of months and last no more than a fortnight as an adult.

Most common of alpine butterflies are the satyrids, known as browns. They lay their eggs on or near grasses. Other groups such as blues, hairstreaks and swallowtails are also represented by a few late-developing highland species.□

A close-up of the wings of an orchard butterfly Papilio aegeus *(above)*

A female Sydney funnelweb Atrax robustus *lurks in her nest, awaiting prey*

A big, dark spider darts about erratically, with jerky movements, over damp ground. Though three or four years old, this funnelweb spider has never left home before. Tonight he has no idea what he is seeking, but if he finds it he will know what to do.

Near a rotting log he scents a female of mating age. Quickly he spins a small pad of silk and squats over it, squirting sperm fluid from organs in his abdomen. Then he places his palps — the feelers in front that look like a short extra pair of legs — on the pad. The ends of the palps work in the manner of eye-droppers, sucking up the

First night out for a funnelweb

Throughout long lives, funnelweb and trapdoor spiders are secretive stay-at-homes — until the mating urge prompts males to roam

fluid and holding it in bulbs.

Now he creeps under the log, disturbing trip lines leading to a purse of silk. It is the opening of the female's nest. She hurries out of the burrow below, hoping for prey, but ready to fight off an invading centipede or scorpion. The male must identify himself or be attacked. He dances back and forth, gaining recognition visually and perhaps also by a pattern of vibrations along the trip lines.

Pacified, the female joins in a mutual touching of legs and palps. Then she raises her front legs high, facing her suitor. He rears against her, embracing and lifting her body with his front two pairs of legs. These are spiny and often spurred for just this purpose. The tips of his sperm-laden palps are thrust into an opening near the front of the female's abdomen. With a squeeze on the bulbs, mating is complete.

The male survives mating

Size and strength are about the same in both sexes, the female having a bulkier body but shorter legs. Unless he is unusually careless and slow in taking his leave, the male survives his mating encounter and may have several more — but only for one season. He will die in a few months, probably during winter. The female, which took four or five years to reach sexual maturity, will breed for three or four more seasons, never leaving the immediate vicinity of her burrow.

Eggs fertilised from this mating will not be laid until spring. A hundred or so are deposited in a pillow-shaped sac of silk at the bottom of the burrow. Hatching in summer, the spiderlings will share their mother's shelter and prey for a few weeks. In hard times she may eat some of them. Survivors disperse in late summer or autumn, a year after their parents mated.

Funnelweb spiders, peculiar to Australia, rely on hiding places that are cool and moist, but not flood-prone. They are largely confined to areas of the southeast that sustain forests, or used to before European settlement. Generally they are summer or autumn breeders, the males emerging on especially humid evenings.

Spurred by public anxiety, most observations and laboratory studies relate to *Atrax robustus*, the so-called Sydney funnelweb. Its habitats are scattered for scores of kilometres beyond the city environs, mostly on wooded slopes and in upland gullies of broken sandstone country. Males of this species are the most lethally venomous spiders known in the world. They wander in search of mates mostly from January to March.

All other funnelwebs also used to be classified as *Atrax*. Recent anatomical studies have shown that only two species are so closely related: a coastal type distributed from southern New South

Wales to eastern Victoria, and a highland version found mostly in the Australian Capital Territory.

At least a dozen more funnelweb species are spread from southeastern Queensland to South Australia and Tasmania. The known ones are now called *Hadronyche*. None has the strange venom component that makes *Atrax robustus* males so feared.

All funnelwebs build some sort of silken tube at the openings of their nests. Often there is more than one entrance to the tube. In ground-dwelling species it occupies a cavity under a rock or a fallen tree, and leads down into an excavated burrow or a natural crevice in rock. Burrows may be up to half a metre deep, depending on the need to retreat from surface heat and desiccation.

Tree-dwelling funnelwebs

Tree-dwelling species of *Hadronyche* start their nests where the breaking of branches or the activities of wood-boring insects have left holes. Tubes disguised with fragments of bark are placed over the holes, which are then enlarged as nests. Tree funnelwebs of northern New South Wales and southern Queensland live high in rainforest trees. In central and southern New South Wales and the Aus-

JUST OUR BAD LUCK

A biochemical fluke makes the male's bite deadly to people

One minor ingredient of a male *Atrax robustus* spider's venom acts as a powerful neurotoxin on humans, wrecking our muscular control and disrupting breathing and blood circulation. Other animals that normally encounter funnelwebs — dogs and cats, for example — are unharmed. The spider can have no real need of this venom component to overpower prey. If he did, females of his species would also possess it. Occurrence of the substance, and our unusual sensitivity to it, seem to be sheer flukes of biochemistry.

Many hospitals in *Atrax robustus* country hold stocks of a completely successful antivenom. Victims need only be pressure-bandaged (as if for snakebite) and kept as still as possible until medical aid is available.

tralian Capital Territory, they usually choose the smaller trees of open forests.

Whether in the ground or up a tree, it is characteristic of funnelwebs to lay trip lines of coarse silk, radiating irregularly from the entrance tube. At night the spider waits just inside the entrance with its front legs touching the lines. Small animals disturbing them are seized, paralysed with venom and carried back into the tube to be devoured.

Insects, snails, slaters, millipedes and other spiders are the usual prey of funnelwebs. Skinks, geckoes and frogs are also taken. Softening fluids are exuded over and into crushed prey, because no spider can digest solids. Natural juices and liquefied tissue are sucked out, filtered by hairs around the spider's mouth.

Funnelwebs and trapdoor spiders belong to an ancient and primitive group that scientists call mygalomorphs. They differ most obviously from all other spiders in the arrangement of their chelicerae — the pair of clawlike appendages at the front of their heads. Tipped with fangs, these are used for biting and then crushing. In mygalomorphs they move up and down in parallel, so a spider has to rear up to strike with them. In more recently evolved spiders, the chelicerae work from side to side like pincers.

There are many other anatomical differences. The breathing mechanisms of mygalomorphs are much like the gills of fish, admitting only a slow transfer of oxygen. Most other spiders breathe through tubes as well, and can lead more

Funnelwebs usually prey on insects, slugs and slaters, but larger prey such as frogs and lizards can also be taken

A female trapdoor spider Anidiops manstridgei *emerging from its nest.* Anidiops *spiders have a second line of defence after the lid: they retreat below a silken tube in the burrow and pull on a thread to cause a landslide behind them*

active lives. In compensation the sedentary mygalomorphs are long-lived — some females exceed twenty years — while no other spider lasts more than two years.

Trapdoor spiders have adapted to the whole gamut of Australian habitats and climates. Except in tropical rainforests, where they may breed at any time, their maturing is phased with the onset of the wettest season in their locality. In arid regions the males may emerge in response to good rains at any time. Long lifespans enable populations to forgo breeding for several seasons if rains fail altogether.

Putting the lid on it

The lids that nearly all trapdoor spiders put on their burrow entrances are usually made of mixtures of soil, leaf debris, silk and digestive juices. Hinged with silk and lined below, as are the burrow walls, they serve principally to maintain humidity. They also prevent soil and litter from falling in and some may act as flood defences (see page 37).

Trapdoors are not of much use against determined predators. Scorpions and centipedes pry them open unless the spiders below move quickly to take a grip and pull downwards. Bandicoots, the leading hunters of trapdoor spiders, simply dig out whole burrows. For some species the

A female Blue Mountains funnelweb Hadronyche versuta

main enemies are wasps that lay eggs in their burrows, producing larvae that eat the spiders' eggs.

The most widely known of Australian trapdoor spiders are mouse spiders *Missulena*. Various species occur all over the mainland. This vast distribution of one genus was possible because dispersal of the young is wind-assisted on strands of gossamer — extremely rare among mygalomorphs. Most have to depart on foot and few go far.

In warm regions, mature male mouse spiders emerge in winter, often by day. Both sexes build burrows with double doors; females' burrows are unusual inside also. Below the halfway point of the main vertical shaft is a side chamber with its own hinged door. The eggs develop and the spiderlings are raised here.

Spiders of the genus *Misgolas*, common from Tasmania to Queensland, are known as brown trapdoor spiders. But they do not build trapdoors. Their habit of topping their burrows with wide tubes of silk, usually propped on grass or litter and easily visible, can lead to needless funnelweb scares.□

A sugar glider Petaurus breviceps *feeding on the blossom of the swamp bloodwood* Eucalyptus ptychocarpa

MARCH

A plague carried on the wind 88
Facts on fungi 92
Mosquitoes are still out for blood 94
When a loner takes the plunge 95
Painted ladies play the field 99
Tough immigrants 101

THIS MONTH'S WEATHER

Rain-bearing cloud systems of the northwesterly monsoon shrink to the north coast. Inland effects are no longer felt, though decaying cyclones may still bring some benefit, especially in the northwest. Rainfall is heaviest in far northern Queensland but starts to decline in middle regions of the east coast. New South Wales enters what is usually its wettest season. Southern regions remain at their driest.

AROUND THE COUNTRY	RAIN (mm)	MAX. (°C)	MIN. (°C)	SUN hrs/day
Adelaide	26	26	15	7.9
Alice Springs	34	32	17	9.7
Brisbane	150	28	20	7.7
Canberra	54	24	11	7.8
Darwin	316	32	24	6.6
Hobart	47	20	11	6.3
Melbourne	52	24	13	6.7
Perth	19	28	17	9.1
Port Hedland	43	37	24	9.7
Sydney	135	25	17	6.3
Townsville	212	30	23	7.2
Weipa	334	32	24	5.3

Australian plague locusts at the hopper stage crowding together on grass stems (main picture), and adults mating (inset)

A plague carried on the wind

Sailing effortlessly from the outback, locusts can transform fertile pasture and promising crops into wasteland

After a sunny spell across the agricultural heartland of the southeast, a cool change is on the way. Behind an anticyclone, now slipping out over the east coast, a cold front angles up from the Bight. Hopes are high for some rain. But on the last fine evening, as hot northerly winds intensify, growers are apprehensive. Next morning their lands and livelihoods could be under attack.

Over bare plains far off in the northwestern corner of New South Wales, the afterglow of sunset is blotted out as big brown grasshoppers suddenly launch themselves in clattering clouds. Heat ebbing from the ground assists a swirling ascent of hundreds of metres. Then the insects abandon themselves to the wind.

By the time the advancing cold front forces the locusts to earth, they may be 500 kilometres or more south of their birthplace. Swarms land in clusters of millions, more tightly packed than when they took off. Where a horde happens to descend on pastures or among crops, it can devour a hundred tonnes a day. And the worst of the plague is yet to come.

Breeding, not feeding, is the primary aim of the invaders. They will accomplish it even if they find little to eat, sustained by reserves of fat accumulated before their journey. Eggs laid now will undergo a winter diapause and hatch in spring.

The new generation will be about four times as numerous. Unless insecticides are sprayed in a concerted and carefully timed counterattack, day-flying swarms in early summer will spread the infestation farther south and east. Another generation will develop in late summer, perhaps breeding a third in autumn. Tens of millions of dollars' worth of agricultural production are immediately at risk. And even if a plague lasts only one season, damaged pastures are slow to recover.

Locusts are short-horned grasshoppers, distinguished by their instinct to migrate in enormous swarms when populations are high. Usually they have two forms, differing in body shape and perhaps in colour. If hoppers going through their nymphal stages do not encounter many of their own kind, they take a solitary form. Such hoppers feed at random and the adults stay close to home.

Hoppers developing in crowded situations, on the other hand, react to one another's chemical secretions by taking a gregarious form. They are drawn more closely together. Feeding bands advance like armies, visible from the air as dark lines. In their final stage, when wings sprout, they disperse — but not for long.

Fledged and fattened locusts take to the air in hot, dry conditions. Overseas research suggests that the urge to fly is a defence against desiccation — muscular effort breaks down the fat and some of it becomes water. If most of a concentrated population are of the same age and have enjoyed an equal share of food, vast numbers migrate simultaneously. Where they will land and what impact they will have are determined by quirks of weather. Sometimes a farmer's prayers are answered: swarms end up in the Simpson Desert or the Tasman Sea.

Drought-resistant grasshopper

Our most mobile and economically menacing grasshopper is the Australian plague locust *Chortoicetes terminifera*. Common in the eastern and southeastern interior, it thrives in semi-arid regions and has a major advantage in surviving droughts that set back many of its competitors, predators and parasites.

Localised outbreaks among resident farmland populations are fairly frequent, typically occurring after a drought is broken. Multiplication can be so rapid that the migratory impulse is sparked in the second well-fed generation. Swarms in a local plague usually travel by day at low altitude, along pathways dictated by the lie of the land. Distances covered are seldom great — even a line of trees along a riverbank may stop them.

Plagues of statewide and interstate dimensions are the result of long-range migrations, made overnight at high altitude. Their buildup is an irregular occurrence that can be likened to the filling of Lake Eyre. The two events stem from the same cause: a drenching of the normally parched mideastern hinterland, thanks to the freakish intrusion of decaying tropical cyclones.

A typical area of origin is the Channel Country of southwestern Queensland. Good rains there induce exuberant grass growth and a sparse locust population multiplies quickly. Migrants swarm in the first of two or three wind-assisted leaps that can establish their descendants beyond the Murray-Darling basin within four months.

The bounty of fertilised pastures and irrigated crops is almost too much for the invaders. The females seek bare, compacted soil in which to bury their eggs. Where they land in great numbers, some have to settle for fallow paddocks or sites among the stubble of recent harvests.

Hard plates at the tip of a female's abdomen are used to penetrate the ground. The abdomen is driven in for its full length and thirty or more eggs are deposited. As the abdomen is withdrawn a frothy secretion is squirted over the eggs.

Hardening, it binds them together and plugs the hole. A female that is feeding amply may lay as many as three such 'pods' of eggs.

Chortoicetes locusts laying in summer make vertical holes with deep froth plugs that keep the eggs moist and insulate them from excessive heat. The eggs hatch in about six weeks. Autumn-laying females curve their abdomens so that the holes run shallowly parallel to the surface, with a shorter plug. This allows the eggs, which are slow to develop in cooler weather and dormant in winter, to receive early warmth when temperatures rise in spring.

Egg beds — bare patches containing the greatest concentrations of pods — are easily identified. But farmers are wise not to interfere with them. In doing so they would thwart the progress of their most effective natural allies. A group of tiny wasps called scelionids are determined parasites of various locusts and other grasshoppers. The most important one to seek out *Chortoicetes* as its specific host is *Scelio fulgidus*.

Adult female wasps burrow through the plugs of egg pods soon after they are made. They pierce all the eggs they can reach and deposit one of their own eggs in each yolk. The wasp hatches first and the larva — smaller than a pinhead but with grotesque jaws and a toothed appendage — promptly destroys the locust embryo. Not all the eggs in a pod are attacked, but the hatching survivors are usually trapped, their way out blocked by parasitised eggs above them.

The wasps multiply at an even greater rate than their hosts, and some travel with them on the same winds. Given time, the wasps can bring about the collapse of a locust outbreak. Where successive generations of locusts breed in one district the incidence of parasitism rises steeply — from fewer than five per cent of egg pods in the first generation to as many as ninety per cent in the third.

Wasp activity has one drawback. The larvae remain in their host eggs through all their stages of development and pupation. Adult wasps do not emerge for at least a week — sometimes a month —

LOCUST MIGRATION

QLD

November

January

SA

NSW

March

VIC

A typical pattern of migration by three generations of Chortoicetes, *each making its major move in one night. Local populations may also multiply to plague proportions in favourable conditions*

A female locust laying eggs (left)

after unparasitised locust eggs have hatched. To avoid wiping out the wasps, landholders must refrain from spraying the hopper bands until they have marched well away from their egg beds.

During summer in dry districts, adult locusts and hoppers in their last nymphal stage are likely to be parasitised by the nemestrinid fly *Trichopsidea oestracea*, of the family Nemestrinidae. The adult flies have such a fleeting career that they never eat. But the females manage to lay as many as 10 000 eggs, deposited in the cracks of dead, standing wood — usually tree stumps or fence posts.

Hairy larvae from the hatching eggs are blown about like plant pollens. If they collide with locusts or other grasshoppers they cling, then bore through soft membranes between the body sections. At-tached by a long, flexible funnel to one of the host's breathing tubes, a successful larva develops in the body cavity, eating away at whatever it can reach. In a female locust, chemical responses to the para-site's presence induce the production of fat instead of eggs.

After about three weeks in hot weather, or as long as five weeks in a cooler climate, the bee-fly larva is ready to pupate in the ground. By this time it is about half the size of the locust host. It gorges itself on the remaining fat and forces its way out behind the thorax of its dying victim.

For the short period of summer in which bee-flies are active they can kill up to eighty per cent of a locust population — mostly females because they make bigger targets for the windblown larvae. Where the flies are capable of doing so well, insecticide spraying is suspended at the final hopper phase of an infestation and not resumed until fledged locusts are about to swarm.

Consistent parasite populations

Another important parasite is the sarcophagid fly *Blaesoxipha pachytyli*. Females incubate their eggs internally and lay larvae directly onto hoppers or adult locusts. The larvae use hooked mouths and backward-pointing bristles to squirm inside. They move around freely, feeding on muscles, reproductive organs and fatty tissues for about five days before eating through the locust's neck membrane.

The strike rate of sarcophagid flies is only about ten per cent, but they have the advantage that they maintain consistent

THE LOCUST-EATERS
For some birds, a locust plague is paradise

Locusts are a favourite food of the straw-necked ibis *Threskiornis spinicollis*. Sudden influxes of the big birds are sometimes the first indication to farmers that they have a plague on their hands. Though water-breeders, the ibises forage readily on dry pastures. And they are the only birds likely to make a significant dent in locust numbers. If the pests descend near flooded inland swamps, particularly in the Murray-Darling basin, there could be huge breeding colonies of ibises nearby.

Other birds that prey regularly on locusts, though never with the mass impact of the straw-necked ibis, include the sacred ibis, ravens, woodswallows, the Australian kestrel and the black kite.

The straw-necked ibis (also known as the farmer's friend) is the most common of Australia's ibises

Australian plague locusts at the hopper stage advance in feeding bands through farmland

populations by using other grasshoppers as alternative hosts. When locusts arrive in their area they take a steady toll from the start. A similar but less significant role is played by tachinid flies *Ceracia* and *Phoroserosoma*.

All the best efforts of parasitic insects, however, cannot quickly halt a widespread plague of *Chortoicetes* locusts. Nor can predators — mainly birds and small marsupials — because their appetites cannot keep up with the locusts' rate of multiplication. Soaking rains, rendering the soil unsuitable for egg laying, may bring relief in limited areas. But only the disciplined use of insecticides gives any assurance of control.

Australia has many other locust species of varying economic importance. They include the plague locust of Old Testament notoriety, *Locusta migratoria*. It breeds continuously in the wettest tropical and subtropical regions but rarely causes serious trouble. The spur-throated locust *Nomadacris guttulosa* is a more significant tropical species. Though adapted to the monsoonal regime of the far north, it has made raids as far south as northern New South Wales.

In many farming areas the most destructive pest is not a migratory locust but the wingless grasshopper *Phaulacridium vittatum*. This species does not swarm, but hungry nymphal hoppers can occur in densities of hundreds to the square metre. They eat the young shoots of introduced legumes and grasses.

Adult wingless grasshoppers — a minority of which do have wings — also attack trees and crops, especially after pastures have dried off in summer. On the tablelands of New South Wales and in Tasmania they breed only once a year, in late summer or early autumn. At lower altitudes in the southeast, and in moist pockets of South and Western Australia, two generations are bred each year.

Wingless grasshoppers do their costliest damage in seasons of below-average rainfall, when they spend more time on croplands or in gardens and orchards. In seasons of high rainfall they suffer heavily from parasitism by nematode worms. The worm eggs, laid on damp vegetation, are accidentally eaten by the insects and hatch inside them. Worms mature in their body cavities for a month or more, hampering their sexual development and killing them as they emerge.□

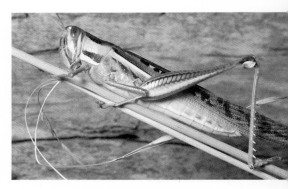

The tropical spur-throated locust has been known to reach New South Wales

FACTS ON FUNGI

The fruits of many fungi are appearing now, in a bewildering variety of forms

A fungus appearing on damp ground or wood is the equivalent of a flower — an ephemeral fruiting growth with the sole purpose of disseminating spores. Hidden below, a long-lived mass feeds on material produced by other organisms. Underground fungal growths supplement the diet of burrowing marsupials such as potoroos and bettongs, and of some native rodents. Certain families of flies, bugs and beetles breed in them. The fruiting bodies attract other insects, springtails, slugs and snails that often help spread the spores.

Far more creatures succumb to parasitism by fungi. Most attacks are by obscure moulds, infecting fishes, insects, spiders and so on at all stages of development. Among prominent fungi, *Cordyceps* grows from insect larvae as deep as a metre below the surface. Common species produce sausage-like fruits more than ten centimetres high. A branching type found in Victorian high country, specialising in the larvae of big moths, is the world's tallest at thirty centimetres.

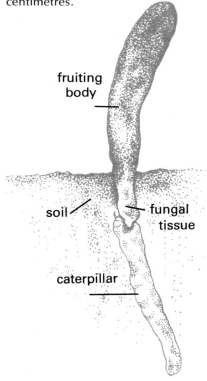

fruiting body

soil

fungal tissue

caterpillar

Vegetable caterpillars Cordyceps gunnii *(left and above) grow from moth larvae, usually under stands of acacias. The club-like fruiting body is attached to the larva near its head by a column of fungal tissue varying from a few centimetres up to a metre in length*

The tables turned: this puffball fungus (right) is making a meal for a leopard slug Limax maximus

Hericium (above) is a rare fungus that grows on wood in damp, shady forests

The starfish fungus Aseroe rubra (above) is found in high grassland and open forest. The brown slime contains spores

Two related fungi growing close together on the forest floor (left): the red one is flame fungus Clavulinopsis miniata and the yellow one is C. amoena. The simple club-like fruiting bodies can be cylindrical, flattened, grooved or forked at the ends in both species

The most common Australian luminous fungus is ghost fungus Pleurotus nidiformis (right); it grows on wood

Mosquitoes are still out for blood

Summer's end can be a boom time for these short-lived insects

With breeding swamps full to brimming, mosquitoes are at their worst now in the monsoonal tropics. To people in other parts of the country, who had their sleep shattered in midsummer, the bloodsucking insects are of diminishing concern. But they are still about — perhaps doing better than before.

Hot, sunny summers in the south do not favour mosquitoes that breed in rainwater. Feeding hours are at their shortest and evaporation rates are high. In early autumn, given reasonable rainfall and mild night temperatures, their populations may well increase. Generations later they will be assured of a good crop of overwintering eggs.

In any part of Australia where mosquitoes are a nuisance, it is worth paying particular attention in autumn to tidiness around houses. Gutters and drains should be clear. Unnecessary articles that could hold water should be removed. Necessary water should be changed once a week.

Inevitable invasions

Householders' efforts can limit the populations of certain mosquito species that share our homes. They include some of the most persistent disease carriers. Many others, unfortunately, have flight ranges of hundreds of metres. Some ride gentle winds — especially evening sea breezes. Near coastal mudflats and interior wetlands, invasions are inevitable.

Adult mosquitoes rarely live for more than a month. Only the females bite: blood proteins and vitamins are essential for egg production. Males may sip plant fluids. Male mosquitoes seldom fly except in answer to a mating summons — the whine of a female's wingbeats. Each species has its own distinctive pitch.

Blood is sought immediately after mating. Sources are located by backtracking warm air currents, exhalations of carbon dioxide and chemical traces in mouth and body odours. Few mosquitoes have a special preference for human blood, though they take it when available. Most would sooner bite wild mammals or birds. Some even seek the 'cold' blood of snakes, lizards and frogs.

Adequately fed females lay batches of a hundred or more eggs at intervals of about a week. The various species favour different laying sites, such as wet soil, holes in trees, gently running as well as stagnant water, and even saltwater rock pools. Temperatures determine the hatching times.

The larvae breathe air through their rear ends, hanging upside-down from the water surface while they use brushlike appendages to sweep aquatic bacteria and plant fragments into their mouths. Growth through four moulting stages takes two to four weeks, and pupation a further two days. Females are ready to mate and feed as soon as their bodies and wings have dried.

Australian mosquitoes can carry many diseases, most of them viral infections that cause fever. The north has been cleared of endemic malaria and the east coast of filariasis, though the carrier species remain. Outbreaks of viral encephalitis are still a danger around the Murray-Darling floodplains, but debilitating dengue fever in north Queensland is the disease that has affected most people in recent years. Health authorities fear the arrival of a potentially lethal Asian form, haemorrhagic dengue.

Old methods of controlling mosquito populations were far from satisfactory. Petroleum products, spread on breeding areas such as swamp surfaces, worked for only one season and interfered with other aquatic life. Chemical insecticides killed even more indiscriminately, and raised fears about accident hazards and dangerous residues. But excellent results have been achieved in recent years with crystals of a bacterial protein that quickly kills mosquito, blackfly and bloodworm larvae and leaves all other life forms unharmed.□

The life cycle of the common banded mosquito Culex annulirostris. *This photograph shows the egg-raft, larval and pupal stages and a newly emerged adult mosquito. Culex species hold themselves parallel to the surface on which they are feeding; Anopheles species hold their bodies at an angle when feeding*

March is the month when greater gliders are brought into contact with one another by mating attempts and rivalries

When a loner takes the plunge

Silent and solitary, the biggest of the gliding possums associates with its own kind only in the autumn mating season

A dark shape flits from the canopy of a tall eucalypt. Silhouetted for an instant against a moonlit sky, the angular form at first resembles a big bat. But an absurdly long tail streams behind, suggesting a child's kite. Seconds later, claws rip the bark near the base of another tree fifty metres away. A greater glider is on the move.

All day he lounged and slept in a lofty, leaf-padded hollow. Now he planes from tree to tree, along a habitual aerial pathway that will take him to certain favoured eucalypts. Like the koala he eats almost nothing but gumleaves. From all the variety in the forest he will choose only one or two species.

He leaps in the manner of all gliding possums, face down and limbs spreadeagled. At the end of the glide he brakes by tilting upright, striking the trunk of the target tree with the powerful claws of all four feet. He can turn in mid-flight, at right-angles if he wishes. But he is not the most accomplished glider. His planing membranes do not stretch from the feet all the way to the hands — only to the elbows.

With this modest canopy area his glide is more of a dive, descending at an angle of about forty degrees, which limits his leaping range. He must avoid the ground for he is clumsy there — and he lives in dingo country. Though the biggest of the gliders, *Petauroides volans* is only about the size of a domestic cat and makes easy prey.

Tonight he may vary his travelling

A male feathertail glider Acrobates pygmaeus *preparing to land*

routine. The breeding season has begun. Scent markings on the home tree of another glider — normally a 'keep out' signal — may tell him that a female is in oestrus. He will scramble up and stake his claim, warning off other males by re-marking the tree with a stronger scent from his own anal glands.

The young are born singly in late autumn or winter and spend three to four months in their mothers' pouches. They are weaned about three months later, some travelling on their mothers' backs in the meantime and others left in nesting hollows. Juveniles begin a solitary exist-ence at nine months, waiting a further year before they are sexually capable.

Greater gliders abound in tall eucalypt forests and flanking woodlands along the Great Dividing Range from the Tropic of Capricorn to Victoria. Though seldom seen — and never heard calling — their presence is obvious from deep scratches near the bases of the trees that they use. Similar animals are found less frequently in tropical forests; they may prove to be a separate species.

Sharing the range of the greater glider, though more restricted to the tallest for-

A rare sight of three types of gliders together (above). At top left is a sugar glider, at left is a feathertail glider, and the other three are all yellow-bellied gliders. They are feeding on the sap of a eucalypt

Sugar gliders have a large canopy of body skin, but glide only about fifty metres

The yellow-bellied glider (above) sleeps in a leaf-lined tree-hole by day

ests, is the rare yellow-bellied glider *Petaurus australis*. It distinguishes itself with a loud, shrieking call that descends to a rattle, along with many other noises. And it makes the longest, shallowest flights of any glider, spanning as much as a hundred metres.

In complete contrast to the greater glider, the yellow-bellied or fluffy glider is compulsively social, living in groups composed of a dominant breeding male, a harem of up to five females and their young. Bonded by exchanges of scent, they share a den and have a long breeding season. Mating — sometimes accomplished while a pair hang upside-down from a branch — can take place at any time from early spring to late autumn.

The principal foods of yellow-bellied gliders are the nectar and pollen of flowering eucalypts, along with sap oozing from holes bitten through the bark. Crawling insects are also taken. Manna gum *Eucalyptus viminalis* is the most favoured tree, though many others are used. An isolated, dwindling population in far northern Queensland taps its sap supply only from red mahogany *Eucalyptus resinifera*.

Sugar gliders *Petaurus breviceps* are common over a vast geographical and climatic range that sweeps in an arc from northern Western Australia to Tasmania. Groups of up to seven adults and their young share nests, huddling together to conserve warmth in cold weather. On high country in the southern part of the range they enter a torpid state in winter.

Predators take a heavy toll

Dense stands of acacias provide the most favoured habitat. Sugar gliders eat acacia resins, eucalypt sap and many insects. Breeding times vary with localities. In the southeast twin young are born in spring. By midsummer they are fending for themselves, and many fall prey to owls, goannas and feral cats. By autumn most of the surviving young are ejected from family nests. Where agriculture has broken up their habitats, predators take a further toll of juveniles forced to traverse open country.

Drier woodlands to the west of the Great Dividing Range harbour the squirrel glider *Petaurus norfolcensis*. Its biology and habits seem much the same as those of the smaller sugar glider. The two are so closely related that captive specimens have produced fertile hybrids.

One other possum in a completely separate family has perfected the art of gliding. The feathertail glider *Acrobates pygmaeus* is a burramyid, allied to the pygmy possums. Its planing membranes are small, extending only between the elbows and knees. But its flattened tail has coarse, stiff hairs at each side, giving it an extra planing area and control surface. This makes it highly manoeuvrable, and a feathertail can end its glide with a spiralling series of turns around the target tree.

Feathertails range from Cape York to Bass Strait, in habitats varying from dry woodlands to tall eucalypt forests. They are much like the *Petaurus* gliders in their food preferences — sometimes stealing sap from the bark incisions made by the other species.

Living in groups of a dozen or more and breeding virtually year-round, feathertails are also amusingly opportunistic in choosing nesting sites. If a suitable tree hollow is not available they take over the abandoned nests of birds and other animals. Junction boxes on telephone poles are sometimes colonised, and even the big plastic bags used to protect ripening bunches of bananas.

Ringtail possums are the closest relatives of *Petaurus* gliders. At this time of year the twittering calls of the common ringtail *Pseudocheirus peregrinus* may herald the onset of the breeding season, which extends through to November. Two litters, usually of twins, may be reared in one year. The young leave the pouch at

Twin young of the common ringtail possum Pseudocheirus peregrinus

eighteen weeks and are independent at six months old.

Colourings, habitats and nesting habits can vary widely. Many zoologists think that the basic type of ringtail, distributed from Cape York to South Australia and Tasmania, with a few in Western Australia, is diverging into different species.

Common ringtails are easily distinguished from other possums by their thin, white-tipped tails. At rest or on the ground the end of the tail is tightly coiled. When the animal is scrambling among branches in its quest for food the tail comes into play like a monkey's, as an extra hand or an anchor. The naked underside of the tip has a pad of roughened skin to improve the grip.

Adult ringtails do not form groups but are socially tolerant. Home ranges, in which each animal may have several nests, often overlap. Leaves make up most of the diet but blossoms and fruits are also eaten. Where there is a cover of dense shrubbery near human settlements, gardens are frequently raided.□

THE CLASH OF ALIEN ANTLERS
Male deer compete fiercely for breeding dominance

Wild herds of deer graze and breed in a surprising number of localities, scattered in all states except Western Australia. Their ancestors were introduced as hunting targets or as ornaments to satisfy the pretensions of landowners.

In the middle of March, with almost clockwork regularity, the males of two of the most prominent species start their preparations for mating. They seek exclusive rights to as many females as possible. In herds with more than one mature male, or where two herds are within earshot of each other, 'rutting' behaviour usually leads to violent confrontations.

In a ritual that is characteristic of most cervids, bucks of the fallow deer *Dama dama* and stags of the red deer *Cervus elaphus* mark

the boundaries of chosen breeding territories by battering shrubs and small trees with their antlers. A scent from glands in front of the eyes is thus transferred to the vegetation. The forefeet are used to scrape shallow ruts within the claimed areas and these are drenched with urine, which gives off an acrid stench that presumably attracts does and hinds in season.

Call like a lion's roar

Loud calling begins — like a lion's roar in the case of the red stag, while a fallow buck sounds remarkably like a courting koala. The roars are advertisements of size and strength, a further enticement to females but intensely provocative to rivals. Competing males put their boasting to the test by locking antlers and trying to force each other to the ground.

Struggles go on for many minutes, and may be renewed over and over until one contestant capitulates — usually without serious injury. Antlers are often smashed, but in any case they are due to be shed in October. Replacement sets will reach full size by the middle of February, in good time for next season's joustings.

Mating takes place from late in March until the end of April. Single young of both species are born in November or December. Most remain in family groups that feed by day if there is no human disturbance, mainly eating grasses but also browsing some shrubs. Other deer surviving in Australia, all of Asian origin, do not show the breeding precision of the two European species. The most numerous is the sambar *Cervus unicolor*, from India. It breeds at any time, but its mating peak is in May and June. This species, spreading from eastern Victoria into mountainous districts of New South Wales and the Australian Capital Territory, is alone in having significantly expanded its Australian range.

A stag of the red deer Cervus elaphus *calling*

A plump painted snipe, surprised in her hideout under dense swamp grasses, offers defiance. Fixing her gaze on the intruder she spreads her wing and tail feathers, suddenly increasing her apparent size. From a windpipe of exceptional length she produces a canine growl — or a snake-like hiss. Males of her kind are not capable of such vocal tricks. They make gentle, clicking sounds more appropriate to nursery duties.

In the muddy world of the painted snipe, feminine superiority is complete. Females are bigger, more brightly plumed, and bolder in every way. The males on whom they bestow their favours — three or more mates are chosen in a good season — carry all domestic burdens.

'True' snipe are starting to leave Australia now. They are fast-flying annual migrants from breeding grounds in north-eastern Asia. The painted snipe *Rostratula benghalensis*, a slower bird that dangles its legs in flight like a rail or a crake, lives here year-round. It is mainly an inland wanderer that seeks shallow freshwater swamps, though in the south it may settle for coastal salt-marshes. It probes in soft mud for insects and worms.

Painted snipe feed and rest alone, but form small nesting colonies where conditions are most suitable. Mating starts in March in the north, as floods from monsoonal rains or cyclones recede. Southern populations, most numerous in the Murray-Darling basin, breed from October to December.

Females make the first move

A female flirts with any unattached male, initiating courtship flights. After they copulate it is up to the male to make a nest — a sheltered scrape padded with plant material. Four eggs are usually laid, and for nearly three weeks the male alone has the task of incubating them. He also broods and guards the hatchlings for the short time it takes them to learn to fend for themselves. Long before then, their mother has found another partner.

Painted snipe are probably fairly common. But few people go into their swampy habitats, where they are furtive and mainly nocturnal. Far more prominent among birds breeding now in the north, around the fringes of swamps or mangrove flats, are bar-shouldered doves *Geopelia humeralis*. Courting males are often seen on display flights, bursting into the air above the pandanus scrub.

Bar-shouldered doves are seed-eaters that feed only on the ground but roost and nest in pandanus palms or accompanying trees. Most stay close to their home areas, changing their diets as different plants begin to seed. Nests are flimsy platforms of twigs. Parents share the incubation of two eggs, which hatch in two weeks.

Painted ladies play the field

Scorning domesticity, female native snipe flit from one mate to the next. Males are left to care for the eggs and chicks

A female painted snipe stands its ground and threatens an intruder

The peaceful dove *Geopelia placida*, mainly grey rather than brown, and noticeably smaller, also starts breeding now in the north. They are seen in flight in the same districts as their relatives, but feed on drier ground and nest in eucalypt woodlands. Both species have southern populations that will breed in spring.

Unmistakable among birds thronging tropical woodlands is the boisterous red-tailed black cockatoo *Calyptorhynchus banksii*. It too is breeding now. Flocks of twenty or so are splitting up into pairs, filling the air with raucous yelps as they wheel about over their nesting trees.

Natural hollows are widened until either bird can enter — tail first, in the manner of all black cockatoos. Wood chewed from the inside makes a bed of chips for a single egg, incubated in about a month by the female, who is brought food by her mate. The young take up to three months to fledge.

Northern and eastern birds eat seeds from countless different trees and shrubs, and groups sometimes alight on the ground to harvest grasses. A population inhabiting the wheat belt of Western Australia is even more given to ground foraging. But races found in tall forests of the far southwest and in an isolated pocket on the South Australia-Victoria border restrict themselves to seeds of the eucalypts in which they live — marri and brown stringybark respectively. These latter birds, breeding in winter and spring, descend to the ground only to drink.

The quiet cockatoo

Only male redtails four years old or more live up to their name. Females, and juveniles of both sexes, have yellow-to-orange undertail bars and can also be distinguished by yellow speckling on the head and shoulders. Similar colour contrasts occur in the glossy black cockatoo *Calyptorhynchus lathami*, another autumn breeder. It lives in eastern and southeastern eucalypt forests and woodlands but eats only the newly ripened cones of some casuarinas. This species differs from the true redtail in having no crest — and in being unusually quiet.

The spangled drongo *Dicrurus bracteatus* ends a long breeding season now. Populations that have lived in Queensland rainforests since last spring inexplicably divide. Most go north, travelling in groups of a dozen or two, and

The spangled drongo builds its nest up to twenty-five metres above the ground

winter in New Guinea. Others are happy to stay where they are. And a few follow the Great Dividing Range south into increasingly chilly latitudes, all the way to the New South Wales-Victoria border. Meanwhile a separate population in the Kimberley and the Top End makes no move at all.

Drongos prey on big flying insects, taking most of them on the wing. Nesting high up, they descend to medium levels to hunt, but are not easily seen in the typical gloom of a rainforest. Calls have a characteristically metallic tone, but a drongo's song can cause confusion because it mimics the sounds of other birds.

Two familiar small species of the south and east make migrations at this time: the silvereye *Zosterops lateralis* and the white-naped honeyeater *Melithreptus lunatus*. Both versatile, agile feeders (hanging upside-down if necessary), they have no trouble sustaining themselves

wherever they have to rest.

Having completed a breeding season that began as long ago as August, silvereyes from every kind of wooded habitat congregate in big flocks. Birds from Tasmania and Victoria travel as far as Queensland, joining sedentary populations there. Long flights are made at night to a constant accompaniment of sharp chirping. By day the travellers work their way through forest or garden shrubbery. They pluck small insects from foli-

Silvereyes feed in small flocks, on insects, seeds, fruit and nectar

Glossy black cockatoos, unlike their more sociable relatives, feed in small groups

The barking owl is the least nocturnal of Australian owls; it may hunt before sunset

THE SCREAMING WOMAN
One bird has a distinctive autumn call

Ninox connivens is aptly named the barking owl. Its usual call is a descending 'woof-woof', often interspersed with growling noises. But a few females occasionally vary this with a succession of high-pitched wails, sounding eerily like a woman screaming for help.

The source of the cries, a bush mystery since pioneering times, was not traced until 1939. A bird on exhibition at Healesville Sanctuary, Victoria, gave vent to a hair-raising series of screams, and investigations in the wild established this as a trait of the species. Still unexplained is the purpose of the calls — and why they are nearly always heard in March or April. Breeding does not start until July.

age, sip nectar, peck seeds and raid cultivated fruit crops.

Silvereyes with their trilled or whistled warblings are among the loudest contributors to a dawn chorus. From cover during the day they utter a variety of whispered songs that often include mimicry. Singing is most noticeable in the long breeding season, during which as many as three broods, each of three young, may be raised. Human hair and animal fur is collected as nest-lining material.

White-naped honeyeaters are prolific breeders in tall eucalypt forests of the southwest and all along the Great Dividing Range. They too use hair and fur, some taken from the backs of livestock.

The major migratory population, from high country between Melbourne and Canberra, moves in thousands, north towards Queensland and west to the South Australian gulfs. Along the way they feed on sap exuding from gums, on honeydew from leaf suckers, other insects, spiders and eucalypt nectar.□

Tough immigrants
Native birds lose ground to unwise imports

All across the southeast from Brisbane to the Bight, huge flocks are forming now of Australia's most unfortunately introduced birds — common starlings. Throughout autumn and winter they will scour every pasture and clearing. Seldom able to find enough insects, spiders, worms and snails to sustain them, they will destroy a good share of soft fruit crops.

Worse will come in early spring when breeding starts. Noisy communal roosts of thousands of birds will break up as pairs seek nesting holes. Spaces under eaves or crannies in walls will do, but all too often native species such as kingfishers, treecreepers and grass parrots are evicted from their tree hollows. Native breeding rates plummet and the starlings prosper, often raising two broods of up to eight young each by midsummer.

In a mid-nineteenth-century frenzy for reminders of England, common starlings *Sturnus vulgaris* were released first in Melbourne in the 1850s and subsequently in every colonial capital except Perth. Across about one-fifth of the country they have gone everywhere that agriculture has gone, stalled only by tropical heat in Queensland. Only zealous observation and destruction keep them out of the west — the Nullarbor is no barrier.

Another misguided introduction through Melbourne was the common mynah — not to be confused with native miners. *Acridotheres tristis*, from Southeast Asia, was encouraged as a supposed scourge of crop pests such as grasshoppers. Releases were made at many points along the east coast. Attempted introductions in Adelaide and in Tasmania in the 1950s did not succeed.

Mynahs are omnivorous scavengers that stay in and around urban areas. On the face of it they harm the chances of native birds' breeding only on

the fringes. But to suburbanites hoping to encourage native species into their gardens, the mynah is a leading stumbling-block — along with the house sparrow *Passer domesticus*.

Sparrows were brought in through Melbourne, Adelaide and Hobart in the 1860s. In a century their descendants were in every settled area in the eastern half of the country, all the way to Cape York. In favourable conditions they breed continuously. Western Australia and the Northern Territory would be overwhelmed too, without strenuous preventive measures by wildlife authorities.

In a similar period the tree sparrow *Passer montanus* has progressed from Melbourne only through the eastern half of Victoria and into the southern Riverina district of New South Wales. It frequents introduced ornamental trees rather than natural vegetation.□

Common starlings Sturnus vulgaris *in a typically energetic squabble over food. They form large flocks in autumn and winter and cause extensive damage to fruit crops. A big flock was destroyed at Nullarbor Station in recent years in order to prevent the starling spreading to previously uncolonised Western Australia*

APRIL

THIS MONTH'S WEATHER

As the anticyclone belt returns northward,
Southern Ocean westerlies are re-established
and rainfall readings soar in Tasmania. In most
other regions this is a month of transition, with
rainfall increasing gradually in the south and
dwindling in the northeast. At the Top End,
monsoonal effects are displaced by a
southeasterly airflow that heralds the dry
season but brings storms at first. Northern
waters remain warm enough to generate the
last cyclones of the season.

AROUND THE COUNTRY	RAIN (mm)	MAX. (°C)	MIN. (°C)	SUN hrs/day
Adelaide	47	22	12	6.0
Alice Springs	14	28	13	9.4
Brisbane	79	27	17	7.8
Canberra	49	20	7	7.2
Darwin	99	33	24	8.7
Hobart	53	17	9	5.3
Melbourne	58	20	11	5.6
Perth	45	25	14	7.2
Port Hedland	23	35	21	9.7
Sydney	124	22	15	6.6
Townsville	62	29	20	7.7
Weipa	114	32	23	6.8

Grey-headed flying foxes at sunrise, roosting in a Sydney suburb

Hunting with a bunch of hangers-on

Tenacity earns wolf spiderlings unique protection. In autumn the strongest of a brood freeload for weeks on their foraging mother's back

Dashing about haphazardly, the wolf spider seems distracted. But she is hunting. In dim light or even in darkness, nothing that moves escapes her notice. Pausing momentarily, she checks the position of a fat cockroach she has sighted. Her attacking rush and pounce are, as usual, deadly accurate.

Observed while she overpowers her prey, this spider presents a curiously woolly appearance. On closer inspection the tangled mat covering her back proves to be a lively, leg-waving mass of scores of miniature spiders.

These are the strongest of her brood, hatched from hundreds of eggs that she produced in summer. Others have literally fallen by the wayside. As weeks go by there will be further attrition. A tenacious minority will stay safe, then dismount and find homes before winter.

Prolonged back-riding by spiderlings is known only in lycosids — wolf spiders and their close relatives. The hatching young of a few other types may accidentally scramble onto their mothers, but are soon dislodged. A female wolf spider, however, is specially equipped to carry her brood without interruption to her energetic hunting activities.

Among normal hairs on the upper surface of the abdomen are some with knobbed ends and spurred sides. The first spiderlings to clamber over their mother trail draglines of silk that are snagged on these hairs. Clamping clawed feet to the spurs, knobs and a mesh of draglines, the young hangers-on are fixed firmly enough to anchor as many as four layers of brothers and sisters above them.

The privileged treatment of these spiderlings began earlier in the year, even before they hatched. The cocoon in which they developed was taken by the mother on every foraging excursion, receiving regular airings. If she hunted in daylight it

A female wolf spider with young clinging to her back; note the characteristic squarish arrangement of the upper four eyes

A large huntsman spider Isopoda vasta with prey (left). Huntsman spiders are usually easily identifiable by their flattened bodies, spreadeagled posture, and their two parallel rows of four eyes

A large nursery-web spider displaying a talent for fishing that is unexpected in a spider (below). Dolomedes species can both walk on the water and dive beneath the surface

was automatically warmed; if she belonged to a nocturnal species she would have spent part of her days sunning it at the entrance of her burrow.

Some other spiders carry egg sacs about with them, usually slung under their bodies. Wolf spiders distinguish themselves by hauling spherical white cocoons behind them, attached to the spinnerets at the rear of the abdomen.

A female wolf spider's ability to feed normally while she takes care of eggs and spiderlings gives her a good chance of living for a second year and breeding again next summer. These advantages to the mothers and young make lycosids a highly successful group. Among ground-dwellers in Australia, only trapdoor spiders rival them in dominance.

Identifying wolf spiders

The two most common and widespread wolf spiders are also the biggest. *Lycosa godeffroyi* and *L. leuckartii* reach three centimetres in length. Boldly patterned with dark chevrons and radiating bands on grey or brown backgrounds, they are most at home in dry woodlands. They dig shallow burrows beside rocks or logs, sometimes erecting entrance funnels of silkbound grass or leaves.

Hundreds of smaller species occur in habitats as diverse as forest floors, sandplains, pastures, swamps, salt-marshes, mountaintops, beaches and suburban gardens. In rich soils they are generally dark, drab and obscure, seldom noticed unless females with cocoons are disturbed. Sand-dwelling species vary from buff to yellow or reddish. Some live just like trapdoor spiders, in deep vertical burrows closed with plugs or topped by parapets, pebbles or piles of twigs.

Whatever its size, colour or habits, any wolf spider can be distinguished by the square arrangement of its four biggest

eyes, high on a rounded head. Four other tiny eyes are aligned in front. Jumping spiders also have a square pattern of eyes on top but their front eyes are bigger.

Lycosids epitomise the hunting spiders — all those that make no use of silk in snaring or subduing their prey. They are aggressors that rely instead on boldness, speed, strength, dexterity, acute vision and good distance perception. Insects are

the usual prey but any small moving creature may be attacked. Big wolf spiders sometimes take on frogs and lizards.

Foraging widely in apparently random directions, frequently criss-crossing their own routes, wolf spiders must have exceptional powers of observation to find their way home. Keen sight in females is also fundamental to their breeding behaviour. Males, attracted by chemical traces, have

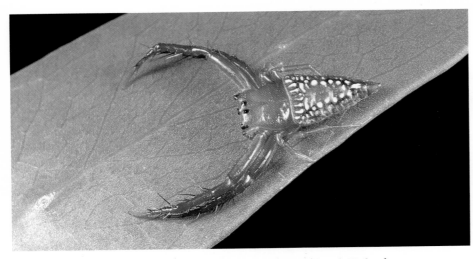

The triangle spider Arcys clavatus *is widespread in New South Wales forests*

to identify themselves from a safe distance. They hold up their palps — the paired sensory appendages in front of their legs — and wave them to create patterns of movement and colour that are exclusive to their species.

In at least one of the smaller species, mating is preceded by aerial dispersal on gossamer, which is highly unusual among mature spiders. Males of *Lycosa pullastra*, common in lawns around Perth, climb up the grass in early summer. Spinning buoyant nets, they allow themselves to drift wherever breezes take them. The young of some wolf spider species also disperse aerially in autumn.

Pisaurid hunting spiders match lycosids in their instinctive protection of the young — hence their common name of nursery-web spiders. Most are vagrants that take shelter where they can find it. A mother carries her cocoon while foraging, held by her palps and fang-tipped chelicerae. But when she senses that the eggs are ready to hatch, she makes a nest of silk among vegetation or under stones. The cocoon is deposited there and she waits outside, guarding it. She abandons hunting until the spiderlings are sufficiently developed to disperse.

Nursery-web spiders are also called water spiders, though they are not truly aquatic. They hunt around and on water — salt as well as fresh. Delicate hairs radiating from the tips of their long legs allow them to walk on water without breaking its surface tension. But they can dive and stay under if they are frightened, breathing air trapped in body hairs.

Dolomedes, the main genus of nursery-web spiders, has species distributed throughout Australia, from tropical mangrove swamps to alpine streams. The biggest, *Dolomedes australianus*, can exceed 2.5 centimetres in body length and with legs extended can span fifteen centimetres. All its kind have a characteristic resting attitude, flat on the ground with legs splayed like the spokes of a wheel.

Big, hairy sparassids — most of which also have a flattened, spreadeagled posture — have probably alarmed more people in Australia than all other spiders put together. They are commonly called huntsmen, giant crab spiders, triantelopes or tarantulas. The last name belongs to a dangerous European wolf spider, not found in this country, and was transferred to a huge American bird-eating spider. Use of the name here has led to unjustified fear of a largely inoffensive family.

The travelling huntsman

Few huntsmen spiders have permanent homes. In natural environments they sidle into rock crevices, cracks in wood or under loose bark to rest. Retreats are constructed only for egg-laying and perhaps for moulting. But these spiders do have habitual hunting territories. In wet weather they frequently enter houses or outbuildings — and if left undisturbed, they take up occupancy.

A huntsman may appear in the same part of a room every evening for months on end. It roves when the lights go out and does a useful job of disposing of insect pests. Equipped to walk upside down on ceilings, it will not drop onto its hosts.

Huntsmen have eight big eyes arranged in parallel rows of four. The most frequently encountered large types are species of *Isopoda* and *Delena* with characteristically flattened bodies. Another common type, *Olios*, is less obviously one of the family. It has a humped body, held high, and hunts on the foliage of shrubbery. All sparassids show a maternal instinct, the females either guarding or carrying their egg sacs.

Sac spiders, so called for the silken chambers in which they brood their eggs and moult, include some species that take up domestic life just as readily as the huntsmen do. Females of the dark, cigar-shaped, white-tailed spider *Lampona cylindrata* are still brooding at this time of year. Another domestic species, the buff-coloured *Chiracanthium mordax*, matures earlier; adults are probably dead by now, but the young are hunting widely. The chambers of household-adapted sac spiders are usually found in the angles between walls and ceilings. Their daytime

Flower spiders are camouflaged to escape the notice of predators and prey

A jumping spider's eyes are arranged to give it all-round vision

hiding places may be elsewhere — behind cupboards and pictures, for example. In natural habitats they shelter under bark or among foliage. A much bigger bushland sac spider, *Miturga*, makes a semi-permanent home in vegetation close to ground level, or under logs or stones.

Flower spiders *Diaea* expend the least energy of any hunting type. They are patient little deceivers that ambush their prey. Exclusive territories are held on blossoming shrubs. Day after day the spiders wait inside flowers, their front legs held up. Generally yellow or white, they escape the notice of predatory birds. Intruding insects, intent on nectar, are bitten before they realise the danger.

Another ambush specialist, successful in spite of its gaudy colouring, is the triangle spider *Arcys*. It waits on leaves by day and hangs from a horizontal strand of silk at night. *Arcys* is an oddity: its anatomy clearly places it among orb-weavers, yet it makes no web at all.

Jumping spiders are the most athletic hunters, capable not only of prodigious forward pounces at prey but also of leaps in any direction to evade predators. Eyes positioned at the top corners of their angular heads give them all-round vision. They usually stalk insects that alight on vertical surfaces but sometimes they hurl themselves out at flying prey. Draglines arrest their fall.

Big and colourful jumping spiders abound in the tropics. Those of the south are small, and drab with the exception of *Saitis* species. Mature males of *Saitis pavonis*, the peacock spider, display their vividly patterned bodies in courtship dances by raising their abdomens.

Lynx spiders *Oxyopes* leap as effectively as jumping spiders in pursuit of their prey. They hunt in foliage, their surefootedness aided by strong spines on their legs. Camouflaged with brown markings on an unusual background of bright green, lynx spiders make no refuges even when moulting. Egg sacs are deposited in a shelter of loosely bound leaves.

Six-eyed spiders

Spitting spiders are hunters that immobilise their prey from a distance by squirting a kind of gum through their fangs. They are also remarkable in having only six eyes. Australia has some native species, which have been little observed. More is known about an introduced species, *Scytodes thoracica*. It is virtually domesticated, inhabiting neglected corners of buildings and undisturbed rubbish.

Female *Scytodes* carry their eggs with them, but not in a cocoon. They dangle in a loosely woven purse of silk bound with gum. Spiderlings simply drop to the ground in early autumn, immediately able to fend for themselves.

Most hunting spiders are excitable and aggressive if disturbed. Bigger types inflict bites that are nearly always painful. Swellings and symptoms of envenomation such as headache, dizziness and vomiting may follow, but there is no threat to life. Wolf spiders, sac spiders, tree-dwelling huntsmen *Olios* and tropical jumping spiders *Mopsus* have the worst reputations for causing illness of this nature. □

WHEN LOOKS CAN KILL
Spiders mimic ants for protection — and prey

Slender, spindly-legged hunting spiders of at least four different families imitate ants — and three of them are known to dine richly on their models. Their adaptations probably evolved as defences against birds, which find ants distasteful. Then the spiders learned to take advantage of mistaken identity, infiltrating ant columns and eating their fill.

The tropical *Amyciaea albomaculata*, relying on colour and false eye-spots, looks like a back-to-front green tree-ant. A species of *Storena* also exploits colour, along with front legs raised to look like antennae, in its imposture of red meat-ants. *Corinomma* has a false waist in its long abdomen and waves its forelegs, though it does not seem to prey on ants.

Most thorough in their mimicry are species of jumping spiders *Myrmarachne*. False 'necks' divide their heads and thoraxes, copying the proportions of their prey. They conceal their palps and hoist their forelegs. Males even have oversized chelicerae that look like the jaws of soldier ants.

Amyciaea albomaculata eating a green tree-ant. The spider's elaborate disguise enables it to infiltrate the ants' pathways and kill at leisure

Insistent whistles sound across a shallow lagoon, the pairing ground of a group of black ducks. Drakes vie for attention, trying to catch female eyes as they perform intricate rituals of splashing and posturing. Approving females approach chosen drakes, then abruptly take flight. Quacking uproariously, they incite the males to pursue them. Sometimes a game of chasing leads to an aerial coupling, despite the fact that the birds are not yet in breeding condition.

Repeated often as weeks go by, courtship displays and pursuit flights establish bonds that will last until eggs are laid. Mating may be delayed until spring or summer, depending on rainfall, but courting nearly always starts in April. Where winters are wet some birds will nest as early as July, so their prospecting for a site will begin almost immediately.

Pacific black ducks *Anas superciliosa* are the most widespread in Australia, and probably the most abundant. Certainly they are the most often shot, making up about two-thirds of legal sporting kills. Following so closely on the open-season losses of May, the assembly and pairing-off of young flocks now are reassuring events. But all too often, scenes of happy activity are subtly flawed. Some of the birds are the wrong kind.

Mallards *Anas platyrhynchos* were introduced from Europe and North America late last century to decorate public parks. They thrive in the southeast and southwest. Some venture to the natural breeding grounds of black ducks, where they are accepted without dispute. During dry seasons, black duck flocks join mal-

The very rare orange-bellied parrot breeds only in Tasmania

Mixed-up ducks court disaster

Ducks begin courting in April. But some risk the future of their species by wooing foreigners

lards on urban ponds and streams.

The mallard is slightly bigger, and in many ways a superior bird. In favourable conditions it lays more eggs. Its juvenile survival rate is higher and its adult life expectancy is greater. In any direct competition with the black duck for habitats and food, it must win. New Zealand's race of black ducks outnumbered mallards twenty to one in 1960. By 1980 there were five mallards to each black duck.

Such an easy supplanting cannot happen in Australia. Our black ducks, accustomed to less reliable rainfall, are nomads at heart. If conditions turn against them they move, and if necessary they adjust their breeding patterns. Mallards lead seasonally regulated lives that depend on permanent water. Nevertheless they present a threat to the endemic species — by genetic takeover.

Courtship behaviour of the two species is much the same. If they happen to be together at an appropriate time there is a chance of interbreeding — especially by black drakes with female mallards. For some reason female black ducks are less impressed by mallard drakes.

Mallard characteristics are strongly dominant in the progeny of mixed matings. They are carried through succeeding generations. It may seem no bad thing to have bigger and more productive ducks. But it is a reasonable assumption that the hybrids also inherit a mallard's static nature. Experts fear that black duck flocks, increasingly 'mallardised', will become helpless in the face of drought.

While numbers are maintained, Pacific black ducks are likely to be found on any body of still or slow-moving water, including some brackish coastal lagoons and salty estuaries. They are surface feeders on aquatic plants and animals, busily dabbling and upending — but not diving — in early-morning and evening sessions. Seeds are stripped from grasses in and around the water.

Nests may be in tree holes, woven cups of grass or reeds, or mere scrapes in the ground. Eight to ten eggs are laid, normally one each morning. They are packed with down, and covered when the mother goes out to feed. The drake accompanies her at first but loses interest in the first of the four weeks of incubation, wandering off in search of unmated females.

Golden-shouldered parrots (below) may die out if trafficking continues

Aquatic insects make up about half of the Pacific black duck's diet

Ducklings are led to the water within hours of the last hatching. But for three weeks their outings are brief — for most of the time they are brooded in the nest. Fledged at eight to ten weeks, they disperse soon after to join various groups. More than half die in the first year. Survivors generally live for two or three more years, though fifteen is possible.

Birdlife on seashores becomes noticeably quieter in April with the departure of migratory species — especially waders — that breed in the northern hemisphere. Many native birds also head north, or move to lower altitudes for winter.

With luck the orange-bellied parrot *Neophema chrysogaster* of western Tasmania may be sighted now and throughout winter near southern mainland shores. This is one of the rarest birds in Australia. A population of a few hundred crosses Bass Strait in small groups that scatter between Wilsons Promontory and the Murray River mouth. They are seed-eaters that forage on tidal flats, saltmarshes and coastal grasslands.

A better-known relative, the blue-winged parrot *Neophema chrysostoma* also leaves Tasmania around April. Other populations normally living in southern Victoria and South Australia are probably on the move as well. Small flocks — whether Tasmanians or mainlanders is not known — reach the Darling River floodplains in New South Wales; in wet years some birds find seeding grasses in the forbidding Lake Eyre basin.

Swift parrots *Lathamus discolor* make the most extensive migrations from Tasmania. After crossing the strait they concentrate for a while in Victoria. A later dispersal takes flocks west to high country near Adelaide, and as far up the east coast as Rockhampton, Queensland. Feeding in the canopies of blossoming eucalypts, they are easily mistaken for lorikeets.

In contrast to the bleak weather and food scarcity that force Tasmania's parrots from their homes, conditions are perfect now for two remarkable grass parrots of the far north. Plants brought on by the monsoon rains are producing their greatest bounty of seeds. And though the rains have retreated, termite mounds are still soft.

Both the hooded parrot *Psephotus dissimilis* of Arnhem Land and the golden-shouldered parrot *Psephotus chrysopterygius* of Cape York Peninsula prepare their nesting holes in April, excavating cosy spaces in the huge mounds. Older birds return to the holes of previous years, undoing the termites' repair work.

The masterbuilder logrunner

Back in the deepening chill and dampness of upland rainforests in New South Wales and southern Queensland, the logrunner *Orthonyx temminckii* chooses a surprising time to start breeding. A small masterpiece of building — a house rather than a nest — is carefully constructed to protect the eggs and hatchlings.

Working alone, the female lays down a thick platform of sticks on the ground, piling more at the sides and rear to make walls that lean together at the top. A pad of moss and leaves is laid above, sloping down to shield the entrance. A further capping of sticks and leaves is added, and the interior is lined.

Laboriousness is a way of life for the logrunner. It spends all its time on the ground or hopping over fallen trees; even when alarmed it flutters only two or three metres. Hour after hour it scuffles about on ferny banks, hunting for grubs, slugs

The southern logrunner spends most of its time foraging on the ground

A male great frigatebird inflates its throat pouch to attract females

and snails. When it comes to a promising spot it props itself on a spine-tipped tail and kicks away leaf litter and humus. A fresh clearing the size of a bread plate may be a bushwalker's only hint that a logrunner is about.

On tropical islands and coral cays boobies are at the peak of colonial breeding activity. In some locations all three Australian species of these sea hunters are close neighbours, each in its own preferred habitat. The brown booby *Sula*

Brahminy kites are solitary, each bird patrolling its own stretch of shore

leucogaster — often seen in mainland estuaries — nests on cliff edges or in small clearings among shrubbery. The masked booby *Sula dactylatra* favours open headlands, where it may merely make a scrape. The red-footed booby *Sula sula* weaves a nest of sticks in trees or bushes.

Boobies attack their prey of fish and squid in slanting dives from as high as a hundred metres. The red-footed and masked species do not plunge far under the surface, often skimming it to take flying fish. The brown booby chases prey underwater, still beating its wings.

Fed twice a day, chicks weigh more than their parents at about ten weeks but cannot fly until they are four months old. Some adults usually remain in a colony

while others are hunting because the chicks are under frequent threat of attack by great frigatebirds *Fregata minor*. Often these predators live on the same islands.

Piratical frigatebirds

Frigatebirds are highly efficient ocean hunters in the same manner as the boobies, and they are better fliers. But they find it easier to prey on unprotected chicks and eggs. They also hijack food and nesting materials by dive-bombing boobies in flight, forcing them to release their cargo and catching it in mid-air.

Some excuse for the rapaciousness of frigatebirds can be found in the care they have to give their own offspring. A young bird may not fledge until it is five months old, by which time it is enormous — and it may not master hunting skills for a further six months. Probably because of this protracted responsibility, adults seem to breed at roughly two-yearly intervals in virtually any season. The spectacular sight of a smoothly gliding male in breeding condition, with a small patch on his throat puffed into a great red ball, is therefore quite rare.

A bird of tropical shores that could be expected to menace wildlife is the majestic, eagle-like brahminy kite *Milvus indus*. It fact it scarcely deserves to be classed as a bird of prey at all. Patrolling mangrove-skirted bays and inlets, it feeds principally on dead fish and other marine creatures cast onto mudflats by the tide.

A brown booby Sula leucogaster *adult and chick at the nest*

The corpses of frogs and small reptiles may also be disposed of, if crabs do not get to them first. Insects are about all that a brahminy is likely to take alive.

April is the start of a long breeding season for brahminies that will last until the return of the Wet. Courtships are vigorous aerial displays common to many eagles and kites. Stick nests lined with softer material are built in the forks of tall trees. The male fetches food for his mate during about seven weeks of incubation and brooding, but soon they part. In Australia, unlike in India, brahminies are solitary when not breeding. □

A shoal of sea mullet — they mature at about three years old and move out of estuaries to the open sea to spawn

Fish breed — and humans feed

In autumn, inshore waters are crowded with fish on their way to warmer spawning grounds. Many end up on our tables

The southern bream is popular with anglers and is also fished commercially

First light casts a silvery gleam across a sheltered river estuary. Quickly the still waters come alive with leaping fish. Their forms cannot be seen yet, but the smacking sounds of re-entry suggest that they are of a respectable size. After three years in enclosed waters sea mullet are massing to embark on the journey of their lives. For many it will be a short one.

Southern populations of sea mullet *Mugil cephalus* are among a great number of fishes to make a northward spawning migration in autumn. It is their misfortune to travel together in coastline-hugging shoals — and to make palatable human food. Mullet catches have long been a mainstay of most Australian commercial fisheries. Though the flesh is not as popular as it used to be, unspawned eggs dominate the smoked roe market.

Reaching adulthood in the brackish upper tidal reaches of rivers, sea mullet frustrate amateur anglers because they rarely take baits and lures. They live on drifting micro-organisms and algae. When they gather at rivermouths, preparing to migrate, some are taken by 'jagging' — casting unbaited hooks and jerking them back through the shoals. The technique is illegal in most states.

Commercial hauls come from travelling mullet. The fish move north in dense shoals within about three kilometres of the coast. Thousands of tonnes are taken each season by beach netting or nearshore trawling. The average weight is not much over one kilogram — about a fifth of what a fully matured specimen could be expected to reach.

Migrations from the southernmost estuaries began early in the year. By April the biggest shoals are off the central western coast and off northern New South Wales. Sea mullet entering Queensland waters will contribute the greatest tonnage of any species to that state's commercial catch. Survivors will spawn just inside tropical waters in about two months' time. Currents will bring the juveniles, and some adults, back to rivers of the temperate regions in spring.

So-called Australian salmon — really members of the perch group — suffer heavily from inshore netting for canneries during their spawning migrations. Adults of the western species *Arripis truttaceus* move out of Southern Ocean waters in summer and form big shoals around the southwestern corner of Australia, where they begin spawning now. Then eggs and small fry are carried east to spend three years of development in estuaries and bays in South Australia, Victoria and western Tasmania. This species is a predator of small fish, especially pilchards.

Australian salmon of the eastern species *Arripis trutta* filter-feed on tiny crustaceans. The young take four or five years to mature in estuarine refuges in northeastern Tasmania. Adults begin a movement to the southern New South Wales coast now, remaining there until they spawn near Cape Howe in summer. Some then resume a northward migration while others return to Bass Strait.

Tailor *Pomatomus saltator* show a pattern of migration similar to that of the sea mullet. Indeed mullet are among the prey they take in slashing, high-speed runs. In the case of tailor the biggest shoals are formed by sub-adults in estuaries and tidal lagoons.

Autumn spawning habits of southern bream *Acanthopagrus butcheri* are exploited by surf anglers seeking the best-grown specimens. These predators of molluscs, crustaceans and small fish move downstream from quiet estuarine reaches to broken water at rivermouths or adjoining beaches. Most go only that far to spawn, feeding afterwards in nearshore gutters and holes. A minority make northward migrations.

Total tonnages and money value of schooling table fish taken at this time of year are dwarfed by the haul of prawns in

The Australian salmon is an important food-fish; its flesh is usually canned

the north. A good day's catches by trawler fleets in the Gulf of Carpentaria alone may be counted in dozens of tonnes. The catch is swiftly transferred to refrigerated carrier ships and landed at purpose-built export packing plants.

Prawns spawn at sea
Prawns too rely on the protection of estuaries or lagoons in their juvenile stages. But with few exceptions they must go to sea to spawn, completing a life cycle that lasts a year to eighteen months. Until the late 1940s no one knew or apparently cared much about the offshore destinations of 'running' prawns. When it was discovered that they made dependable migrations in vast, tightly packed swarms — and that remote tropical waters held bigger and more lucrative species — a major industry took off.

The species of highest export value is the pale yellow banana prawn *Penaeus merguiensis*, reaching about twenty-five centimetres in length. Huge quantities are trawled in late autumn and winter between the Gulf and North West Cape in

waters up to forty metres deep.

Rivalling it in size and exceeding it in weight is the tiger prawn *Penaeus esculentus*, found in deeper tropical waters and as far south as Sydney. The giant tiger or panda prawn *Penaeus monodon* is less abundant; it reaches thirty-three centimetres.

The king prawn *Penaeus plebejus* gave the modern industry its impetus. Previously no one familiar with juveniles in east coast estuaries had imagined that mature females in deep seas could reach thirty centimetres and weigh more than 200 grams, the fattest of all species. The much smaller western king prawn *Penaeus latisulcatus* is named for a similarity of appearance rather than its size.

Metapenaeus species of the subtropical east and southeast include several that are trawled only for local marketing. Best known are school prawns *Metapenaeus macleayi* and various greentail or greasyback prawns. The latter are able to reach maturity and spawn without leaving brackish water, though most go a short way out to sea. □

PRUDENT PRAWNING
Take only what you need

Prawning with small handnets is a favourite summer holiday pastime on coastal waterways in the southeast. Sub-adults 'run' at night on ebbing tides, usually under a full or new moon. It is great fun to bring them to the surface with a light and then scoop up a suppertime snack. But these are breeding stock, about to begin the ocean phase of the life cycle. If too many are taken — especially with illegal outsize nets — populations in subsequent seasons are bound to decline.

The eastern king prawn Plenaeus plebejus — *easily caught and easily eaten*

The eastern race of mangrove gerygone Gerygone laevigaster *cantator* has a rust-tinged back and is bigger than the western race

The collared kingfisher snatches its prey from the surface of the mud or from shallow pools

Oysters grow among the mangrove roots, filter-feeding when the tide comes in

The home of the parchment-tube worm (right), which it shares with a pea-crab Polyonyx transversus

The chestnut teal feeds by dabbling in mangrove-lined estuaries

The green-grey form of the striated heron lives in mangroves around the northern and eastern coasts

A realm that oozes riches

Animal life thrives on mud and mangrove litter

Mangroves are trees and shrubs of many different types, all adapted to daily flooding by salt water. Australia has about fifty species; many can be found growing together on broad coastal mudflats. Tangled roots trap outflowing river silts and incoming marine sediments, stabilising shorelines and adding to the land.

Each square metre of mangrove forest sheds about a kilo of leaves and wood in a year. Decomposed particles feed tiny marine life forms that in turn support crustaceans, molluscs, worms and insects. Crabs of all shapes and sizes breed here, and prawns come in on the tides to feed, along with the juveniles of many commercially important fish species. The food web reaches up and out to rats, bats, reptiles and many different bird species — a wealth of wildlife in this muddy world.

Mangroves at Careel Bay, Pittwater, New South Wales (above)

The life forms on this small section of rotting log (left) include shipworm, crab, pill-bug and gastropods

The semaphore crab Heloecius cordiformis waves its white-tipped claws to attract a mate or warn off a rival

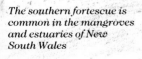

The southern fortescue is common in the mangroves and estuaries of New South Wales

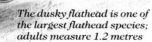

The dusky flathead is one of the largest flathead species; adults measure 1.2 metres

Two male fiddler crabs Uca temporarily share a hollow in the mud

Too close for comfort

Flying fox communities are so crowded that there is scarcely elbow-room for mating — let alone any peace and quiet for this autumn ritual

For over a week the flying fox has been grooming himself ostentatiously for much of each day, showing off his genitals. At last his intended mate's interest is aroused. Foreplay is perfunctory — a few nibbles at the neck and some licking precede a copulation that lasts about a minute. There is no room here for elaborate courting behaviour. All around, as close as half a metre away, other couples hold mating territories.

Sometimes these bats snap stout branches with their combined weight. Any of them could find unoccupied trees within easy flying distance. But they are wholly conditioned to communal living, on the principle of safety in numbers. They tolerate crowding that would place most other mammals under disastrous stress. Only in cool regions where food runs short in winter do communities break up — into groups whose roosts may be just as tightly packed.

We take it for granted that bats sleep by day, weary from their night-long feeding expeditions. But sleep is at a premium in this camp of flying foxes, especially now at mating time. Against a conversational background of squeaks and twitterings, the treetops resound to the snarls, squawks and screams of innumerable territorial squabbles. In a colony that may number tens of thousands, the racket never ceases.

Mating is strongly seasonal among flying foxes and related fruit and blossom bats. Males as well as females come into breeding condition only once a year. In three of the four flying fox species — grey-headed, black and spectacled — mating activities peak around April and most births occur in October. Only the little red flying fox varies from this cycle; its females are giving birth now, having mated in summer.

Black flying foxes *Pteropus alecto* are common all around the tropical coast and in southeastern Queensland. They occupy year-round camps, congregating in enormous numbers where tall mangroves grow densely on rivermouth islets and

The Queensland blossom bat is restricted to the east Queensland coast

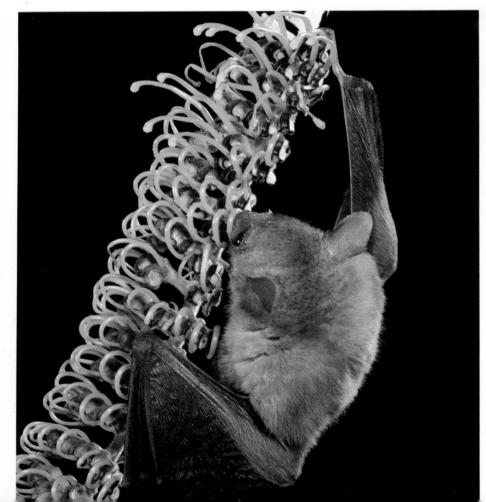

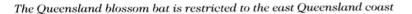

Black and spectacled flying foxes share a

mudbanks. Smaller communities occupy the melaleucas of paperbark swamps or roosts in lowland rainforest canopies.

Northern skies at dusk are filled with their flapping shapes, streaming inland at more than thirty kilometres an hour. Parties journey up to fifty kilometres to reach known stands of eucalypts and other native trees whose blossoms provide their principal food. Individual scouts head off in various directions to look for new supplies.

The general diet of blossoms is common to all flying foxes. Soft native fruits are also enjoyed — especially the purple berries of lilli-pillies *Acmena* and *Syzygium*. Cultivated fruit crops are raided if natural foods are scarce. All food is crushed and the fibrous material spat out. Only nectar, juices and pollen are digested. Small seeds, incidentally swallowed, pass rapidly through the gut and are helpfully dispersed.

Pale eye-rings distinguish the spectacled flying fox *Pteropus conspicillatus*, which is restricted to tropical eastern Queensland. Its camps are also occupied year-round, the biggest communities favouring tall rainforest and swamp trees more than mangroves.

daytime roosting site in coastal forest; at night they fly inland to feed

Grey-headed flying foxes *Pteropus poliocephalus* breed from mid-Queensland to southern New South Wales, foraging as far south as Bass Strait. Camps are formed in forests or mangroves in early summer, when females are still nursing the young born in October. Mature bats — in their second year or older — organise themselves into mating pairs, and camp accommodation is arranged according to a social order: couples, unpaired adults and juveniles occupy separate areas. Sentinel positions on the outskirts are taken by aged males, no longer breeding.

Pregnant bats are segregated

Southern camps break up with the onset of winter, soon after the mating season. Small groups and solitary bats scatter to find food opportunistically. In the warmer part of the range camps are maintained but pregnant females segregate themselves in spring, in preparation for giving birth.

Little red flying foxes *Pteropus scapulatus* are the most nomadic, overlapping the feeding ranges of the other species and travelling farthest inland to harvest the blossoms of arid-adapted eucalypts. They congregate in big camps only during summer. Females leave soon after mating to form maternity and nursing groups of their own. Late in the year they may found new colonies, though many will join the camps of other species.

Development of the young — always born singly — is much the same in all flying foxes. For four or five weeks a baby is carried on foraging expeditions, clinging to its mother's fur with its mouth fastened onto one or other of her armpit teats, so that it appears to be tucked under her wing. Later it is left hanging from the roosting branch overnight and fed when its mother returns. Juveniles can fly at eight weeks or so and become independent at three months. They may have fifteen years or more of life ahead of them.

The rare bare-backed fruit bat of Cape York Peninsula, *Dobsonia moluccense*, is the only plant-feeding bat to roost in caves or among boulders. It is bigger than any of the flying foxes. The common Queensland tube-nosed bat *Nyctimene robinsoni*, on the other hand, is less than half their size.

An autumn breeder, the tube-nose is effectively camouflaged in its daytime roosts, wrapping itself in wings that are dappled with green and gold. It proclaims itself in flight by whistling. Unlike flying foxes, the tube-nose prefers banksia blossoms to eucalypts. The function of its large, protruding nostrils is unknown.

Australia's two tiny blossom bats feed exclusively on nectar and pollen. They have sharp muzzles and long, bristling tongues for the purpose. Weighing only about fifteen grams, they can hover like hummingbirds while they feed. Teeth are ill-formed and weak but the bats can bite holes in trumpet-shaped flowers that are too long for their tongues.

The Queensland blossom bat *Syconycteris australis* roosts in dense, high-rainfall forests throughout that state. On the move it follows tracks among the trees, flying as low as three metres from the ground. The northern blossom bat *Macroglossus lagochilus,* found from the Kimberley to Cape York Peninsula, lives in monsoon forests, paperbark swamps and stands of tall bamboo.

Flying foxes and their relatives are thought to have evolved from an early branch of insect-eating bats that lived in tropical forests. They are physically more primitive than their modern insect-eating, cave-dwelling counterparts — though they do have better sight. Not needing the special skill of echolocation in total darkness, they communicate with many different calls in a normal auditory range.

Both types have problems with high energy expenditure in flight and rapid loss of heat and moisture through their exaggerated surface area. Insectivorous bats overcome these by an ability to lower their temperatures and metabolic rates, lapsing into torpor while at rest and hibernating where winters are cold.

Bats of the herbivorous group can do neither. They compensate to some extent by wrapping their wings tightly round them when they roost, and their diet of plant sugars gives them a high input of energy. But they must stay where winters are mild and trees blossom and fruit year-round, or else adopt migratory habits. □

Queensland tube-nosed bats eat blossoms and fruit — in this case, guava

The wanderer or monarch butterfly can be seen in late autumn in Victoria, New South Wales and Queensland

MAY

THIS MONTH'S WEATHER

South Australia and the southwest enter their rainiest period. Night temperatures fall to chilling levels in the high country of the southeast and Tasmania. Little rain is recorded in tropical regions, though the Top End and the Queensland coast remain humid. Air off the Indian Ocean may create disturbances generating storms in arid areas around the latitude of the Tropic of Capricorn.

AROUND THE COUNTRY	RAIN (mm)	MAX. (°C)	MIN. (°C)	SUN hrs/day
Adelaide	76	19	10	4.8
Alice Springs	17	23	8	8.4
Brisbane	85	24	14	6.6
Canberra	48	15	3	5.5
Darwin	17	32	22	9.5
Hobart	49	14	7	4.1
Melbourne	58	17	8	4.5
Perth	123	21	12	6.1
Port Hedland	29	30	17	8.7
Sydney	121	19	11	6.0
Townsville	36	27	17	7.3
Weipa	16	31	21	7.5

Soon after sundown a short-legged animal breaks from woodland cover and scuttles across a farm paddock. In long grass little can be seen but the tail, waving extravagantly. Near a hayshed the intruder halts, rearing on its hind legs and sniffing the breeze, before darting inside. During that pause, even in failing light, bold white spots on its fur reveal it unmistakably as a quoll. No other Australian mammal has such markings.

Quolls are the marsupial counterparts of northern hemisphere mustelids — weasels and the like. Often called 'native cats', they are aggressive carnivores that seek live prey at night, mainly by scent. A quoll can dispatch any mammal up to its own size, as well as birds and reptiles, with a bite to the back of the neck.

But such rewarding kills do not present themselves regularly, and quolls are obliged to have catholic tastes. Insects contribute most to the diet of the best-studied species, the eastern quoll *Dasyurus viverrinus* of Tasmania. Other food sources are vegetation and carrion, plus what people may unwittingly offer.

When quolls invade farms and bushland homes — perhaps even using outbuildings as dens — their primary interest is in rats and mice. They may help themselves to livestock feed or kitchen scraps, often showing little caution or cunning. One temptation they can never resist is domestic poultry.

Seasonal changes in diet are fairly clear-cut among eastern quolls. The animals abound where farm pastures are adjoined by eucalypt forests, and introduced blackberries grow on the forest's edge. The brambles make excellent cover for the quolls' dens. And two to three months ago the ripe berries provided almost all of their food.

In spring the quolls will eat grass grubs emerging on the pastures, then feast on caterpillars and beetles. As summer approaches they will eat young mammals and ground-nesting birds and their chicks.

Tastes to suit all seasons

Quolls, the most ferocious of meat-eating marsupials, forage for humbler fare in their autumn mating season, when wild prey is scarce

Juvenile snakes, lizards and frogs widen the variety in midsummer. In autumn the quolls will rely increasingly on seeding grasses and wild fruits.

Pickings are slimmest now and through winter. A quoll must call on all its resourcefulness in hunting, foraging and scavenging because its energy demands are at a peak. Not only does it have to resist deepening cold in Tasmania, but it must also maintain maximum fitness for breeding. A mating season only a month long starts in the middle of May.

Breeding when times are hardest may seem illogical. But it brings to the fore the strongest males — the winners in bouts of savage fighting that break out now. It occurs when there is the least probability of drought interfering with the milk supplies of mothers. Above all it means that the next generation will start an independent life late in spring, when caterpillars and other crawling insects will be most abundant.

Quolls become sexually active in their first year and do most of their breeding then, though they may live for many more seasons. The onset of maturity in female eastern quolls is signalled in March by surface changes towards the rear of the abdomen. They do not have complete, permanent pouches. Folds of skin develop annually beside the mammary area, giving partial protection to the newborn. By the time the young outgrow these flaps of

Despite a non-prehensile tail, the western

THE CAN-OPENER RAT
Big rats flourish on fruits and seeds

Australia's biggest rat — half as long again as familiar urban pests and twice as heavy — makes itself heard now, high in the canopies of north Queensland rainforests. The white-tailed rat *Uromys caudimaculatus* feeds on the ripe seeds of silky oak, cracking the tough shells with explosive noises and showering the husks on the ground. A spring breeder, it eats mostly fruits and seeds but readily tops up with insects, frogs, lizards, birds' eggs and fungi. And in bold nocturnal raids on

camps or bush homesteads it will even use its powerful incisors to tear open cans of food and garbage bins. Breeding farther west at this time, mainly in Arnhem Land, is a rat nearly as big and even heavier. The black-footed tree rat *Mesembriomys gouldii* normally sleeps by day in tree hollows but may use the ceilings of buildings. It seems to be strongly vegetarian, living off fruits, seeds and flowers. The huge fruits of pandanus palms, ripening in midwinter, are among its favourites.

The white-tailed rat grows up to nearly seventy centimetres long, including tail

quoll or chuditch is an agile climber. It has five toes on the hind foot; the eastern quoll has only four

skin, they are sufficiently developed to be left in dens while their mothers forage.

Knowledge of mating behaviour is based mainly on observations of captive quolls. Females, coming on heat for about three days, advertise their condition by scent-marking. They lick themselves and rub their faces and hindquarters against tree trunks, rocks, tufts of grass and sometimes other quolls of either sex.

A male pursues any female that he sees, to check her smell. He may attempt to mount one that has already mated, clamping his teeth on the back of her neck and gripping her body with his forelegs. He will meet a hissing, snarling resistance, but may succeed because he is usually much more powerful.

An unmated female is quietly compliant, raising her rump and turning aside her tail. Eyes half shut, she goes into what seems almost a trance during a session of copulation that may last for eight hours. Some females are dragged from one place to another, uncomplaining, though their necks may be torn and bleeding.

Only the strong survive
Three weeks later as many as thirty young are born, about the size of long grains of rice. But the mother has only six nipples on which to feed them. Such a waste can be explained only as a strategy for selecting the most viable candidates.

The fortunate few remain attached to the teats for eight weeks. Then they are

deposited in a grass-padded den and suckled during the mother's resting periods. After their eyes open at three months or so the young devote almost every waking moment to pouncing, biting, wrestling and chasing one another's tails, perfecting their hunting skills. Weaned at about five months, they fend for themselves without any protection or tuition from the mother.

A female occupies only one den while she has young to nurse outside her pouch. Otherwise quolls of both sexes move between many dens, sometimes spending only a day in each. Although they are solitary hunters their home ranges overlap, so two or three animals may use the same dens on different days. There is even some doubling-up, but without any consistency that would suggest companionship between particular individuals.

Dens are commonly nothing more than convenient spaces in hollow logs, rock crevices and piles of boulders. Only nursing dens are grass-lined. Eastern quolls are also accomplished burrowers, however, and some forest-dwellers in southern Tasmania excavate complex warrens with multiple entrances, connecting tunnels and several sleeping chambers.

Eastern quolls can climb trees, but they rely almost entirely on ground feeding. They were fairly common over a wide area of the southeastern mainland, from the region of Adelaide to northern New South Wales, until around the end of last century. Then they quickly became extinct in South Australia, and recent sightings in Victoria and New South Wales have

been extremely rare.

Loss of habitats no doubt contributed to the decline but it occurred so swiftly that zoologists believe an epidemic must also have been involved. Competition from introduced foxes and feral cats could not have helped. It is significant that Tasmania, the last stronghold of the species, has no foxes — nor any dingoes.

Mainland populations of the spotted-tailed or tiger quoll *Dasyurus maculatus* were almost as severely depleted. They have vanished from South Australia and much of Victoria but maintain a sparse distribution through eastern New South Wales and parts of Queensland. They too

The eastern quoll (right) used to be widespread on the southeastern mainland, but is now restricted to Tasmania. The satanellus (below) continues to thrive in the north

remain common in Tasmania, though are less likely to be seen near settlements.

An inhabitant of rainforests as well as eucalypt country, the spotted-tailed quoll is by far the biggest of the family, and the best climber. It has enlarged great toes on its hind feet and ridged pads on all paws. With easy access to arboreal mammals and a greater variety of birds, it enjoys the most reliable supply of sizable live prey.

A permanent pouch

Mating by this species started in April and will continue until July, with unmated females coming on heat at three-weekly intervals. Permanent folds of skin in the female's mammary area form a better-developed pouch than in other species, but the young vacate it just as soon. Male parents occasionally retain some loyalty to their mates, bringing food to the den during the out-of-pouch nursing period.

What used to be the most widely distributed mainland quoll is now the scarcest. The western quoll or chuditch *Dasyurus geoffroii* had a nineteenth-century range that virtually encircled the continent and included hostile northwestern regions such as the Pilbara.

Confined today to forests and woodlands of the far southwest, the chuditch still shows facets of its adaptability to harsh climates. It burrows more than the other species, retains the ability to compensate for extremes of temperature (for example by shivering, or panting and salivating), and apparently has no need to drink if live prey is plentiful. But the remaining population is fully attuned to the winter rainfall regime of the southwest, breeding from late May until early July.

Most secure of the family is the northern quoll or satanellus *Dasyurus*

hallucatus. Its tropical range and abundance seem little affected by European settlement or agricultural development. There are no foxes in its region and relatively few feral cats. The greatest potential threat could be the relentless spread from Queensland canefields of giant toads, whose toxic secretions take less than half an hour to kill quolls that bite them.

Northern quolls thrive in sparsely wooded, rocky country. They mate in June when water is scarce, and the females are not nearly as fecund as their southern relatives. Rarely are there enough newborn to claim all six or eight teats. The protective flaps of the rudimentary pouch area are so skimpy that well-grown young simply dangle, and some are lost. The overall success of the species indicates that mortality after weaning must be exceptionally low.□

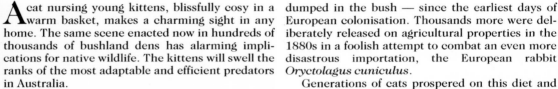

Pets that mastered a continent

No other predator succeeds as widely as the feral cat

A cat nursing young kittens, blissfully cosy in a warm basket, makes a charming sight in any home. The same scene enacted now in hundreds of thousands of bushland dens has alarming implications for native wildlife. The kittens will swell the ranks of the most adaptable and efficient predators in Australia.

Feral cats have established themselves in every habitat, from snowfields to tropical rainforests to deserts, encompassing a range attainable by no other single animal species. They prey on mammals up to the size of possums and wallabies, as well as birds, reptiles, frogs, insects, fishes and crustaceans. The direct toll they take may not be of huge importance. The competition that they force on less versatile carnivores is.

Kittens reared at this time are second-litter offspring, born in late summer or early autumn. An earlier batch came in spring. A mature, well-fed mother usually produces eight or ten kittens a year. Her daughters will breed before they are a year old, the young toms becoming sexually mature a few months later.

In wooded areas where prey is most plentiful, adult feral cats — always solitary hunters — can thrive in densities higher than one per square kilometre. They carry more weight than domestic cats but are otherwise not much bigger. In arid regions, however, under the rigorous discipline of natural selection, some cats are twice as tall as their forebears and three or four times as heavy (see page 27).

Whatever domestic strains they descended from, after a few generations of breeding in the wild cats wear the tabby camouflage stripes of basic *Felis catus*. Forest cats are most often grey and plains cats ginger, juveniles of unsuitably conspicuous colour having been weeded out by foxes, eagles or dingoes.

Cats have escaped from ships and strayed from settlements — or unwanted kittens have been dumped in the bush — since the earliest days of European colonisation. Thousands more were deliberately released on agricultural properties in the 1880s in a foolish attempt to combat an even more disastrous importation, the European rabbit *Oryctolagus cuniculus*.

Generations of cats prospered on this diet and took to using rabbit burrows as their daytime dens. But they could never keep pace with the rabbits' rate of increase. Even though the pests virtually disappeared from the most important farming areas after the spread of mosquito-borne *Myxoma* virus in the 1950s, they continued to be the principal food of many feral cats.

Now the effects of myxomatosis are clearly waning and rabbits are once more on the increase. That could mean that cats will eat rabbits more often, slackening their competitive demand for the natural foods of native carnivores. On the other hand, it may simply mean that there will soon be many more cats.□

Another Australian native bird bites the dust...

LIFE IN A MOUND SPRING

Oases under threat

A small world in water more than a million years old

Artesian springs well up in some of the driest parts of the hinterland. Originating as rain in the eastern highlands, the water has seeped along a layer of porous rock deep within the earth on a journey that has taken at least one million years. Sometimes as it discharges and evaporates it leaves deposits that solidify as a type of limestone, building up by a few millimetres each year.

Clusters of mounds discharging streams of water were stepping-stones in exploring the centre and setting up transcontinental communications, especially in the north of South Australia. They became the first basis of arid-land agriculture. Lately — perhaps too late — they have been found to support rare forms of life. New species were being discovered as recently as the 1970s, and many of them have not yet been given names. Most mound springs now are damaged by livestock, vehicles or people, and all are threatened by a general lowering of the water table after a century of outback bore-sinking.

Button grass Eriocaulon carsoni *found growing at Hermit Hill springs is extremely rare and grows only around some mound springs*

SPRING OUTLET
water discharges to drain in swamp or salina

channel and swamp formed by discharge

CONFINING BED fine-grained mudstone and siltstone

water table

partly or mostly saturated

CONFINING BED fine-grained mudstone and siltstone

water table

movement of artesian water

fracture zone

aquifer 200-300 m below surface

Algae, a source of food for aquatic invertebrates

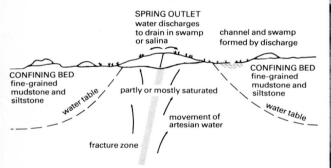

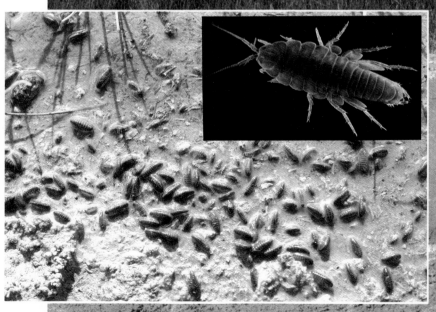

Small black snails are plentiful (above). The crustaceans (right and inset) are isopods Phreatomerus latipes, *slater-like animals about one centimetre long*

Some mounds like Julie Springs between Elizabeth Springs and Kewson Hill are rock-hard, the sediments bound into calcrete

Blanche Cup, west of Lake Eyre, is a flowing mound spring. Its round pool is 25.5 metres wide

A male desert goby Chlamydogobius eremius (left) and a spangled perch Leiopotherapon unicolor (below). Seven species of fish are found in mound spring waters

125

The male malleefowl takes great care over incubating its eggs, but ignores the hatchlings; they dig their own way out of the mound,

Grit and twigs fly as the big bird demolishes a vast pile of debris. His raking backward kicks are mechanical — four or five strokes with one foot, then a similar flurry with the other, over and over again. All the while his gaze seems to be fixed on a point in the distance, as if he would rather be somewhere else.

No bird works harder than this malleefowl cock. The daily demands of the previous breeding season ended only last month. Now he has to start renovating a burial mound for next season's eggs, even though his mate will not begin laying them before September.

Once the eggs are deposited, neither parent will touch them again. Successful incubation will depend on warmth inside the mound. In the cool weather of early spring the heat has to be manufactured. It will come from the fermentation of rotting plant material, which the bird must toil to find in his barren habitat.

Slaving over a warm stove

Fatherhood for a malleefowl means a life sentence of hard labour, perpetually building, tending or wrecking huge incubators

Mound incubation, a technique shared with crocodiles, is practised by a group of birds called megapodes, which means 'great-footed'. Resembling turkeys in physique, they are found from Australia to the Philippines and Malaysia. Our malleefowl *Leipoa ocellata* leads the

hardest life: it is the only megapode that copes with semi-desert conditions.

In its sandplain domains, reaching from the midwestern coast to inland New South Wales, the most significant trees are mallees — the various species of stunted, ground-branching eucalypts that give the bird its name — and the arid-adapted acacia known as mulga. Summers are dry and fiercely hot. Meagre, patchy rains may come now, in late autumn, and during a chilly winter.

Adult malleefowl mate for life. But partners are seldom together except at the egg burial site. It is chosen from four or five existing mounds in the pair's feeding territory of about fifty hectares.

Perhaps with some help from his mate, the cock bird wrecks the old mound, scratching out a hole three to four metres wide and a metre deep. Then he or both of them must gather leaves, twigs and bark to refill the excavation and pile in a heap

and emerge fully independent

high above it. They rake the ground over a radius of twenty-five metres from the site to accumulate enough material from the sparse growth of trees and shrubs. The work takes about four months.

If winter rains should miss the area, all the effort is in vain. The pair will not breed that year. But if the dump of plant litter holds some moisture the cock bird hollows out a cavity at the top, roughly his own size. Then he knuckles down to his next big task — covering the whole pile with a thick layer of sand and other debris. The completed mound is about five metres in diameter and stands more than a metre above ground level.

The hen will offer no help as spring approaches. She roams all over their territory, intent on feeding. Relying mainly on the fallen seeds of mulga and buds produced by smaller plants, she has to build herself up for a laying season that may last five or six months.

She visits the mound to inspect the finished work. The two birds take part in a brief courtship on top of the mound and then copulate. After that the female returns only to lay eggs. Depending on how well she feeds, they are produced at intervals ranging from two days to two weeks. As many as thirty may be laid — a total production equivalent to twice the mother's bodyweight.

Eggs are laid soon after daybreak, the cock first opening the top of the mound to give his mate access to the cavity that he made in the rotting plant matter. Each egg, about twice as long as a domestic fowl's, is pushed into the loose sand of the chamber so that it stands vertically, the broader end up. Incubation will take seven weeks or more.

A built-in thermometer

As long as there are eggs in the mound, from spring to autumn, the cock is on hand for most of every day. He defends the site against rival males, uttering loud, booming calls. But his main duty is to keep a regular check on the temperature inside the mound — ideally about 33°C. He pecks at the mound and plunges in a part-open bill, apparently gauging the temperature with the inside of his mouth.

In spring the heat of fermentation may be too great. If so the cock opens the top of the mound for a while. In summer the effects of fermentation will have waned but the sun is often too hot: extra sand is piled over the mound and it is opened at the coolest time of morning. When air temperatures fall in autumn the mound is opened during the middle of the day to let in direct sunlight.

If the hen arrives to lay an egg in weather that the cock judges too chilly for the mound to be breached, he drives her away. The unwanted offering, presumably abandoned in the scrub, will make a good meal for a snake, goanna or feral cat.

Near the time of hatching, the shells of the eggs become extremely fragile. When early researchers tried to incubate some under domestic fowls, all their specimens were crushed. It was discovered recently that hatchlings break out so effortlessly

that they do not even need to draw breath. Megapode eggs, unlike those of all other birds (so far as is known), contain no air sac from which hatchlings gain oxygen to activate their muscles.

Finding enough air in the frequently worked sand above the egg chamber, a hatchling wriggles straight up to the top of the mound, emerges and flops about until it tumbles down the slope. Covered in slime and debris but highly developed, it is soon able to walk to shelter. It receives no attention from its parents, nor from sibling chicks.

Independent feeding starts within hours. The chick can also fly almost immediately. Its body is downy but the wings are fully feathered. It is more likely to run, however. Megapodes flutter into the air only to reach roosting branches or to escape extreme danger.

The habitats of malleefowl remained unusually secure throughout the nineteenth century and half of the twentieth, simply because European settlers could find no use for them. But the development of drought-resistant wheat strains had disastrous consequences for many of the birds when their territories were cleared, ploughed and sown. A backlash in the 1960s, centred on northwestern Victoria, led to the dedication there and in other states of special parks to save the species.

Logging and agricultural clearance of eastern upland forests and coastal scrubs has diminished the southern range of the malleefowl's bigger and more eye-catching relative, the Australian brush turkey *Alectura lathami*. This bird's habits are broadly the same, but in well-watered subtropical and tropical bushland it has a markedly easier time. Fruits, seeds and insects are plentiful all year round, and there is more litter for mound building.

Pairs use the same mound year after year, adding to it each season. Sometimes the male replenishes the material during incubation. In forest shade the heat of fermentation has to be prolonged but the season is less extensive. The hen, opening and closing the mound for herself, lays about twenty eggs at intervals of two or three days.

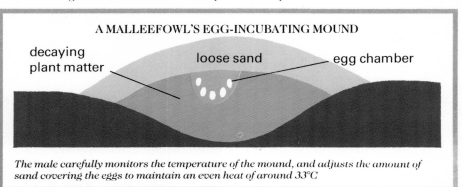

A MALLEEFOWL'S EGG-INCUBATING MOUND

decaying plant matter

loose sand

egg chamber

The male carefully monitors the temperature of the mound, and adjusts the amount of sand covering the eggs to maintain an even heat of around 33°C

raised as an identification signal when birds meet, and invariably when they land after their short, low-level flights.

A tree-hollow nest is lined with bark stripped from the entrance, and padded with crumbled fragments of dead wood. Most often three eggs are laid. Parents share incubation, which takes about a month, and the feeding of chicks for six weeks before they fledge. Seeds of cypress pine and acacias, taken from trees and the ground, make up most of the diet.

Generally to the north of the Major Mitchell's range, the spectacular red-winged parrot *Aprosmictus erythropterus* also starts breeding now. It is especially common in eucalypt woodlands along permanent watercourses. Feeding only in trees, it takes blossoms, buds, seeds and fruits. Females lay five or six eggs.

Gang-gang cockatoos *Callocephalon fimbriatum* make a cheerful invasion of Melbourne, Canberra and other urban areas of the far southeast around May, retreating from their breeding grounds in alpine forests. Flocks of up to a hundred descend not only on native trees but also on introduced ornamentals. The birds have acquired a special liking for pine nuts and hawthorn berries. They will depart in spring, breaking up into smaller groups for their breeding season.

With a boisterous confidence that seems almost menacing, big pied currawongs *Strepera graculina* make a

The biggest mounds are constructed by the smallest of the Australian family, the orange-footed scrubfowl *Megapodius reinwardt*. Generally built around tree trunks, some reach three metres in height and may be seven metres across.

Scrubfowl live in hot rainforests along the Queensland coast and in monsoon vineforests of the Top End and the Kimberley. The huge mounds are often shared by several pairs, though they have separate feeding territories. Egg-laying may start as early as August. Only about ten eggs are laid, at intervals of more than a week — sometimes nearly three weeks. The laying season in the far north is likely to span parts of both the dry and wet seasons, with the position of eggs in the mound accordingly lower or higher.

Major Mitchell — a regular drinker

Pink cockatoos *Cacatua leadbeateri* — better known popularly as Major Mitchells — start breeding now in the northern part of their inland range. Some share the sandplain habitats of the malleefowl, but only if there are waterholes nearby. They need to drink at least twice a day. Populations are happily sedentary near permanent water; otherwise the birds are nomadic in permanent pairs and small family groups, sometimes accompanying galahs or corellas.

Courtship by the male pink cockatoo, shuffling along a branch towards his mate, is a lively display of bobbing and weaving with the head. He of course erects the gorgeous, forward-fanning crest which has made both sexes of this species a prime target of illegal trapping. The crest is often

Orange-footed scrubfowl probably mate for life. Both sexes help build and maintain the egg-incubating mound

The pink cockatoo (below) is very territorial when breeding, seldom tolerating rivals near the nest

Grey currawongs breed in isolated pairs; both parents help to feed young

similar migration to southeastern lowlands. Birds may travel 200 kilometres or more from forests high in the Great Dividing Range, forming wandering flocks that forage in urban gardens and roost communally. Their indiscriminate diet may include smaller birds.

Tasmania's black currawong *Strepera fuliginosa* also makes a move to lower altitudes, flocking on farmland, in parks and gardens, and even along shorelines. The Tasmanian race of the grey currawong *Strepera versicolor* also comes down to settled areas now. Populations on the southern mainland, however, largely remain in their dry forest and woodland homes, breeding as early as July.

Among the most attractive smaller birds of wet high-country forests, forced to find kinder climates for the coming winter, is the spotted pardalote *Pardalotus punctatus*. Flying silently in small flocks, some merely move to sheltered lower valleys, or inland where cold westerlies seldom reach. But many from the southeast migrate as far as the central coast of Queensland.

Pardalotes, peculiar to Australia, are specialised to glean sugary substances and small insects from foliage. They feed nearly always in eucalypts, flashing from tree to tree. Most species have white-spotted heads and wings that led to their being called diamond birds. But the most widespread, the striated pardalote *Pardalotus striatus*, carries streaks and stripes. An inhabitant of drier forests and woodlands, it too migrates from the coldest part of its range. Tropical populations, however, prepare now for a breeding season that starts in June.

A lark-like pipit

Richard's pipit *Anthus novaeseelandiae*, a drab, lark-like bird, retreats from the Snowy Mountains and Tasmanian highlands in late autumn. Remarkably, this is the only climatic concession made by a species that is seen in open country throughout Australia, from tropical grasslands to southern beaches, from alpine heaths to arid saltpans.

A busy feeder on insects from the ground or low foliage, the pipit dashes about erratically with teetering pauses like those of wagtails. But the resemblance to a lark is reinforced in the breeding season, in spring or early summer. Males advertise their territories and display to their mates with song flights, soaring high and trilling as they dive.

Most black swans *Cygnus atratus* begin breeding in May, while in the northeast and northwest their season is coming to an end. Bad temper, especially in crowded colonies, is given full rein when birds are ready to mate. A female provokes her partner into a threatening display against a neighbouring male, or cob. When he retreats the pair celebrate with a protracted face-to-face duet of wing-raising, neck-stretching and loud trumpeting. A long sequence of ducking actions follows before they proceed to copulation.

Swans do not rush into long-term relationships. They mate for the first time in their second or third year and are promiscuous. Either sex may desert while the other is incubating eggs. A female may breed with as many as four cobs in her first season. Later matings generally lead to permanent pairings.

The nest, built beside or over shallow water, may be a scanty circle of plucked grasses placed in reeds or shrubbery, or a luxurious mound if material is plentiful. Swans nesting in colonies have no compunction about stealing one another's material, sometimes destroying nests where eggs are already laid.

Clutches of three to five eggs take about six weeks to hatch. The cygnets take quickly to water but may not fledge for as long as five months. During this period, typically between September and February in the south, the parents are undergoing their moult and are also flightless. That is when they flock in their greatest numbers on open waterways.

The introduced mute or white swan *Cygnus olor* has a natural Australian breeding season in late winter and spring, but park flocks that are fed year-round include breeding pairs at any time. In spite of its name the species does not lack a voice: it can trumpet almost as loudly as the black swan.□

Two male black swans square up with threat displays in the breeding season

A red-tailed tropicbird's precarious nesting site on Lord Howe Island

Confrontation and combat on the cliff edge

Tropicbirds engage in beak-to-beak wrestling matches for precipitous nesting sites

Angry screaming has failed to dissuade a late-arriving tropicbird, hovering over the already-crowded clifftop colony. Ready for his first mating, he insists on landing close to the nesting scrape of older birds that are already paired. Battle must be joined. The defending male confronts the interloper and they glare at each other, black eye-streaks emphasising the threat in their gaze.

Suddenly and silently the rivals lock bills and begin a test of strength, wings flailing as they try to maintain balance on webbed feet that were not made for walking, let alone for holding ground in a wrestling match. After a few seconds, convinced of the resident bird's determination, the newcomer retires — taking flight by simply flopping off the cliff edge.

Red-tailed tropicbirds *Phaethon rubricauda* spend eight or nine months of the year at sea, expertly snapping up fish and squid and resting on the water. Pairing for life, they return each year to traditional coastal nesting sites. Scrapes are made as close as possible to cliff edges, to ease take-offs and landings. Populations are only loosely social — neighbours nearer than twenty metres away are not tolerated.

Daily aerobatic displays

Groups of pairs often join, however, in daily courtship displays of aerobatics. Soarings and swoopings are punctuated by a manoeuvre in which birds face into the wind, raise their heads and let themselves be carried backwards — showing to best advantage the tail streamers that signify sexual maturity and may grow longer than the birds' bodies.

Occupants of sites along the tropical Queensland coast arrive now to breed in winter. Subtropical populations, south to just beyond the New South Wales border and along most of the west coast, breed mainly in summer. Pairs seldom raise more than one chick, which hatches in six or seven weeks and fledges a month or so later.

Off all non-tropical shores at this time of year, Australasian gannets *Morus serrator* start to appear in great numbers. Most have just completed their breeding season in New Zealand, where they form vast, close-packed colonies. A few breed on rocky islets off Tasmania and Victoria.

A similar pattern of movement, generally westward or northwestward, is shown now by the white-fronted tern *Sterna striata*. This is a New Zealand breeder with small outpost colonies established fairly recently on islands at the eastern end of Bass Strait. Wintering flocks feed close to the southeast coast, some venturing north of Brisbane or as far west as the South Australian gulfs.□

LIGHT AT THE END OF THE TUNNEL
Bee-eaters lend a hand around the house

White objects such as bones, shells and even buttons are sometimes found in the burrows of bee-eaters — narrow tunnels often more than a metre long, ending in a spacious nesting chamber. It is conjectured that patterns of light reflected from these articles may identify a burrow to birds outside, or that the absence of reflection may signal that a burrow is occupied. Perhaps the relief of darkness by little points of light is a simple pleasure for sun-loving birds. Rainbow bee-eaters *Merops ornatus* start a second breeding season in May across mid-northern Australia, where populations live year-round. They also breed in spring.

Other populations are seasonal migrants, breeding in summer in the south. Communities of dozens of birds show a striking degree of cooperation, helping one another with burrowing, incubation, and brooding and feeding the chicks. Brilliantly acrobatic fliers, bee-eaters capture all their food in mid-air. Any insect up to the size of a dragonfly may be taken, but bees and wasps are strongly favoured. The prey is taken to a tree and bashed against a branch to force out its venom sac and sting. Bee-eaters are unpopular with apiarists but are gaining acclaim for their efforts against dangerous European wasps.

A rainbow bee-eater returns to its burrow with food for its chicks

Starting with a clean sheet

The deadly arts of platform-building and net-throwing spiders

On misty mornings in eucalypt forests of the southern mainland, water droplets glisten on what look like white scarves suspended just above the ground or over low shrubbery. Made of tightly latticed silk, they form the floors of elaborate snares set by young platform spiders *Corasoides*. Each strip curls into a funnel at one end, disappearing into the ground. Above the sheet is a tent of haphazardly tangled threads suspended from an overhanging branch. Guy lines to the surrounding earth keep the platform taut and flat.

No part of the structure is sticky — there is no need. A flying insect blundering into the upper tangle exhausts itself trying to get out and eventually drops onto the platform. The spider, watching from the funnel, rushes out. The victim is quickly paralysed by a bite and dragged into its captor's burrow to be drained of its juices.

To avoid desiccation in the hot, dry summers of the south and southwest, platform spiders hatch in autumn. Many fall foul of predators themselves, but as the survivors grow during winter and spring the snares of forest species reach a surprising size, up to twenty centimetres wide and over a metre long. Slung across shrubs or clumps of grass, they may form arches well clear of the ground.

Maturing and mating in early summer, the platform-builders reach the size of the larger wolf spiders, to which they are distantly related. Egg cocoons are made in the female's burrow and stay there after her death, bound with soil particles to disguise them.

Sheets of silk are made on a much smaller scale but used to devastating effect by net-throwing spiders *Dinopis*. They fix crimped, elastic silk onto a framework only about as big as their own bodies. Holding this construction between its front four feet, a spider dangles upside-down at night from one of its runway threads, within reach of a surface where insects crawl.

These webs of the platform spider Corasoides australis *(inset) can be up to twenty centimetres wide and stretch for a metre over tussocks and shrubs*

A net-throwing spider Dinopis subrufa *(below) in ambush position. The twig-like appearance gives it one of its common names, stick spider*

When suitable prey approaches, the spider spreads its legs to stretch the sheet and lunges, flinging the net over its victim. All manner of prey is snared and then deftly parcelled up, including cockroaches and big hunting spiders.

Flying insects such as moths may be snared in mid-air. Net-throwers have exceptional night sight and distance perception, thanks to two eyes so enlarged that they obscure the other six. The grotesque appearance of these, together with folded biting parts that look like horns, give dinopids another common name, ogre-faced spiders.

If a night's waiting brings no result and the net has been damaged, the spider eats it. Otherwise it is left intact, suspended among foliage, for re-use next evening. The nets are at their biggest now, in late autumn, with the spiders nearing the end of their lives. Seen unstretched, however, they are seldom more than about 1.5 centimetres long and a centimetre wide.

The owner — a light brown, angular-bodied spider with exceptionally long legs — will be somewhere close by, more or less hidden by foliage. Even fully exposed it may not be noticed because of its resting posture. Its legs are usually arranged in such a way that it resembles a dead leaf or a twig — hence yet another of its common names, stick spider.

Dinopids hatch in spring and mate in late summer. Eggs are encased in spherical cocoons somewhat larger than peas. Golden and soft when they are made, they quickly go nut-brown and leathery. A cocoon can nearly always be found close to an ambush area, fastened to a branch or a timber structure and disguised by the attachment of one or two dead leaves.□

JUNE

THIS MONTH'S WEATHER

Storms intruding from the Southern Ocean may bring snow to the southeastern highlands, and offer hope of isolated rains in the southern part of the arid zone. Rain falls liberally in southwestern and southern regions, but the east coast north of Sydney and all northern regions become increasingly dry.

AROUND THE COUNTRY	RAIN (mm)	MAX. (°C)	MIN. (°C)	SUN hrs/day
Adelaide	79	16	8	4.2
Alice Springs	15	20	5	8.4
Brisbane	83	21	11	7.4
Canberra	37	12	1	5.4
Darwin	2	30	20	9.9
Hobart	57	12	5	3.9
Melbourne	49	14	7	4.1
Perth	183	19	10	4.9
Port Hedland	18	27	14	8.6
Sydney	131	17	9	5.5
Townsville	22	25	14	7.9
Weipa	4	30	19	7.5

This young common wombat, newly emerged from the pouch, will forage with its mother for another nine months or so

The kookaburra's wild cackle is cut off abruptly. Almost immediately, from the same hidden spot in the forest, comes the sweet lilting of a shrike-thrush. Bell miners exchange chimes, then a whipbird gives out a resounding crack. Robins and scrubwrens churr and chatter. They are drowned out by a screeching squabble among lorikeets.

Melancholy flutings are heard from a currawong that ought to have left for the lowlands weeks ago. Migratory honeyeaters mew and twitter softly, though their kind should be wintering far to the north. To dispel a listener's remaining illusions, an owl hoots in the middle of the day. The fantastic medley races on, embroidered with strange plonkings, gurglings, raspings and yappings. It is all the work of just one artist.

Lyrebirds, the most accomplished vocal mimics in Australia, commandeer the songs and calls of virtually any other birds they hear. Performing alone, one bird can imitate the group communication of another species. Even wingbeats, feather rustlings, bill rappings and the sounds of feeding can be reproduced through an unusually flexible voice box.

Both sexes are mimics. But only the cocks are methodical, compulsive entertainers, advertising themselves before and during the breeding season. Recitals begin around April in dense forests from the eastern outskirts of Melbourne to southern Queensland. They are most frequent and extended — up to an hour without stopping — in June and July when mating is at its peak.

Young lyrebirds copy not only from genuine sources but also from their elders. A concert by one bird may seem to be a haphazard string of sounds. But comparisons among the birds of any one locality show similarities. There are patterns in the interweaving of their own song cadences and territorial calls with sequences of mimicry. Some sounds are consistently favoured more than others, and certain borrowed songs are embellished with special musical effects peculiar to a district.

The talking lyrebird?

Lyrebirds have been said to imitate the grunts, snarls and screams of koalas and possums. Doubt is cast on claims that they copy the barking of dogs, the rasping of saws, the thudding of axes and the shrilling of sawmill whistles. Such sounds can just as easily come coincidentally as part of their natural repertoire. Even less credence is given nowadays to old stories of lyrebirds imitating human speech. But where the birds were more or less tame, it seems not too far-fetched.

Snatches of man-made music, heard repeatedly, could well be picked up by

A rhapsody of stolen sounds

Heard loud and clear but rarely seen, the lyrebird announces his winter mating season with virtuoso concerts of copied songs and calls

lyrebirds. In the early 1980s a forester was intrigued by a melodic phrase whistled by birds near Dorrigo in northern New South Wales. Its tones and measure suggested part of a human song, but no one in the locality knew what it was. Aired on a national radio programme, the tune was identified by a man in Victoria. His family had farmed in the Dorrigo district. The song had been the favourite of his brother, who whistled it habitually while working outdoors — four decades earlier.

Though clamorous in calling attention to themselves, lyrebirds are seldom seen. They run quickly to hide in undergrowth

---

A LYRE — OR A LIE?
Early artists gave a false impression

Lyrebirds never hold their tails up in the shape of a lyre — an ancient Greek harp. A displaying male spreads the broad outer feathers sideways, more or less horizontally, and throws the others forward over his head. As the tail is erected there may be — but seldom is — a moment in which the lyre shape can be glimpsed.

Tails from slaughtered birds, arranged artificially, used to be sold as ornaments. Early artists, not having witnessed the display, took these as models for the bird itself. Their work, slavishly copied by designers of emblems, product packaging and even postage stamps, spawned a fallacy that has persisted ever since.

A misleading lyrebird stamp

if people approach. Determined enthusiasts endure hours in concealment, hoping the birds will come to them. To observe the principal species, the superb lyrebird *Menura novaehollandiae*, they wait near the low mounds of scratched-up soil that breeding males build as concert platforms. About a metre across, these bare hummocks are fairly obvious to a practised eye. But one bird could have half a dozen of them scattered over a wide area, and may not visit each one every day.

The first sighting is an anticlimax. The superb lyrebird, built much like a domestic fowl, is plain and dark. Even the long, bundled-up tail, carried like that of a pheasant, appears ordinary.

The cock bird strolls into his little clearing and ascends the mound. He gazes

The lyrebird beginning its display (above). The outer feathers are spread out to the sides and the lacy fan flung forward over the head (left)

around for a few moments, then takes a rigid, angry-looking stance, head thrust forward and short bill partly open. Out pours a string of songs and calls — an overture that may last only a few seconds.

He pauses, perhaps assessing whether a hen may be watching from the forest depths. Then the recital is resumed to the accompaniment of a slow opening of the tail. The outer feathers are pushed side-ways, twisting to show their brightly barred undersides. Between them are erected two dark, wiry central plumes and twelve other feathers that are bordered with delicate filaments, which are coloured silver underneath.

A lacy fan rises over the bird and spills forward, concealing his back and head. Still holding a steady pose, he vibrates this silvery canopy from time to time to make it shimmer, singing all the while. Well into the performance he begins to prance and skip, sending out resonant 'clunk-clunk' calls in all directions.

Male lyrebirds, reaching maturity and gaining their full array of display feathers at three or four years of age, hold feeding territories of two to three hectares. Hens have smaller ranges that overlap these. Both sexes forage in deep forest litter that is rich in insects, worms and snails. Though she will lay only one egg in a season a hen may defend several prospective nesting sites: in banks or rock clefts, on ledges on the ground among ferns or up

This male emu has starved for eight weeks while incubating its brood

to three metres high on a tree stump.

A cock bird mates with any females that he can attract to his display mounds, afterwards showing no interest in them or their nesting arrangements. Hens take three or four weeks to build and line a big dome of sticks, and at least six weeks to incubate the egg. The chick is brooded and fed for a further six weeks.

Small groups forage quietly

Long before then the cock's concerts have ceased. He will be in moult, with tail feathers gone. His display mounds, left to fall into disrepair, will be disappearing under litter. No longer defending territories, small parties comprised of a cock, some hens and their young will forage quietly, raking the ground with sideways sweeps of their feet. Most will go unheard and unseen until next autumn.

Out-of-season clues to their presence, however, may be given by the ringing whistles and cracks of pilotbirds *Pycnoptilus floccosus*. In forests from the Blue Mountains in New South Wales to the Dandenong Ranges in Victoria, these small ground-feeders follow lyrebirds about to take advantage of freshly raked litter. Their song gives rise to an alternative common name, 'guinea-a-week'.

A smaller, reddish species of lyrebird, *Menura alberti*, is found only in subtropical rainforests on the volcanic ranges embracing the southeastern corner of Queensland. Albert's lyrebird does not scratch up mounds. Males call and display from small clearings among vines or from fallen branches (superb lyrebirds also may do this). The northern bird has a less

ornate tail, but is a good match in mimicry and the duration of its concerts.

Far to the north, in lowland rainforests between Townsville and Cape York, cassowaries start to breed in June. Sharing a remote ancestry with emus, they stand about as tall but are much heavier. They too are flightless; stubby vestiges of wings are armed with long, naked quills like curved knitting needles.

The female of *Casuarius casuarius* is bigger and more vividly coloured around the head and neck than the male, and totally dominant. Solitary for most of the year, she easily scares off the opposite sex. But for the past few weeks she has tolerated the company of a chosen mate.

Now she shows him the nest she has made — a simple scrape on the forest floor, lined with leaves and grass. It is to be his nest, not hers, for he will take care of the eggs and young. After he has signified his commitment with a circling dance they move away and copulate.

Eggs the size of mangoes are laid, usually in a clutch of four. That task completed, the female wanders off. She may mate once or even twice more this season. The male spends about two months incubating the eggs, forsaking his usually wide feeding area and seldom leaving the nest.

Hatchlings are soon led out along their father's habitual trails and helped to feed. Under his supervision for about nine months, the striped, downy young develop quickly into big, brown sub-adults resembling emus. By the time the father chases them away to find feeding grounds of their own, his instincts are driving him

again to seek the favours of a female and the burdens of parenthood.

The shiny black plumage and horny head-blade of an adult cassowary take about three years to develop fully. The blade is used to butt through vine thickets and shrubbery. The plumage, made up of coarse, hair-like feathers, does not get entangled. Gaudy colours on the head and neck, and on the throat wattles, presumably help the birds recognise their own kind in the deep gloom of tall forests.

Fallen fruits of trees and vines make up most of the diet of cassowaries, but they are not averse to fungi, insects and snails, and even the carrion of dead birds and mammals. Feeding areas are defined vaguely; more than one bird may forage in the same spot at different times.

Accidental encounters between males can result in threatening confrontations, both birds making a rumbling noise, erecting their plumage and stretching to their fullest height before one retreats. Occasionally they charge at each other, leaping into the air and kicking with both feet simultaneously. The thick plumage prevents serious injury.

Hunting dogs and humans who harry cassowaries may not get off so lightly. The claws on the inner toe of each foot are spikes twelve centimetres long. Many people have been killed in New Guinea, where the birds are traditionally hunted.

Bushwalkers have nothing to fear from a roaming cassowary, provided they make no attempt to interfere with its freedom. A bird hearing unfamiliar noises utters a loud rumble of curiosity. When it finds the source it simply stands and stares. Approached too closely, it will fluff out its plumage and issue a stretching, hissing challenge. If the intruder persists the cassowary ambles off, perhaps venting its displeasure with an exaggerated stamping.

The nomadic emu

Inquisitive and skittish, but never threatening, the emu *Dromaius novaehollandiae* is also a winter breeder across most of the mainland. Its style of life — generally nomadic in open country where rainfall and food supplies are unreliable — is in marked contrast to the sedentary luxury enjoyed by cassowaries. But sexual roles are strikingly similar.

Emus of breeding age pair off early in the year, spending as long as five months together. Females develop nuptial plumes during autumn: black feathers cover their heads and necks and the body colour darkens. Males continue to show the blueish skin of their necks.

Grass, leaves, bark or twigs are gathered to make a nesting bed on the ground. An exceptionally well-nourished emu can lay as many as twenty eggs, but eight or nine is more usual. The male begins his

Southern cassowaries usually lay four eggs — the male incubates them for about two months, then looks after the young

White-bellied sea-eagles build huge nests of sticks up to four metres deep, lined with green plant material. Both sexes help with the construction

task of incubation even before the clutch is completed. He sits almost continuously for about eight weeks, eating very little and suffering a severe loss of weight, even though he saves energy by lapsing into near-torpor. Meanwhile his mate may breed again or join a travelling mob. Some females are said to stay nearby and associate with their new families.

When the chicks hatch the father takes them with him wherever he goes, brooding them under his outspread feathers at night. In arid regions or during a drought he may continue to escort and help his offspring until they are eighteen months old and as big as he is. By doing so he misses a breeding season, but the survival of the young will make up for that.

Emus move about in family groups or loose mobs of up to a hundred. They are principally vegetarian, taking the fresh shoots of grasses and the leaves, flowers, fruits and seeds of native herbs and shrubs. Cereal crops are raided too, perhaps justifying control measures in some areas. But emus also have a taste for insects, and have often proved to be farmers' friends by gorging on caterpillar and grasshopper pests. In Queensland, emus used to be blamed for spreading the seeds of prickly pear. During an official campaign of slaughter, the stomach contents of some birds were examined. One had just eaten 2991 caterpillars.

Also condemned and ruthlessly persecuted on an ill-founded suspicion was the wedge-tailed eagle *Aquila audax*. Seeing eagles picking at the carcasses of sheep and lambs, graziers held the birds responsible for killing the stock. With the inducement of government bounties, thousands of eagles a year were being destroyed as recently as the 1960s.

Widespread research has now established that wedge-tailed eagles hardly ever attack fit lambs, let alone full-grown sheep. They dispose of dead or dying animals. More significant, as far as farmers are concerned, is the toll they take on the resurgent rabbit population. Other pests such as fox cubs and the kittens of feral cats are also killed.

Wedge-tails are scavengers

Traditional prey includes small marsupials, but the eagles are not especially fast or agile and their success rate is low. Ground-nesting birds, waterfowl and slow-moving reptiles offer easier targets. Rarely is an attempt made to catch birds in flight, as a falcon does. On the whole Australia's biggest bird of prey — a female's wingspan often exceeds two metres — is a scavenger of carrion.

Nesting began in autumn in the north; June is the start of peak breeding across the southern mainland. Paired for life and together year-round, birds nevertheless precede each season's mating with spectacular courtship flights. The male makes high-speed dives at his partner, pulling out at the last moment, and she responds by turning over in mid-air and presenting her claws. Often they 'loop the loop' together. Some birds play an aerial game with a stick or a strip of animal skin, dropping it, diving for it and passing it from one to the other.

Nests are massive platforms of sticks placed in the forks of trees or on cliffs. Each pair has several in a territory of up to three square kilometres. One is chosen at the start of each breeding season, added to, and refurbished with a lining of green leaves. There are usually two eggs, incubated mainly by the female for six to seven weeks. One or two chicks are brooded for a month and may stay in the nest for up to two months more. The male brings fresh leaves every day, relieves his mate on the nest occasionally, and fetches all food until the brooding is over.

White-bellied sea-eagles *Haliaeetus leucogaster* are also nesting now, not only on coastal cliffs and offshore islets but also in trees lining rivers, lakes and swamps. Most often they swoop for fish from high perches or during soaring flights. But freshwater turtles, waterfowl, sea bird nestlings, sea snakes and some small land mammals are also taken. In courtship, breeding biology and nesting behaviour sea-eagles are very like wedge-tails, but their young are fledged more quickly. □

BLOOD BROTHERS
The struggle for survival begins in the nest

In a season of exceptionally good feeding, wedge-tailed eagles may succeed in rearing chicks from two eggs. More often there are lean times. One hungry chick survives by killing its sibling.
Sea-eagles are less murderous. The first of two chicks, hatched several days apart, simply intimidates the other and seizes all the available food. The smaller brother or sister starves to death.

Wedge-tailed eagle chicks on the nest

A rough ride home for fairy penguins

Male birds struggle ashore before their partners to reclaim their former nesting sites

Dark shapes appear and disappear, bobbing up and down in the sparkle of moonlit surf. They are the bodies of penguins, swimming steadily but overtaken by an endless roller-coaster of shoaling waves. Now and then the last line of breakers spills out one or two birds so tiny that they are engulfed in the backwash of the shallows. Paddling frantically, they propel themselves ashore.

Early arrivals shuffle about idly or stand eyeing the surf, to gauge the progress of other birds. When twenty or thirty have landed — some exchanging bows of recognition — they form a tight group and waddle inland. They are bound for nesting burrows in cliffs or tussock-covered dunes probably up to 300 metres away.

Little or fairy penguins *Eudyptula minor* breed communally on islands and isolated mainland coasts all across the south of Australia. Standing only thirty centimetres tall, they are the smallest of the world's seventeen penguin species. Even closely related races in New Zealand, where they are called blue penguins, are significantly bigger.

Colonies are never entirely deserted. At any time some birds roost ashore. But the autumn months were marked by a decline in daily comings and goings. Most birds stayed at sea for extended periods of feeding, before and after a fast of two or three weeks that was forced on them by their annual moult.

Now it is time to prepare for a new breeding season. More and more birds land each night, about an hour after sundown, both newcomers and residents that have been out for a day's feeding. Males predominate at first, intent on reclaiming the

Beach scene by moonlight: little or fairy penguins Eudyptula minor, *intent on breeding, paddle through the shallows to the shore*

The wandering albatross is an expert flier

Shy albatrosses take nine weeks to incubate their single egg (below)

burrows of previous seasons or on finding favourable digging sites. Disputing birds stand chest-to-chest, jostling each other.

The dominance of stronger males is probably well established by the time females arrive in force, but their advent is signalled by uproar at the nesting grounds. Both sexes advertise by braying loudly while they thrust their bills upwards and wave their flippers.

Pairings of previous seasons are usually renewed. Birds mate repeatedly over the many months during which they cohabit. Egg-laying starts as early as July, and the loss or failure of a first clutch is often followed by the laying of a second. Some pairs even rear two families.

Sand burrows up to a metre long, or shallower nests in cliff faces and crevices, are lined with grass or seaweed. Two or sometimes three eggs are laid. The parents share incubation duties for five or six weeks, one going to sea while the other fasts, in shifts of up to ten days. Continuous care of the hatchlings is alternated daily for two weeks. After that the appetite of the young is so great that both parents have to hunt on their behalf every day, swallowing whole fish or squid and regurgitating them when they return.

Fledglings go to sea to hunt for themselves at about eight weeks of age. They are soon skilful divers, pursuing shoals of fish to depths of about forty metres. But for all the bullet-like perfection of their streamlining, little penguins are relatively slow swimmers, achieving only about six kilometres an hour. This makes them easy prey for sharks, sea-lions and big predatory sea birds.

Death rates in the first few months are high. Nevertheless some penguins succeed in dispersing over remarkably wide areas: banded specimens less

The world's biggest birds, wandering albatrosses *Diomedea exulans*, frequent southern and eastern coastal waters in winter. Their wings span more than three metres. Single birds may be seen making effortless glides just off the wind or soaring into it — they beat their wings only in calm air. Awkward on land, they rest and feed on the ocean.

Almost as big is a visitor from New Zealand or its island territories to the south, the royal albatross *Diomedea epomophora*. Other albatrosses seen in winter are smaller types that are commonly called mollymawks. Best known is the black-browed albatross *Diomedea melanophrys*. It feeds close to the coast, sometimes in flocks.

One albatross breeds in Australia, on islands at the western end of Bass Strait and off southern Tasmania. Reaching a length of nearly a metre with a wingspan of more than two metres, the shy albatross *Diomedea cauta* breeds in loose colonies in September and October. During the rest of the year it can be found as far afield as the midwestern coast and northern New South Wales.

Another winter breeder on southern islands, from the eastern end of Bass Strait to the Recherche Archipelago off Esperance, Western Australia, is the Cape Barren goose *Cereopsis novaehollandiae*. It has some duck-like anatomical features but avoids water, grazing like a goose and often nesting high in shrubbery.

Cape Barren geese insist belligerently on wide spaces between their breeding territories, which they defend until their chicks — often four or five in a brood — are about six weeks old. Abandoned then while their parents moult, the young gather together in creches which become the basis of nomadic flocks.

Adults out of season and immature birds turn up on mainland coasts fairly near their island homes. They used to be shot and poisoned for damaging pastures and crops. That slaughter, along with an earlier toll taken by sailors and sealing gangs, reduced their numbers to a perilously low level of about 5000. Populations have recovered under total legal protection. □

than a year old have been picked up over a thousand kilometres from home. The penguins mature at three years, probably returning to breed at or near their birthplaces in most cases, and can live for twenty years.

Bigger and generally more colourfully marked penguins are occasionally washed onto southern Australian shores. Breeding around New Zealand or on subantarctic islands, they disperse to our waters in winter. Most commonly found are species of *Eudyptes*, distinguished by pairs of yellow crests projecting sideways from over their eyes.

The piratical skua

A deadly enemy of all penguins is the southern skua *Catharacta antarctica*. At its subantarctic breeding grounds in summer this fiercely predatory bird raids penguin nests, eating chicks and eggs. Wintering in Australian waters, it attacks swimming penguins. It is also commonly seen acting as a pirate, terrorising smaller sea birds in flight and forcing them to disgorge food.

Penguin chicks are also preyed on by winter-wandering giant petrels *Macronectes* from subantarctic islands and mainland Antarctica. These bulky birds are distinguished by long nostril-tubes above huge, hooked bills.

Immature southern giant petrels of the dark colour type (above)

Cape Barren geese moult and become flightless after raising chicks

Spanish mackerel are moving north along the east coast, returning to their tropical spawning grounds. One school, still off New South Wales, has left its run too late. As the fish dally over a meal of pilchards, a big shark, bright blue on the back and with pectoral fins of extraordinary length, knifes into their midst.

Within seconds the mackerel are attacked from all sides as more sharks arrive. Torn bodies are flung about in a spreading haze of blood. Excitement among the raiders mounts into a frenzy. Twisting and turning and snapping blindly, they bite one another — and even themselves.

Blue sharks *Prionace glauca*, often exceeding three metres in length, are the world's most widely distributed sharks and probably the most abundant of the bigger species. In the North Atlantic, where they have been closely studied, they are known to make journeys of at least 6000 kilometres. Their migrations take them right around the ocean, exploiting its circulating current. Similar circular migrations presumably occur in the South

Cold-water sharks are frenzied feeders

A winter migration brings huge numbers of blue whalers, white pointers and makos to southern waters

Pacific and Indian Oceans, where the sharks range to about forty degrees south — the latitude of Bass Strait.

The blue shark, sometimes called the blue whaler, prefers cool water. In mid-ocean in the tropics it is found at considerable depths, but in temperate zones it comes in over continental shelves and feeds on or close to the surface. Off

southeastern and southern Australia in winter it appears in numbers, becoming the most dominant shark species.

Notorious for following ships, blue sharks are foremost in a group that seafarers used to call requiem sharks, in the belief that they waited to receive the bodies of dead sailors. The sharks' attention to shipping makes them the leading suspects in the killing of survivors of wartime sinkings; on that score alone, they may be the greatest man-eaters on the globe.

The voracious pack behaviour of blue sharks, often leading to feeding frenzies, is most often observed in Australian waters when they attack trawling hauls. Nets and their. contents are torn to pieces. The sharks remain a nuisance to commercial fishing crews — but a popular challenge to game fishing enthusiasts — until about November. Fortunately for surfers and skin-divers who brave southern waters in winter and spring, the sharks rarely come close to the shore.

Little is known about the biology of most big oceanic sharks. Thanks to work

The blue shark is often confused with the mako; the distinguishing features are its smaller gill slits and longer pectoral fins

done mainly in North America and Britain, this species is an exception. Most of what has been discovered is probably common to the majority of requiem sharks or whalers.

Blue sharks are born live and immediately capable of an independent existence. They are nurtured to this stage of development in a way that is surprisingly like that of most mammals — through a placenta and umbilical cord. A litter may consist of more than a hundred, each up to fifty centimetres in length.

A painful courtship

The gestation period is nine months. Females near full-term pregnancy are found in Australian waters in spring, so mating must take place in tropical depths around January or February. As far as is known all sharks mate the same way: the male introduces sperm into the female reproductive tract with one or other of twin organs called claspers. These are extensions of his pelvic fins, rotated forward during copulation.

Females are stimulated to mate by a courtship of biting. In blue sharks it is severe, often leaving deep lacerations in a female's pectoral fins and along her back and sides, behind the dorsal fin. To withstand wounds in these areas, females have skin and subcutaneous tissue twice as deep as a male's.

Blue sharks show one of the fastest known growth rates, reaching 1.5 metres in three years and three metres in ten

The mako Isurus oxyrinchus; *its teeth are slim, smooth and dagger-like*

years. The biggest on record, a North Atlantic specimen measuring 3.83 metres, was probably about fifteen years old. Uncommonly among sharks, female blues tend to grow larger than the males.

The second most dominant shark in southeastern waters in winter, moving in from the Pacific, is the shortfin mako *Isurus oxyrinchus*. Game fishermen call

it 'blue dynamite' in recognition of its explosive fighting energy. Mako can summon up running speeds of more than thirty-five kilometres an hour, and when hooked can leap metres out of the water.

The mako owes its power to warm-bloodedness. Along with a very few other shark species it can maintain a body temperature as much as 8°C above that of

TOURING TUNA

Southern bluefins grow as they go

Fish preferring warm waters are in full retreat up the east coast with the onset of winter. Not so in the west, where the reverse surface flow of the Leeuwin Current brings heated water south from the Timor Sea. This phenomenon enables southern bluefin tuna *Thunnus maccoyii* — spawned in the Indonesian region — to make the first stages of a remarkable migration. Growing all the time, bluefins travel south along the west coast in winter and across to South Australia in spring. Later movements take them around Tasmania and up to New South Wales where they appear each summer. At eight to ten years old, the mature fish, now weighing more than 100 kilos each, head westward on a return run to the spawning grounds.

A typical haul of migrating southern bluefin tuna; these fish are around the fifteen kilo mark

the surrounding water. The advantage over other sharks and 'true' fish is enormous: scientists calculate that every 3°C of extra muscle heat yields a doubling of strength.

Mako employ, as a component of their reproduction system, a fairly rare process known as oviphagy. The first few young to be conceived feed on a continuing supply of eggs. Highly developed young are born around November off the New South Wales coast, in litters of about ten.

About seventy centimetres long at birth, male mako are sexually mature at two metres. But the females do not breed until they are nearly three metres long. Females caught in Australian waters average slightly more than that and weigh nearly half a tonne. The maximum seems to be about four metres. Any mature mako is potentially exceedingly dangerous, but the species does not come inshore.

During late autumn and winter the most feared shark of all, the white pointer or great white shark *Carcharodon*

carcharias, moves out of the Great Australian Bight and around to cool waters off the southwestern and southeastern coasts. Juveniles are also occasionally trapped in meshing off the beaches of Queensland's Gold Coast. The white pointer is also warm-blooded. Nothing is known of its breeding patterns or reproduction; it can be assumed that it is live-bearing, and because it belongs to the same small family as the mako, perhaps also oviphagous.

Creatures of habit

White pointers are comparatively rare. Though distributed worldwide in temperate seas, they are thought to be most numerous in the Bight. There they show signs of having a territorial habit; researchers recognise the same sharks in the same places, returning year after year.

The attraction is the region's many seal colonies. White pointers prey heavily on seals and dolphins, along with big school fish such as tuna. They are the only

sharks given to lifting their heads out of the water to inspect objects on the surface. This habit is thought to be linked with their taste for marine mammals, whose flesh and energy-rich blubber help meet enormous appetites.

No other shark has a natural taste for mammals. The white pointer's unusual interest may contribute to the danger it presents to swimmers and divers. And the shark grows so big that even a trial bite — before it knows what the target is — can cut a person in two. From records of attacks in which the culprits have been convincingly identified, it is the deadliest shark species.

Female white pointers in Australian waters reach about six metres in length. At that size they would weigh about three tonnes. Elsewhere, tales are told of the 'white death' reaching prodigious dimensions. The biggest to be reliably measured was caught in the middle of the North Atlantic in 1978. Nine metres long, it was estimated to weigh 4.5 tonnes. □

The white pointer is the only shark to lift its head out of the water to investigate possible prey; it has a voracious appetite

Common wombats usually raise one young, which stays with the mother until its successor is ready to leave the pouch

Winter sun brings out the wombats

Snow lies patchily in a woodland clearing, defying the feeble rays of a low-angled sun even at noon. A wombat and her cub amble along a worn trail, swinging their massive heads from side to side and exchanging soft grumbles. Occasionally they snuffle among browned clumps of frostbitten grass or the bases of shrubs.

Wombats restrict themselves to nighttime activity in summer, avoiding high temperatures by spending their days in deep, humid burrows. The colder the weather at other times, the more likely they are to feed in full daylight and bask in sunshine near their burrow entrances.

On densely forested slopes in the southern part of the Great Dividing Range — the stronghold of common wombats *Vombatus ursinus* — their daytime excursions go largely unseen. People notice them more in Tasmania, on heaths and in wooded lowlands and coastal scrubs.

The biggest burrow-dwellers in the world usually emerge at night. But in bitter cold they change their habits

The female seen now with her cub has another in her pouch, probably newborn. Breeding in the south seems to peak between April and June. Cubs, nearly always born singly although there are two teats, are nursed in the pouch for about six months. They may stay with their mothers for most of the following year, until their successors are about to leave the pouch.

Maternal bonds and brief mating encounters aside, common wombats have no social relationships. Each forages over a home range of many hectares. Ranges overlap, but within them the wombats establish private preserves, scent-marking the boundaries and attacking intruders.

Burrows are common property, however. One animal's overall range may include a dozen or more. It uses several as resting places during each feeding excursion. Others use them too at various times. A multi-chambered burrow can be shared by several casual occupants, all doing their best to ignore one another.

Growing to more than a metre long — without a tail worth speaking of — and sometimes weighing well over thirty kilos, common wombats are the biggest burrowing animals in the world. They dig with their front paws, then lie on their sides to push back the debris with all four feet. In soft soil, gnawing through tree roots if necessary, one wombat can excavate a simple refuge three or four metres long in a few hours. The best-developed burrows, with many chambers and entrances, are the work of successive generations.

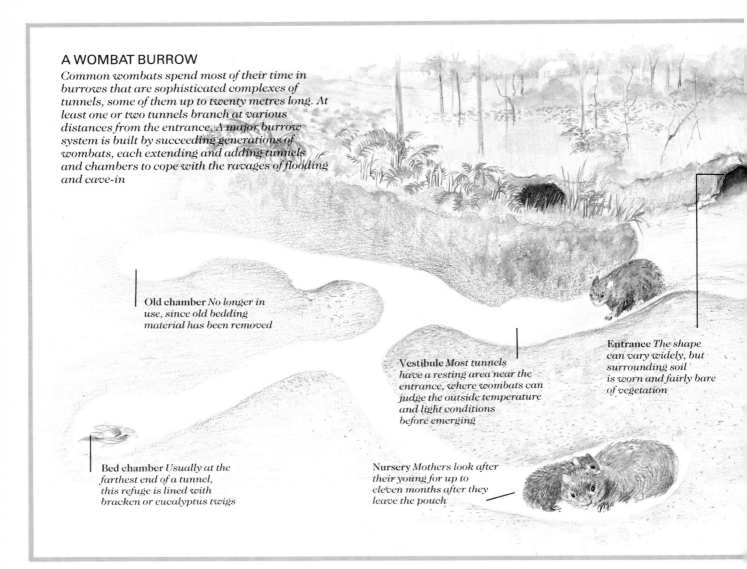

A WOMBAT BURROW

Common wombats spend most of their time in burrows that are sophisticated complexes of tunnels, some of them up to twenty metres long. At least one or two tunnels branch at various distances from the entrance. A major burrow system is built by succeeding generations of wombats, each extending and adding tunnels and chambers to cope with the ravages of flooding and cave-in

Old chamber *No longer in use, since old bedding material has been removed*

Bed chamber *Usually at the farthest end of a tunnel, this refuge is lined with bracken or eucalyptus twigs*

Vestibule *Most tunnels have a resting area near the entrance, where wombats can judge the outside temperature and light conditions before emerging*

Nursery *Mothers look after their young for up to eleven months after they leave the pouch*

Entrance *The shape can vary widely, but surrounding soil is worn and fairly bare of vegetation*

The northern hairy-nosed wombat Lasiorhinus krefftii *is extremely rare*

If frightened — by dogs, for example — apparently bumble-footed wombats can turn on astonishing bursts of speed. They normally show little fear of humans, allowing a close approach and sometimes even letting themselves be touched. But it is unwise to try to hold wild wombats or to block their path. They are immensely strong, bite severely, and can bowl a person over in a charge.

Wombats' teeth grow continuously, like those of rodents, enabling them to cope with a diet high in abrasive silica. Native grasses provide most of their nutrition, along with some sedges, rushes, herbs, leaves, roots and fungi.

Common wombats reach sexual maturity at two years and probably live to five or more in the wild. Some captive animals have reached the age of twenty. Dingoes on the mainland are their only natural enemy. Agricultural clearances have reduced their range, but they seem secure in most high-country habitats.

Hairy-nosed or plains wombats have

The southern hairy-nosed wombat Lasiorhinus latifrons *is the smallest of the three wombat species. Hairy-nosed wombats join together their burrow systems to form a warren. The tunnel entrances are grouped together, or linked by a network of trails*

been hurt much more severely by agricultural development. At home on drier grasslands, they lost most of their food supplies to livestock. And in most areas they were persecuted because their burrows undermined rabbit-proof fences. Now the main species, *Lasiorhinus latifrons*, is confined to the Nullarbor Plain and isolated pockets of South Australia. The last remaining population of a northern species, *Lasiorhinus krefftii*, exists in a fenced-off sanctuary within a central Queensland cattle run.

Hairy-nosed wombats lead sedentary lives, in small communities based on complex arrangements of burrows. They are arid-adapted, with an unusually low rate of metabolism and little need of drinking water. They breed in spring if they get enough to eat — which is far from certain in the harsh country left to them. With luck their populations may remain stable. Scientists calculate that any increase would require at least three successive seasons of good rainfall. □

SMALL WONDER

Tiny marsupials are ferocious insect-hunters

Winter in eastern high country brings out by day — along with wombats — an animal so tiny that it could nest in a wombat's ear. The common planigale or pygmy marsupial mouse *Planigale maculata* averages only eight centimetres in head-and-body length. A quicksilver killer of insects, it shows disconcerting ferocity if disturbed — baring its teeth even at people. This planigale is normally nocturnal in varied habitats from mid-New South Wales to Cape York and across the Top End. Captive specimens have borne as many as twelve young, but nothing is known of its seasonality. In the Kimberley and across the Gulf Country it has an even tinier relative that breeds in the wet season and is equally fecund. At an average length of six centimetres the long-tailed planigale *Planigale ingrami* is Australia's smallest mammal and the second smallest in the world — undercut by an African shrew.

The common planigale eating a slater

JULY

THIS MONTH'S WEATHER

All regions record their lowest average temperatures, and snowfalls may be widespread on southeastern high country. Good rains are maintained in the south and southwest, but readings tend to decline in New South Wales. Queensland enters its driest season, while at the Top End the Dry is already so well established that grasslands fires break out.

AROUND THE COUNTRY	RAIN (mm)	MAX. (°C)	MIN. (°C)	SUN hrs/day
Adelaide	75	15	7	4.3
Alice Springs	17	19	4	9.0
Brisbane	64	21	9	7.3
Canberra	39	11	0	5.7
Darwin	1	30	19	10.0
Hobart	53	12	4	4.4
Melbourne	48	13	6	4.5
Perth	173	18	9	5.3
Port Hedland	10	27	12	9.0
Sydney	101	16	8	6.4
Townsville	15	25	13	8.5
Weipa	2	30	19	7.5

The female brown antechinus drags its young around attached to its teats for about five weeks

A strange start in life

Newborn echidnas are hatched from eggs, then suckled in pouches — a process unique in the animal kingdom

Gradually since autumn, the echidna's temporary pouch has been developing. Behind the deepening, muscle-walled recess in her belly surface, milk-producing glands are expanding. She has mated with one of several males that began to follow her about recently. Now, two weeks later, she curls up in her den and produces one small, soft-skinned egg.

A mammal that lays eggs in the manner of reptiles and birds is strange enough. Only the platypus has a similar method of reproduction. In hatching their eggs in pouches, where the young remain to be suckled, the echidnas of Australia and New Guinea are unique.

We cannot watch the laying of an echidna's egg — all there is to see is a convulsing ball of spines. So no one is sure how the egg gets into the pouch. Presumably the curled-up female is able to fold her abdomen so that her vent is close to the pouch opening. Perhaps the end of the vent turns inside-out to push the egg into position. Wet and sticky, the egg then becomes fastened to the mammary hairs inside the pouch.

In a week to ten days the skin of the egg breaks down. A hatchling less than two centimetres long is left tucked securely between the pouch walls. At the same time the pores in the skin of the mother's belly begin to ooze a rich supply of thick, yellow milk.

The young echidna develops in the pouch for about three months. By then it is some ten centimetres long and its sharp spines are growing — no doubt to the discomfort of the mother. While it is still virtually helpless she claws it from the pouch and beds it down in a den.

Visiting the den every day or two, the mother uses her snout and one forepaw to nudge the offspring into a feeding position below her arched body and suckles it for about half an hour. Maternal care seems to last for a long time: juveniles are not usually seen in the open until they are about a year old.

The formal name for *Tachyglossus aculeatus* is the short-beaked echidna, to distinguish it from a bigger animal that died out thousands of years ago in this country. (It survives in the New Guinea highlands, where it lives on earthworms.) The alternative common name for the short-beaked species, spiny anteater, is apt only in the south; throughout most of Australia it eats mainly termites.

The echidna is our most widespread mammal. It thrives wherever termites or ants are abundant — from wet forests to parched sandplains — and withstands the greatest extremes of temperature. Populations in tropical and arid regions are generally light in colour, with little fur noticeable among the spines. Echidnas of the eastern and southern mainland are darker and more heavily furred, while Tasmania's near-black subspecies has hairs so long that many of the spines are concealed beneath them.

Solitary except at breeding time, echidnas forage in overlapping areas that include a choice of casual sheltering places. Dense shrubbery, hollow logs,

A young echidna in its nursing den. Adult males weigh up to seven kilograms

A short-beaked echidna in Barakula State Forest, Queensland. In addition to its more obvious defences, it is well camouflaged

caves, crevices or heaps of litter are used. Some burrows are made, mainly as nursing dens. Desert-dwellers are nocturnal. In most other regions echidnas look for food around dawn and dusk, except in winter, when they emerge in daylight.

In snow-covered habitats, echidnas hibernate. Sydney University researchers discovered in 1987 that the species is capable of falling into deep torpor. Five animals in the Perisher Valley area of the Snowy Mountains were fitted with radio transmitters to track their movements and monitor their temperature and heart rate. The readings plunged so suddenly at the onset of winter that the first animal to be checked was thought to have died.

Body temperatures drop
Alpine echidnas are among the biggest animals in the world to hibernate in such heavy torpor, with body temperatures falling more than 20°C. The hibernation of northern hemisphere bears, on the other hand, is merely a long, well-fed sleep with only a slight drop in temperature.

Where winters are milder, echidnas breed in July or August. By the time the young are making heavy demands for milk, mothers are richly fed on the spring and summer explosions of ant or termite populations. In spring the bodies of new, virgin queens of meat-ant colonies, for example, contain nearly fifty per cent fat.

Echidnas have been credited with acute senses of hearing and smell, enabling them to find termites and ants in heavy concentrations. They may also have an instinctive knowledge of the tem-

Echidnas use their extensile, saliva-coated tongues to catch ants and termites

perature preferences of their prey. Studies of echidnas near Canberra showed that in late winter and spring they always attacked ant mounds from the northern side, where they were warmest.

A long, sticky tongue
The forepaws and snout are used to break into a mound or nest. The long snout, with nostrils and a tiny mouth at the end, is thrust into an inner gallery. Out flicks a narrow, extensible tongue, heavily coated with sticky saliva. Any insects in the gallery are picked up and drawn back into the mouth, to be ground between horny plates behind the tongue. A lot of soil is also swallowed; the cylindrical droppings of echidnas, sharply broken at the ends, consist mainly of earth.

Echidnas and platypuses are the sole members of the primitive order Monotremata, and in spite of the contrast in habits and appearance, they are broadly the same sort of creature. The echidna even has partly webbed feet. And like the platypus a male echidna develops spurs on its hind legs, though its venom glands no longer function.

Echidnas and platypuses are thought to share a common heritage, dating back perhaps 200 million years to the early emergence of mammalian characteristics in some kind of reptile. Monotremes (members of the order Monotremata) were not the ancestors of the more advanced marsupial and placental mammals, however. They represent a separate evolutionary branch that in global terms proved unsuccessful.

The failure of such an ancient order to diversify and flourish, except in our region, is put down to a primitive brain structure. Monotremes show little learning capacity or adaptability in behaviour. But in the case of the echidna there has been no pressure to change. It succeeds through the staggering abundance of its food supply — for which there is no significant competition — and the excellence of its passive defences.

Goannas may occasionally prey on baby echidnas in their nursery dens. Dingoes sometimes attack foraging adults, but their long spines make them virtually invulnerable. If alarmed on soft ground they immediately dig with all four feet, sinking vertically so that within a minute only the tips of their back spines are showing. In rocky country they retreat into crevices, or if stranded without a refuge they simply curl into a spiky ball.

Over their general range the future of echidnas seems as secure as any animal's can be. They are scarce in settled areas, however, because roads and fences have interfered with their movements. People building on bushland blocks have reason to regret their absence, because ant and termite populations can reach pestilential levels without this natural control.

Bandicoots are not such welcome visitors — these little marsupials are the principal hosts of ticks. Apart from that their night raids on gardens, especially frequent in winter, can be damaging. Conical pits are dug in a quest for worms and insects.

Winter for most bandicoots is the start of a long and prolific breeding season during which females commonly bear three litters. Towards the end of it, the progeny too will have begun to breed. Those that establish feeding territories may continue for two further seasons.

The reproductive biology of bandicoots blurs the distinction between marsupials and placental mammals. Gestation periods are extremely brief — about twelve and a half days in the best-studied species, the shortest of any mammal in the world. Yet the embryonic newborn have umbilical cords, by which they were attached to uterus walls in the manner of placental foetuses. These shrivel when the young have found the pouch, fastened onto a nipple and begun to feed.

Usually born in litters of two to four, bandicoots are weaned at about two months. The mother mates again a week before, so production is almost continuous. Mortality among the young is high, however. Relatively few can find territories not already held by aggressive adults. Native predators abound, though domestic and feral cats probably take an even heavier toll.

Bandicoots favour habitats offering a cover of low vegetation, whether or not there are trees above. They nest by day in shallow depressions, lined with grass and leaves and usually covered with litter. At night they gallop and bound about energetically, often to an accompaniment of squeaks or shrill grunts.

The commonest species are the northern brown *Isoodon macrourus* and the long-nosed *Perameles nasuta*. In warm, well-watered eastern bushland these are the carriers of paralysis ticks. The southern brown *Isoodon obesulus* has suffered heavily from agricultural development. The prettiest of the group, the eastern barred bandicoot *Perameles gunnii*, is found only in Tasmania and the Western District of Victoria.

Male antechinuses mate — and die
Antechinuses, looking much like small bandicoots but in fact closely related to quolls, enter a hectic phase of synchronised breeding in July or August. It lasts only about two weeks in any community. Within another fortnight every male is dead, leaving the field clear for pregnant females and their litters of up to twelve young, born after a month's gestation.

Exhaustion alone, from copulations that last as long as twelve hours and are repeated with all available females, must weaken the males severely. There may also be a hormonal effect that undermines their immune systems, putting them at the mercy of already-acquired parasitic and bacterial infections.

Competitive stresses were thought until recently to be a major factor in the early deaths of male antechinuses. On the basis of observations in captivity they were assumed to fight continually as the breeding season approached and to spend a lot of time pursuing females. But a study by Australian National University researchers of a community of brown antechinuses *Antechinus stuartii* has cast doubt on such notions. Males congregated peaceably enough in big groups and waited for the females to come to them.

All three of the most abundant species have their main concentrations in the southeast, but do not directly compete. The brown antechinus, for example, prefers dense forests with ample ground cover, leaving woodlands and heaths to the yellow-footed antechinus *Antechinus*

A young northern brown bandicoot emerging from its mother's pouch (above). The eastern barred bandicoot (below) is now rare on the Australian mainland

Swamp wallabies Wallabia bicolor *may congregate to feed but are usually solitary*

THE ONE TRUE WALLABY COMES TO TOWN
Winter hunger brings out a browser with strange tastes

Starved of fresh plant growth in their natural habitats, swamp wallabies roam far on cold winter nights in the south. It is not unusual to see them on the outskirts of country towns, sampling bushes and shrubs and whatever crops may be growing. They will eat pine seedlings, hard ferns and brackens, and even hemlock.

Wallabia bicolor, distributed from Cape York to Bass Strait, is a unique type of marsupial. Others that are called wallabies are simply small kangaroos, and are classified as species of the genus *Macropus*. The swamp wallaby's tooth formation, reproduction and behaviour are all different from theirs, and this distinction has been borne out by genetic studies.

It lives where it can shelter by day in dense undergrowth — not necessarily in forests or woodlands, but also on heaths and among boggy stands of ferns. Coming out at night to feed, it prefers to browse taller plants rather than graze on the ground.

The species takes advantage of embryonic diapause (in which a cell cluster's development is suspended at an early stage) in a way known in no other marsupial. The gestation period is longer than the female ovulation cycle, so re-mating takes place some days before the birth of the embryonic joey produced by the previous mating. Born at any time of year, a joey remains in the pouch for up to nine months and is suckled at foot for a further six.

The dusky antechinus Antechinus swainsonii *grows up to 330 millimetres long. This female is devouring a large cricket*

After mating, the female common dunnart develops a pouch in which to carry its young. This is a nesting female with juvenile

flavipes. And in wetter areas the dusky antechinus *Antechinus swainsonii* occupies forest floors, and the brown antechinus takes to the trees.

Insects and spiders, found at night among litter or captured on branches, make up most of the diet of all antechinuses. But they can eat flowers, berries and other plant matter and also prey on small birds and mice. If they eat such vertebrates they leave the skins inside-out — often the only sign of their presence in the bush. Their nests of grass or leaves are well hidden, typically in or among fallen logs.

Females of most species have rudimentary, backward-opening pouches where the young stay for five to eight weeks. But the brown antechinus has only an area of exposed nipples. The young are dragged over the ground clinging to the nipples — incredibly, most survive. In different localities this species has as many as ten or as few as six nipples; litter sizes vary according to the number provided.

In a curious contrast to the frenzied pace of the antechinus's breeding schedule, births of the common dunnart *Sminthopsis murina* (which in Victoria has an adjoining range) are spaced from August right through until March. Females normally have two litters of up to ten young. Males of this species compete ferociously for mating opportunities, often inflicting wounds, and copulation is almost as savage.□

Two little pygmy-possums Cercartetus lepidus *in a state of torpor during cold weather. They are also able to store fat in their prehensile tails in order to cope with the harsh winters where they live, on Kangaroo Island, South Australia, in Tasmania and northwest Victoria*

COPING WITH COLD
Some animals spend winter in a state of torpor, their body mechanisms barely ticking over

Few Australian animals are subjected to long freeze-ups that directly threaten their lives. But faced with winter food shortages, many have to reduce their energy demands. They find safe places and lapse into torpor, allowing their body temperature to drop. The processes of metabolism — chemical changes within the body — are slowed, along with heartbeat and breathing.

Torpor is automatic in cold-blooded creatures, which are unable to regulate their temperature. Snakes and lizards become inactive in cold weather. Insect life cycles usually include a phase of winter dormancy in the development of eggs or larvae. Mammals, on the other hand, have ways of maintaining their temperature in defiance of surrounding conditions. But for many smaller ones — and one surprisingly big one, the echidna — it can be uneconomical to try to fight heat loss. Therefore some trigger mechanism switches off their bodies' thermostats.

Pygmy-possums, antechinuses, dunnarts, planigales and bats can slip in and out of torpor as part of a daily cycle, or suspend all activity for extended periods where winters are hardest. Some bats that remain in the southeastern highlands during winter allow their body temperature to fall close to freezing point. Their rate of metabolism may be as little as one per cent of what is normal during flight.

In all classes of land animals there are some that show extraordinary responses to severe cold — insects that hunt on snow, for example, or tiny mice that continue to run around underneath it. As always, food is the key to seasonality. The exceptional animals have habits or physiques that enable them exclusively to exploit certain resources.

Southern populations of Gould's long-eared bat Nyctophylus gouldi *favour the disused mud nests of fairy martins as winter refuges. Their body temperature falls in stages as the cold deepens, and torpor is maintained until the air temperature rises to about 16°C. A reviving bat warms its blood by flexing its chest muscles*

As far south as eastern Victoria, the common jezabel Delias nigrina *is often more abundant in winter than at any other time. Large numbers may be seen migrating along the dune lines of beaches, or, when breeding, fluttering high among the foliage of trees*

The common wombat
Vombatus ursinus
abandons its normal
nocturnal habit in very
cold weather, coming out
of its burrow by day to
feed on native grasses

Apteropanorpa tasmanica
(above) is a wingless
scorpion-fly peculiar to
Tasmania. About the size
of a meat-ant, it is found
on snowdrifts, where it
presumably feeds on small
flying insects

Even with snow still on
the ground the
copperhead Austrelaps
superbus (below) comes
out to bask in sunshine. It
prefers colder regions,
spending less time in
torpor than any other big
snake. Copperheads
favour swampland and
prey largely on frogs

Tasmania's long-tailed mouse Pseudomys higginsi (left) defies winter
temperatures that are often 10°C or more below freezing. Under snow it
remains active in tunnels among forest litter, eating insects, spiders and
a wide variety of plant material

Driven off by shotguns and sugarcane

Tropical pigeons have been slaughtered by hunters and starved of rainforest fruits. Dismally depleted flocks now shun their old nesting grounds

Wings beating powerfully in defiance of a stiff southeasterly, bulky white birds stream in over the waters around Cape York. Groups of thirty or so veer inshore to make clattering, cooing landings in mangroves and vine thickets. The Torres Strait imperial-pigeons are back.

Day after day during July, more flocks make the crossing from winter quarters in New Guinea. In successive waves they pass through the cape area, parched at this time of year, to seek luxuriant lowland rainforests farther south. There they hope to feed on fruits until autumn. During their nesting season they will commute each day from offshore islets and coral cays.

Tens of thousands of birds take part in the annual migration. To witness the noisy arrival of a flock is a heart-warming experience — until one learns that not so many years back, the travellers were more likely to have been numbered in millions.

In the first decade of this century imperial-pigeons *Ducula bicolor* fed and bred in teeming abundance as far south as Mackay, almost to the limit of the tropical zone. A cluster of islets near Dunk Island, for example, not much more than a hundred hectares in total area, used to accommodate up to 100 000 birds. Only a few hundred come now, in the best of years.

Over what seems to have been only a decade, during and soon after World War I, the birds virtually relinquished some 700 kilometres of their Queensland range.

Islands northeast of Mossman became, and remain, the southern limit of mass breeding. Significantly, Mossman is the northernmost district of sugarcane cultivation. Beyond the township, protected forests reach to the shores of the Coral Sea in Daintree and Cape Tribulation National Parks.

The clearing of lowland scrub by settlers, battling for meagre livelihoods from cane or dairying, was undoubtedly the principal factor in the pigeons' withdrawal. Their feeding trees vanished from wide areas. But agriculture does not deserve all the blame. Half as big again as domestic pigeons, well-fed birds are fat and delicious. Shooters collected them by the bagful, both from the remaining forests and from nesting islands. The fact that former southern breeding grounds remain almost deserted suggests that the persecution has continued.

Flocks occupying sites off the northeast of Cape York Peninsula are secure. Others make their way in modest numbers to lonely shores in the Gulf of Carpentaria, Arnhem Land and the northwest. Many birds have abandoned

The Torres Strait imperial-pigeon performs bowing displays, with loud cooing, in aggressive and courting situations

The wompoo lives high up in rainforest foliage and never comes to the ground

their migratory patterns, staying in New Guinea to breed. The species seems to be in no danger. But in the more accessible parts of our tropical coast we have squandered the opportunity to enjoy the sights and sounds of a splendid form of birdlife.

The flocks that come as far as the Daintree rainforests arrive in the second week of August. They stay put for a month or so, combing the canopies for fruit. Though they were commonly called nutmeg pigeons, they show no special preference for this tree. Lawyer vine, laurel, scrub turpentine, native olive and walnut are their favourites. Courting begins on crowded branches, the booming calls of chest-puffing males drowning out any other daytime sound of the forest.

In the course of a few afternoons around the middle of September the scattered flocks head out to sea. Fattened birds skim less than a metre above the languid, reef-sheltered waters. All make for the same low-lying cay, ten to fifteen kilometres offshore. Twenty hectares of tide-washed coral rubble support nothing but mangroves. But in some years as many as 12 000 pairs come here. They choose the most inhospitable cay for good reason: it is free of the menace of resident goannas, snakes, rats and butcherbirds.

Pairs take about a week to build platform nests in the mangroves, using green-leafed twigs and fallen branches. A single egg is laid. The sexes share its four-week incubation, flying back to the mainland to feed on alternate days. By the end of October, with the wind now in the northeast and wet-season storm clouds gathering, the first yellow-downed chicks are waiting each evening to feed from a parent's bulging crop.

The young fledge in less than a month but the flocks maintain their offshore base until the end of January, risking some mortality if violent squalls should strike during their daily feeding flights. In spite of the attentions of sea-eagles, many pairs raise two successive chicks and some even manage three. Parents and young loiter on the mainland for two more months before the flight back to New Guinea.

The colourful wompoo

The decline of imperial-pigeons over so much of their Queensland range has brought the wompoo fruit-dove *Ptilinopus magnificus* to the forefront in remaining lowland rainforests. Essentially a sedentary bird, it roams locally to follow the irregular fruiting of trees, and will move into upland forests if necessary.

Agricultural clearances and hunting have hurt the wompoo most in New South Wales, where it once ranged south of Sydney. Now it is rare except in the far north of the state. Though their brilliant plumage is disguised among dense foliage, the big birds invite the attention of shooters by their loud, persistent calling.

Wompoos also begin their nesting in winter, some as early as June. They assemble flimsy stands of tangled sticks near the ends of high branches, inside a screen of leaves. The single egg probably takes about a fortnight to hatch.

THE PLUCK OF A HONEYEATER

It will take the hair from your head

Most honeyeaters seek soft materials to line their cup nests. Some are content with plant down, flowers or feathers. Others such as the white-eared honeyeater *Lichenostomus leucotis* collect animal fibres.

Long accustomed to plucking the growing fur from placid, daytime-sleeping wild animals such as koalas, possums and wallabies, white-ears have taken to doing the same thing to domestic livestock. Failing any other source of supply, some even suspend their natural fear of humans. They alight to take hair from the heads of compliant people.

Australia has more than sixty species of honeyeaters, characterised by brush-tipped tongues that help them gather nectar. In spite of their collective name, the white-ear and many others live largely on insects and their secretions, and on the sap exuding from insect-damaged trees.

Honeyeaters breeding as early as July include the biggest, the wattlebirds *Anthochaera*, and the noisiest, the miners *Manorina* and the friarbirds *Philemon*. In general these are not colourful birds, but the male scarlet honeyeater *Myzomela sanguinolenta* is the brightest of all.

Scarlet honeyeaters are the smallest of Australia's honeyeater species

A flock of tree martins Hirundo nigricans at rest. Their feet are tiny and weak and are used only for perching

Martins declare an early end to winter. Both species, the tree martin *Hirundo nigricans* and the fairy martin *Hirundo ariel*, flocked north in autumn. Now they are appearing in the south to prepare their nests. Often the two types feed together, hawking for insects that fly above streams or swamps. But there is no competition for nesting sites, except in neglected buildings. In natural environments their preferences are distinctive.

Breeding colonies of fairy martins collect pellets of mud to build tightly packed clusters of bottle-shaped nesting chambers on cliff faces or under rock overhangs. Tree martins also use mud, but only to modify the entrances or inner shapes of the tree hollows that they favour. Both kinds of nests allow the birds to dive inside in full flight — a remarkable sight when a flock comes home. On emerging they simply fall out and fly; their claws can cling in gravity-defying attitudes, but martins cannot walk.

Nests are repaired and freshly lined for reoccupation year after year, though not necessarily by the same birds. It is likely that during the long season, lasting until midsummer in most regions, new pairs move in. About four eggs are laid by both species, hatching in just over a fortnight.

Robins feed on insects

Robins have an equally long season, each pair commonly raising three broods of about three young. Sedentary species such as the scarlet and red-capped robins *Petroica* and the yellow robins *Eopsaltria* start nesting in July; migratory species will arrive in the south a little later. All are insect-eaters, taking them mostly on the ground but also on foliage or in flight.

Female robins build cup nests, usually of bark strips bound with cobweb. In their efforts to camouflage them they produce

The male scarlet robin has a darker back and a brighter chest than the female

examples of charming artistry. Nests may be adorned with flakes of lichen, sprigs of moss or dangling pieces of bark. The scarlet robin often adds pieces of charred wood, while the red-capped species uses the egg sacs of spiders.

Similar arts of decoration are practised by the jacky winter *Microeca leucophaea*. It is an everyday sight on the edges of eucalypt woodlands, hunting for insects during fluttering, hovering flights. While breeding, which starts now among some birds but can occur as late as February, jacky winters sing all day long — even during their feeding sorties.

The far-carrying melody of the grey shrike-thrush *Colluricincla harmonica* rings out at frequent intervals during the day when it starts to breed, which may be at any time from now until late summer. Out of breeding the bird is heard less often, usually early in the morning. Though principally a forager for insects, the grey shrike-thrush may take lizards, mice and the nestlings of other birds. Its nesting bowls of bark and grass are placed at low level, usually in stumps or logs.

Whipbirds also nest close to the ground, in the densest undergrowth they can find. Though the unmistakable whistle-and-whipcrack call of the male eastern whipbird *Psophodes olivaceus* often seems to come from high up, this is a

Male and female jacky winters share nest-building and feeding of young

ground-feeding species that rarely flies. A brief chirruping heard at the end of the call is the female's response.

In spite of its close relationship, the western whipbird *Psophodes nigrogularis* makes no whipcrack sound at all. Differ-

ent tinkling calls are exchanged between pairs, often for minutes at a time. Once widespread but now severely affected by agricultural clearance, the species is confined to pockets of mallee heathland in South and Western Australia.

A male eastern yellow robin Eopsaltria australis *flies in to feed the female incubating the eggs in the nest*

All across the southern mainland west of the Great Dividing Range, winter rains encourage early breeding by the white-browed babbler *Pomatostomus superciliosus*. Nest building and the feeding of chicks are joint efforts by groups of up to fifteen birds, only one pair of which breeds. The others are earlier offspring, awaiting their turn but perhaps never getting it. Families live together year-round, roosting in permanently maintained dormitory nests. The grey-crowned babbler *Pomatostomus temporalis* of northern and eastern regions has similar family ties between a breeding pair and as many as ten non-breeders, earning the species the alternative common name of 'twelve apostles'.

The sedentary ringnecks

In a band of reliable winter rainfall from the southwest to the South Australian gulfs — including the Nullarbor Plain — the Port Lincoln parrot *Barnardius zonarius* starts breeding as early as July. Birds of these regions are part of one race of a more widespread species collectively known as ringnecks. Many of the others, farther inland, are opportunistic breeders.

Where there is no risk of drought, ringnecks are among the most sedentary of parrots, roosting and nesting in the same places throughout their long lives. A powerful flight action gives them access to wide feeding areas and they have catholic tastes. Along with the seeds of eucalypts, acacias, cypress pine, grasses and herbs, they eat buds, blossoms, fruits and sometimes insects. Holes and hollows in eucalypts are exploited as nests, where two clutches of up to six eggs may be laid.

One of Australia's four races of ringneck, the twenty-eight parrot, which lives in the forests and woodlands of the southwest

A female white-fronted chat feeds its two nestlings with a juicy caterpillar

ACTING IN HASTE
Chats feign injury to protect their young

Pretending to be injured in order to draw a predator's attention away from eggs or chicks is a common ploy of small birds that nest on or near the ground and lack the protection of dense vegetation. Among the leading exponents are chats, which live in low shrubs in open country — a habitat often shared with snakes.

In loose colonies of white-fronted chats *Epthianura albifrons*, which start to breed in July, the impulse is so ingrained that even the non-breeding neighbours of a threatened family may take part. The birds flutter to the ground and scramble and flop about, apparently suffering some severe handicap. But their movements carry them steadily away from the nest, and they are ready to take to the air in an instant.

Over the vast range of the masked lapwing *Vanellus miles* — roughly the eastern two-thirds of the mainland, and also Tasmania — many birds are obliged to breed opportunistically, whenever marshlands or pastures are sufficiently wet. Populations enjoying regular rainfall start breeding as early as July. They normally nest in scrapes on the ground. But some that have moved into southeastern urban centres, exploiting parks and beaches in their search for insects, spiders, worms and small crustaceans, have taken to nesting on high buildings.

The Australian shelduck *Tadorna tadornoides* is well into its breeding season now. Many started in June, having moved into southern nesting areas as long ago as March. Permanent pairs defend their chosen territories belligerently throughout the autumn. Shallow, brackish coastal lagoons are preferred. Shelducks graze on land — sometimes destroying crops — as well as nibbling aquatic plants and taking insects. Most nests are in the hollows of tall trees, though the birds rarely perch there. Incubation of as many as fifteen eggs, by the female, takes up to seven weeks.□

Both sexes of the masked lapwing cooperate in building the simple nest

Australian shelducks probably mate for life, forming a bond as sub-adults but not breeding until they are twenty-two months old

A boobook returns to its nesting hollow carrying a large flying insect; they also catch and eat small birds and mammals

When a boobook comes of age

It doesn't give a hoot until it's old enough to breed

The barn owl occurs throughout Australia

The 'mopoke' call of the boobook, Australia's most abundant owl, may be heard on any night of the year. But July brings a sharp increase in hooting, as if there were suddenly twice as many birds. In effect there are. Young boobooks, hatched late last year, have been capable since autumn of a cat-like crying. Now they acquire adult voices and join their elders in a pre-breeding clamour to claim territory and win mates.

Southern boobooks *Ninox boobook* live wherever trees provide vantage points for their hunting. Urban gardens serve just as well as forests, and offer a bonus in introduced birds and mice. If daytime shelter is scarce in the most sparsely wooded arid regions, the owls use caves or rock overhangs. Moisture is gained from the blood of prey animals. Though boobooks love to bathe every morning, they do not need to drink.

Courtship by the male is chiefly a long, patient repetition of soft, staccato sounds, to which an interested female will respond by approaching closely and trilling in a low tone. Paired birds usually continue to hunt and roost separately, keeping in touch by hoots that can carry for more than a kilometre. Many different roosts are used within a territory as large as ten hectares.

Even on an exposed branch in daylight a roosting boobook is unlikely to be noticed. On the approach of an intruder it stretches up, flattens its feathers and averts its distinctive face, presenting a slim, stick-like appearance. Noisy heckling by a resentful mob of smaller birds is often the best clue to the presence of a boobook.

Nesting takes places in August or September, the male cleaning out a deep tree hollow and padding it with wood chips, twigs and leaves. Incubation of two to four eggs by the female takes around a month, during which her mate brings food. Chicks fledge in five or six weeks but remain with their parents through summer, relying on them to catch prey and to tear up bigger kills.

Sallying out from high perches, generally soon after dusk or before dawn, keen-sighted boobooks seldom miss in their swoops on small birds and mammals. Insects make up a major part of their diet, however — especially moths and beetles.

Such humble fare cannot sustain the powerful owl *Ninox strenua*. Twice as big as a boobook, it needs an average of about half a kilo of flesh a day. Pairs maintain territories of hundreds of hectares in wet eucalypt forests of the southeast, snatching ringtail possums, greater gliders and sugar gliders from their feeding trees. Young brushtail possums and birds are also taken occasionally, and ground forays are made in pursuit of rabbits and rats.

Powerful owls start nesting in May, so most young will have hatched by now. Apart from the adults' persistent 'woohoo' calling, especially during the breeding season, they are extremely secretive birds. Sometimes a favourite roosting site is revealed by pellets of excreted fur and bone on a whitened patch of forest floor.

The barking owl *Ninox connivens*, notorious for its 'screaming woman' calls in autumn (see March, page 101), may show itself in daylight at this time of year. It starts hunting before sunset under overcast skies. The barking owl too is a winter breeder, as is the rufous owl of tropical forests, *Ninox rufa*.

Australia's only other owls are *Tyto* species with broad, flat faces. Their call is a screech rather than a hoot. Best known are the masked owl *Tyto novaehollandiae* and the barn owl *Tyto alba*. All are erratic, opportunistic breeders.□

A menace still on the march

Giant toads advance relentlessly across the north, their prodigious breeding and voracious appetites threatening ecological disaster

Twelve toads the size of avocados sit contentedly on a doorstep, snapping up the moths and beetles that fall after flying into an outside light. This nightly scene is set not in a drenched coastal Queensland sugar town, but on a dry and dusty cattle station in the Gulf Country. It is all the same to *Bufo marinus*.

Originating in Central and South America, giant toads were brought in from

The giant toad Bufo marinus — *a biological success and an ecological catastrophe*

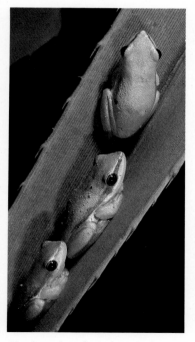

Northern dwarf tree frogs Litoria bicolor *congregating on a palm leaf*

Hawaii to control a beetle damaging sugar crops. They were released around Cairns in 1935, and in other districts including northern New South Wales a little later — before it was discovered that they ate almost anything rather than the beetles.

With females spawning up to 35 000 eggs a year — and males turning into females wherever they found a shortage of mates — the toads quickly formed a continuous band of population along the tropical and subtropical east coast. People called them cane toads, but that term is no longer appropriate. Giant toads have spread well into the semi-arid west of Queensland, all the way up the Cape York Peninsula, and across the Gulf into the Northern Territory.

Active year-round, they spawn and advance in flood seasons and survive dry intervals in billabongs, farm dams, rainwater tanks and lavatories. The amenities of human settlement suit them: because of their bulk they can hunt more easily in gardens and on roads, paths and pastures than they can in dense vegetation.

Constant activity means constant eating, with an appetite that can produce toads twenty-five centimetres long. They gorge on discarded foodstuffs and on human and livestock dung. Flying and crawling insects and practically any small forms of aquatic life are taken. Native frogs are preyed on to some extent, though they presumably suffer greater harm through being robbed of their food supplies.

Damage to the ecology

Immeasurable damage must already have occurred farther up the food chain. Fish and birds have less to eat. Fewer flowers are fertilised by insects. Ecologists fear that the toads will reach the monsoonal wetlands of the Northern Territory — the most unspoiled of their kind in the world. The consequences for wildlife in Kakadu National Park, for example, could be catastrophic.

Giant toads have glands that secrete a potent toxin. Most wild birds, reptiles and carnivorous mammals can be killed if they attack the invaders. Ravens and magpies are said to have learned to feed safely on the entrails of dead toads, but no predator offers hope of a natural control.

Researchers have no doubt that biological counters can be found. The answer could well be a virus or a parasitic worm. But if it has to be introduced from overseas, scientists will be a long time proving that, this time, the cure will not be worse than the complaint.□

AUGUST

THIS MONTH'S WEATHER

The anticyclone belt reaches its northernmost point, at about the latitude of the New South Wales-Queensland border. Good rains continue in the southwest and south but falls dwindle in the southeast and subtropical Queensland. The tropical east coast is at its driest, though the southeasterly trade winds still bring some moisture. The same winds, passing overland, arrive at the Top End hot and utterly dry.

AROUND THE COUNTRY	RAIN (mm)	MAX. (°C)	MIN. (°C)	SUN hrs/day
Adelaide	69	17	8	5.3
Alice Springs	12	22	6	9.7
Brisbane	43	22	10	8.4
Canberra	48	13	1	6.7
Darwin	6	31	21	10.2
Hobart	52	13	5	4.9
Melbourne	51	15	6	5.1
Perth	137	18	9	6.4
Port Hedland	4	29	13	10.1
Sydney	80	18	9	7.1
Townsville	13	26	15	9.0
Weipa	2	32	19	8.3

A humpback whale sounding as it nears its breeding grounds around the Great Barrier Reef

The peregrine falcon has recently become rarer because of the effect of some insecticides in thinning the shells of its eggs

A falcon that stoops to conquer

When a peregrine dives out of the blue, its quarry may never know what hit it

A mere speck in the sky, 200 metres up, the peregrine falcon circles. Infrequent shallow wingbeats keep him aloft; mostly he glides. At last a plump duck is spotted in flight far below. The peregrine tilts down, flapping his wings powerfully now, then snaps them back and goes into a plummeting dive that will intersect the path of his quarry.

The duck has no hope of escape. Within seconds the peregrine is upon it, pulling out of the dive but still travelling at high speed. As he passes over the quarry he strikes out with heavy, black-clawed feet.

Sometimes prey is grasped in the talons and carried to the ground. More usually, it is simply knocked down — stunned and with its neck or back broken. Then the peregrine circles back and alights beside his victim, immediately plucking and disembowelling it.

He is capable of dispatching birds up to the size of geese and swans. If the kill is big he will eat part of it on the ground, but prefers to carry as much as he can to a cliff ledge or perhaps a tree. At this time of year he has a mate — much bigger than he is — to look after. She has begun to incubate a clutch of three eggs. He will relieve her occasionally during the coming months, but at this early stage he concentrates on hunting. Food is usually dropped to the female or left near the nest.

Sometimes she flies out to greet him and takes her share of the kill in a talon-to-talon aerial pass — a manoeuvre that they practised often during their midwinter courtship. When the hatchlings are well advanced, and at other times outside the breeding season, the pair may join forces in hunting.

Mammals and ground-feeding birds in open country are attacked, as well as flying prey. Screens of trees or shrubbery are the only protection. No bird in level flight, let alone a running animal, is capable of anything like the speed that a peregrine can achieve at the bottom of its dive — guessed by some observers to exceed eighty metres a second, that is, around 300 kilometres an hour.

Purists call the attacking dive of *Falco peregrinus* and some other birds of prey a 'stoop'. Later confused with 'swoop', the word was used in medieval England by falconers, who tamed and bred the birds for sport. Training of peregrines is carried out on a small scale in Australia — but the main sporting impact of the birds is in the menace they present to racing pigeons.

Mating for life, peregrines hold hunting territories as extensive as fifty square kilometres and occupy the same nesting sites year after year. Most often these are shallow recesses scraped in high rock ledges. Tree hollows and the abandoned nests of other big birds are also used. Peregrines occasionally take possession of the tops of tall urban buildings if there is open country nearby.

Many other falcons are bigger than the peregrine, but none dives as far or as swiftly in attack. Some brown and black falcons have almost completed the rearing of their young by now, having started breeding as early as June. Much alike in appearance, these two differ markedly in their feeding habits.

The brown falcon *Falco berigora*, one of the most commonly seen birds of prey in Australia, is largely a hunter of small mammals and reptiles and big insects. Some birds are also taken in its sallies

Brown falcons prefer to take their prey, such as this rabbit, on the ground

The grey goshawk has two colour phases in Australia; this is the white phase

The slowest flier of the group is the Australian kestrel *Falco cenchroides*. But it can maintain a hovering position for minutes on end, eyeing open ground from ten to twenty metres up. Gradually moving lower and then dropping head-first on its target, it preys on a wide variety of small birds and mammals, reptiles and insects.

Goshawks and sparrowhawks *Accipiter* are adapted to more heavily timbered country. They ambush all kinds of prey from the cover of leafy foliage. And unlike the falcons they are industrious nest-builders, constructing big saucers of twigs in the high forks of trees. Most often seen, from around August in the south, is the largely migratory brown goshawk *Accipiter fasciatus*.

Harriers *Circus* hunt by systematic quartering of their territories, usually flying no more than five metres from the ground. Best known is the swamp harrier *Circus approximans*, which patrols reed-beds and wet pastures, nesting on platforms of sticks and aquatic plant material. It preys especially on breeding flocks of waterfowl, and includes frogs in its diet.

Buzzards and kites rob nests

Among the biggest birds of prey to start its breeding season now is the black-breasted buzzard *Hamirostra melanosternon*, which frequents the river red gums of inland watercourses. It makes low swoops from a perch. Most prey — said to include wallabies — is taken on the ground, but buzzards frequently rob the nests of other birds.

The square-tailed kite *Lophoictinia isura* flies close to the upper foliage of eucalypts, picking off lizards and insects and raiding the nests of small birds such as honeyeaters. They hunt hundreds of metres away from their own nesting trees, oddly leaving near-neighbours unmolested. Though many are nomadic, established pairs become sedentary in areas of reliable rainfall.

Little eagles *Hieraaetus morphnoides*, about half the size of wedge-tailed eagles, are similarly inclined to a sedentary life after they mate. Outside the spring breeding season pairs hunt together over woodlands, taking a variety of ground-dwelling prey. Where rabbits are abundant their young make up most of the diet. Big nests of sticks, placed as high as possible in trees, are lined every morning with fresh leaves brought by the male. He does nearly all the hunting while his mate incubates one or two eggs and cares for

An osprey Pandion haliaetus *(right) returns to its precarious clifftop nest, built of sticks and lined with seaweed and grass. Two or three eggs are laid*

from high perches. It has adapted easily to human settlement, readily making use of power poles and outbuildings as vantage points.

Black falcons *Falco subniger* are nomadic birds that roam sparsely wooded inland plains, borrowing the nests of other species during winter or spring. Drought occasionally forces them to coastal regions. They pursue some birds in flight — occasionally rushing at bushes to flush out prey — and also take

mammals, but ignore snakes and lizards.

A few kestrels and hobbies may be breeding now, though their main season does not begin until September. The Australian hobby or little falcon *Falco longipennis* sometimes makes power dives like a peregrine, knocking down sizable birds, but it is just as happy to lurk in a tree and take small ground-feeders or to snap up swarming insects. Often a hungry hobby waits for the twilight flights of bats.

the single surviving chick — duties that take up a total of three months each year.

The female osprey *Pandion haliaetus* devotes an even longer time to the care of two or three young. She incubates the eggs for about five weeks, feeds the chicks consistently for six weeks, and continues to supplement their catches with some of her own food even after they leave the nest at eight weeks old. Later in the brooding phase, the male may have to bring home as many as six big fish a day.

Sparsely distributed on all but the southernmost coasts, ospreys can easily be taken for the white-bellied sea-eagle *Haliaeetus leucogaster* but are only about three-quarters the size. They feed exclusively on marine fish and a few sea snakes, whereas sea-eagles are just as likely to take turtles, waterfowl and the nestlings of sea birds, or even go inland in search of rabbits.

A hunting osprey may swoop from a clifftop or a tall tree on the shore, or patrol at a leisurely pace about twenty metres above inlets or nearshore ocean waters. Spotting a fish near the surface, it briefly hovers over it, then drops feet-first on half-closed wings. As well as long claws an osprey has spiny toe scales to aid it in grasping slippery quarry that may weigh up to two kilos. It carries off its catch head-first in a characteristic fore-and-aft grip with both feet.

Spectacular courtship flights by ospreys may be seen at this time of year over temperate coasts, or a month or two earlier in the tropics. Pairs soar as high as 300 metres above their nesting sites, then swoop and dive and tumble. Sometimes a male breaks off to catch a fish, passing it to his mate near the nest while flying upside down or backwards.

Enormous stick nests, added to year after year, are lined with seaweed and grasses. The male supplies most of the material while his noticeably bigger mate does the building. High rocky headlands and cliff faces are preferred, but some nest in tall trees.□

Strangers on the shore
Sandpipers dominate the first wave of immigrant waders

Spindly-shanked wading birds from high northern latitudes — many from inside the Arctic Circle — start streaming into Australia late in August. They are sandpipers or closely allied types, retreating from the ice that will soon claim the inland waterways and marshes of their breeding areas. In this country for seven to nine months, few are able to find similar habitats. The majority will stay on seashores, stalking over tidal flats and

Curlew sandpipers Calidris ferruginea *forage along a coastal shoreline, accompanied by, at left, another visiting wader, the ruddy turnstone* Arenaria interpres

probing for small marine creatures.

Numbers involved in the annual influx defy estimation. From northern shores — especially the Timor Sea coast — some species disperse over or around the entire continent and even reach Tasmania. Australia is believed to receive all or nearly all of the world's population of certain species. But breeding in regions such as the Siberian tundra, few are seen, let alone counted.

Nor is much known about the routes the birds take through Southeast Asia, or the time spent travelling. But the journeys are probably very fast. Other sandpiper species migrating from the Arctic to South America have been intercepted and banded in the United States. A world long-distance speed record was claimed in 1985 for a bird released in Massachusetts and shot less than four days later in Guyana — 4480 kilometres away.

Sandpipers complete a moult before migrating and arrive here in subdued non-breeding plumage. Some of the common names bestowed on them in the northern hemisphere — red-necked stint and red knot, for example — are meaningless to most of us. Occasionally in far northern Australia in late autumn, when the last birds are assembling for their return journey, richer nuptial colours and bolder markings are seen. A few birds that may remain during winter are almost certain to be immature, retaining sombre plumage.

Fairly typical of the group, and among the most abundant, is the curlew sandpiper *Calidris ferruginea* from Arctic Siberia. Though some birds range to swampy or flooded inland districts, this species keeps mainly to tidal flats and estuaries. Flocks varying in numbers from dozens to thousands tend to stay in the same area for months, and become especially sedentary around December when they moult their wing feathers.

Another very common species, especially in the southeast, is the sharp-tailed sandpiper *Calidris acuminata*. It shows a stronger preference for fresh or brackish water and feeds in shallows. The red-necked stint *Calidris ruficollis* favours barely inundated mud, and the terek sandpiper *Xenus cinereus* waits for the tide to retreat. Flocks of any of these and of other sandpipers, along with waders such as godwits, curlews, greenshanks and whimbrels, are frequently mixed.

Longer legs for deeper water

Migrant waders finding inland habitats provide stiff competition for native-breeding stilts and avocets. But the latter have one advantage — even longer legs that enable them to forage in deeper water. The natives are at least partly nomadic and opportunistic in their breeding. Where there are dependable winter and spring rains, however, the black-winged stilt *Himantopus himantopus* starts nesting in August. Eggs, usually in clutches of four, are laid in mud depressions beside lakes or swamps, or sometimes on islands or plant platforms built in shallows. Hatched in three or four weeks, the young scramble into the water on their first day but return to the nest at night.

On ocean shores, the most prominent native waders to start breeding now are oystercatchers. Their specialised, chisel-shaped bills give them exclusive access to hard-shelled molluscs that the immigrant waders cannot open. Mussels, oysters, pipis and so on are dredged up and broached by one or other of two techniques, apparently passed on from parents to their young. Some birds place their catch on hard ground and hammer it open; others carefully insert their bills to prise open the shells. In either case they skilfully snip the mollusc's adductor muscle before pulling out the flesh.

Pied oystercatchers *Haematopus longirostris*

The black-winged stilt can feed in water up to fifteen centimetres deep. Its tiny mouth restricts its diet to minute organisms

A pied oystercatcher (below) sampling a crustacean as a change from its staple diet of molluscs. Oystercatchers mate for life, but forage alone or in dispersed pairs

are common on all sandy beaches, whether on the ocean front or around bays and estuaries. The all-black sooty oystercatcher *Haematopus fuliginosus* prefers rocky coasts, stony beaches and coral reefs. It flies to nearby islands to breed, while the pied species stays on the mainland. Habits and breeding patterns are otherwise much the same.

Pairs of oystercatchers, permanently mated, perform territorial and courtship displays in which they rush about side by side, piping shrilly. Nests are scrapes in sand or depressions in rocks. Two or three eggs take about a month to incubate. The young are quick to enter the sea but may not fly for six weeks or more. Adults feign death or injury to divert threats to the nest, or else pretend to be brooding in another place.□

A dangerous intruder in the nest

Nature plays its cruellest trick on cuckoos' hosts. Their own young are destroyed and they toil to feed oversized aliens

Scrawny and sightless, two squabs nestle inside a fur-lined globe of dry grass. Both are a day or two old. Yet they are strangely ill-matched. One is pink-skinned with some fringes of pale grey down. It is the season's first offspring of a pair of speckled warblers. The other chick, slightly bigger, is dark and naked. There is a cuckoo in the nest.

Until now the two youngsters have lain together quietly. But the baby warbler stirs and stretches, disturbing its companion. This will cause it to be cast out of the nest, to die from exposure, starvation or the attentions of a predator.

The cuckoo squab squirms to the lowest part of the nest and spreadeagles itself beak-down. There it twists and turns until it feels the weight of the warbler on its back. Drawing its skinny wings up behind it to clasp the other chick, it braces its legs and starts pushing backwards. The warbler chick is manoeuvred to an opening at the side of the nest and heaved over the edge.

Two or three of the speckled warblers' chocolate-coloured eggs may also lie in the nest. Chicks of some cuckoo species automatically roll out any eggs that they touch, using the same technique. The young of the black-eared cuckoo *Chrysococcyx osculans*, the specialist parasite of speckled warblers, are more inclined to wait for hatching and dispose of the chicks later.

With the nest to itself the cuckoo devours all the food that the parent warblers can bring. They were content to incubate the egg because it looked very like one of their own. The chick's alien appearance now does not concern them — nor, evidently, does the sight of a corpse or two outside the nest. All their energies go towards filling one great, ever-gaping mouth.

By the time the impostor is fledged, in less than three weeks, he is bigger than the foster-parents and scarcely able to squeeze out through the nest opening. Lingering outside for weeks longer, he still demands to be fed. Often the help of other adult warblers is needed to keep up the supply of insects. Finally, twice the size of his hosts, the cuckoo flies off to join his own kind.

Ten species of parasitic cuckoos breed in Australia, victimising about a hundred kinds of smaller birds. With little or no effort by the parents the young are reared in most cases from single eggs, laid in various nests during a long season. Some of the exploiters are smaller than a budgerigar. One is bigger than most ducks, and bold enough to invade the nests of currawongs, magpies and ravens.

A cuckoo squab's compulsion to eliminate all competition, and its efficiency in doing so while it is still blind and relatively puny, are remarkable. There is as much to marvel at in the behaviour of the adults. Mostly migrants, they arrive in their favoured localities in late winter or spring and start at once to spy on the nesting activities of prospective hosts — those whose incubation periods are best matched to their own, and generally those whose eggs look similar. Close observation pays off in fine timing. A female cuckoo is ready to lay an egg at the perfect moment, usually just as her chosen foster-mother is completing a clutch.

If both hosts do not leave the nest of their own accord the male cuckoo reveals himself and incites their aggression, drawing them away from the site. The female flies in, depositing her egg directly into a cup nest, and makes off with one of the natural clutch in her beak. If the nest is a domed type with a side entrance that is too small for her, she lays her egg on the ground and uses her beak or the claws of one foot to insert it, removing a genuine egg in the same way.

The boarding-out of baby cuckoos raises intriguing questions about their acquired behaviour. They could be expected to copy the calls and some of the mannerisms of their foster-parents, but they do not. On the limited evidence available, it seems that the natural parents spend a lot of time in the vicinity of their young, and may supplement their feeding when the hosts are away.

A persistent parasite

Among the most persistent and successful of the parasites is the shining bronze-cuckoo *Chrysococcyx lucidus*, found in the southwest and in heavily wooded regions of the south and east, all the way from Tasmania to Cape York. Between August and January a female may lay as many as sixteen eggs.

Each egg is laid well after those of the hosts because this species needs less time for incubating. There is seldom much resemblance between the eggs — instead, the cuckoo squab looks much like the chick it has replaced.

Fine arts of egg mimicry are practised by the brush cuckoo *Cacomantis variolosus*. It ranges in a north-to-southeast arc from the Kimberley to Victoria, where it starts to breed as late as October. Colourings, markings and even

This newly hatched common koel Eudynamys scolopacea *is removing the last of three figbird young from the nest of its foster-parents*

the shapes of eggs vary according to the hosts that the cuckoos are likely to find in a given region. Flycatchers are most commonly copied, but many eggs in the northwest imitate those of a rufous fantail. In the northeast the model is a honeyeater, while in the east and south it is often the grey fantail.

The calls that inspire European clockmakers and writers of letters to newspapers are not heard from Australian cuckoos. Ours give piping or trilling whistles. The most distinctive call — sometimes heard disturbingly in the dead of night — is the drawn-out, rising 'coo-ee' of the male common koel *Eudynamys scolopacea*. Adults of this species, arriving from the north around September, feed on fruiting trees rather than the insects that most cuckoos seek. But the young eat virtually anything that their foster-parents offer.

Ripe fruits — especially figs — are similarly favoured by the biggest and most easily seen of the cuckoos, the channel-bill *Scythrops novaehollandiae*. Migratory flocks of these heavily built, massive-billed birds begin to cross into northern Australia from New Guinea and Indonesia in August, working their way as far as southern New South Wales.

Channel-billed cuckoos sometimes consume the eggs and nestlings of other birds, along with large insects. Insects also play a part in courtship, being offered by the males to their intended mates. Exceptionally among cuckoos, a female channel-bill may infiltrate more than one egg into a host nest. Two are commonly laid, and as many as five

The young pallid cuckoo's loud squawks can induce complete strangers to feed it

A female tawny frogmouth with two well-camouflaged chicks at the nest

NIGHT BEAT
Frogmouths are easy to hear but hard to see

Soft booming sounds like muffled drumbeats throb monotonously in the still air of a bushland night. Frogmouths are announcing their choice of nesting sites. The most widespread species, the tawny frogmouth *Podargus strigoides*, remains in the same few hectares of woodland or drier forest all its life. Brief communications between permanent pairs may be heard at any time of year. But with the onset of breeding their noise becomes persistent, with bursts of as many as fifty quickly repeated calls.

When daylight comes, these nocturnal insect hunters seek shade but make no effort to hide. They rest on tree stumps, bare branches or occasionally on the ground. Motionless, feathers drawn in and the eyes closed to slits, they pass easily for the stumps of dead branches. Approached too closely, however, or disturbed at the nest, a frogmouth puts on a sudden and disconcerting display. It fluffs out its plumage, snaps its big beak alarmingly, and may hiss and growl. Glimpses of its broad mouth, a vivid yellow inside, suggest not so much a frog as an enraged lizard.

have been recorded. So the young have to tolerate some rivalry. Presumably as a consequence of this, they show no inclination to throw out remaining natural eggs or hatchlings. Faced with the competition of greedy and fast-growing interlopers, squabs of the host species simply starve to death.

Grisly feeding habits

Butcherbirds — another menace to smaller species — start their breeding well before winter's end. By now the dawn chorus of woodland birdsong is often dominated by their fluting duets, the sexes interweaving their melodies and embroidering them with distinctive personal flourishes.

The bigger of the two main species, the pied butcherbird *Cracticus nigrogularis*, avoids Tasmania and the southernmost parts of the mainland. Elsewhere its range overlaps that of the grey butcherbird *Cracticus torquatus* but there is a fine distinction in habitats, the smaller bird favouring more cover, with denser thickets and tree canopy.

A grey butcherbird feasting off the remains of a New Holland honeyeater

Grisly feeding habits earned butcherbirds their name. Their principal food is insects, taken on the ground in swooping dives from high perches. But they readily pounce on mice, lizards and snakes as well as helpless birds and nestlings. They cannot use their short, weak legs to anchor a sizable catch as true birds of prey do while eating. Instead they wedge it into a tree fork or impale it on a sharp twig or thorn.

Pairing for life, butcherbirds hold year-round territories and frequently hunt together. They spend a month building a sturdy cup nest of twigs in a high tree fork. The female incubates three to five eggs that hatch in about twenty-five days. The young fledge in a month but many stay in their parents' territory until the following spring, when they help to feed a new brood. Brownish where their parents are black, they do not gain adult plumage and sexual maturity until nearly two years old.

Welcome swallows *Hirundo neoxena*, most of which make a northward shift during

White-breasted woodswallows Artamus leucorhynchus *often sit in groups, preening one another. They also roost communally*

Male and female dusky woodswallows share nest-building and feeding duties. The young stay in the nest for up to twenty days

winter, begin to reappear in their breeding areas around August. Hunters of flying insects, usually over water, they build cup nests of mud and rootlets plastered to vertical surfaces. Before European settlement they were limited to caves and hollow trees.

Now they exploit sheds, bridges, tunnels and mine shafts, and two or three broods may be reared in a season, from clutches that usually number up to six eggs.

The white-backed swallow *Cheramoeca leucosternum* also begins to breed now.

Peculiar to Australia, it roosts and nests communally in burrows dug into creek banks. The species is unusually sedentary: huddled together in their sleeping chambers and able to lapse into torpor, white-backed swallow communities withstand the worst weather that winter can bring.

Woodswallows *Artamus* include both sedentary and migratory species, along with thoroughly nomadic inland types that respond to erratic rains and follow locust plagues. Best-known of the migrants, appearing at this time in the southwest and southeast, are dusky woodswallows *Artamus cyanopterus*. They too are communal, clustering in tree-hole roosts. Their cup nests of grass and twigs are often surprisingly exposed, however, in shallow recesses where trees have been damaged, on stumps or even on fence-posts.

Migratory pink or red-breasted robins *Petroica* move now towards high-country breeding areas in the southeast. This may mean the disappearance from urban gardens of birds that have been wintering at lower altitude, or the abrupt appearance in passing of birds travelling south. The rose robin *Petroica rosea* is the only one of the group whose breeding habitat extends to lowland forests. It may nest three times in a good season — but often all it raises is a murderous and greedy young brush cuckoo.

From feeding territories as big as a thousand hectares in eastern and

KEPT IN SUSPENSE
A unique warbler that hangs about in caves

Origmas — rock-hopping warblers peculiar to the central and southern sandstone country of eastern New South Wales — start life in extraordinary nests that dangle and sway like Chinese lanterns. Big boxes of plant material, attached at one corner to long masses of cobweb, are suspended from rock overhangs or the ceilings of dark caverns.

Dedicated to searching cliff faces and crevices for insects and seeds, *Origma solitaria* has no close kinship with any other birds. Its evolution seems to have been a specialised response to the rugged, river-cut terrain of its region. One of its oldest common names is cataract-bird, since its nesting sites are often screened by spills of water. Adjusting to European settlement, origmas have extended their fondness for dark places to tunnels, culverts and disused buildings.

The unusual design of an origma's nest

southern woodlands, groups of white-winged choughs *Corcorax melanorhamphus* withdraw to vigorously defended breeding areas of only twenty hectares or so. A typical group of about eight includes only one breeding pair and their surviving young of the previous three or four seasons. They forage together on the ground, probing and digging for insects, spiders and molluscs, and remain close in everything else they do. At this time of year they collaborate in building a big nesting basin of bark-stiffened mud.

The senior female lays three to five eggs that are incubated in just under three weeks, all birds taking their turn to sit. There is similar cooperation in feeding the hatchlings. In the occasional bigger group with two breeding females, all the eggs are laid in the one nest.

In drier country, almost identical nesting habits and communal behaviour are displayed by another bird of the

Before they can fly properly these white-winged chough nestlings will flutter to the forest floor to beg food from the older birds in their breeding group

The Australian magpie-lark is found near water, as it needs mud for its nest

same family, the apostlebird *Struthidea cinerea*. The common name stems from an old notion that groups always comprised twelve birds. That is a fair average, among groups whose numbers may range from eight to more than twenty. In a clear contrast to the chough, the apostlebird has a very short bill and takes its food from the ground surface.

Large flocks of magpie-larks

Another bird that constructs a mud nest is the Australian magpie-lark or peewee *Grallina cyanoleuca*; southern populations are increasing rapidly now. Established breeding pairs remain in their territories year-round. They are joined as winter ends by big flocks of younger birds — migratory or nomadic until they reach breeding age.

On the ground or perching on a branch, the magpie-lark often flicks its tail. The motion is up and down rather than from side to side — a point that helps distinguish it from the equally abundant and widespread willie wagtail *Rhipidura leucophrys*. Closely related to fantails, the willie wagtail is a flycatcher that makes hawking sallies from low trees, stumps, fence-posts, boulders overhanging creeks, and even the backs of livestock.

Wagtails become fiercely territorial while breeding. A dispute is worth close observation, for it shows a curious use of the species' white eyebrow streaks. An angry or defiant wagtail stretches its facial skin to expose and enlarge the streaks; a bird conceding defeat or acknowledging social inferiority frowns in a way that hides them.

Small cup nests of grass bound with cobweb are placed on horizontal branches. Many clutches of two or four eggs are laid in a long season but predation of eggs and hatchlings is high. Sometimes an unsuccessful nest is dismantled and re-erected in another place.

Fairy-wrens delight the eye now as the males come into their brilliant breeding plumage. Females are drab, as are non-breeding males. Western Australians see an iridescent blue species that is arguably the most beautiful, the splendid fairy-wren *Malurus splendens*. Most common in heavily populated parts of the east and south is the superb fairy-wren *Malurus cyaneus,* which has happily adapted to urban parks and gardens.

The high cost of cuckoos
These and various other species live in small, sedentary groups, foraging on the ground for insects and occasionally soaring from bushes to catch prey in mid-air. Their warbling or trilling songs are among the first bird sounds of the day, starting long before dawn. Many successive broods are reared through spring and early summer, with the help of non-breeders to feed the young. But because of predation and the impersonations of cuckoos, only about twenty per cent of fairy-wrens are thought to survive their first year of life.

For sheer gaudiness among all the birds that are beginning their breeding season now, Western Australia takes the prize again with its red-capped parrot *Purpureicephalus spurius*. Restricted to the forests of the far southwest, this bird nearly always nests in the hollows of marri eucalypts and relies heavily on their seeds for food. Males feed their mates in courtship and while they incubate and brood about five young. Immature birds wander in small flocks but adults, probably paired for life, hold a territory throughout the year.

A male splendid fairy-wren Malurus splendens *of the black-backed eastern race*

Red-rumped parrots are sedentary and appear to mate for life

Breeding ends in August for northern Australia's nomadic flocks of cockatiels *Leptolophus hollandicus*. Southern populations, however, are just beginning their season after a return flight from winter quarters far inland. Cockatiels live mainly on the seeds of acacias and grasses. They are a type of cockatoo, but they have tapered wings and tails that resemble those of parrots.

Many grass parrots of the southern hinterland begin breeding now. Perhaps the best known, ranging into settled areas and even to some coastal fringes, are the red-rumped parrot *Psephotus haematonotus* and the elegant parrot *Neophema elegans*. Grass parrots nest in hollow stumps and logs as well as in living trees. They can survive in very sparsely wooded country, but not without drinking frequently.□

Clusters of sawfly Perga affinis *larvae are a common sight in eucalyptus foliage*

The brown mantid Archimantis latistyla *grows up to 100 millimetres long*

Like the wedge-tail, the little eagle's legs are fully feathered down to the toes

Both the adults and the caterpillar-like larvae of this leaf beetle Paropsis *feed on eucalyptus and wattle leaves*

More than meets the eye

The flood-loving river red gum supports ceaseless animal activity

A tree can be seen as many things: a pleasant relief to a landscape, a giver of shade, a source of fuel or building material — even a nuisance standing in the way of settlement or agriculture. To animals a tree means food, shelter and a great deal more. It provides the structure for a teeming society of vast complexity, comprising hundreds of species. Relatively few of these catch the eye of a casual observer.

Shown here are river red gums *Eucalyptus camaldulensis*. They are the most widely distributed of eucalypts, lining permanent and temporary watercourses in all regions of moderate to low rainfall. These are located in the Flinders Ranges of inland South Australia, where they endure a harsh regime of winter flooding and parched, fiercely hot summers. Even here, the trees enable wildlife not merely to survive but to flourish in abundance and diversity.

River red gums Eucalyptus camaldulensis *in the Flinders Ranges of South Australia*

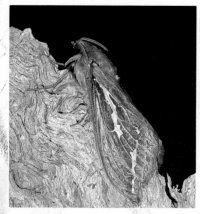

The larvae of the Murray River ghost moth Trictena argentata *feed on eucalyptus roots*

The little corella's favourite nesting place is a hollow in a river red gum

Gould's wattled bat roosts in tree-holes by day, and hunts flying insects at night

The brown treecreeper Climacteris picumnus *spirals up tree trunks in search of insects*

Flat cockroaches are found in damp leaf litter at the base of trees

An eastern spiny-tailed gecko Diplodactylus intermedius *shows its wood-grain camouflage*

An easy rider finds his feet

Freeloading comes to a sudden end for many brushtails. Rejected by re-mating mothers, they are forced into perilous exile

Well before sun-up, the lightening eastern sky and a swelling din of birdsong warn the brushtail possum that it is time to return to the den where she rests by day. Her half-grown offspring feeds nearby, on the same high branch of an ironbark. For once she does not make the soft, grunting call that summons him to climb on her back. As she starts to descend the trunk alone he scrambles after her, but is rebuffed with a hiss.

Coming into season for the second time this year and already courted by males, the mother no longer wants her young around. Even if he manages to make his own way back to the den she will chase him away — or worse, an aggressive suitor may attack him.

Alone and inexperienced, the little outcast will be easy meat for predators unless he soon finds secure places where he can shelter between sessions of feeding. If he lingers on branches he may fall foul of a python, a lace monitor or even a bird of prey. Moving on the ground, he is also at the mercy of dingoes, cats and quolls. But unoccupied tree-holes or other suitable retreats are hard to come by.

Nor is it easy for the abruptly weaned juvenile to get all the food he needs. The leafiest eucalypts and other big trees are on the regular visiting rounds of hostile adults. Many trees are scent-marked to warn of the dangerous presence of breeding males. Wandering ever more widely in search of a territory to claim as his own, the youngster may have to survive on bark or run the extra risks of ground-feeding as he grazes herbage or browses shrubs.

Audacity born of desperation makes the common brushtail *Trichosurus vulpecula* the most widely seen of all marsupials. Young animals forced to disperse take eagerly to urban gardens and parks, using exotic ornamental trees as travelling routes even if they do not feed from them. They frequently commandeer the ceiling spaces of houses as their dens. Gardens are raided for fruits, flowers and vegetables. Household food stocks and garbage, including raw or cooked meat, may be plundered. Given regular access to food without interference, the possums can become semi-tame.

This young common brushtail possum Trichosurus vulpecula *will ride on its mother's back for up to two months before being abruptly abandoned*

three years, even while succeeding brothers or sisters are being raised.

Mountain brushtails are less prolific than the common type, occurring in densities only about one-tenth as great. Many young die in the pouch, presumably because preceding offspring are still being suckled. But the survivors live longer — females to fifteen years or more, compared with about ten years for the common brushtail.

August in Tasmania sees the start of a single breeding season for the eastern pygmy-possum *Cercartetus nanus*. On the mainland this species and most of its relatives breed twice a year, in spring and autumn. Litters of four are usual, but the western pygmy-possum *Cercartetus concinnus*, found across a wide area of South Australia as well as in the southwest, rears as many as six at a time.

Pygmy-possums, the size of mice, use their long, naked tails for balance or extra grip as they leap and scramble about in shrubbery at night. Most are predominantly hunters of insects. But the eastern species has a brush-tipped tongue and a strong preference for nectar and pollen. Low in body mass, all species lapse easily into torpor in cool conditions or when food is scarce, instead of expending energy to maintain their temperatures.

Many native mice *Pseudomys* begin a busy annual breeding period as winter ends. These are not marsupials but placental mammals, part of a big group of rodents whose ancestral type is thought to

Brushtails can breed at any time of year but in their natural woodland and open forest habitats there is a pronounced peak in autumn and a secondary season in spring. Females, giving birth after a gestation period of about seventeen days, carry their single young in their pouches for four to five months, and on their backs for a further one or two.

The western pygmy-possum (above) is, at twenty grams, smaller than the eastern pygmy-possum

More females survive
Starting around August, about half of the autumn-born riders are abandoned by fecund mothers ready to breed again in spring. Other females do not re-mate until next autumn or even the following spring, permitting their young to feed and rest with them until then. Whenever separation occurs, young females find easier social acceptance and fare better. Young males suffer high mortality and in adult populations are outnumbered two to one.

A clear contrast is seen in the mountain brushtail or bobuck *Trichosurus caninus*. Occupying densely forested slopes of the southern half of the Great Dividing Range, the species is much the same as the common brushtail in appearance and general habits. But it has only a single breeding season, nearly always confined to autumn. There is an equal sexual distribution of adults, which are thought to form pair-bonds. And the young are tolerated in their home areas for as long as

The delicate mouse Pseudomys delicatulus *is one of the smallest native mice*

The New Holland mouse is restricted to the southeast, living in heathland

have reached Australia through the Indonesian region about fifteen million years ago. Different species have evolved to survive in all types of climate and every kind of habitat.

Usually born in litters of three or four — sometimes six — native mice are pre-

cocious. They can gain sexual maturity in less than two months, long before they are full-grown. Though they live for only eighteen months to two years their breeding season can last all through spring and summer. With gestation periods as short as one month, many females breed once

or twice in the season of their birth and have three or four litters a year later.

In suddenly improved conditions — after a drought breaks, for example — native mice have a typical rodent capacity to increase their numbers with great speed. A more specialised adaptation to Australian conditions is shown in the reliance of some species on bushfires (see page 18). Thriving on the earliest shrubs to grow in regenerating forests, their populations explode in the second breeding season after a fire.

Native mice are perhaps the least noticed of mammals living close to human habitations. They are secretive and largely nocturnal, retreating into burrows by day. Among the most thoroughly studied in recent years is a species that went missing for more than a century. The New Holland mouse *Pseudomys novaehollandiae* was rediscovered in the 1960s on the northern outskirts of Sydney and subsequently found to be common in patches of coastal New South Wales, Victoria and northeastern Tasmania.

The New Holland mouse lives on a seasonal variety of plant matter, fungi, insects and spiders. Invading areas recovering from fire, populations are prominent for a year or so while they flourish on the seeds of low-growing legumes. Then as other plants and animals take over, the mice return to obscurity. □

THE WILD BUSH HORSES
Former four-legged slaves now run free

On the foothills around the Snowy Mountains, the slow coming of spring is heralded by the whickering and whinnying of mares and newborn foals. Alpine brumbies are nearing the end of their winter sojourn. Within a month or so they and their latest offspring will start a leisurely journey back to the high plains, where their runaway ancestors took up residence a century ago. The wild bush horses, as Banjo Patterson called the mountain mobs in *The Man from Snowy River*, are small but stocky — apparently a mixture of the agile types needed for stock mustering on steep, rocky slopes and the draught horses that were used for hauling timber. They are a tiny, isolated minority among hundreds of thousands of feral horses *Equus caballus*, spread mostly over the centre and north of the continent. These are called plains brumbies — more rangily built and often downright scrawny, but hardy in the face of drought.

Feral mares foal once a year, generally in early spring. Fillies can breed in their second year but colts have to wait a lot longer before they are strong enough to challenge for dominance of a mob, usually numbering between twenty and forty.

Some brumbies are said to maintain pure bloodlines — including those of 'Walers', the mounts bred in New South Wales for supply to Britain's Indian Army. Even so, feral horses are largely unwanted except as pet food. Most pastoralists condemn them for the damage they do to fences and water sources, and for their consumption of precious pasture grasses.

Even greater numbers of donkeys *Equus asinus* roam arid and monsoonal regions. The descendants of pack animals, used mostly in Western and South Australia, they attract little attention because they less often come into conflict with agriculture. But in dry seasons they gather around waterholes in mobs of hundreds. Their local impact on native wildlife, by monopolising the water supply, overgrazing the vegetation and compacting the soil, must be devastating.

Plains brumbies digging for water in a riverbed

Nursery of the gentlest giants

Humpback whales come all the way from Antarctic waters to breed. While adults fast, calves indulge a gargantuan appetite for milk

Swimming effortlessly in the slipstream of its mother, the newborn humpback whale calf sidles up to her flank. Below the bases of her pectoral fins — each far bigger than a man — are huge mammary glands that produce about 600 litres of fatty milk every day. The hungry calf gently nuzzles a teat. It has no need to fasten on and suck. The mother pumps out the milk under muscular pressure, and the water is quickly clouded.

Born after about a year's gestation, the calf is highly developed. It was immediately expert in swimming, thrusting away to break the umbilical cord and needing only a nudge to direct it towards the surface for its first breath of air. Already bigger than a bull elephant, it could attain a weight of fifty tonnes and exceed fifteen metres in length at maturity.

This ocean marvel, peaceful and playful however big it gets, could live for over fifty years and procreate many more of its kind. Its chances rest on enlightened conservation policies — international as well as our own. The humpback needs the continued security of its Antarctic food resources and of its Australian breeding grounds, and safe passage between them. This and many other whale species have formerly been hunted to the very brink of extinction.

Long haul to the breeding grounds

Humpback whales *Megaptera novaeangliae* from separate subpolar populations — two of probably nine in the world — migrate annually along each side of the Australian continent. They travel north from late May and return in September, the last of them being seen off southern coasts in November.

Throughout August the humpbacks lounge — but do not feed — at the breeding grounds. Small groups are sparsely scattered in relatively shallow tropical waters, above the continental shelf. In the west they occur within an arc between Shark Bay and Port Hedland. Eastern grounds extend from Hervey Bay, in the lee of Fraser Island, over most of the Great Barrier Reef region.

A humpback whale Megaptera novaeangliae *breaching off Coffs Harbour, New South Wales, on its long journey south from the breeding grounds*

An urge to retreat from iced-over feeding areas is understandable. It is hard to say why the whales should go so far to the other extreme. Perhaps the variation in water temperatures kills off the marine organisms that form encrusting growths on the whale's skins. Whatever the reason the compulsion is strong — most females make the long voyage annually, still guarding the calves of earlier seasons, even though they mate only once every two or three years.

Also surprising is a humpback's apparent squandering of energy while it travels. Periods of shallow submersion and frequent breathing are interspersed with deep dives. The animal rises to the surface with its back arched, airs its enormous tail and plunges almost vertically. After four or five minutes at great depth it shoots up and performs a corkscrewing back-flip, returning to the water with an impact like a bomb blast.

Old-time whalers called these actions sounding and breaching. Humpbacks in Antarctic waters sometimes feed in such a manner, spiralling up from below. At other times it could be taken as a display of sheer exuberance. But deep sounding is also a humpback's main defensive manoeuvre. Because it makes unusual physical demands — the blood stops flowing, except between the heart and brain — it may require regular practice.

Even such a colossus has mortal enemies. Orcas — the so-called killer whales — and sharks attack humpbacks and other slow-moving, toothless whale species. So of course did we, within living memory of

Female southern right whales with calf

One of the large school of bottle-nosed dolphins Tursiops truncatus *that live at Monkey Mia, Shark Bay, in Western Australia*

many of the whales themselves. Significantly, sounding is said to become more frequent if a boat is near.

Explosions of air from a 'blowing' whale — cooling and condensing in cold weather so that they look like jets of steam — are evidence of a breathing system far more efficient than any land mammal's. The whale exerts tremendous muscular power to expel about ninety per cent of the used air in its lungs, compared with only about fifteen per cent expelled by humans. Breathing in, it takes advantage of modified body chemistry to store a much higher concentration of oxygen in its muscles and blood.

Leaping humpbacks and other big whales have capsized boats and drowned people. A wounded whale could use its tail with destructive force. Otherwise these massive cetaceans (members of the zoological order of Cetacea) are as tolerant and friendly as dolphins. A swimmer or board rider has nothing to fear if a whale should appear nearby. At worst, if people come between calves and their mothers, they may be gently bumped aside or hoisted with a tail fluke.

Deliberate interference with whales is forbidden by law. If the animals linger near populated areas, wildlife authorities impose rules to keep away the curious — especially those in motor-driven boats or low-flying aircraft. Excessive noise distresses whales and could disrupt their migration or breeding.

Whales and other cetaceans use sound to identify themselves to one another. The vocal feats of humpback bulls, presumably for the purpose of attracting and keeping together harems of cows, are the most famed of all. They communicate over long distances by singing songs.

At close quarters the sounds are so powerful that they resonate through the hull of a boat or inside the body cavities of a diver. Heard from greater distance, through a hydrophone placed in the water, the noises made by one whale can be distinguished as various rumbles, squeals, chirps, moans, hoots and whistles. They usually last for ten minutes or so, resuming after a pause.

If a tape recorder is used or notes taken — researchers invent their own shorthand — a pattern emerges. The sounds are always produced in the same sequence. It is the whale's individual signature tune, broadcast for hours on end during migration and at the breeding ground.

A humpback's theme tune

Other bulls of his tribe compose their songs from the same repertoire, but each puts the noises in a different order. Any other tribe of humpbacks — our west coast breeders as opposed to the eastern population, for example — makes up its variations from a different theme. And to the further confusion of scientists, all tribes make changes to their basic themes, season by season.

Humpbacks and other toothless whales are specialised to eat small marine organisms, filtered from the water. Australia's humpbacks feed almost exclusively on Antarctic krill — small prawn-like crustaceans that occur in dense swarms.

Fringed sheets of a horny material called baleen, similar to that of our fingernails, hang like curtains from the roof of a humpback's mouth. When feeding it takes huge gulps, then uses its tongue to push the water back out through the baleen. Hundreds of kilograms of krill are caught in the fringes.

Humpbacks were hunted not only for the oil in their blubber but also for baleen, which became the 'whalebone' stiffeners in corsets. Their numbers declined alarmingly. Original stocks were thought to be about 15 000 on the west coast and 10 000 on the east. By 1962 the highest estimates were 800 and 500 respectively. Protection in Australian waters was followed by international bans, and by the late 1980s the recovering populations exceeded a thousand on both coasts.

Before whaling, humpbacks are thought to have consumed more than ten million tonnes of Antarctic krill each summer. With their decline the krill proliferated. This apparent surplus of highly edible protein has attracted the attention of nations such as Japan and the Soviet Union. If proposals for massive harvesting proceed, expanding populations of protected humpbacks may face a new jeopardy — starvation.

Another baleen species, the southern right whale *Eubalaena australis,* was hit even harder by whaling. Breeding in temperate waters and given to seeking winter shelter in bays, it was easy to catch even by the old-fashioned methods of the early nineteenth century. Australian-based whaling was founded on this species, which gained its common name because it was the 'right' whale to catch.

Stocks were commercially exhausted before 1840. In this century no Australian sighting of a southern right whale was reported until 1983. Since then small numbers have been seen fairly regularly, generally around August and September, in bays between Sydney and Perth.

Toothed species such as the sperm and beaked whales and the various dolphins are loosely grouped with baleen whales but probably evolved from a different land-mammal ancestor. Fast-moving, they chase fishes and squid. Prey is identified and obstructions are avoided by a system of ultrasound echolocation, comparable with that of bats. The bigger toothed whales are extremely rare sights in Australian waters — unlike the dolphins.

Dolphins are annual breeders, generally in winter, after gestation periods of about eleven months. Females bear their young tail-first to avoid drowning them — a process that may well apply to all whales. Herds are migratory in colder waters but fairly sedentary in the tropics. In some secluded spots they form resident populations — most notably at Monkey Mia, in the sheltered shallows of Western Australia's Shark Bay. There some 150 dolphins are virtually tame, coming in to be fed by hand and letting people play with them.

These are bottle-nosed dolphins *Tursiops truncatus,* the world's most familiar species because of its coastal habits, its taste for sporting in the bow-waves of boats, and the ease with which it adapts to captivity and accepts training.

Bottle-nosed dolphins have provided most of what is known to science about dolphins in general. Publicity has focused on studies of their 'language' — the various clicks and squeaks with which they communicate. Separate purposes can be distinguished for certain sounds, but they are not put together in any way that can be truly described as a language.

Dolphins are big-brained

Special interest in the intelligence of dolphins derives from the fact that they have the biggest brains, in relation to body size, of any creatures other than humans. But there is little evidence that they think like us except in one respect. They seek sexual gratification for its own sake — aside from reproductive activity — and are far from fussy about how they get it.

After studying the Monkey Mia herd in deeper water, American zoologists reported in the authoritative journal *Science*: 'constant sexual interaction, both heterosexual and homosexual'. Males persistently mounted one another and also females not in season, they said.

Other scientists have collected reports of dolphins mounting small boats, and of masturbation both in the wild and in captivity. Erections have been observed in calves two days old, though they do not breed for at least ten years. And teams of adult males have been seen to capture a female and keep her with them as a sexual partner, regardless of the season.

Usually farther from the coastline, the common or saddleback dolphin *Delphinus delphis* is often seen. This is a cosmopolitan type, known from classical Greek statuary. It does not exceed two metres in length, while the bottle-nosed species can reach 3.5 metres.

Some dolphins of the far north frequent estuaries, lagoons and mangrove swamps and even enter the freshwater reaches of rivers. Our most common tropical dolphin is the Irrawaddy or snubfin *Orcaella brevirostris*. This grows to three metres, and in Asia it has been seen a thousand kilometres from the ocean.

The Irrawaddy dolphin has cold-water relatives so big that most people call them whales. Notorious among these is the orca *Orcinus orca*, reaching nine metres. Seals are its favourite food but it is occasionally a whale-killer. In a slow process, packs harass ailing or trapped baleen whales, tearing at their lips and tongues so that they can no longer feed. Both the orca and the smaller false killer whale *Pseudorca crassidens* frequently become stranded in winter storms in the south. □

STINGING SHARKS
Spring visitors breed in the shallows

Bullhead sharks *Heterodontus* evolved more than 200 million years ago and haven't changed a bit, according to fossil evidence. They are shellfish-eaters, equipped with crushing and grinding teeth and small mouths that cannot harm people. But among their primitive features is a defensive armament found in no other sharks — venom-charged spines at the front of each of the two dorsal fins.

Australia has two species: the Port Jackson shark *Heterodontus portusjacksoni* in all temperate mainland waters, and the crested Port Jackson shark *Heterodontus galeatus* off tropical Queensland. Bottom-dwellers, they usually live well out at depths as great as 200 metres. But around August they come inshore to breed in shallows. Treading on a spine — younger sharks have the sharpest — can result in severe localised pain and hours of muscle weakness in the leg.

Other August visitors from the deep, moving inshore to spawn, include various types of cuttlefishes. Closely related to squids, they are of interest to east coast fishermen because they are followed in by snapper. Albatrosses also feast on them. Often the birds' activity in the surf zone is the first sign of the arrival of cuttlefish. Soon the beach is littered with their stripped internal shells, which are shaped like little surfboards.

A Port Jackson shark (above) in a rock-pool – note the spines in front of both the dorsal fins. The giant Australian cuttlefish Sepia apama (right) also spawns inshore

SEPTEMBER

THIS MONTH'S WEATHER

Rainfall is at its lowest in the tropics and all along the east coast. This is the driest month, on average, for both Sydney and Brisbane. Rains in the south and southwest start to dwindle. Average daytime temperatures rise noticeably in all regions, but nights remain chilly in the southeastern high country.

AROUND THE COUNTRY	RAIN (mm)	MAX. (°C)	MIN. (°C)	SUN hrs/day
Adelaide	57	18	9	6.2
Alice Springs	10	27	10	9.9
Brisbane	34	24	13	8.9
Canberra	52	16	3	7.3
Darwin	18	32	23	9.8
Hobart	53	15	6	5.7
Melbourne	59	17	8	5.6
Perth	80	20	10	7.4
Port Hedland	1	32	15	10.8
Sydney	69	20	11	7.1
Townsville	11	27	17	9.4
Weipa	6	33	20	8.6

A rainbow lorikeet Trichoglossus haematodus *of the eastern race feeding on nectar*

The Queensland lungfish has many unusual features, including large, flipper-like fins, which it uses to walk along the riverbed

Old-fashioned fish get frisky

In spring, as rivers shrink and backwaters stagnate, the lungfish takes a deep breath before breeding

Murky water churns in a weed-choked pool. A stout, cylindrical fish surfaces, its tail formation suggesting a strangely shortened eel. But it has obvious scales, and pairs of fleshy side fins like the flippers of a seal. Its actions are even more odd. Mouth gaping, it exhales with an audible gasp. Then it takes a gulp of air and submerges.

The Queensland lungfish *Neoceratodus forsteri*, equipped to breathe out of water though it also has gills, is a rare relic of ancient natural history. Sharing an ancestry with amphibians such as frogs and salamanders, lungfishes flourished worldwide until about 200 million years ago. Isolated descendants of different types are found in Africa and South America. Many kinds used to live in the Australian region but only this one survives. It is identical to fossils more than 100 million years old.

European colonisers of southeastern Queensland came across the lungfish in only two rivers and their tributary systems: the Burnett, flowing out through Bundaberg, and the Mary, which gave Maryborough its name. They feasted on what they called 'Burnett salmon' up to 1.5 metres long, some weighing more than forty kilos. For once the fine eating qualities of a newly discovered animal worked in its favour. Envious settlers farther south introduced young lungfish into their own waterways. Now totally protected, the species thrives in many creeks and streams around Brisbane.

Lungfish are normally sluggish bottom-dwellers, lying in deep pools of still or slow-flowing water. Rainfall in their region is scantiest in winter and spring. Flows weaken and some creeks stop running. Oxygen is depleted by the rotting of organic matter, and further lowered at night by the activity of aquatic plants and algae. Then fish come up for air, refilling their single lungs once or twice an hour.

Spring is also their breeding season. Sexually mature fish, probably many years old, start pairing up in June. Constantly together in their movements, some pairs spawn as early as August. A weed patch is chosen in shallow water near a bank. The female swims over and through the plants, followed closely by the male. He repeatedly bumps her cloacal area with his snout. Then, in a gesture reminiscent of many courting birds, he signals his readiness by shaking a plant stem in his mouth. The pair spawn for up to an hour, diving in and out of the weeds with their tails wagging vigorously.

Lungfish in miniature

The fertilised eggs — coated in jelly like those of a frog — cling to the weeds for three to six weeks, depending on water temperatures. Embryos and hatched larvae develop in much the same way as those of amphibians but there is no sudden transformation (such as when a tadpole turns into a frog).

Larvae feed on egg-yolk for six to eight weeks, then start to eat tiny insects and crustaceans. In their fourth month they can breathe air and their fins start to form. By autumn they are miniature replicas of their parents. Subsequent growth is slow: the biggest lungfish are thought to be over a hundred years old.

Counterparts in South America and Africa can live for months without water,

A lungfish egg containing an embryo a few days before hatching

surviving drought by cocooning themselves in mud. The Queensland lungfish cannot do this, though it can live in the open air if it is shaded and its skin is kept moist.

Tolerance of drought or the seasonal drying of streams is a notable feature of many crustaceans, including most freshwater crayfishes. Well-known species such as the yabby *Cherax destructor* and the Murray lobster *Euastacus armatus*

burrow into the mud of drying creekbeds. Western Australia's marron *Cherax tenuimanus* does not have this capability and is restricted to permanent bodies of water. Some smaller species, on the other hand, need no standing water at all — they live in damp pastures and regularly sprinkled lawns. During the winter in colder regions, hibernation in riverbank burrows is common among crayfishes.

One Australian fish is known to aestivate, becoming dormant in summer as part of its normal cycle. The salamanderfish *Lepidogalaxias salamandroides* lives in seasonal streams and pools on coastal sandplains in the southwest, east of Cape Leeuwin. As its habitat dries it burrows into the bed and secretes a sheath of mucus. Its rate of metabolism drops and what little energy it needs is taken from its own fat. Revived by winter rains, it breeds early in spring and dies soon after.

There is some evidence that the Tasmanian mudfish *Galaxias cleaveri* may also aestivate. Its species was unknown to science until an Ulverstone farmer dynamited a tree stump and found a slender little fish among the roots — 350 metres

One of the most common freshwater crayfishes is the yabby Cherax destructor *which grows up to 150 millimetres in length*

The salamanderfish is found in Western Australia and is distinguished from Galaxias *species in possessing scales*

from the nearest creek. Kept for months in a tin of water, it persistently jumped out and had to be retrieved from the farmer's tomato patch.

This galaxias is one of at least twenty species of small, scaleless fishes that are often called native minnows. Various types are found throughout the southern half of the mainland as well as in Tasmania. Their contrasting habits and breeding styles are of interest not only to naturalists but also to freshwater anglers,

because they are a major food source for introduced trout.

Several galaxias species migrate up and down rivers and spend their larval and juvenile stages at sea, while others are stay-at-homes. And a few species exhibit both habits, depending on their locality. The most intriguing of the travellers is the climbing galaxias *Galaxias brevipinnis*, the type from which all the others are thought to have developed.

Adults of this species live in the upper

reaches of rivers, where they spawn in autumn. Larvae are carried downstream and out to sea. They develop there for about six months, re-entering rivers in spring as transparent juveniles. If they encounter waterfalls or boulders on their way upstream they skirt around the water flow and wriggle up rock faces, using their pectoral and pelvic fins.

Juveniles of the most widely known species of native minnow, the common jollytail *Galaxias maculatus*, also return from the oceans in early spring. But their life began differently. Their parents migrated downstream in autumn, to estuary margins where they waited for the spring tide following a full or new moon. Then they spawned in shoals. Each female jollytail deposited thousands of eggs among flooded riverside plants, as far from the main flow of the river as she could get. With tides weakening, the eggs were stranded for two weeks. Flooding by the next spring tide triggered their hatching and out to sea went the larvae.

The life cycle of eels

Freshwater eels also have a marine phase. In their case it is for the purpose of spawning, and it comes towards the end of very long lives. Female short-finned eels *Anguilla australis* migrate at anything from ten to thirty-five years of age, according to New Zealand studies; on average they spend more than twenty years in rivers. Males of their species are said to average fourteen years before migration. Our biggest freshwater eel, the long-finned *Anguilla reinhardtii*, has a New Zealand relative that is thought to wait sixty years before going to sea.

Though little is known in detail, Australia's major eel species are believed to spawn in deep Coral Sea waters near New Caledonia. Larvae drift in the East Austra-

The common jollytail Galaxias maculatus *is probably the most widespread of the family Galaxiidae, occurring throughout southern Australia*

The short-headed lamprey's mouth is a sucking disc lined with horny teeth

but for an unexplained reason, both show peaks at three-yearly intervals.

Fairly predictable upstream runs and gatherings can be observed in certain districts. On September nights, for example, long-finned elvers are likely to be travelling in groups up Sydney's Hawkesbury-Nepean river system, swimming close to the banks where the flow against them is weakest. They mass in enormous numbers at the foot of the Warragamba Dam. Many manage to squirm up steep, even vertical barriers, but where possible they move up through bordering vegetation. Older eels often travel long distances over wet ground to avoid obstacles or escape drying pools.

Migratory lampreys climb barriers easily, using the sucking discs with which they attach themselves to marine fish. The cycle of these parasites is a reversal of that followed by eels. They live in the sea but migrate into rivers to spawn, scooping holes in upstream beds and covering the eggs with sand or gravel. The larvae stay in fresh water for three years, eating micro-organisms, before metamorphosing into the sea-going, parasitic form.

Australia's two migratory lampreys, the pouched *Geotria australis* and the short-headed *Mordacia mordax*, generally arrive to spawn in early spring. A third species, *Mordacia praecox*, spends all its life in fresh water and is not parasitic.

Also on their way up southeastern rivers in September, to the delight of anglers, are Australian bass *Macquaria novemaculeata*. Big adults are returning from a winter season of spawning in estuaries. But these fish are not climbers. Unless the rivers are in flood, many will be thwarted by weirs, dams and silting. Their new young, struggling upstream later in spring and summer, will have an even harder time.□

lian Current for up to three years, feeding on other plankton, before reaching Australian waters. Crossing the edge of the continental shelf they transform into transparent cylinders called 'glass eels', toothless and unable to eat. When they reach estuaries they take on colour, grow new teeth and rapidly gain size.

Elvers, as these recognisable juveniles are called, may head upstream almost immediately, or wash back and forth in estuarine tides for weeks. There is no particular season for their invasions, or for that matter for the departure of adults. Both movements are frequently associated with local changes in water levels —

A FISH THAT SCALES TREES

Mudskippers crawl, hop — and climb

Mudskippers spend all the time they can on land, hunting insects and other invertebrates on tropical mangrove flats or the banks of tidal rivers. They crawl using their fins, and if alarmed they hop — not necessarily to the water but often to safer ground.

If they are still hungry when the tide comes in, they elbow their way up the aerial roots or trunks of mangroves. Males, raising colourful dorsal fins, even do their courting in the open air. It is hard to believe that they do not breathe it.

In fact mudskippers are gill-breathing fish and have to return to the water frequently. They buy their time on land by carrying extra supplies of water in their gill chambers. By rolling their heads about, they slosh the water through the gills and extract its oxygen.

Two mudskippers Periophthalmus *square up to one another with a threat display*

The water rat Hydromys chrysogaster *hunts mainly around sunset and sleeps in a burrow at night*

Tooth beats claw in an underwater duel

On a riverbed somewhere in Australia's southwest, a marron — one of the biggest of freshwater crayfishes — crawls ponderously among the granite boulders. It is hungry, having just emerged from the burrow where it spent the winter in hibernation, and its massive claws rake patches of silt for morsels of decaying flesh or plant matter. A water rat dives down, her fast-moving shadow and trail of bubbles the only warnings. Her incisors snap at the marron's head, menacing its feelers and protruding eyes.

The two are matched in size and weight, but the marron's reactions are slow. As it raises its claws to protect its head the rat dodges and darts in from the side. With chopping bites she detaches one claw at the base joint. In a second attack the other claw is severed.

After snatching a breath at the surface the rat dives again and immobilises her disarmed victim by biting off its legs. The marron is dragged to the riverbank to be deposited in a favourite eating place, screened by a heavy growth of sedges. Satisfied that no intruder is around to steal her food, the rat goes back into the

In spring and summer water rats claim easy pickings among the animals of streams, swamps and dams

The false water rat lacks webbing on its hind feet and grows to 230 millimetres

water to retrieve the flesh-filled claws. As darkness falls she will dine at leisure.

The female water rat is feeding herself up as she enters her breeding season, and she is among the most versatile of flesh-eaters. Next time she feels hungry her prey may be a duckling — seized by the legs from below — a fish, a frog or a turtle. For snacks she takes aquatic snails and bugs. On land she may eat lizards, small mammals and crawling insects, or raid birds' nests for eggs and nestlings.

What the British call a water rat is really just a type of vole. *Hydromys chrysogaster*, peculiar to the Australia-New Guinea region, is a true rat adapted to swimming. The broad, paddle-shaped hind feet are partially webbed, the tail is flattened to aid steering, and the fur is so dense that it sheds water.

Though seldom abundant, the species occurs around permanent bodies of water all over the country. Swamp draining has cost it some old habitats, but irrigation and dam-building have provided new ones. Some water rats hunt from the shores of brackish estuaries, harbours and even sheltered ocean beaches. Among

their favoured foods are mussels — marine or freshwater — wrenched from rocks. They can easily crack them with their teeth, but in secure feeding territories they prefer to leave them in the sun so that the dying shellfish open of their own accord.

Reaching the size of a rabbit, the water rat is among the biggest of native or introduced rats. It is also one of the least nocturnal, hunting mainly around sunset but sometimes in broad daylight. This is because its relatively small eyes are probably not very effective at finding underwater prey in poor light.

Burrows for resting and maternal nesting are tunnelled into banks. Maturing at about eight months of age, a well-fed water rat is capable of breeding at any time of year. But for most the season starts when prey is most abundant, in spring in temperate and subtropical regions and summer in the monsoonal north. Up to five litters of three or four young, spaced about six weeks apart, may be produced in an exceptional season. Two litters are more usual.

Suckled for about four weeks, young water rats are largely dependent on a share of their mothers' prey for a further month. Only after that do their coats become fully waterproof. Water rats moult twice a year. The heavier winter coat of soft, fine hairs, likened to that of a beaver, was commercially prized before the species came under legal protection.

Males especially are fiercely combative in defence of feeding territories. This tends to limit the growth of populations. Predators also impose a control, many water rats falling foul of snakes, bigger fishes, cats, birds of prey, and, in the north, crocodiles.

The false water rat *Xeromys myoides*, not much bigger than a house mouse, seems to be very rare. It has been noticed in scattered locations between the Top End and southeastern Queensland, among tidal mangroves as well as around grassy freshwater swamps. At least partly carnivorous, it has water-repellent fur but its feet lack webbing.

The vegetarian swamp rat

The swamp rat *Rattus lutreolus* too was originally supposed to be semi-aquatic. But it swims only to flee from flooding. Largely vegetarian — though never averse to eating insects — it chews through dense grasses or heaths to make runways that enable it to move around under cover, often by day.

Common near eastern and southern coasts and also in Tasmania, swamp rats are thought to have been an important source of Aboriginal food. Their breeding starts in early spring, its success depending on good rains and the sustained

The female bush rat Rattus fuscipes *has eight teats and rears about five young*

growth of grasses. The gestation period is only three weeks — compared with five for water rats — and females can reproduce at three months, so the species is potentially much more prolific. However, most swamp rats die after only one breeding season.

In forests with dense undergrowths of ferns and shrubs, a similar breeding pattern is shown by the closely related bush rat *Rattus fuscipes*. It is more strictly nocturnal and relies heavily on insects in its diet. But it readily eats fungi, one of the few foods quickly available after bushfires.

Juveniles colonising burnt areas in the following season establish populations that attain freakish densities, in the same way as native mice (see page 18).

Altogether Australia has seven native *Rattus* species, adapted to every climatic regime. They are fundamentally much the same as the black and brown rats that came as stowaways in ships from Europe and America. All share the one Asiatic ancestry. The native species have evolved from rats that reached Australia through Indonesia no more than fifteen million years ago.□

The prehensile-tailed rat grows up to 360 millimetres long

LOOK WHAT THE CAT BROUGHT IN

A rat with a telling tail

For a long time prehensile-tailed rats *Pogonomys mollipilosus* have been known in New Guinea, and noted for the softness of their fur. But they were not recognised in Australia until 1974, when a pet cat took one home to a hotel on the Atherton Tableland. Many more have been found since in upland rainforests on the Cape York Peninsula.

These rats climb trees at night to eat leaves and nuts. They curl their long tails upwards — unlike any other Australian climber — to grip branches and twigs. By day they shelter in burrows, perhaps in big family groups. Breeding is probably confined to spring and early summer. The species' closest evolutionary link is believed to be with the water rat.

Safe within the coils of a constrictor

Female pythons show a devotion known in no other snake, and brood their eggs for months

Bloated with her last good meal of the season — a doe rabbit and her entire litter of young — the carpet python remains coiled in the victims' nesting chamber. At intervals of half an hour or more the mid-section of her body convulses and she lays a long, soft-skinned egg. After depositing twelve or fifteen she coils more tightly around them, compressing them into a sticky cluster, and goes to sleep.

Her close guardianship of the eggs will be virtually constant until they hatch in two months or so. She is unlikely to move except to void her excreta or to investigate vibrations that could signal the approach of an intruder. Marauding rats or goannas will stand no chance against her.

Pythons are the only snakes to display any instinct for maternal care. Other egg-layers hide their clutches as best they can, then get on with their own lives. Live-bearing species abandon their young immediately — if, indeed, they refrain from eating some of them.

In spite of what may seem to be an advanced strategy for the survival of their kind, pythons are primitive. They belong to the same family as South America's boas, sharing with them the strongest anatomical reminders of a lizard ancestry. Visible evidence of this includes vestigial hind legs that stick out as tiny spurs on each side of the cloacal vent. They are more prominent in males, and are used to aid penetration during mating.

Lacking venom, pythons also share with boas a method of overpowering large prey by constriction. A victim is grasped first by biting, then coils are thrown around it and relentlessly tightened. It may be strangled by pressure on the windpipe or suffocated because it cannot inflate its lungs. No prey is crushed to death — though blood vessels may burst.

As soon as a victim stops struggling it is gradually swallowed. Double rows of back-curving teeth draw the python's head over its prey. Jaw connections are so loose and the skin so elastic that a python with a head smaller than a man's hand can devour a wallaby.

Pythons are as shy of people as any other snake. They flee if they detect footfalls nearby, but may be surprised while basking on the branches of trees. No python will coil around a human unless it is being held, or bite unless it is cornered. Bites rarely do serious damage in themselves, but the deep multiple punctures carry a high risk of infection.

Mainly nocturnal and fairly slow-moving, pythons rely heavily on finding sleeping prey — especially birds. They hunt both in trees and on the ground, also seeking mammals of manageable size and in some cases frogs, lizards and other

The amethystine python is found in northern Queensland in a variety of habitats

The children's python (left) is one of the smallest of Liasis species, averaging only seventy-five centimetres in length. It is widespread throughout the northern two-thirds of Australia. The green python Chondropython viridis (right) is a nocturnal tree-dwelling snake that preys on small mammals and birds. This is a juvenile — it will gradually change colour from lemon yellow to emerald green over a two-week period. The common tree snake (below) is found around the north and eastern coasts, and for some distance inland

snakes. Hollows in trees and logs are favoured daytime resting places, but rock crevices and the dens of burrowing animals are often used.

The boldly patterned carpet python *Morelia spilota* is the most widespread and best-known type. Averaging about two metres in length but sometimes reaching four metres, it is equally at home in rainforests, on arid sandplains or in any kind of habitat in between, except where winters are coldest. Markings and colours vary regionally: a distinctive subspecies in coastal New South Wales is called the diamond python.

North Queensland's amethystine python *Morelia amethistina* — also called a scrub or rock python — is among the world's biggest snakes. Average specimens measure three to four metres and weigh more than twenty kilos. Authorities have reservations about a record of 8.4 metres, claimed for a monster shot in 1948, but reliable measurements of snakes over six metres have been made.

Pythons shed their skins about every six weeks. The amethystine species, basically brownish with darker bands, gets its name from the iridescent green sheen of a fresh skin, which is especially brilliant if the snake is seen basking in sunshine. Its habitats range from rainforests to grassy woodlands, and even to the poor scrubs of coral cays in Torres Strait.

Wet and dry habitats

Prominent among other widespread and sizable pythons are species of *Liasis*. One stays close to water, dropping or creeping in if it is alarmed. Others occupy habitats so parched that they live inside termite mounds, preying on geckoes.

Tree snakes, although completely unrelated, show a pythonish ability to use their coils to subdue larger prey. They too are egg-layers in spring. The nocturnal brown tree snake *Boiga irregularis* is fierce and venomous, but its fangs are at the rear of the jaws. Common or green tree snakes *Dendrelaphis punctulatus*, which are active by day and sometimes shelter in houses in the north and east, are not venomous.□

Swallowed for their own protection

The inside story of our oddest frogs

In certain mountain streams of southern and central Queensland, and perhaps in other places, gastric-brooding frogs spawn in early spring. At least, biologists suppose that they are doing so — they are hardly ever seen.

These frogs spend all day submerged, hidden under rocks. Even at night they do not leave their streams but sit on or cling to rocks. The first species, *Rheobatrachus silus*, was not discovered until 1973, in the Blackall and Conondale Ranges. Specimens taken in 1982, 800 kilometres to the north near Mackay, turned out to be a different type and were named *Rheobatrachus vitellinus*.

There is nothing remarkable about the frogs' appearance. But the revelation of their method of

The male gastric-brooding frog Rheobatrachus vitellinus (above) grows up to fifty-five millimetres, but the female is larger, up to eighty millimetres long

Fletcher's frog (right) grows up to fifty millimetres

The brown-striped frog (below) has a call like a hammer striking an anvil

raising young astonished the scientific world. Immediately after spawning, females gulp down their own fertilised eggs before they can be swept away in the fast-running waters. The eggs hatch and the young go through a full tadpole stage in their mothers' stomachs before being regurgitated as self-sufficient froglets. Somehow the flow of digestive juices is cut off while they are inside.

More prominent amphibians that start to breed early in spring include the brown-striped frog *Limnodynastes peronii*. Often misleadingly called the Sydney bullfrog, it occurs throughout the east from tropical Queensland to Tasmania. The spotted grass frog *Limnodynastes tasmaniensis* has an even greater range, extending west into South Australia.

Fletcher's frog *Lechriodus fletcheri*, found in subtropical eastern forests, emerges onto roads and tracks to exploit puddles forming in wheel ruts and horses' hoofprints. The easy opportunism of its breeding does little to boost this frog's populations, however — the tadpoles eat one another.□

Birth control: a strategy for survival

A stick insect's eggs are programmed so that hatchings are spaced over a period of months — or even years

A woody capsule, easily mistaken for a big seed, has lain in ground litter for months. Now, under cover of darkness, one end is pushed open. A nymphal stick insect wriggles out, stretching its slender body and flexing its limbs before crawling slowly to a nearby plant stem. It may spend the rest of its life munching the leaves of the first shrub that it climbs.

In all likelihood this will be the same shrub that its mother lived in. Last autumn she dropped hundreds of eggs from the branches. But whatever influences of temperature, humidity or lengthening daylight brought on this nymph's development and cause it to break out now, they do not work on all of its brothers and sisters. Many will not emerge for a month or two. Some will wait until next spring — or the spring after that.

Confinement to the one tiny area, generation after generation, is common among stick insects. Such species cannot afford to destroy their food supply by overpopulation. Nor can they risk having their whole annual crop of young coming out when the food may be missing — because of a bushfire, for example.

Somehow, during the weeks that it takes individual females to produce and discharge their eggs, genetic variations are introduced. These bring about different environmental responses in the eggs, causing them to hatch at different times.

Physical variations too show up in the nymphal stages and in adult forms. In the one species, some individuals may have horns, spines or lumps and others not. Some may be green, others brown. The simplest way to identify many types is through their distinctive egg cases.

Species vary widely in size and build. The longest, reaching twenty-five centimetres, is the east coast's *Acrophylla titan*. But *Eurycnema goliath*, found mostly in the north, is the heaviest. A flattened type in tropical rainforests imitates leaves; most others have very slender forms that help them escape notice among stems or twigs. One group is so thin that its members rest on grass stems.

Feeding mainly at night, nymphs and adults — generally not much different in size or form — climb instinctively, waving

The mainly tropical Eurycnema goliath *is shorter but heavier than* Acrophylla titan

Both sexes of the giant stick insect Acrophylla titan *have large mottled wings*

their forelegs above them and hooking onto anything they touch. At rest by day they 'freeze', often in grotesque attitudes. But if slightly disturbed they rock or sway rhythmically. If more alarmed, they may drop to the ground and not move for hours.

Even the types that feed on trees and have functional wings — usually only the males — do not use them to escape danger. They fly occasionally to light on summer nights, diverted from mating missions. Parthenogenesis — reproduction without sexual intercourse, from unfertilised eggs — is common.

Winds may scatter eggs dropped from taller trees. In some seasons species such as *Didymuria violescens* and *Podacanthus wilkinsoni* breed so successfully that extensive areas of eucalypt forest are entirely stripped of leaves. Such population surges, showing peaks every second year, peter out as the insects exhaust the food supply or fall victim to birds such as currawongs and cuckooshrikes — sometimes providing the bulk of their diet.

September in most regions outside the tropics is also a peak month for the hatching of grasshoppers and crickets, again to the great benefit of birdlife and many small mammals. The 'singing' that most species are known for will not be

Myrmecia, the workers growing to between one and three centimetres long, are a deadly exception. They paralyse and tear apart crawling insects and other invertebrates of relatively huge size — not to feed themselves but to take home for the older larvae in their nests.

Ant ancestors are wasps

Bulldog ants, which are known variously as bull ants, jumpers, jackjumpers or inchmen according to the region, belong to a primitive family that survives now only in Australia and New Caledonia. They form an evolutionary link with ancient wasps, which are thought to have been the ancestors of all ants and bees.

The sheer length and penetrating force of the venomous sting in a bulldog ant's tail (most other ants have them too, in proportion to their size) make it a potential menace to public safety. Stings inflicted on more than one occasion, or perhaps the first sting received by someone already sensitive to wasp venom, can induce a dangerous allergic reaction. A nip by the sawtoothed mandibles — the ant needs to get a grip before inflicting its sting — is harmless.

Worker bulldog ants are usually not aggressive unless a threat arises close to their nests in warm weather. Wider-ranging foragers mind their own business, but should not be picked up. Nests start as simple holes, the size of five or ten-cent coins, in the soil of well-drained slopes. As they develop, cones of excavated soil build up around the entrances. In their social order and breeding patterns, bulldog ants are much like other ants (see November, page 276).□

The stick insect Didymuria violescens *is a pest of eucalypts. Only the male can fly*

A bulldog ant Myrmecia gulosa *with the head of a long-horned grasshopper or katydid*

heard until they mature in weeks or months. Various methods of noisy scraping, called stridulation, make use of special adaptations to legs or wings and are usually employed in courtship. Cicadas (see December, page 298) do not stridulate; they are sap-suckers from another insect order, with their own exclusive sound equipment.

The order of grasshoppers and crickets comprises more than 1500 species in Australia. Adapted to all climates, some feeding by day and some at night — nearly always on plant matter — they take forms so varied that in many cases their relationship could not be guessed. One group looks like stick insects, others like cockroaches or lice.

Along with prominent long-horned grasshoppers such as katydids, the migratory short-horned grasshoppers that we usually call locusts (see March, page 88), and the various prolific species that leap and creep in lawns and pastures, come obscure burrowers and cave dwellers. Three species of tiny crickets *Myrmecophila* live their whole lives in ants' nests, licking their hosts' secretions.

Ants of many kinds eat the eggs of grasshoppers, crickets and stick insects. Few are big enough to seize and sting the nymphs and adults. Bulldog ants

A male satin bowerbird Ptilonorhynchus violaceus *puts the final touches to his love-nest — the blue objects emphasise his colouring*

Playboys with an urge to paint

Companionable hisses are exchanged as a weary band of satin bowerbirds alights in a stand of negrohead beech. All winter long the birds were foraging on east coast lowlands, plundering many an orchardist's crop. September's rising temperatures have brought them back to their breeding territory, at the edge of a rainforest on the Great Dividing Range.

These are creatures of the tall timber. They feed on fruits and insects in the forest canopy, and roost and nest on lofty

Seeking the favours of wandering females, bowerbirds fuss over custom-built boudoirs, with particular attention to colour schemes

branches. Yet they and other bowerbird species — found only in Australia and New Guinea — choose to mate on the ground. And this is the most elaborately staged ceremony in the world of birds.

Most satin bowerbirds wear greenish plumage. They are females, or else males less than six or seven years old. Senior males, eager to breed, are a glossy blueblack. As the homecoming group disperses, each of these darker birds makes directly for his own private estate.

A layer of sticks occupies most of a small clearing, shielded by logs and shrubbery. It provides a firm platform for more sticks, wedged in so that they stand upright. Twin rows, less than ten centimetres apart, are aligned north and south. Arching over at the top, the bower that they form is about forty centimetres high and similarly long — just the right size to accommodate a visitor. Inside it, as spring progresses, the builder hopes to mate one by one with as many females as he can attract to the clearing.

Over past seasons he has met many a crisis. Falling branches have flattened his construction; dingoes once wrecked it while chasing a wallaby. This year there is only some tidying-up to do. Sagging sticks in the walls are tweaked back into position, and a few new ones added.

Next the bird works on the platform aprons at both ends of the bower. These will be stages from which he entertains his guest, cavorting and singing to excite her sexual urge. He is busiest at the sunny northern end. As he clears away a rotting carpet of leaves, fallen since autumn, colourful objects appear. Along with hard fruits, feathers, snail shells and moulted insect casings are manmade oddments. For years the bird has collected pieces of glass, plastic, cardboard and so on — nearly all of them blue.

Throughout spring and summer he will take every opportunity to brighten the decor. Blue flowers will be brought home. Blue or purple berries will be strewn over the platform — and promptly thrown out if they are of a kind that ripens to red.

A few items of ornamental bric-a-brac may be creamy yellow. But the preference of the satin bowerbird *Ptilonorhynchus violaceus* is overwhelmingly for blue. This

The brightly coloured regent bowerbird displaying to a female in his bower

The golden bowerbird displays to females from a perch between twin towers

sets off his colouring, which is itself an advertisement of male maturity and sexuality, to best advantage.

Other species adorn the forecourts of their bowers with objects of different colours. In the case of the spotted bowerbird of the inland, *Chlamydera maculata*, males simply collect whatever is whitest or shiniest. Small, sun-bleached bones of sheep, favoured since the expansion of European agriculture, are rivalled now by ringpull tops from beer and soft-drink cans.

Painting and decorating

Before remote upland homesteads received electricity, and washing machines replaced coppers and tubs, the satin bowerbird's most prized baubles were laundry bluebags. Used much like teabags, they contained soluble blocks of dye and other chemicals to prevent the yellowing of white clothing. Foresters commonly came across bowers surrounded by the gaudy little bags, cheekily snatched from farmhouse windowsills where they were put to dry.

Some birds discovered another use for bluebags. Pecking them open, they moistened the contents with saliva and daubed the paste on the inside of their bower walls. (They were not alone in this

innovation: in far-off Arnhem Land, mission supplies of Reckitt's Blue, used with traditional ochres, also inspired a new look in Aboriginal rock painting.)

Charcoal is a more natural colouring agent, employed by most satin bowerbirds in sprucing up their boudoirs. They fly to dry, fire-prone woodlands and nibble off the more powdery parts of burnt logs and stumps. By the time they get home their bills are full of a runny mixture of carbon and saliva. The side of the bill, slightly open and oozing this solution, is wiped against individual sticks in the bower.

Close observers may see a piece of bark picked up and held inside the bill just before the painting starts. In earlier days this was thought to be used as a brush — a sensationally rare example of birds employing tools. More plausibly, it plugs the front of the bill and prevents a wasteful spilling of the mixture.

The urge to paint is powerful. Satin bowerbirds that cannot find charcoal resort to mashing up dark-juiced berries. A captive bird in a New York zoo chewed dry wood into a grey paste and applied it to his bower. He would not have been pleased with the colour, however. Only dark pigmentation satisfies the satin bowerbird. Other species select plant materials that produce yellows, greens and so on.

When work on the bower and stages is complete the bird spends long periods of each day perched on a branch overlooking the site. If a female is drawn to the clearing by his persistent calling and enticed into the bower by the decorations, he flies down and immediately starts a courtship display. Eyes bulging and glistening, he rises on his toes and prances about stiff-legged. Wings are raised and drooped in alternating shows of aggression and supplication. Bright objects are picked up and waved, and sometimes tossed in the air. He emits buzzing and whirring noises almost nonstop, occasionally introducing the mimicked calls of other birds.

After copulation the female flies to a distant nesting site that the male probably never sees. She alone has built the nest, a leaf-lined bowl of twigs placed in a fork of an upright branch or against a trunk. Unaided she will incubate her eggs — usually two — for three weeks and tend the nestlings for a similar period. Fledglings are led to a sheltered nursery area where the mother feeds them for a further two months.

Males are busy at their bowers all through summer, long after there is any likelihood of mating. Their activity seems to be recreational. Immature males have a communal playground where they make mock displays to one another and practise their building skills on a rudimentary bower. Females also gather in a common area, usually just a clearing.

Mature male regent bowerbirds *Sericulus chrysocephalus*, found in rainforests near the mid-east coast, are the prettiest of the Australian group. Their bowers are painted inside with yellow leaf juices, complementing the brilliant colour of their heads and flight feathers.

But this bird maintains other, bowerless clearings over an extensive territory. He also calls from these and if a female approaches, he displays and mates on the spot. His construction work does not seem really necessary: a dancing exhibition of his plumage is stimulus enough.

A bridge-and-tower bower
Enormous bowers are erected by the smallest species, the golden bowerbird *Prionodura newtoniana*. Found on steep slopes in the highest ranges of far northern Queensland, they are made altogether differently from others of the group. Towers of sticks are assembled around the trunks of two young trees about a metre apart. The towers reach as high as three metres to meet a branch or a buttress root. This forms a bridge on which the courting bird sings and displays.

Some New Guinea bowerbirds build single 'maypole' towers, encircling them with rings of other vegetation. Their style

During breeding the male green catbird actively defends a small area around the nest

and that of our 'avenue' builders (such as the satin bowerbird), diverging in the remote past, are thought to have a common origin in the 'bridge' method practised by the golden bowerbird.

The drably coloured tooth-billed catbird *Ailuroedus dentirostris*, occurring in the same part of Queensland, is zoologically classed as a bowerbird but acquired a different name because of its wailing territorial call. And it does not build. The male 'bower' is simply a small level area kept clear of litter. He decks it with about a dozen big leaves, cut from their tree with a notched bill and carefully laid to show their pale undersides. The leaves are replaced daily.

Much more colourful are green catbirds *Ailuroedus crassirostris*, which retain a similar practice although they have abandoned polygamy. Pair-bonds are apparently formed for life and courtships in early spring are uncomplicated routines of displaying, chasing and preening. The female alone builds the nest and incubates the eggs, but receives her mate's help in feeding the young on fruit and beetles. Either parent will respond to a threat to the nest by dropping to the ground and feigning injury.

Birds-of-paradise, nearly always polygamous and occupying habitual courting places, are usually identified with New Guinea. But that island cannot lay claim to all of them. Australia has four species. Three of these, all exhibiting typical bird-of-paradise mating behaviour but lacking the extravagant male nuptial plumes of their New Guinea relatives, are called

riflebirds. The name is thought to derive from the best-known species bearing colours reminiscent of British infantry uniforms in the Napoleonic Wars.

Mature males of this species, the paradise riflebird *Ptilorus paradiseus* of sub-

The mating display of Victoria's riflebird

tropical Queensland and northern New South Wales, start in September to call and display from high branches of rainforest trees. Wings are fanned and flapped, belly and flanks are puffed out, the head is thrown back and wagged and the long, curved bill is opened and shut to give vivid flashes of pale lime inside the mouth.

Feeding at this time of year mainly on spiders, insects and grubs — most fruits will come later — paradise riflebirds move silently in the rainforest canopy and are generally hard to see from below. Glimpses may be caught of birds hanging upside down to snatch berries or probe under bark.

Flock-feeding parrots

Even more acrobatic in the treetops — and often notoriously noisy — are the flock-feeding parrots that start to breed in early spring. Lorikeets form the biggest flocks, and together with rosellas are dominant in virtually every well-watered and wooded area of Australia.

Lorikeets are given the scientific name *Trichoglossus*, meaning 'hairy-tongue'. Their tongues do not in fact have hairs but small, fleshy protuberances that work like a brush in mopping nectar and pollen from the blossoms of a huge range of native trees and many introduced species. Insects are eaten incidentally, and sometimes fruits are taken.

The rainbow lorikeet *Trichoglossus haematodus* is the most widespread of its group and shows typical characteristics. Birds roost communally in hundreds, breaking up into feeding flocks of up to about fifty when they go out at dawn.

A USE FOR CAST-OFF CLOTHING
Riflebirds go in for exotic nest decoration

Female riflebirds lay two eggs in crude, bulky bowls made of almost any available plant material. Two species commonly add a curious finishing touch. They wrap or drape the outside of their nests with sloughed-off snakeskins.

No New Guinea members of their bird-of-paradise group do this — nor, in a land where snakes are so abundant, does any other Australian bird. In Africa, Asia and the Americas, on the other hand, several species do.

It has been suggested that the skins may scare off predators or help returning birds locate their nests. Some ornithologists lean to the view that the practice began accidentally and gives the birds pleasure. Paradise riflebirds of mid-eastern Australia sometimes also decorate nests with moss, ferns or flowers.

The female paradise riflebird builds and decorates the nest with no help from the male

They may cover more than a hundred kilometres in daily round trips to stands of blossoming trees. Each flight is direct and accompanied by incessant screeching.

The homecoming reunion each evening is noisiest of all. Excited birds alight in the roosting trees, chatter to neighbours and preen their mates, then take off for flitting sorties so that they can come back to do it all again. Rushing to and fro, they may socialise for half an hour before settling down for the night.

Animated behaviour among big flocks makes individual studies difficult. Some aspects of the rainbow lorikeet's breeding in the wild are not known with certainty. Birds are thought to pair up for life, courting as early as August by huddling and squirming together on a perch. The female probably incubates her two eggs alone, but is given regurgitated food by her mate during the twenty-five days that it takes. Bedded on wood dust in tree-holes or hollow branches, the chicks fledge two months after hatching.

Rosellas *Platycercus* are less gregarious and more sedentary, though immature birds and some adults outside the breeding season may form foraging bands of up to about thirty. They are versatile feeders but mainly eat seeds — not only those growing in trees but also the grains that fall from various grasses and herbs. So they are seen on the ground far more often than lorikeets are.

The white-cheeked 'Rose Hiller'

The white-cheeked rosella *Platycercus eximius* was the first to be scientifically studied and the first to be given the common name — said to have been a corruption of 'Rose Hiller' after Sydney's earliest farming outpost, Rose Hill. It is found as far afield as Cape York Peninsula and the Kimberley, where its breeding starts in March to coincide with the peak of seeding after the wet season.

Spring breeding in the southeast is marked by the breaking up of feeding groups but an increase in overall noise from roosts and nesting trees. Permanent pairs re-establish private territories and court with little shrugging, bobbing or tail-wagging movements. Gifts of food by the male — common among many different groups of parrots — usually form some

The several different races of the crimson rosella vary widely in colour

part of the courtship ritual. (In a more unusual demonstration of affection, paired western rosellas *Platycercus icterotis* feed each other occasionally at any time of year.)

Rosellas are prolific breeders, in marked contrast to lorikeets. A white-cheeked female may lay as many as nine eggs, though about five would be more usual. Incubated in tree-holes by the mother alone, they hatch in less than three weeks and the chicks fledge in only a month. In seasons of very good feeding, this leaves time for some pairs to raise two broods. Young birds remain with their parents until the following season, when they form small flocks of their own.

Australian king parrots *Alisterus scapularis* breed now in highland forests almost anywhere from the tropical Atherton Tableland to western Victoria. Normally feeding in the outer branches of tall trees, they occasionally come to the ground for fallen seeds or fruits. Small groups seem able to do disproportionate damage when they decide to raid orchards or descend on cereal crops.

The western rosella is the smallest of the rosellas, growing up to 260 millimetres

Australian king parrots feed all day in the outer branches of forest trees, and fly to communal roosts just before sunset

Ground parrots Pezoporus wallicus *have long legs and can run and climb with ease*

Courtship feeding by the male king parrot starts weeks ahead of mating. But pairs show no interest in each other before winter or after their three or four young are reared to fledging. Unusually among parrots, they may not be permanently bonded.

Indifference to the other sex for most of the year is also shown by regent parrots *Polytelis anthopeplus*. Even during the spring breeding season, pairs do not preen each other. Regent parrots, feeding mostly on the ground, form widely separated populations in the southwest and along middle reaches of the Murray River. They differ in colour, males of the eastern race being brighter, with golden plumage.

An affectionate mate
Male superb parrots *Polytelis swainsonii*, closely related to regent parrots, are attentive and indulgent to their mates, at least while courting, breeding and rearing four or five young. Part of their courtship ritual, easily observed, is a playful flight by the male around a perching female. He continues to feed his mate long after her eggs are hatched, and later helps feed their four or five chicks. The species is seasonally nomadic and partly migratory, within a fairly confined area of inland New South Wales.

Ground parrots *Pezoporus wallicus* breed now in scattered locations near the coast of Tasmania and the southeastern mainland, and also in Western Australia. Though they are capable of strong, sustained flight they roost and nest on damp heathlands and pastures, climbing low vegetation to pick seeds.

Voluntary flights are made only at dusk and dawn, when the birds flutter about for half an hour or more, calling persistently. Between times they forage in the dark. By day they hide in tussocks, taking to the air vertically if flushed out. Their ground-dwelling habit has one advantage: the young can leave the nest before they can fly, hiding and fending for themselves.

Convincing sightings of the night parrot *Pezoporus occidentalis*, a relative that has adapted to the arid hinterland, have not been recorded for many decades. Bearing in mind that it is not only just as secretive but also nomadic, and its habitats in samphire and spinifex country are seldom visited, it is reasonable to suppose that small numbers still exist.

Many ground-dwelling birds of grasslands and forest floors are normally just as obscure and elusive. But they give themselves away at the onset of breeding by urgent bursts of singing and territorial calling. In September across a vast area of natural grasses and agricultural pastures in the south, male singing bushlarks *Mirafra javanica* rise in soaring and hovering song flights, day or night. They perform a repertoire of tinkling melodies — some borrowed from other birds.

In eastern rainforests the rufous scrubbird *Atrichornis rufescens* proclaims his territory with piercing, ringing notes. Scarcely able to fly, this bird spends all its life in the cover of dense, damp undergrowth, poking about for insects, worms, snails and seeds. It has anatomical links with lyrebirds, and possesses some of their skill in mimicry.

Pairs of diamond finches *Stagonopleura guttata*, exclusively ground-feeders in woodlands and wooded grasslands, have been exchanging insistent calls for weeks. Now the male begins a charming courtship. Characteristic of most finches, his display centres on the waving and offering of a grass stem to stimulate the nest-building impulse.□

Diamond finches Stagonopleura guttata *forage on the ground for seeds and insects*

Over and over, all day long, the golden whistler has piped his loud and lively song. Near evening, when surely he should be tired of it, the roar of a passing jet airliner fills the sky. Far from being cowed into silence, the little bird cocks his tail angrily, puffs out his breast and sings louder than ever.

The golden whistler *Pachycephala pectoralis* and a relative with very similar habits and needs, the rufous whistler *Pachycephala rufiventris*, can-

The sound and the fury

When a whistler turns up the volume

movement is not consistent even in the far south: while many birds leave high ranges on the mainland, some members of the same species in Tasmania remain to endure just as hard a winter.

Zonal migration is most common among flycatchers, including the beautiful types called monarchs. Species such as the black-faced monarch *Monarcha melanopsis* and the spectacled monarch *Monarcha trivirgatus* take all kinds of insects from foliage and bark, rarely hawking for them in mid-air. Much more active is the aptly named restless flycatcher *Myiagra inquieta*, which sallies out on zigzag flights or hovers over foliage, making a continuous rasping noise. Oldtimers called it the scissors grinder. Leaden and satin flycatchers *Myiagra rubecula* and *Myiagra cyanoleuca* are also migratory. So are southern fantail populations. The grey fantail *Rhipidura fuliginosa* is the first of the flycatcher group to return, usually establishing its breeding territory in August.

One of the most musical of spring singers — quiet at other times — is the white-throated gerygone *Gerygone olivacea*. It too is eager to get back, settling in by August. But the early nesting of this gerygone and of the grey fantail is not entirely to their advantage. They are among the main hosts of cuckoos (see August, page 174), losing many eggs and squabs.

White-winged trillers *Lalage tricolor* are among the most noticeable migrants arriving in the south. Scores may travel together, and as they sort out their territories the males advertise them with circling, fluttering display flights. Out in grassier woodlands, the rufous songlark *Cinclorhamphus mathewsi* gives a similar display, singing nonstop. It makes one of the longest zonal migrations, birds from the far south wintering in the tropics.

The olive-backed oriole *Oriolus sagittatus* is also migratory, returning to the south to breed as early as September. It is principally a fruit-eater, but at this time of year relies heavily on insects gleaned from eucalypts.□

not bear to be drowned out. If any loud noise interferes with their singing, they increase the volume. Or if they were not already performing, the noise is their cue. Early settlers, noting their response to the rumblings of distant storms, called them thunderbirds.

Competitive singing is ingrained as part of the breeding behaviour of both species. It stems from an intense territorial rivalry that erupts suddenly in early spring when the birds return from winter travels. In the case of southeastern high country populations, there is an annual movement to southern Queensland and back.

By early September forest and woodland trees fill with returning birds, urgently intent on breeding. Not an hour passes without noisy disputes. Males face off less than a metre apart and do their utmost to out-sing each other, meanwhile bobbing and rocking in threatening postures. Where pairs have already formed the females join in the uproar, which sometimes concludes with a furious chase. Once they start nesting the females quieten, but loud contests continue among the males.

Most groups of smaller, insect-eating forest birds include species that take part in what is called zonal migration. They do not leave the country but make a shift each autumn to regions where winters are milder. Their northern populations stay put.

Some birds may simply descend to lowlands; others travel a thousand kilometres or more, stopping to feed and roost on the way. The

An adult male golden whistler at the nest (above) and an olive-backed oriole feeding (below)

Home from a good day's hunting, the kookaburras have already performed the raucous chorus that proclaims their family territory. Now two of them engage in a fluttering game of aerial chasing, alighting finally near the tree-hole in which they have chosen to make their nest. They perch close together, feathers fluffed out as they clatter their bills and exchange soft chuckles. Their brief courtship display is well-practised; the two have been paired for ten years.

Half a dozen other kookaburras look on

A long wait for the last laugh

Kookaburras spend years in their parents' shadow, acting as nursemaids and guards, awaiting their chance to breed

from roosts nearby. These are the progeny of past seasons, in the prime of physical maturity. But they are sexually inactive. For the four or five years that they remain in their birthplace under the parents' eye, their breeding urge is suppressed.

Instead the unmated birds serve as family helpers. This spring all will take turns to relieve their mother as she incubates a new clutch of eggs and broods the squabs. Later the helpers will fetch about two-thirds of the food eaten by the young nestlings and fledglings.

Kookaburras are capable of living for over twenty years. They can afford to sacrifice some breeding potential in favour of social security. The auxiliary birds provide a high degree of care and protection for the few young needed to maintain populations. Their presence also ensures a permanent hold on ample territory. The more birds joining in a chorus at dawn or dusk, the less likely is an attempt at encroachment by any other group.

No young birds are more indulged than kookaburras. Reared commonly in pairs, after three or four weeks' incubation of the eggs in a bare hole, they are fledged in five weeks. But their elders will give them food for a further two or three months or even longer. The progeny from eggs laid in September will not hunt independently until January or February.

Kookaburras are kingfishers, with a hunting method characteristic of their group. Most of their day is spent perching up to ten metres above the ground, gazing downwards. When prey is seen they drop gently and pluck it up in their bills. Insects such as grasshoppers make up most of the diet but mice and small reptiles are often taken. Some families develop a habit of robbing other birds' nests: one observer saw nineteen wood-swallow nestlings snatched in an hour.

A big snake-killer?

Doubtful tales are told of epic struggles between kookaburras and big snakes. But the birds are ill-equipped to capture large prey, and not capable of tearing it up unless two of them cooperate in wrenching it apart. Even a small snake, swallowed whole, may take hours to eat. A kookaburra perched with a tail-end dangling from its bill is a common sight.

Kookaburras are widespread in eucalypt woodlands and forests. Not all of them nest in trees, however — some use termite mounds. They love to bathe in warm weather, often splashing in and out of urban swimming pools, but need no drinking water.

Dacelo novaeguineae, the laughing kookaburra of the eastern and southeastern mainland, was successfully introduced to the southwest and Tasmania last century. Northern regions are home to the

This laughing kookaburra Dacelo novaeguineae *is about to swallow a young rat*

blue-winged kookaburra *Dacelo leachii*, a smaller-bodied bird with a bigger bill. Its territorial call is more of a howl than a laugh. In Queensland the two species overlap, often perching together.

Other Australian kingfishers are markedly smaller than the kookaburras, but more colourful. Though generally migratory or nomadic, they have consistent spring breeding seasons. Nesting chambers are made by burrowing into termite mounds, the tree nests of arboreal termites, or banks of earth. The birds break open chosen sites by flying at them and spearing them with their bills. Feet are used to continue the excavation.

Of commonly seen kingfisher species, only one has a true fishing habit. The azure kingfisher *Alcedo azurea* is restricted to forests bordering streams and inlets, and does all of its hunting over water — perching within a metre of the surface. Crustaceans and big aquatic insects are taken, along with small fish.

The widely distributed sacred kingfisher *Todiramphus sanctus* may also catch fish or crustaceans if it happens to be over water. But it is essentially a land bird, living off insects and small reptiles in virtually any open, wooded area. There is a marked migratory movement in the south. Sacred kingfishers start arriving at the end of August for a long breeding season in which two broods are usually raised. They depart around March to winter on islands to the north of Australia.

Similar patterns of migration are shown by the more southerly populations of the collared kingfisher *Todiramphus chloris*. In a wide overseas range from the Middle

Three young azure kingfishers Alcedo azurea, *newly fledged, perch over the water (above). A Pacific baza brings food to its young (below)*

East to Polynesia this is a versatile bird of woodlands and forests. But in Australia it is strangely restricted to the tidal margins of mangrove stands. It does not dive into the water; aquatic prey is picked from mudflats and pools at low tide.

Along forest edges of the north and east, as far south as Sydney, the habitats of kookaburras and other kingfishers are often shared with a small but highly distinctive bird of prey. The Pacific baza *Aviceda subcristata*, sometimes called a crested hawk or lizard hawk, does not compete for ground-dwelling prey. Hunting by day, bazas snatch their food from the outer foliage of tree crowns. Some small reptiles and tree frogs are taken but the staple diet is insects and their larvae. In early spring they feast on stick insects.

Bazas are seldom noticed as they hunt, but around September they attract attention with their courtship flights. Soaring and tumbling manoeuvres are accompanied by loud calling. The nest, a saucer of sticks built by both sexes, is set on a horizontal limb at least fifteen metres from the ground. Incubation of two to four eggs, taking more than a month, is also shared by the parents. Nestlings are cared for by the mother, who zealously cleans out refuse and renews a bed of gumleaves, while the male bird brings food.□

Mitchell's water monitor Varanus mitchelli
grows up to sixty centimetres long, including
the keeled tail

This ornate burrowing frog Limnodynastes
ornatus is calling while afloat in the water

A billabong on the Mitchell
River, northern Queensland

All except very old specimens of the
saw-shelled turtle Elseya latisternum
have a serrated edge on the rear
of their shell

The freshwater crocodile
Crocodylus johnstoni

Under siege from the sun

For the inhabitants of drying rivers, time is running out

All across the far north, early spring brings a crisis for water-dependent animals. With little if any rain for six months or more, most rivers have long since ceased flowing. Here and there the deeper holes of their meandering beds hold pools of turbid, oxygen-poor water. Under cloudless skies, as days lengthen and temperatures rise, these little reservoirs evaporate rapidly.

The billabong shown here forms part of a river system draining into the Gulf of Carpentaria. Its catchment is in highlands on the opposite side of Cape York Peninsula, near Cairns. So the river should be flowing again by November, though patchy local storms could replenish the billabong before then. If not, the life that it supports will come under increasing threat. Birds will be able to find a better place. So may the reptiles – even the crocodiles. Drought-adapted crustaceans and insects will hold out in mud. But the fish may well die.

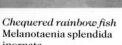

Chequered rainbow fish Melanotaenia splendida inornata

Water-fleas Daphnia carinata. *The black spots are eggs*

Freshwater mussels Velesumio ambiguus

Toothless catfish Anodontiglanis dahli

During drought, Australian pelicans have reached Indonesia and New Zealand in their search for water

211

Dressed up for the big occasion

Courting spoonbills and egrets show off their distinctive ornamental plumes only during the breeding season

Frills of spiny breast plumes are raised and lowered as two spoonbills court. They bob their heads and noisily clap the mandibles of their great yellow bills. The female pretends to peck at her suitor but is soon submissive, letting him nibble her bill. From this moment they are paired.

Their swampside perch overlooks a clump of rushes that the female has already chosen for her nest. She leads the male to it and squats down, pushing and pulling at fallen twigs. They copulate, both grasping the same twig in their bills.

His next task firmly imprinted in his mind, the male immediately sets about collecting more sticks for his mate to arrange on the trampled rushes. As soon as a shallow construction is completed they return to their perch and preen each other. Now if a third bird should approach they abruptly raise their breast frills, scaring it off.

Nuptial plumes, important in courtship and various nest displays, are common to spoonbills of both sexes and to several of those members of the heron family that are usually called egrets. Among populations nesting in the south the special feathers start growing in winter, about two months before the onset of breeding in September. They are moulted soon after the young leave the nest.

Breast plumes of yellow-billed spoonbills *Platalea flavipes* are distinctive of their species alone. Royal spoonbills *Platalea regia*, which have black bills and nest in the same areas but rarely assemble before October, develop longer and finer plumes behind their heads.

The showiest nuptial plumage is displayed by the intermediate egret *Ardea intermedia*. Quills with lacy filaments, like those of a lyrebird's tail, fan out from the back and breast. The great egret *Ardea alba* has only back plumes, extending past its tail. The little egret *Ardea garzetta* grows two narrow ribbons from the back of its head.

Courtship among these and allied swamp-dwellers is often also attended by temporary changes in skin colouring. Under hormonal influences the flow of blood is altered, and naked areas of skin

A royal spoonbill with nuptial plumes on the nest; up to four eggs are laid

change colour. In species with yellowish eyes, the irises redden. The pale face of the yellow-billed spoonbill takes on a blue tinge, reverting to white the moment that the pair-bond is made. The yellow facial skin of great and intermediate egrets turns blue-green — but that of the little egret goes red. Light leg and bill colourings darken in many species.

The straw-necked ibis *Threskiornis spinicollis* has spiky neck plumes year-round, raising them as a threat to drive off unpaired birds. In courtship it displays red patches at each side of the breast and behind the eyes. At other times the breast patches are yellow and the patches behind the eyes dark.

Most such birds are nomadic when not breeding, relying on animal food picked from or around large areas of fresh water. In the south they congregate where spring flooding is most likely, to breed in loose colonies. Many species may nest in the one area. The biggest colonies, sometimes numbering tens of thousands, are formed by straw-necked ibises.

The breeding pattern of ibises is fairly typical of the whole group. All build stick platforms on vegetation, laying up to five eggs, and in all cases both sexes share incubation duties for three or four weeks. Fledging varies from four to seven weeks.

A variety of diets

Feeding preferences vary subtly among birds that are frequently seen together. The sacred ibis *Threskiornis aethiopicus* forages always in water, seeking crustaceans and other aquatic animals but also taking earthworms and terrestrial insects from flooded ground. The straw-necked ibis feeds on dry as well as wet pastures, widening its diet to caterpillars and grasshoppers. Huge flocks sometimes mass to exploit plague locust outbreaks (see March, page 91). Both ibises can eat shellfish such as mussels, breaking them open by holding them against rocks and striking with their bills.

Royal spoonbills are predominantly fish-eaters, catching them by swinging part-open bills from side to side in the water. Yellow-billed spoonbills have a more varied diet, eating proportionately more aquatic insects. Both crush hard-shelled prey with knobs located inside the bases of their bills.

Egrets rely on their vision to hunt for

A sacred ibis feeding on a fish carcass

aquatic creatures. Much of their time is spent standing motionless and gazing into the water, or slowly stalking until prey is seen. Their size determines their foraging depth, the great egret naturally feeding in the deepest water and catching the biggest fish. The intermediate egret is more limited and the little egret has humble tastes,

often settling for worms. It sometimes stirs the beds of muddy shallows with one foot, or follows spoonbills to take advantage of the disturbance they cause.

One watch-and-wait hunter is distinguished by its dark colouring and strictly nocturnal habit. The rufous night heron *Nycticorax caledonicus* bears two or three fine, white neck plumes throughout the year, raising them as part of its courtship display. It feeds just after dark and again before dawn, sometimes shaking its bill in the water to attract fish. Though mainly reliant on aquatic prey, it occasionally eats the eggs or takes the nestlings of other birds.

Night herons are often branded as the chief hosts of the virus of Australian encephalitis, which in sporadic outbreaks has killed over a hundred people this century — mostly young children — in Queensland and the southeast. Infected by mosquito bites, the birds incubate the virus without harm to themselves and pass it on to other mosquitoes.

While it is true that night herons are the most infected birds in outbreak areas, they are not the most abundant. By weight of numbers ducks are more likely to harbour and transport the virus.

Ducks too are drawn to the teeming aquatic life and lush plant growth of flooded swamps and pastures. In the southwest and southeast many species

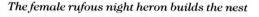

The female rufous night heron builds the nest

Intermediate egrets nest in colonies in trees

follow a fairly regular spring breeding cycle like that of the herons, spoonbills and their allies. The ducks tend to settle in sooner, however. Some are already paired, having begun their courting in autumn (see April, page 108). Boisterous male displays may have been repeated all through winter, on whatever water the birds could find.

Two unusual fan-tailed ducks arrive predictably at the breeding swamps in August and start their mating in September. The blue-billed duck *Oxyura australis* lives up to its common name only in spring — at other times its bill is grey. The musk duck *Biziura lobata* is so-called because of a heady smell, very strong during breeding, that comes from an oil gland on the rumps of drakes.

Neither species is permanently paired. Males display vigorously, tails stiffly erected and necks puffed out, to attract the attention of females. Musk drakes, inflating the grotesque sacs under their bills, start displaying as early as March though females are never receptive then.

Mated females trample down reeds to make deep cup nests on or just over the water. The blue-billed duck lays up to a dozen eggs — normally five or six — while the musk duck seldom produces more than three. Incubation, by the mother alone, takes about a month. Ducklings are led into the water at about one day old. Young blue-bills feed themselves immediately but musk ducklings depend on their mothers for a few days, sometimes riding on their backs.

Feeding is almost invariably by diving and prolonged submerged swimming in search of aquatic animals, though some seeds and shoots are stripped from plants.

Dusky moorhens Gallinula tenebrosa *feed their chicks for nine weeks after hatching*

The blue-bill eats mostly insects and larvae. Musk dusks are more varied feeders, preying also on molluscs, crustaceans and frogs. Both of these ducks are fully at home only on the water. They sleep there at night, floating with their tails widely fanned. When birds disperse after breeding their flight action is laboured; they cannot perch in trees or walk.

Deep-diving ducks

The deepest divers, also totally aquatic, are hardheads *Aythya australis*. They arrive in thousands on bigger swamps and lagoons and on flooding inland rivers. Submerging for as long as a minute, they eat insects, molluscs, crustaceans and fish along with plant seeds. Nests woven from sticks and reeds are placed on flooded vegetation and up to a dozen eggs are laid.

Seen in twos or threes among other spring-breeding ducks, Australasian shovelers *Anas rhynchotis* are surface-feeders that strain water or mud through hair-like fringes on their broad bills. They go into deeper water to court and copulate, but nest ashore among tussocks.

The greatest landlubber among ducks breeding in the south now is the maned duck *Chenonetta jubata*. Related to the pygmy geese of the tropics, with clawed feet that are only half webbed, it walks and perches more ably than it swims. Once it is fledged this bird takes to the water only to flee danger, and to bathe and copulate. No doubt to the annoyance of woodland birds such as parrots and kookaburras, it takes over big tree-holes

A musk drake Biziura lobata *giving his remarkable mating display*

SWELLING WITH PRIDE
The inflatable musk duck

The black bladder of skin hanging under a musk drake's bill becomes so big during winter and spring, even when not inflated, that a distant shape on the water is not easily recognisable as that of a bird. While the drake is displaying to females — rocking back and forth, kicking water more than two metres behind him, then spinning and piping shrilly – the bladder balloons to as much as fifteen centimetres in diameter.

Monsters have been made out of mystifying glimpses. As recently as the 1960s Sydney newspapers revelled in claims that 'bunyips' inhabited the city's Centennial Park lake. Such stories are often made more believable by eerie boomings at night — the calls of Australasian bitterns sharing musk duck habitats.

EXCESS BAGGAGE

*Marine cormorants struggle
under a heavy load*

Buoyancy in salt water makes life hard for Australia's only exclusively marine cormorant, the black-faced shag *Leucocarbo fuscescens*. To weigh it down during dives that last up to forty seconds in pursuit of fish and squid, it is believed to swallow pebbles.

That seems to be the only explanation for the extraordinary difficulty the bird has in flying. At the end of a day's fishing, when it takes off to head for its roost, it flaps with all its might, but can barely clear the wave-crests.

Black-faced shags roost and nest in colonies on rocky islets off southern coasts. They mould big cup nests from seaweed and other plant matter and both sexes incubate the eggs, of which there are usually around three. The young are raised in creches, but each is fed by its own parents until it is old enough to go to sea.

Black-faced shags live around the south coast, and grow up to seventy centimetres

and hollows for its nesting sites.

Maned ducks pair up for life. Although the drake gives no help during a month-long incubation of about ten eggs, he guards the nest and later defends flightless young. Summoned by the parents, hatchlings topple fearlessly out of their tree and sprawl on the ground below. They are led to water and remain there for about seven weeks, nibbling on aquatic plants and taking insects, until they are able to fly. Older birds graze on land like geese.

Mingling with herons and ducks on and around swamps, and usually slightly ahead in their breeding, are various members of the rail family. The most visible, feeding and sleeping in open water, are Eurasian coots *Fulica atra*. After lively courtships and noisy fights over territory,

nests are made from loose heaps of sticks among fringing vegetation, or sometimes as floating rafts.

In contrast to ducks, male coots help in nest-building and incubation of the eggs. Clutch sizes vary widely, from four to fifteen. Males also assist in feeding the young, which cannot dive for three weeks and take another month to become fully competent. Attentive males often build themselves roosts, close to their nests.

Two female coots sometimes form a family with one male. Communal living and polygamy are practised more systematically by purple swamphens *Porphyrio porphyrio*. These are nomadic in many regions, but where water lies permanently, groups of up to ten occupy year-round territories. Dominant males mate

with most of the females, all of which build the one nest and lay their eggs together. Subordinate males help brood the chicks in a nursery nest and teach them to forage.

Swamphens can swim but are seldom seen in the water. They clamber about in dense beds of fringing reeds, chopping off the tenderest young stems and eating them held in one foot, in the manner of parrots. Moving away from swamps to graze wet grasslands, they walk rather than fly — and if alarmed, run for cover.

Smaller and less colourful, the dusky moorhen *Gallinula tenebrosa* shares the habitats of swamphens but feeds mainly in the water. It is also found on lakes, including those in urban parks. Dusky moorhens live in groups of up to seven adults, most of which are males. Females initiate courtships and mate with any or all of the males in their group.

Native-breeding plovers

Salt marshes bordering inland lakes provide breeding grounds for a bird that is more commonly associated with seashores, the red-capped plover *Charadrius ruficapillus*. It is sedentary along coasts and around other permanent waters, often raising three broods in a season. Some inland populations exploiting temporary waters are nomadic and nest at any time.

In the east of its southern range another native-breeding bird, the hooded plover *Charadrius rubricollis*, is confined to sandy shores that are backed by lagoons. In Western Australia, however, it ranges hundreds of kilometres inland to the shores of salt lakes.

Both birds nest in ground scrapes that they line with shell fragments, pebbles, leaves or dried seaweed. Feeding on beaches — picking at flotsam strewn along the high-water line or taking insects from

A maned duck Chenonetta jubata *with ducklings — both parents look after young*

Silver gulls Larus novaehollandiae *are the best-known of Australia's sea birds*

immatures stay in the north all year.

Many gulls and native terns begin breeding in September. The most widespread and numerous species, the silver gull *Larus novaehollandiae*, starts in winter in the south, while in the extreme southwest some birds breed twice a year, in spring and autumn.

Well suited to human ways, this is the species most likely to scavenge at urban garbage dumps and mob people eating in the open air, taking virtually anything edible. It also ranges far inland to permanent or temporary water and hunts insects in ploughed paddocks. Birds feeding more naturally float in rafts on the sea surface, taking plankton, or patrol the water's edge for crustaceans and insects.

Silver gulls reaching three years of age nest in crowded colonies on sandspits and islands, preferring to build their shallow cups on the ground but using bushes if necessary. Older birds have habitual spots

Caspian terns are the largest of the terns

and are permanently paired. About three eggs, incubated by both parents, hatch in three to four weeks. Chicks leave the nest before they are fully fledged, sheltering under nearby plants to avoid the attacks of other gulls. During their immature years they face a difficult life, constantly bullied and driven from feeding areas by dominant senior birds.

The heavy-billed Pacific gull *Larus pacificus*, the biggest of its group, breeds on headlands and islands of the south and west. Birds in their first two years wander north in small· groups, along the New South Wales coast — where their ancestors used to breed — and, in Western Australia, beyond North West Cape. Once paired they become fairly sedentary.

Pacific gulls are versatile feeders on beaches, reefs or at sea. Later in the year they will wreak havoc on the nesting colonies of smaller birds such as shearwaters, destroying eggs, taking young and robbing the adults of food. Though they rarely fly far inland they seek rocks on

wet sand — they are outnumbered by migratory waders. New arrivals in September include one close relative, the Mongolian plover *Charadrius mongolus*, which breeds in eastern Siberia.

From the same region, and also from Alaska, come loose groups of ruddy turnstones *Arenaria interpres*. More common in the north, they are perhaps the busiest of all shore waders, using their bills and sometimes their whole heads to flip over shells, stones, driftwood and seaweed in search of insects and worms. They also catch small fish, and can hammer or prise open most shellfish.

Godwits, also from Siberia, wade in the shallows or on the wet flats of tidal inlets, probing for molluscs and worms. The species most commonly seen here is the bar-tailed godwit *Limosa lapponica*. Breeding plumage, a rich reddish-brown in the males, will be seen on many birds by the time they leave, around April.

As is the case with many migratory birds, grey-tailed tattlers *Tringa brevipes* are better known here than in their native land — a mountainous region of Siberia where it took ornithologists until 1959 to discover eggs. Tattlers in Australia frequent the same areas as godwits. Some

A crested tern feeding its young. Usually only one egg is laid, and after a few days' brooding, hatchlings are reared in creches

which to drop and break hard-shelled prey. The same places are used year after year, and the heaps of shells have been confused with Aboriginal middens.

Some terns range for surprising distances across the hinterland. Gull-billed terns *Sterna nilotica* and whiskered terns *Chlidonias hybrida* are adapted to a nomadic and migratory life, moving south in September to breed where they can on swamps, freshwater or salt lakes and flooded ground. They hunt on the wing, gliding down to take insects and lizards as well as fish and crustaceans.

Huge Caspian terns *Sterna caspia*, with wingspans of nearly 1.5 metres, also roam the eastern hinterland between the Gulf of Carpentaria and the Murray River. There they breed in response to floods. But most populations are coastal, and those in subtropical and temperate regions have a regular season starting in September.

Courting Caspian terns

Small colonies may be formed, but Caspian terns often breed in solitude. Courting pairs execute synchronised twists and turns while diving towards their nesting sites at an alarming speed. Nests are bare scrapes, often in very exposed situations, but there is always some low vegetation nearby to shelter the chicks when they leave. Only one or two eggs are laid, but the loss of a clutch or brood is quickly followed by a further laying.

Roseate terns *Sterna dougallii* breed twice a year on islands off the northwestern coast, in September and again in March. Northeastern populations frequenting the Great Barrier Reef region have only a spring season. New tourist developments are a great threat to them.

Western populations of crested terns *Sterna bergii* have a similar pattern of

Sooty terns feed in flocks at sea, especially at dusk, skimming the water surface

Black noddies Anous minutus *leave their nests in the morning to feed at sea*

twice-yearly breeding, while birds in the south breed only in spring and tropical populations in autumn. These are the most coast-bound and familiar of big terns, patrolling inshore waters in search of the small, surface-swimming fish that make up practically all of their diet.

Crested terns breed on nearshore islands all around Australia, in densely packed colonies that may comprise thousands of birds. Courting males exhibit fish to their mates, then pairs take part in the diving display flights that are typical of terns. Hatched in scrapes a metre apart, chicks gather in creches after a few days. When southern colonies break up around December, the new generation disperses far and wide. Some southern-born birds may end up as tropical breeders.

In contrast to the coast-hugging habits of crested terns, the sooty tern *Sterna fuscata* comes inshore only to breed on islets. The rest of its life is spent at sea, apparently even sleeping on the wing. Though adults may not travel far from their breeding grounds, juveniles have been found thousands of kilometres away. Between their third and sixth year they start breeding, usually at their birthplace.

Sooty terns are cautious breeders
In preparation for breeding, flocks of sooty terns overfly their nesting islets for as long as two months. They inspect the sites night after night, and later day after day, before small groups start to land and court. September and March are peak arrival times at many colonies. But landings and layings — in scrapes a mere fifty centimetres apart — can occur at any time except midwinter. Their unpredictability was baffling until it was discovered that these birds have a breeding cycle of about nine-and-a-half months.

Tropical islands, coral cays and some remote coastal headlands are breeding grounds for noddies — dark-plumaged terns that hunt by skimming the sea rather than diving from a height. Queensland's black noddy *Anous minutus* and the more southerly populations of the common noddy *Anous stolidus*, which occurs all around the tropical coast, breed in spring. In another contrast with conventional terns, they make cup nests of seaweed and other plant material. The common noddy presses its nest into a ground scrape, while the black noddy uses tree forks.□

These young of the song thrush Turdus philomelos *are nearly ready to fledge*

Sweet echoes of the old country

European songsters have adjusted to an unfamiliar climate

Hopping daintily from the shrubbery of a Melbourne garden, the song thrush peers around to see that the coast is clear. A big snail, shell intact, is held delicately in his bill. Assured that no cats are about, he rushes to a rockery stone — always the same one — and pounds his prize against it. The mollusc is extracted whole from its shattered shell and gulped down. Then the bird flies to a high branch and begins a delightful song sequence of varied phrases, each repeated three or four times.

Immigrants flooding in from the British Isles in the second half of last century yearned to hear again this harbinger of spring, advertising his breeding territory. Introductions of *Turdus philomelos* were attempted in many Australian communities. Only in and around Melbourne did they succeed, in liberally watered locations offering deep shade in summer. The thrushes breed prolifically from September on, but they cannot cope with prolonged heat or drought.

Introduced finches have been similarly success-ful in the southeast, though they do not range as far inland as the blackbird. The European goldfinch *Carduelis carduelis* has also established itself in Western Australia, evidently after birds escaped from aviaries in Perth and Albany.

Both the goldfinch and the European greenfinch *Carduelis chloris* still rely on exotic trees for their nesting, however. The two species compete for sites, especially in pine trees. Greenfinches, bigger and more belligerent, usually win. Their ruthless tactics include the destruction of their rivals' eggs — if they have not already wrecked the nest.

Spotted turtle-doves *Streptopelia chinensis*, of Asian origin, were introduced in all settled areas last century. They have succeeded in most coastal districts and along permanent waterways, in some places pushing out native bar-shouldered and peaceful doves. The laughing turtle-dove *Strep-topelia senegalensis*, a native of Africa and Asia, occurs only in Western Australia. Its cooing has a distinctive rippling quality.

Red-whiskered bulbuls *Pycnonotus jocosus*, perky and playful, are amusing additions to many public parks and home gardens in central and southern coastal New South Wales. A few are seen around Melbourne. Brought from China last cen-tury, bulbuls were peddled as cage birds — 'Persian nightingales'. Their song is bright, but their endless repetition of one phrase, in the confines of a house, must have driven many a buyer to distraction.□

Nostalgic settlers had more luck with the black-bird *Turdus merula*, an equally melodious singer. The species thrives in Tasmania and across the southeastern mainland, and is beginning to show physical adaptations to various climatic conditions. As is the case with thrushes, only male blackbirds sing. And only the males are black — females look like unspeckled thrushes.

Clockwise from top: a European goldfinch feeding on thistles; from China, the red-whiskered bulbul Pycnonotus jocosus; *the spotted turtle-dove* Streptopelia chinensis

Four male crimson fiddler crabs Uca flammula *on a Queensland mud-flat*

OCTOBER

THIS MONTH'S WEATHER

Occasional storms signal the beginning of the far north's transition back to the Wet. The southwest and south join the generally drying trend of the southeast — though Melbourne, which has the most even rainfall of all the capitals, experiences a slight peak now. Good rains return to southern Queensland but the state's tropical coast remains fairly dry.

AROUND THE COUNTRY	RAIN (mm)	MAX. (°C)	MIN. (°C)	SUN hrs/day
Adelaide	51	22	11	7.2
Alice Springs	22	30	15	9.9
Brisbane	102	26	16	8.4
Canberra	69	19	6	8.3
Darwin	74	33	25	9.4
Hobart	63	17	8	6.5
Melbourne	68	20	9	6.7
Perth	54	22	12	8.9
Port Hedland	1	34	18	11.4
Sydney	78	22	13	7.1
Townsville	25	29	20	9.7
Weipa	27	35	21	9.3

Seduced by a perfumed impostor

Nectar entices wasps and bees to pollinate most flowering plants. But some wasps are led up the garden path....

Legs braced, clawed feet gripping tightly and slender body arched, the wasp probes with his rear end at what his senses convince him is the genital region of a receptive female. But there is no other wasp in sight. By superb natural artifice, he has been lured into attempting to copulate with an orchid blossom. When he tires of his vain efforts he will carry off some of the plant's pollen — and pass it on as soon as he is tricked by another of the same kind.

Native ground orchids of several types imitate female wasps. They have developed floral forms and patterns that suggest antennae, eyes or wings. Even more compellingly, they produce scents that resemble the wasps' exclusive chemical sex-attractants. And the structure of their flowers dictates the way in which deluded male wasps must grasp them. Attempts at sexual intimacy always lead to contact with the pollen-bearing anthers.

Best known of the floral frauds are slipper orchids *Cryptostylis*. Some widespread species are commonly called wasp orchids. Flowers of various slipper orchids entice different *Lissopimpla* species, a group of parasitic wasps whose females mostly lay their eggs in the larvae of wood-boring beetles. Bearded orchids *Calochilus* are also prominent in their seduction of wasps. These and a few other orchid groups with similar abilities flower at varying times from early spring to the end of summer, brightening damp, wooded regions from mountainsides to the margins of coastal swamps.

Wasps and bees — closely related to each other and to ants — are on the whole the most beneficial insects on the face of the earth. Bees are the leading pollinators of trees and shrubs, as well as wildflowers, pasture plants and crops. Wasps do a share of this work; although most young are raised on animal tissue the adults seek nectar and incidentally transmit pollens. More importantly, the wasps help to control the populations of other insects, many of which could be very destructive if their numbers were to get out of hand.

Australia has well over 6000 described wasp species. No doubt more await discov-

This ichneumon wasp Lissopimpla semipunctata *will carry away a load of pollen after attempting to mate with the large tongue-orchid* Cryptostylis subulata

ery. The lives of the vast majority — more than 5000 species — are based on a parasitic larval stage. Eggs are laid in other eggs, other larvae, or sometimes in or on living adult hosts. Between them the parasitic wasps have an enormous impact on practically everything else in the insect world, from mealy bugs and aphids to cockroaches and locusts. Spiders and their relatives are also parasitised.

Some primitive wasps feed on plant tissue at their larval stage. The young resemble caterpillars and are highly active — not like the immobile grubs of other wasps. Most native plant-eaters are known as sawflies because the female egg-depositing organ doubles as a tool to cut into leaves. Some females, notably those of *Perga* species, show a maternal instinct. They stay with their eggs and guard the larvae. Sawfly larvae can strip eucalypts, but the trees are not killed unless other insects are also involved.

We have a few native wood-boring wasps, but the most destructive of this kind, *Sirex noctilio*, is an accidental introduction from the northern hemisphere. It damages pine trees — also introduced — by exposing the heartwood to a fungus. Fortunately the fungus often supports worms that parasitise the wasps' eggs.

Aggressive predation of other insects or spiders — only by female wasps — occurs in hundreds of species. Many are seen carrying victims off to nests as food for their young. This group commands the major share of public attention because it includes the most prominent nest-builders and the most worrying stingers.

Predation at first must have been a simple matter of parasitic wasps moving insects or spiders to laying sites, rather than laying eggs in the hosts wherever they were found. That led to the nurturing of larvae in permanent retreats, and then the construction of protective cells.

Among some wasp families individual species have advanced to different levels of sophistication. Some pompilids (wasps of the family Pompilidae) drag off big spiders that they have stunned with their venomous stings. They make their way to existing retreats in burrows or under bark, or else will quickly make nests. Some burrows will be lined with mud.

Parasites and hijackers

But many other pompilids go unseen. They remain parasites, attacking spiders in their own retreats or burrows and laying their eggs there. And a few members of the family are not so much parasites as hijackers: they lay eggs in other wasps' prey before it is placed in nests.

Wasps that tackle prey as big or bigger than themselves are relatively primitive. They have no trouble overpowering their prey with venom. But having to carry their captives back, gripped in their mandibles, puts them at a disadvantage. They are limited in their hunting range, and in order to open their nests they have to put down the prey, exposing it to parasites. Such wasps place just one insect or spider in each brood cell, as fuel for the larva's entire development.

Predatory wasps at the next levels of advancement choose smaller prey that they can carry with the middle and hind pairs of legs. They provide each larva with a number of food animals. And some of them have adopted habits of progressive provisioning, reopening their brood cells at intervals to supply fresh prey.

These stages have been reached by the Sphecoidea group of wasps (known as sphecoids), some of which are big enough to provision their brood cells with cicadas. *Exeirus lateritius*, a ground-nester, can exceed thirty-five millimetres in length. *Sceliphron* species are nearly as big. They use mud to daub nesting cells not only on tree trunks but also on posts, fences and the walls of buildings.

Eumenid wasps (of the family Eumenidae) prey on caterpillars, and are also prominent mud-daubers. Mason wasps *Abispa* plaster clusters of big brood cells to Queensland buildings — sometimes inside. Potter wasps *Eumenes* attach jug-like mud vessels under logs or the eaves of houses.

Eumenids and sphecoids are solitary wasps that as adults lead independent lives. But some show an inclination towards nesting in colonies. Sphecoid *Bembix* species excavate their fly-stocked brood cells in groups. Eumenids such as *Pseudozethus* go further, groups of females pasting together leaves or plant fibres to form clusters of cells. In doing so they are approaching the next stage in the evolution of wasps — social organisation.

One severe restriction confronts all

FATTENING FIGS
Fleshy 'fruit' is produced by tiny wasps

Fruit bats, birds and climbing marsupials have wasps to thank for the succulent flesh of native figs. What they enjoy is not a true fruit but a growth that forms like a gall, through a chemical response to penetration by the insects. Otherwise the figs would be small, dry and hard — and the trees would face a doubtful future.

Fig flowers never see the light of day. They develop inside cases called synconiums. Female agaonid wasps (of the family Agaonidae), none more than three millimetres long, enter through ready-made holes and lay eggs. In doing so they transfer pollen from male to female flowers. Their progeny complete all their development inside — many males never emerging. Meanwhile the synconiums swell and ripen. Each fig species has its own wasp. The Moreton Bay fig, for example, accommodates one of the biggest of the agaonids, *Pleistodontes froggatti*.

Animals digest the fleshy growths but excrete the real fruits — tiny balls containing seeds. In their travels they establish seedlings far from the parent trees, or give parasitic strangler figs starting-points high in the branches of promising new hosts.

Young sawfly larvae Perga lewisi *feed while their mother stands guard*

Many wasps provision their egg-cells with food for the developing larvae; this pompilid wasp Cryptocheilus *is trying to subdue a wolf spider for the larder*

insects. Unless new breathing systems are evolved, none of them can attain significantly greater size. Their present mechanisms are efficient in transporting oxygen only over very short distances.

Among the Hymenoptera — wasps, bees and ants — the limit to growth is overcome by interaction. Many species form communities in which roles are predetermined and every member must cooperate. There can be no choice, because no individual is functionally complete. But together the members become a superorganism, theoretically unlimited in size if climatic conditions are suitable and food is abundant.

'Blue ant' Diamma bicolor

WINGLESS WASPS
Blue and velvet ants that aren't

Dashing about on the ground, conspicuous with their glistening dark green or purple bodies, female wasps of *Diamma* species are commonly called 'blue ants'. They belong to a parasitic group in which all females are wingless burrowers. Most lay their eggs in the larvae of scarab beetles, but *Diamma* species apparently pick on mole crickets.

Winged males are the same size — about twenty millimetres long — and bring nectar and honeydew to the females. But in many related species females are smaller and are carried by males to feeding sites.

Hairy 'velvet ants', some also reaching twenty millimetres, are seen on grass stems, tree trunks and twigs. They are the wingless females of *Ephutomorpha* species, from a family that parasitises bees as well as other wasps.

'Velvet ant' Ephutomorpha rugicollis

Cooperative instincts are reinforced by chemical signals, from glandular secretions called pheromones. Many insects use them for species recognition and to stimulate mating. In societies of the order Hymenoptera, where pheromones are passed in exchanges of food, they are constant reminders of each member's role. And they work as a continuous census, keeping egg-laying females informed of the population make-up. Any imbalance is automatically corrected through an adjustment to fertilisation.

The sphecoid wasp Sphecius pectoralis *uses cicadas to provision its egg-cells*

Male Hymenoptera hatch from unfertilised eggs. They lead short lives, with sperm production and mating their only role. Fertilised eggs produce females, but in social species most of these are neutered. Probably under the influence of another pheromone, the ovaries fail to develop, and they become the workers. Their primary functions are to build and repair nests, gather food, nurture larvae and tend the egg-layers. Their wasted reproductive systems produce venoms and their egg-depositing organs become stings — needed for hunting by predatory wasps and ants, and used to defend the nest by workers of all societies.

Long-lived queens

A minority of females — in some communities only one — are sexually complete. Their lives are devoted to egg production. Activity of the rest of a developed community centres on the feeding of these 'queens' and the construction of cells into which they lay their eggs; and then on the nourishment of the grubs.

Most queens live for many years, but their supporting populations swell and dwindle annually. In the coldest climates only the queens may survive winter, in hibernation. In spring they start the community anew, feeding themselves and their first crop of larvae. In temperate and warm climates some workers survive winter and there is faster population growth in spring.

Such communities can get bigger by the year, but to avoid running short of food they split up and found new colonies. In some species lone queens make fresh starts. In others senior queens are followed to new sites by swarms of workers, leaving daughters to maintain old nests.

Social wasps all belong to the family Vespidae. Australia has only two native groups, both called paper-nest wasps.

This mud-daubing eumenid wasp is laying eggs — its egg-cells contain caterpillars

Some *Polistes* species reach twenty-five millimetres in length; *Ropalidia* species do not exceed ten millimetres. Both kinds renew their populations annually in the south but breed continuous generations year-round in the tropics. But even the biggest nests contain no more than a few hundred brood cells.

Paper-nest workers scrape fragments of weathered wood from trees or posts and chew them up. Mixed with saliva, the material is slowly built up to form combs of hexagonal cells. It dries out to resemble paper. The combs are suspended by narrow stems from branches, rock overhangs or occasionally from the eaves of houses. *Polistes* combs hang horizontally and are always open. *Ropalidia* combs usually hang vertically, though a tropical Queens-

land species builds horizontal tiers and adds a papery covering.

Both kinds sting severely if their nests are touched — an accidental risk in dense bush, where the structures are often hard to see. The stings, which can penetrate clothing, are not normally dangerous but some people become sensitive to them.

Of far greater concern in recent years has been the spread of introduced wasps. *Vespula germanica*, the so-called European wasp, is also native to North Africa and parts of Asia. *Vespula vulgaris* is called the English wasp — which is even more meaningless because it ranges across Europe and through Asia and has become widespread in North America. Both species are thought to have expanded their ranges with the help of cargo movements during and after the Second World War. Hibernating queens concealed in packing cases could have survived weeks of transportation.

Vespula vulgaris appeared in Tasmania and southern Victoria in the 1950s. It has not spread north of Melbourne. *Vespula germanica* seems to have arrived a little later, probably from New Zealand. First noticed in a Melbourne suburb in 1958, by the late 1970s it was widely established in Tasmania, Victoria and New South Wales and had made isolated appearances in South and Western Australia.

In Tasmania and the coldest parts of Victoria the workers die off in autumn and the queens abandon their nests, which seldom exceed the size of a person's head. The queens hibernate under bark, in stacks of timber or firewood, in outbuildings or in the ceilings of houses.

Warm spring weather brings surviving

SEXUAL SABOTAGE
A plan to neuter insect pests

CSIRO researchers in 1988 stepped up a programme to isolate the pheromone, or chemical communicator, that European wasp queens use to neuter other females of their species and turn them into workers. They took hundreds of queens from a nest about 1.5 metres long and almost a metre deep, discovered at an inner-Sydney vehicle depot.

The scientists want to know how the pheromone is constituted and whether it works on non-social insects. If so, and if quantities can be synthesised, they could be used to suppress the breeding of crop pests and of health hazards such as flies and mosquitoes.

The European wasp Vespula germanica *is a pest*

queens out in a search for nectar and nesting sites. The minority that succeed in establishing nests feed their larvae on chewed-up insects — chiefly caterpillars — and spiders. They may also take meat from animal carcasses or help themselves to prepared foods.

Workers are seen after a few weeks, taking over the foraging, enlarging nests and feeding new larvae while the queens concentrate on egg-laying. Nest expansion continues until late summer, when there is a final flurry of activity and the workers become pests not only outdoors but also in houses and shops. At this time they seek sugars rather than animal protein, to feed a special batch of larvae in enlarged brood cells. These become new queens, which leave their nests on mating flights, then find refuges for hibernation.

In warmer climates mated queens return to their nests instead of hibernating. Nest expansion is virtually continuous, the same construction growing year after year. Along sheltered river valleys in the Sydney region, some nests have exceeded three metres in length. Communities can number hundreds of thousands.

Possible wasp invasion

Inland aridity prevents the northward spread of the wasps, except in the east. For years it was assumed that their limit would be subtropical because they could not tolerate too much summer heat. But CSIRO researchers have found that the wasps are capable of reversing their European cycle and aestivating in summer. Tropical Queensland may yet be invaded.

Worker wasps have a foraging range of up to a kilometre. But conditioned by thousands of years of close association with humans — in much the same way as houseflies and bushflies — the queens like to nest near houses, schools, sports grounds and picnic areas. Foodstuffs and sugary drinks are irresistible lures.

Most nests start in holes dug in the ground or behind rockeries. But tree clefts and hollows, hedges, tussocks, compost heaps, stacks of cartons or building material and the ceiling spaces or wall cavities of houses may also be chosen.

Combs of brood cells are made of the same papery material as those of the native vespids (wasps of the family Vespidae). They are extended horizontally during a colony's first season of growth, but in succeeding years new combs are added in parallel tiers. The cells are open at the bottom but the nest has a stiff covering, usually grey but sometimes brown.

The wasps are harmless when they are foraging, and fairly tolerant of movement or noise near their nests. But if a nest is touched the workers storm out and attempt to sting whatever they see. Each

Paper-nest wasps Ropalidia *on their vertical comb*

can sting repeatedly. People attacked on two or three separate occasions can develop a life-threatening allergy, and it is possible that wasps may oversensitise some people to bulldog ant stings.

Property owners are obliged under pest control regulations to destroy European wasps' nests. This has done little to allay public health fears in urban areas — and nothing to stop the advance of *Vespula germanica*. Most hope of control rests on a tiny parasitic wasp, also from Europe, but it has proved difficult to breed.

Thousands of bee species

The alien wasps have a devastating impact on honey bees. They plunder honeycombs and kill worker bees trying to defend them — not only in domestic and commercial hives but also in wild nests. Introduced wherever European settlers went, the honey bee now has feral populations in woodlands and heathlands all over the country. They nest mainly in hollow trees and logs, rock crevices and holes in banks.

Bees are thought to have descended from sphecoid wasps that adapted to feeding their young on the products of flowers instead of animal tissue. Australia probably has well over 3000 species, only about half of which have been scientifically studied.

Most are solitary types that nest in individual burrows. A few have primitive social links but native bees forming advanced societies occur only across the northern half of the continent. Elsewhere the honey bee *Apis mellifera* is the sole species with a caste system to match that of vespid wasps; it also has methods of food storage and preparation unrivalled in the insect world.

Successive generations of worker bees maintain communities year-round. In

A single honey bee Apis mellifera *(above); and a swarm clustered on an acacia preparing to colonise a new hive (left)*

A bee of the family Braconidae using its long ovipositor to lay eggs in the trunk of a fallen rainforest tree

cold weather they are inactive, cramming together to conserve body heat, with their long-living queen always in their midst. In hot weather they cooperate in fanning the brood cells with their wings, and bring in water to cool the nest by evaporation.

From about October worker bees are especially busy gathering food for expanding populations of larvae. While they sip and swallow nectar from flowers, protein-rich pollen collects in little baskets on their hind legs. Some also take plant resins and saps for sealing joints and weatherproofing the nest covering, which consists of clustered cells of wax secreted from glands in the bees' skins.

Back at the nest the food gatherers regurgitate the nectar, which has undergone a chemical conversion in their stomachs and comes out as honey. It is deposited in some storage cells; the pollen

DANCING FOR DINNER
How a honey bee shows the way

A honey bee worker, returning to her hive, pinpoints the direction of a far-off food source by dancing on the honeycomb. She prances in a figure-of-eight pattern, emphasising the centre of the figure by waggling movements. The angle between the line of that central movement and the vertical is the same as the angle between the sun and the food plants. All her attentive co-workers have to do is match it when they fly out. If the food is closer than about a hundred metres, however, the guide simply walks in a circle. The others then know that they will soon find it by flying in increasing circles around the hive.

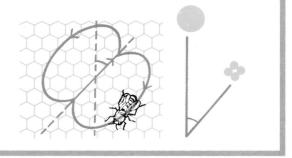

The banded bee Amegilla *belongs to the carpenter bee group*

goes into others. When brood cells are provisioned the two are mixed into what is called 'bee bread'.

Young workers produce a further secretion from glands in their throats. This 'royal jelly' is fed to all larvae for three days after they hatch. Later it is given only to a few larvae in oversized cells — the future queens.

Queens take to the air on single mating flights, generally in late summer. Drones pursue them, competing for the privilege of having their copulatory organs wrenched out, which occurs as a part of the mating process. In any case their lives are short.

Each queen stores the sperm of one chosen drone. As her community expands, she may lead a swarm of workers to find a site for a fresh colony. Her daughters stay in the old nest, the strongest of them quickly killing all her sisters. Less often a daughter queen leads the emigration to a new nesting site.

Only queens can sting more than once. Workers have barbed stings that remain trapped in their targets. When a worker breaks off an attack her entire venom apparatus is torn from her abdomen, the poison sac still pumping. The wound kills her within a day or so.

Domesticated bees become accustomed to disturbances of their hives when honeycombs are removed. Feral populations resent the touching of their nests but retaliation is generally carried out by only a few workers — they cannot risk mass suicide by attacking in the manner of wasps.

Migrating swarms settle quietly wherever their queens alight, entrusting a few scouts to look about for nesting sites. They do not buzz around furiously unless they are interfered with. Control is simply a matter of trapping the queen, but it takes skill and protective gear. State and territory agriculture departments keep registers of expert apiarists who are volun-tary bee-collectors. An ill-prepared attempt to drive away an invading swarm could have painful consequences.

To the delight of northern Aborigines, native social bees *Trigona* produce tasty honey and do not have stings. Small and dark, they nearly always build their horizontal combs in hollow trees. They do not migrate by swarming — their old queens get too fat to fly. Instead they establish outposts in a gradual process that takes weeks, with workers flying back and forth between sites. Eventually a daughter queen moves into a completed nest.

Carpenter bees

A rudimentary form of social organisation occurs among some of the plant-burrowing types that are commonly known as carpenter bees. Groups such as *Allodapula* and *Exoneura* do not make cells but place all their larvae together in holes bored into pithy stems, or in wood that has been bored by other insects. There seems to be some specialisation among females, the larger ones mating and laying eggs and the others foraging and tending the nest. This group also includes 'cuckoo bees' that practise social parasitism, laying their eggs in the nests of closely related species.

Many other carpenter bees are solitary. Prominent among them are big, hairy *Xylocopa* and *Lestis* species. They excavate grasstree stems, rotting wood and sometimes sound timber for their nests. Separately stocked brood cells are placed end to end and paper membrane parti-

Two egg-cells of the leafcutter bee Megachile, *taken from an underground nest*

WASPISH WAYS
Predators leave look-alikes alone

A *hoverfly* Baccha *mimicking a eumenid wasp*

Because birds, spiders, mice and other predators are wary of stings, wasps are the leading models for mimicry by insects that have no such weapons. This kind of evolutionary adaptation is especially notable among robber-flies, hoverflies, bee-flies and longhorn beetles.

Not only are the warning colours of common stinging wasps copied, but also their shapes — and if a slender 'wasp-waist' cannot be achieved, it may be faked by shading. Imitations extend to behaviour, with many mimics attempting to discourage potential predators by adopting waspish ways of vibrating their antennae and flicking their wings.

A *longhorn beetle* Hesthesis *mimicking* Hyleoides concinna, *a wasp-mimicking bee*

tions are constructed between them.

Australia is the world's greatest stronghold of colletids (bees of the family Colletidae). All solitary, they burrow deeply into soil or sometimes into rotten wood. Females are unique in their secretion of a translucent material like cellophane, which they apply with their tongues as a lining for brood chambers.

Megachilid bees (of the family Megachilidae), also very common, are noted for transporting various lining materials for brood cells. These are usually constructed in natural cavities or burrows made by other creatures. Best known is the leaf-cutting bee *Megachile*, which lines clusters of cells with neatly trimmed fragments of leaves. *Chalicodoma* collects resins, and according to overseas observations carries back to its nest tiny pebbles and blobs of mud.□

A black mark for ticks
Spring is the season when females are biting

Life cycles of ticks, including the infamous paralysis tick *Ixodes holocyclus*, vary with climate and weather. The paralysis tick can breed at six months of age in tropical Queensland, or take more than fifteen months in Victoria, at the limit of its east coast range. In New South Wales and southern Queensland, where it has caused most trouble — killing many people before the Second World War — the life cycle is roughly one year. October and November are the danger months.

Ticks are zoologically connected with spiders but are totally parasitic, like lice and many mites. Female paralysis ticks feed three times in their lives, males normally only twice. Both sexes need nutrition from feasts of extra blood to transform from larva to nymph and from nymph to adult. The mature female needs a further intake for egg production. The male simply mates and dies.

Preferred animal hosts
Paralysis ticks and their close relatives rely on warm-blooded vertebrate hosts. Bandicoots, probing in forest and woodland litter, are prime targets. But any furry native mammals — or introduced pets and livestock — will do just as well. Humans are less suitable unless a tick finds shelter in hair, beneath clothing or in folds of skin.

A tick injects its saliva to aid the flow and digestion of blood from its host. By accident the paralysis tick's saliva contains a substance that works on humans as a powerful neurotoxin. Native hosts are immune, at least in tick-infested districts. Serious diseases may also be transmitted in the saliva. In general, problems arise only at the third

The size of this tick feeding on a magpie's head suggests that it is a female about to lay eggs

and last stage of feeding by the female, though small dogs have suffered mild paralysis from nymphal tickbites.

In warm, moist eastern areas, tick eggs hatch mostly in January. Six-legged larvae, barely visible

A tick of the family Ixodidae feeding on the shingle-back lizard Trachydosaurus rugosus *of arid Australia*

to our eyes, climb to the outer foliage of low plants around March. Whatever fibrous surface brushes past, they cling to it. They seek darkness, and if they find moist skin, they push in a barbed tube and feed for a week.

Replete, the larvae drop into moist litter to undergo their first moult, emerging as eight-legged nymphs about the size of pinheads. Usually in July in the east, they climb plants again to claim another ride and their second meal. More than doubled in size if successful, they drop off again.

Adult females when they start to seek blood again in October are about the size and shape of match-heads. Eyeless, they are attracted to mammals by carbon dioxide in exhaled breath. On their new hosts they encounter wandering males who mate with them. If a female has already been feeding, a copulating male may sneak an unofficial snack by biting her.

Usually starved, the males drop off and quickly die. Meanwhile females try to feed for at least six days — sometimes twenty. They become enormously engorged, expanding to the size of a gardener's best peas. After three weeks back on the ground, fertilised females lay as many as 3000 eggs. Then their life too is over. ☐

A female tick that successfully completes its life cycle may lay 3000 eggs

Awaiting a favourable wind

For an orb-weaving spider, constructing a web of startling beauty and complexity is all in a night's work

Insects zoom and flit about in the still air, not knowing how lucky they are. A hungry spider squats among the outer foliage of some low shrubbery. Patient as always, she has waited half the night for a puff of wind. Unless it comes she cannot start to set up her web.

She holds a long strand of fine silk, heavily sticky at the end. At last a breeze springs up and she releases the thread. The end catches a twig on a neighbouring bush and holds fast. Quickly the spider draws in the slack and secures her end of the line to her perch.

In a skittering tightrope act she dashes back and forth across the bridge she has made between the bushes, laying more silk to reinforce it. Next she spins a longer strand and fastens it at both ends of the bridge. Moving to the middle of this slack thread, she lets her own weight stretch it and pull it down into a V shape. Then she attaches a new line and lowers herself — to wait again for the wind.

If she is swung towards one other anchoring point and can grasp it with her forelegs, the rest of her task is routine. Working in and out from the centre of the Y formation that she has created, and from one anchorage to another, she trails and tightens new lines of silk that eventually complete a pattern of radiating spokes within an angular frame.

Starting from near the centre and still using dry silk, the spider strengthens the structure by linking up the spokes with a wide spiral. Then she spins sticky silk, working her way back towards the centre in a much tighter spiral. At the same time she rolls up and removes the dry one — perhaps eating it. As a final touch she loops swathes of dry silk into two broad ribbons that cross in the centre of the

Some spiders build distinctive silk ribbons into their webs: St Andrew's cross spider Argiope aetherea *(left);* Argiope picta *(right)*

web. This is the trademark of the St Andrew's cross spider.

Legs together in pairs, aligned with the cross, she will wait in the centre of her web day and night as long as the structure lasts. Wear and tear from the struggles of trapped insects will probably render it useless within three or four days. Something big may blunder into the web before then or strong winds may buffet the supporting bushes and tear it apart.

As spiders grow, so do their webs. The elaborate constructions of many orb-weavers are easily noticeable by October. But across the north and along most of the east coast, no spider makes itself more conspicuous than the female *Argiope aetherea*. Her cross is a lustrous silver. She herself, about a centimetre long at this time of year, is vividly patterned and covered with hairs that reflect sunlight.

Hanging out in daylight in such an eye-catching fashion may seem dangerous. But the total effect apparently confuses predatory birds. To make sure of that, if the spider is alarmed by a sudden shadow or noise, she shakes her web so rapidly that her appearance is blurred.

Ribbon overlays on the webs of related species are usually less obvious. In the south, where the St Andrew's cross spider does not occur, its name is often given to *Argiope trifasciata*. The teardrop spider *Argiope protensa*, with an elongated and pointed abdomen, is another well-known member of the group.

These and dozens of other kinds of orb-weavers have broadly similar annual life cycles. Most reach maturity and mate in summer or autumn, dying soon afterwards. The male is always minute in comparison with his mate, and often not recognisable as the same species. His courtship, to placate the female and avoid being attacked as prey, consists of a rhythmical tweaking or strumming on a guy-line of her web, sometimes for hours.

Spiders don't get stuck

The spiders run no risk of being caught in their own or a neighbouring web. As they move about over the adhesive spiral, its silk slips smoothly between hard bristles on their feet. Other parts of their bodies are protected against accidental contact by a coating of oil.

Soon after hatching in winter or early spring, spiderlings are all capable of wind-blown aerial dispersal on strands of gossamer. But although they cannot be called social animals, many orb-weavers have a tendency to cluster. Lines of bushes or trees may be linked by one web after another, all of the same type.

In city parks and suburban gardens almost anywhere in Australia, the biggest and most perfectly symmetrical orbs are usually those spun by *Eriophora* species.

Tiers of webs made by tent spiders Cyrtophora. *These webs are very strong, and prey is ensnared by the labyrinthine tangle rather than by sticky silk*

The brightly coloured jewel or Christmas spider Gasteracantha minax

These webs have a hole in the centre — bitten out and eaten after all the spokes are in place. The hairy, boldly banded owners grow to two centimetres long.

Some smaller species commonly seen in gardens have extraordinary body forms. Spines on the jewel or Christmas spider *Gasteracantha minax* give it the shape of a star. This is one of the types most given to clustering. *Cyclosa trilobata*, most abundant in cool regions, has a very long abdomen divided into three lobes at the rear. Though highly conspicuous with a broad, bright stripe down the back of the abdomen, like the St Andrew's spider it hangs in its web all day.

Some orb-weavers leave a segment out of their webs, like a wedge out of a cheese. This is not a sign of inferior ability but an advanced adaptation — demonstrated most obviously by the builders of the biggest and strongest webs of all, golden orb-weavers *Nephila*.

Golden orb-weavers like to build in high, windy situations, most often in dry forests and woodlands or coastal scrub. Mature females of some species exceed four centimetres in length. Their orbs are about one metre across but other webbing gives a total span of up to four metres.

strength. A person walking into such a web with a hat on is likely to have it plucked off. Small birds are sometimes caught — and trussed up and bitten like any other prey. Bigger birds are greeted by a violent shaking of the whole enormous structure — an awesome sight.

Leaf-rolling spiders

Other notable weavers of incomplete circular webs are the leaf-rolling spiders *Phonognatha*. They roll up dry gumleaves and place them in the missing segment, attached at one end to the hub. A female leaf-roller has not only a weatherproof retreat and a screen against birds, but also a place to lay eggs and brood spiderlings. Other weavers have to attach cocoons to nearby foliage.

A few orb-weavers make horizontal webs. The best known are tent spiders *Cyrtophora*. They build tangled labyrinth traps and draw the hubs of their orbs up inside, so that they form peaks. The webs are meant to last: they have branching spokes and retain the dry spirals of their original scaffolding. But there are no sticky spirals. The prey exhausts itself trying to escape from the labyrinth, and then the spider rushes out to bite it, in the manner of sheet-web weavers (see May, page 131). Young tent spiders sometimes cluster so closely that their strange webs form tiers in the foliage.

Nearly all orb-weavers belong to the family Araneidae. But one small and completely unrelated family, the Uloboridae, has hit on the same technique. The webs tend to be lopsided, however. A more remarkable fact about *Uloborus* species is that they are among the very few known spiders that do not have venom. They have to enswathe their prey completely with silk to overpower it. All other orb-weavers are venomous, but their toxins do not need to be especially potent because their prey is already helpless. None is dangerous to humans. □

This golden orb-weaver Nephila *has just added another corpse to its garbage dump*

Through a wide segment at the top of the orb, where the sticky spiral is interrupted, a single line runs out from the hub. It appears to be abnormally thick and bumpy. This is the spider's garbage dump. Rather than have the sucked-dry skeletons of her prey blowing about and perhaps cluttering the web, she carries them here and attaches them.

Again with tidiness in mind, she permits tiny dewdrop or quicksilver spiders or other *Argyrodes* species — not weavers themselves — to live in her web. They dispose of trapped insects that are too small for her to manage.

Golden orb-weavers build their webs to last indefinitely. About halfway from the hub to the anchorages, the spokes are branched, giving the structure extra

A two-spined spider Poecilopachys bispinosa

SPINNING IN SECRET
A new web every night

Until late in the 1960s a common but bizarre-looking spider of the east coast, the two-spined *Poecilopachys bispinosa*, was believed not to make a web. At the cost of much lost sleep, the Sydney naturalist and photographer Densey Clyne proved otherwise. This little orb-weaver has an unusual method of laying its snare threads in segments rather than in a continuous spiral. The adhesive is exuded at intervals, forming a coating on the threads. None of this work starts until well after midnight — and the spider destroys it all before dawn.

The web of a leaf-rolling spider Phonognatha, with the leaf at top right, an egg-sac at top centre, and newly hatched young

A yellow-billed spoonbill at its nest

Floods – a blessing in disguise

Wetlands are vital to waterfowl survival throughout the continent

To our settled way of thinking, floods are disruptive and often disastrous. But in nature they are an essential element of the life force. Where they occur with some regularity, creating what scientists call wetlands, they provide the food resources and breeding conditions for innumerable animal species. In particular, our few mainland wetland areas ensure the restocking of waterfowl populations that roam all over the country.

The floodplain forests shown here, beside the middle reaches of the Murray River, are inundated by spring snowmelt from catchments to the south and east. Elsewhere in the system, summer overspills come from rains in southern Queensland. Natural cycles of flooding and drying bring a variation of water depths, accommodating the needs of different birds. Salting, silting and pesticide pollution all pose a threat to wetlands – but their worst enemy is injudicious flood control.

Koorangie Game Reserve in northern Victoria

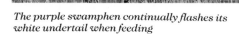

The purple swamphen continually flashes its white undertail when feeding

These water scorpions of the family Nepidae breathe air from the surface through their long, tail-like snorkels

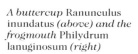

A buttercup Ranunculus inundatus *(above) and the frogmouth* Philydrum lanuginosum *(right)*

The darter sinks underwater to hunt, using its sharp bill to spear prey

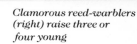

Clamorous reed-warblers (right) raise three or four young

Damselflies, unlike dragonflies, fold their wings over their backs when at rest

The purple-spotted gudgeon Mogurnda mogurnda

The mosquito fish Gambusia affinis, introduced to control the spread of malaria

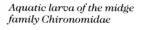

Aquatic larva of the midge family Chironomidae

The blue-billed duck's courtship display is spectacular, ending in a high-speed chase. Midge larvae (left) make up about twenty-five per cent of this duck's diet

Squirming inside their small, purse-like nest until they are almost standing on their heads, mistletoebird triplets less than a week old thrust their rumps out of the entrance hole. Their mother, perched beside the nest, gently presses her bill around the pinkish vent area of each chick, causing the muscles to relax. The youngsters are being house-trained.

At first the nestlings were fed on insects. Now, a week or so before fledging, they are about to be converted to the diet that will be their staple for the rest of their

A diet for clean-living chicks

Within a few days of hatching, young mistletoebirds are taught to dispose of dangerous waste

lives: the pulp of mistletoe berries. But unless they are taught to crane out as far as they can while taking berries from their parents, and always to defecate well clear of the nest, this food could be dangerous.

Mistletoes attach themselves to trees, taking water and nutrient salts from their hosts. Beneath a tasty, jelly-like flesh their seeds are heavily coated with one of nature's strongest adhesives. When a ripe berry falls and splits open on striking a lower branch, or when a seed is excreted by an animal, the adhesive secures it to a new site for germination.

Forest hunters of many cultures learned long ago to use mistletoe glue to catch birds. The English called it 'bird-lime'. Smeared on branches and twigs where smaller species alighted, it would cement them to their perches. For a mistletoebird to drop food or excrete a seed in its nest could be suicidal.

Mistletoebirds belong to a family called flowerpeckers, occurring worldwide in tropical regions. Australia's single species, *Dicaeum hirundinaceum*, has spread itself — and its food plants — all over the mainland. Many native trees are killed by the parasites, which in times of drought take all the available moisture.

Dozens of mistletoe species are exploited and disseminated by the birds. Berries are bitten open at the ends, then delicately nibbled at the bases so that the contents are squeezed out, leaving the empty skins hanging. A simplified digestive system extracts nutrients from the flesh and passes out the sticky seeds within an hour.

Populations are locally nomadic, moving around because fruiting times vary. The birds also eat a few insects, especially in winter. Their breeding starts when ripe berries become most abundant — generally from October through into summer in temperate and subtropical regions, or autumn in the monsoonal zone. In good seasons successive broods are reared.

The female builds and decorates
Side-opening nests are slung from twigs among foliage that may be more than ten metres from the ground or as low as a metre. The female spends a week weaving fluffy plant fibres and caterpillar hairs into a dense, durable fabric that resembles felt. The structure is matted with cobweb and decorated with insect cases, dry flowers or lichen. Eggs are incubated by the female with no help from the male bird.

One other Australian bird, though classed as a honeyeater, shares the mistletoebird's tastes. The painted honeyeater *Grantiella picta* is even more particular, feeding on a few species of mistletoe that parasitise casuarinas and eking out its diet with flying insects.

Ranging in a belt from the Gulf

A male mistletoebird Dicaeum hirundinaceum *feeds a berry to one of its chicks*

Both sexes of the noisy pitta help to incubate and feed the three to four young

Country to western Victoria, painted honeyeaters are highly nomadic for most of the year. Males move into southern districts in October to establish breeding territories, advertising them with a loud two-note whistle that sounded to early settlers like 'Georgie', which became the bird's popular name.

Both sexes help to build an apparently flimsy basket of roots, grass or casuarina branchlets at the end of a drooping branch. This task takes as long as three weeks, much of the time being spent in tying the nest to twigs with cobweb, securing it in as many as twenty places. Parents share the incubation of two eggs.

In eastern rainforests the noisy pitta *Pitta versicolor* starts to make its presence known around October. Its loud territorial call is a questioning whistle of three syllables, likened by some people to 'walk-to-work?' or 'want-a-whip?'

Incessant calling by noisy pittas in the north of their range coincides with the early rains of the approaching wet season. So along with the rainbow pitta *Pitta iris* of the Top End and the red-bellied pitta *Pitta erythrogaster*, which migrates from New Guinea in October to breed on Cape York Peninsula, it enjoys a reputation as a weather forecaster.

Out of breeding, pittas are not heard and rarely seen in spite of their vivid colouring. They are furtive ground-feeders, turning over forest litter in search of insects, woodlice, worms, and especially snails. Sometimes called anvil birds, they each select a single stone or log on which to smash the shells of snails.

Pittas' nests are side-opening domes of various plant material on or close to the ground, most often among the buttress roots of rainforest trees. They are strangely characterised by aprons of soft mammal dung that the birds collect and spread around the entrances. Sexes share the incubation of three or four eggs.

Courtship by fruit-eating rainforest pigeons, reaching a peak around October, is marked by persistent cooing during the bowing displays of the males. Two species, the white-headed pigeon *Columba leucomela* and the brown cuckoo-dove *Macropygia amboinensis*, draw further attention to themselves with display flights high over the forest canopy. Both species do most of their feeding in the trees, in pairs during the breeding season or in groups of about a dozen.

More given to ground-feeding on fallen fruits are the wonga pigeon *Leucosarcia melanoleuca* and the emerald ground-

The wonga pigeon is a sedentary bird, and solitary when not breeding

The emerald ground-dove gives an eye-catching bowing display when courting

The dollarbird or broad-billed roller Eurystomus orientalis *is essentially a tropical bird that comes to Australia to breed*

dove *Chalcophaps indica*. These two are generally solitary, though small groups are sometimes seen in clearings. Nesting habits are much the same in all four species. Pairs nest repeatedly in good seasons, on platforms of twigs and vine tendrils in tall shrubbery, tree forks or vine tangles. But there is a striking dis-

tinction in productivity — the tree-feeders lay only one egg, the ground-feeders two.

Flying as high as 2500 metres, flocks of dollarbirds *Eurystomus orientalis* enter Australia from the north in mid-October to breed in woodlands and along rainforest edges. Having wintered in northern New

Guinea, some will work their way as far south as eastern Victoria.

Dollarbirds are conspicuous on the highest bare branches of tall trees or sometimes telephone wires, perched motionless because the structure of their feet does not encourage walking or hopping. Around dawn and dusk they sally out on

Despite its size, the Australasian bittern is a stealthy bird and is seldom seen

flights in pursuit of insects, showing the blueish-white wing patches that resemble coins and give them their name.

Pairs chatter volubly during the breeding season and both sexes give cackling territorial calls. They choose high tree-hollows for nesting. About four eggs are laid on wood dust. Both parents are thought to incubate them; feeding duties are known to be shared.

Migrating pratincoles

Another migrant that feeds voraciously on swarming insects, taking them in mid-flight, is the oriental pratincole *Glareola maldivarum*. From breeding grounds on the Asian mainland, enormous flocks arrive over northwestern coasts during October and November and spread inland. They exploit flushes of insects brought out by isolated storms reaching the southern and eastern margins of the monsoonal zone. Floods must be avoided because the birds need firm ground for roosting.

The native-breeding Australian pratincole *Stiltia isabella* catches insects on the ground as well as in the air. It is a zonal migrant that winters in the north and returns to the inner southeast in spring. Loose groups nest on bare, stony plains. Parents share incubation in brief shifts, often exposed to fierce heat. They resist it by spreading their feathers and panting. Hatchlings are placed in the shelter of low vegetation, or sometimes in burrows.

Wherever spring floods have filled freshwater swamps of the southern mainland, waves of clamorous reed-warblers *Acrocephalus stentoreus* arrive in September and October to set up a din of competitive singing. In winter they were dispersed across the far north, but now they return to beds of reeds and

bullrushes where pairs forage and nest less than ten metres apart. Males proclaiming their territories sing all day long and well into the night.

Scattered in the more permanent swamps are the nesting platforms and roosting pads of Australasian bitterns *Botaurus poiciloptilus*. These birds, related to herons, spend their entire existence in the cover of dense growths of reeds and rushes, feeding mainly at night. If disturbed they are reluctant to fly; instead they 'freeze' with their bills pointing to the sky, so that the streaked

plumage of their slim bodies merges with the surrounding vegetation.

Well before the onset of breeding in October, male Australasian bitterns give booming nighttime calls that can carry more than two kilometres. The sound, uttered with the bill closed, is like the lowing of a cow. Males probably mate with more than one female; they are not dutiful parents, and give no help in incubation or the care of the young.

Four to six eggs are laid at two-day intervals, so there may be as much as ten days' difference in the age of hatchlings. Regurgitated food is doled out systematically. A female studied in New Zealand was seen to feed her young in order of age. Each was given a frog — the first a fresh one, the others in progressive stages of predigestion.

Bitterns are entirely carnivorous, taking mice, lizards, insects, snails and worms from among the reeds, as well as fish, crustaceans, amphibians and molluscs from the water. Frogs and mice are stabbed with the bill; sizable fish are seized between the mandibles and killed by shaking and biting.

The little bittern *Ixobrychus minutus*, less than half the size of *Botaurus*, frequents similar habitats and also breeds in October. It seems to be monogamous, the male starting the nest and helping with incubation. The male black bittern *Ixobrychus flavicollis* also shows a devotion to his mate and family. This species, nearly as big as the Australasian bittern but distinguished by plain dark colouring and straw-coloured neck

Black bitterns usually build their stick nests in a tree over water

Coastal colonies of pied cormorants often gather in numbers on shoals of fish

in groups, whistling and splashing to attract attention. Nests are usually scrapes in the ground among grass or rushes, but sometimes rock crannies or tree-holes are used. As many as ten eggs are incubated by the female alone. Hatchlings take to the water on their second day, and are guarded by both parents until they can fly.

Sea-feeding storm-petrels
On islands off the southern coast between Geraldton in Western Australia and Port Stephens in New South Wales, white-faced storm-petrels *Pelagodroma marina* start a breeding season as regular as that of shearwaters (see November, page 260). They are alike in many other ways, raising their chicks in burrows and when not on incubation or brooding duty, spending their days far out at sea. Dense breeding colonies disband in late summer. Out of breeding, the birds are thought to spend their time in the northern Indian Ocean.

The sea-feeding storm-petrels and shearwaters, along with terns, gulls and gannets, make choice targets for jaegers — the leading pirates of temperate coastal waters in late spring and summer. These are slender, agile skuas that breed north of the Arctic Circle and begin to arrive off Australia in October. They terrorise other birds in flight, forcing them to drop food, as well as scavenging refuse and doing some fishing of their own. Two species are regular visitors; the more commonly seen, because it follows boats and enters harbours, is the smaller of the two, the Arctic jaeger *Stercorarius parasiticus*.□

plumes, lives along the forested margins of rivers and coastal inlets.

Spring flooding in the south expands the breeding opportunities of cormorants. The little pied cormorant *Phalacrocorax melanoleucos* is at home near any body of calm water — fresh or salt, temporary or permanent. Like all cormorants it swims underwater in pursuit of fish or crustaceans, and spends much of the rest of its day perched with wings spread out to dry, from time to time preening the feathers with oil from enlarged glands at the base of the tail.

Colonial cormorants
Cormorants nest in colonies, their species often mixed. Males gather sticks and debris and females build platforms, usually in trees but occasionally in shrubbery or on the ground. Both sexes share the incubation of three to five eggs, taking about a month.

The biggest birds seen nesting or hunting with cormorants are often not true cormorants but darters *Anhinga melanogaster*. They are closely related but have anatomical differences — most noticeably a double curvature of the neck that gives them the quick-striking ability of a snake. They can wait for prey underwater, during dives lasting up to a minute, rather than having to chase it.

October is the peak breeding month for chestnut teal *Anas castanea*, though some populations begin as early as July. They are sedentary ducks where easy conditions prevail but readily move if threatened by drought — often joining flocks of nomadic grey teal. Drakes court

Male and female chestnut teal form a pair-bond, and both look after the young

Australian magpies of the white-backed race feeding chicks at the nest — young beg food from all adults in the group

The black and white blitz

Territorial anxiety drives magpies to aggression

Aerial attacks by magpies, sometimes in big mobs, can occur unnervingly at any time of year. They intensify in mid-spring when the majority of breeding birds are incubating eggs or brooding hatchlings. Though serious injury is rare, life outdoors can be made difficult for adults and terrifying for children.

Magpie aggression in Australia is often displayed far from any nest and without apparent provocation. But our magpies are not concerned with nest defence. Their aim is to hold secure feeding territories, on which their place in the social order and their chances of breeding depend.

The Australian magpie *Gymnorhina tibicen* has no links with its European counterpart. Closely related to butcherbirds and currawongs, it has adapted to feeding on the ground and spends most of its day on foot. Insects and other invertebrates provide most of its diet but lizards, mice and small birds are sometimes taken.

Successful groups, comprising up to ten adults in the east and sometimes more than twenty in the southwest, hold ample territories year-round. Only these groups can be relied on to breed — and even then not all of the members take part. One dominant male mates with some of the females, while non-breeders assist him in defence.

Other groups try to establish themselves in areas where the availability of food or shelter is marginal, and their hold is usually temporary. They seldom attempt to breed and very rarely succeed. In the least favourable areas adults and immature birds form nomadic flocks, never breeding.

Territorial magpies see any larger animal walking on their feeding grounds as a threat. Their anxiety is heightened during breeding because weak-flying magpie fledglings will flutter to these grounds when they are only about a month old and incapable of looking after themselves. Any available member of the group tries to keep the territory clear of intruders, swooping at their heads from behind in what are most often mock assaults, without contact.

Mated females build basket nests high in trees or occasionally on power pylons. Sticks are the natural structural material and grasses are the conventional lining, but magpies have taken a strong liking to all manner of things that people may provide. Offcuts of fencing or electrical wire are favourites. A nest found in Western Australia in the 1950s consisted entirely of wire — 243 pieces with a combined length of more than a hundred metres. Other materials commonly incorporated in nests include hair, string, cloth, cardboard, rubber and plastic. Shiny items such as cutlery and shards of glass or crockery are used as decorations.

As many as six eggs may be laid, taking about three weeks for the female alone to incubate. But it is unusual for more than two or three hatchlings to survive. The young remain dependent on the adults in their group all through summer. In autumn they are driven out to take up with wandering flocks. They may get a chance to breed at three or four years old, and could live to over fifteen.□

243

Numbats, unlike other ant and termite eaters, lack the strong forelimbs and stout claws needed to break into termite mounds

Two kittenish numbats, separated from their mother for the first time, scamper across a gravelly, forested slope of the southwest's Darling Range. Among the tall wandoo and jarrah, a recently fallen log is a welcome discovery. It may contain a nest of termites — the numbats' only food. Better still, it could also make a cosy den.

But this log already has a casual tenant. A fox is dozing, hungry and ill at ease because his foraging last night yielded only a few insects. As the numbats snuffle hopefully at the entrance to his hiding place, he stirs and leaps out. In the ensuing slaughter, neither of the marsupials gets a chance to use the sharp claws on its forepaws — a numbat's only defensive weapon.

Myrmecobius fasciatus is unique among marsupials. It is remotely related to quolls, antechinuses and other small carnivores that can bite ferociously. But a

Slaughter of the innocents

Extinct across most of their former range, termite-eating numbats attempt a shaky last stand in a corner of the west

numbat's teeth are small and blunt, useful only for carrying nesting material or for shifting sticks that interfere with its quest for termites. A fast-flicking tongue — sticky, cylindrical and half as long as the animal's head and body — draws up the insects. On a good day one numbat may eat 20 000 termites, swallowed whole.

Most are taken from the soft nests in hollowed-out branches of tree-dwelling species, after limbs or trunk have fallen to the ground. Numbats do not have an echidna's ability to break into the hard nests of mound-building termites. But they eat plenty of them, sniffing out the shallow runways that radiate from the mounds and scratching away the leaf litter, stones and soil that cover them.

Though numbats usually sleep in logs, an adult female also digs a burrow. A tunnel a metre or two long leads to a nesting chamber lined with plant material. In common with some quolls, the female has no pouch. Her young, born in late summer, attach their mouths to teats that are protected by long belly hairs and surrounded by short, bent bristles to provide footholds.

When their fur has grown the young are placed in the nesting chamber, to be suckled during visits by their mother. For a few weeks after weaning they go out to feed with her, riding on her back. Independence comes in October, and juveniles wander away to find their own feeding ranges during summer.

Just as termites are active by day, so are numbats. They occupy their log dens at night and may shelter in them on the hottest afternoons, but in milder conditions they keep busy through all the hours of daylight. Boldly marked — with banded backs that only the thylacine or Tasmanian 'tiger' could match, if it still exists — they are the most conspicuous of marsupials. Sadly, all too few are seen.

Last century numbats with redder fur

The western brush wallaby is one of the largest of the wallabies

were found in western New South Wales and at points in South Australia and central Western Australia that suggested a broad band of distribution across the southern arid zone. Their habitat was a virtually continuous belt of mulga scrub. This type, regarded as a subspecies, is believed to be extinct.

Extinction of the scrub numbat

Foxes, cats and dingoes must have played their part in the disappearance of the scrub numbat — called *walpurti* by western desert Aborigines. But the chief cause was probably the breaking-up of the habitat for agricultural purposes. Isolated populations would have found nowhere to go after bushfires.

Under close national park protection numbats have been reintroduced to some western parts of the mulga scrub belt. Their only other habitat is dry eucalypt forest behind the Darling scarp, which backs the populous Swan coastal plain on each side of Perth.

These refuges too are fire-prone and fragmented. Some are increasingly impoverished by cinnamon fungus, which not only causes jarrah dieback but also kills many understorey plants, and so reduces the available cover. Foxes abound, their populations having exploded in the wooded southwest around 1973. Once a common sight, numbats now are rare.

Another heavy sufferer from the predation of foxes in the southwest is the western brush wallaby *Macropus irma*. Its young emerge from their pouches in October and November, and many are taken soon after. The species remains fairly common, however. Solitary animals or pairs can be seen in broad daylight, grazing in woodlands and open forest.

Ghost bats Microderma gigas *are unusual in having good eyesight*

Drastic disturbance of a habitat — by blasting with explosives — has drawn unusual public attention to some of our most obscure mammals, the cave-dwelling bats. In 1988 the national media became interested in a long conservation battle near Rockhampton, Queensland, where a cement company was mining a fissured limestone outcrop.

THE ONES THAT GOT AWAY
Foxes thrive in Australia's open spaces

European foxes *Vulpes vulpes* have been almost as successful as feral cats in their conquest of the mainland. Descended from animals introduced in the 1860s by southern gentry with a penchant for riding to hounds, they have spread right across the continent and into the tropical northwest and northeast. They have no discernible preference in habitats provided there is water to drink. And though they are a scourge of small mammals and ground-nesting birds, they will settle for scavenged carrion, insects and wild fruits.

Cubs are born and reared in dens — most often the enlarged burrows of an even more foolish import, the rabbit. Well-fed females, sexually mature in their first year, whelp four or five young. The cubs emerge in October to hunt or forage at night in family groups. By autumn they seek territories of their own, pushing the range of their kind wider every year.

Unlike so many other creatures, foxes have prospered in spite of hunting

Grandly called Mount Etna, the hill contains roosting and breeding havens for five kinds of bats, including Australia's only carnivorous species, the ghost bat *Macroderma gigas*. It is not threatened with extinction, but disruption could make it extremely rare. Colonies scattered throughout the tropical zone usually comprise a few dozen animals, or a few hundred at most. Only in limestone formations at the southeastern limit of their range do thousands of bats congregate.

At Fitzroy Caves, not far from Mount Etna, one of the biggest communities is under national parks guardianship. Various caves include one that the bats use only from October to January. It is reserved for mothers, first as a maternity ward and later as a nursery when their young get too heavy to carry.

A few minutes after sunset, when the cave-dwellers pour out to feed, the ghost bats among them can be distinguished by their pale grey colouring and low, direct flight. They seize their prey mainly on the ground, enveloping it in their wings and then biting with long, sharp teeth that give them the alternative name of false vampire bat. Frogs, mice, lizards, birds, big insects and sometimes other bats are taken. Prey is carried not to the home caves but to habitual feeding roosts, below which are found heaps of animal remains.

Grotesque ghost bats

Ghost bats have big eyes and seem to see well. They navigate by echolocation, but do not rely on it continuously in flight as other cave bats do. Grotesque, leaf-like protuberances of skin above the nostrils and in the ears direct the transmission and reception of calls.

Diadem horseshoe bats Hipposideros diadema *are the largest of our horseshoe bats*

Even more bizarre nose-leaf formations are seen in insect-eating horseshoe bats *Rhinolophus* and *Hipposideros*. Orange or reddish in colour, these bats flutter about like butterflies and can hover. Insects are taken on the wing and carried to feeding roosts. The bats echolocate continuously even with their mouths full, because the sounds are snorted through the nose.

Our eight species of horseshoe bats are almost entirely tropical in their distribution. Only the eastern horseshoe bat *Rhinolophus megaphyllus* ranges into the southeast, where small colonies in high-country forests are obliged to hibernate in winter. All species studied have a regular cycle of births in October or November.

Females have pairs of teats in their pubic area that do not bear milk. Single young fasten to these while they are carried in flight; they are suckled on chest nipples while their mothers are at rest. After about two weeks the young are placed in clusters on their cave ceiling. They are weaned at two months, by which time they are almost the size of adults. They are soon able to hunt for themselves, though they stay with their mothers.

Horseshoe bats are sexually mature at

The eastern horseshoe bat's strange nose-leaf formation helps it in echolocation

two or three years of age. Mating occurs in autumn in cooler regions, before communities break up for the winter. Females store the sperm, not fertilising themselves until they ovulate in spring. Ghost bats on the other hand are directly fertilised.

Sperm storage in colder climates is common among wattled bats and other *Chalinolobus* species. Wattled bats are not normally cave-dwellers, except where vegetation is scarce. They favour tree-hollows. But many roost opportunistically in domed birds' nests or the ceiling spaces of buildings. The group includes Australia's most widespread species, Gould's wattled bat *Chalinolobus gouldii*. It occurs from Tasmania to the Top End and practically everywhere else but Cape York Peninsula. Birth times vary with latitude, but the peak is around October. Twins are quite common.□

Gould's wattled bat hunts moths, flying beetles and other insects

The persistence of a lopsided lover

Excitement runs high in the mangrove fiddler colony. Usually the little crabs are peaceful foragers on the lowest reaches of the mudflat. But at this time of year dozens are running about or popping in and out of burrows. Some are fighting or chasing, waving their claws up and down. Others caress partners tenderly — then scuttle off to new engagements.

This is a common scene beside warm, mangrove-lined creeks and estuaries during the lowest tides of spring and summer. The crabs perform in daylight. The most energetically mobile are nearly all males — easily distinguished by vividly coloured claws of comically unequal size. The right-hand claw of each male is about as big as his body, the other insignificant. Females also have colourful claws, but both are small.

Fiddler crabs are found worldwide on tropical and subtropical shores. They are named for their claw-waving habit — practised only by the males of most

Communal courting by fiddler crabs looks like a free-for-all. But the most successful males are those that keep trying

species as a courtship display. But both sexes of Australian mangrove fiddlers *Uca vomeris* brandish their claws as a threat. Thanks to a detailed study by a visiting American authority, many curious aspects of their behaviour can be explained.

Professor Michael Salmon of the University of Illinois spied on colonies near Townsville, Queensland, throughout their breeding season, from late October until early February. He observed matings nearly every day, but group activities peaked at roughly fortnightly intervals, around full and new moon.

Professor Salmon tagged scores of crabs so that he could record individual encounters. He found that both sexes were promiscuous, mating with many

partners. They reserved most of their claw-waving displays of aggression for members of the same sex, and frequently fought. Female battles over burrows and foraging areas usually lasted longer than tests of strength between rival males.

In any case the females were not impressed by size or fighting ability. They mated with males smaller than themselves as often as with bigger ones. Yet they were choosy. From his observations of a population in which the sexes were fairly evenly divided, Salmon calculated that for every successful courtship, the average male suffered seventeen rejections.

Certain males, though, did exceptionally well. Sometimes they mated with one female after another within a few minutes. Salmon discovered that these were the ones that consistently worked hardest, approaching most females, courting them ardently and returning to them often. He offers a theory that the persistent fervour of such males is a trait that their sons

Male and female fiddler crabs Uca vomeris *in a mangrove swamp. The male is the one with the enormously enlarged claw*

A mud crab Scylla serrata *among mangrove roots. This one has lost a claw*

several minutes. If the female is responsive she allows herself to be grasped and lifted out, then turned to face her suitor. Both raise their bodies and tilt them back, bringing their abdomens together. Grasping his mate with his walking legs, the male begins a slight but steady movement from side to side. Copulation lasts for up to seven minutes.

Eggs are produced and incubated in fortnightly cycles. Clutches adhere to the female's pleopods — small, non-walking abdominal legs that are sometimes called swimmerets — until the larvae hatch. These are released into the water at night, before the full moon or coinciding with the new moon. The tiny larvae do not join drifting plankton but swim for a time, growing and moulting until they take a form intermediate between a crab and a prawn. At that stage they sink to the seabed, probably returning to the mud-flats as juveniles about a year later.

Many fiddlers are preyed on by fish, birds and bigger mangrove crabs, including the mud crab *Scylla serrata*. This, the most prized of eating crabs, is less often seen because it hides in its burrow when the tide is out. *Scylla's* rival in commercial importance, the blue swimmer or sand crab *Portunus pelagicus*, stays mainly in deeper estuarine waters.

Both of the big table species also begin mating in October. Pairs show a devotion in marked contrast to the play-the-field policy of fiddlers. Males find mates by tracking sex-attractant chemicals in the water, emitted by females two days before a pre-nuptial moult. The females are clasped by their partners throughout this time and for three or four days afterwards. Only then does copulation take place.

Unrecognised rock lobsters

Similar patience in mating is shown by rock lobsters *Jasus* and *Panulirus*. Maternal care is also lengthy. Fertilised females carry eggs fixed to their swimmerets for more than three months. Even then the hatching larvae are only the size of pinheads, with five years or more to go until they will be mature lobsters. In their early years they drift on the ocean surface as flat, transparent creatures called phyllosomas. Their connection with lobsters unrecognised, these were once classed as adults in a group of their own.

Another transparent ocean-dweller coming to prominence at this time of year is the chironex box jellyfish *Chironex fleckeri*. Along the tropical Queensland coast, October is the month when maturing chironexes may become big enough to inflict severe stings on people in the sea. Across the northern coast their threat arises earlier.

By late summer the box-shaped body of a chironex can be as big as a man's head

inherit. So the females choose them to give their own genes the best chance.

Fiddler crab burrows are more or less temporary. Males change theirs frequently — perhaps several times a day during breeding peaks when they are anxious to cover as much ground as possible. Most matings take place just outside the females' burrows. Sometimes the female crabs are intercepted while going to or from their feeding grounds near the waterline, and shepherded back to their homes. On a rising tide when they retreat and close up their burrows, enthusiastic males may dig them out for a final fling.

A courting male gently strokes the sides or top of the female's carapace with his legs and smaller claw. She is usually crouched just inside her burrow entrance. The wooing may go on for a few seconds or

A painted crayfish Panulirus ornatus *on the Great Barrier Reef*

and its tentacles can extend for three metres when it is feeding. Yet it is so hard to see in the water that its existence was not established until 1955. Deaths before then were blamed on *Physalia*, the stinging hydroid that is known as the Portuguese man o' war or bluebottle.

It took until the 1980s to unveil the complicated annual life cycle of the chironex. In autumn, towards the end of their lives, large adults enter estuaries. They are presumed to spawn in pairs, though this has not been observed. Hatched larvae take the form of microscopic balls called planulas. These have hairs to propel themselves, and search upriver for sheltered places to settle.

Transforming into crawling polyps, much like tiny slugs, they move off again to find even more secure spots in rock crevices or indentations. There they attach themselves for a long stay. Like coral polyps and sea anemones they feed by stinging minute organisms, and reproduce without sexual activity, by budding.

In early spring another metamorphosis occurs. A total change in muscle and tentacle structure and in the digestive and nervous systems is completed in no more than two weeks. The outcome is a miniature medusa or jellyfish, less than a millimetre across and possessing only four small tentacles. Its attachment decays and it swims downstream.

Dispersing in coastal waters, fast-growing chironexes may be dangerously armed with multiple tentacles within two months or so. As an animal matures, up to sixty tentacles develop in four clusters, each clump trailing from a corner of the hollow jelly box.

Every tentacle is covered with millions of capsules called nematocysts. Triggered instantly if any other living creature makes contact with the protruding bristles, some capsules fire barbs or discharge adhesives at whatever has touched them. Most release venom-injecting threads, in densities of over a thousand from areas no bigger than a pinhead.

The venom contains an immensely powerful neurotoxin, along with components that destroy skin and damage red blood cells. Since the primary purpose of the capsules is merely to anchor and paralyse shrimps and prawns — the natural prey of the chironex — the awesome potency of its venom seems unnecessary. But the jelly must protect itself from collisions with big fish. If they are not quickly paralysed, their struggles could wrench off many tentacles.

The world's most advanced jellyfish

In the event of humans blundering into the tentacles with exposed skin, the clinging appendages are invariably torn off. The inevitable result is excruciating pain, but the outlook for the victim depends on what total length of tentacles adheres. Drenching with vinegar for thirty seconds deactivates undischarged stinging cells, and antivenom — stored at most popular beaches — should be administered as soon as possible.

Chironex fleckeri is by far the most dangerous of an uncertain number of Australian box jellyfish species. At least one other occurs as far south as Brisbane. All sting painfully, but none has as many tentacles or as potent a venom.

The chironex is also the world's most advanced jellyfish, with sensors that 'see' its surroundings and the ability to swim strongly in the manner of an octopus. It does not depend on tides or wind-forced currents, so these are no guide to its presence or absence. Strong wave action may drive it from very shallow waters — but not necessarily far.□

A chironex box jellyfish Chironex fleckeri *with prey in a mangrove swamp*

A tasty fish that changes sex

Male barramundi can never grow old — they reverse roles instead. Heading for the sea in spring, last year's fathers are mothers-to-be

Powerful tail lashing, the big barramundi surges from its hiding place, hard against the riverbank among the branches of a fallen tree. Its great mouth gapes like a bucket as it literally sucks in a passing pair of rainbow fish. They are only a snack. Day and night the barramundi will continue to ambush fish, prawns, frogs, aquatic reptiles and even small waterfowl.

The fish is feeding avidly in preparation for a long downstream journey, the third of its life. When it swam out of the broad, muddy estuary of its tropical river both last year and the year before and schooled with others of its kind, it spawned male sperm. Now it needs to put on even better condition. It is a female, about to produce thousands of eggs.

Sex changing is fairly widespread among several families of fishes. Their reproductive organs develop and shrivel up annually in any case. No great alteration in anatomy is needed for ovaries to develop instead of testes, or vice versa. No change is called for in breeding technique — simply the spawning into the water of a different batch of genetic material.

Most often the transition by other species is from female to male, in response to urgent population needs. In schools of some sedentary reef fishes, for example, the disappearance of a dominant male during the spawning season leaves a vacancy for the next biggest fish. If that happens to be a female, it promptly becomes a male. The transformation is complete in less than two weeks.

But all barramundi *Lates calcarifer* are born male. All, if they live long enough, become female. This inevitable, automatic change is unusual. It means that small male barramundi must invariably spawn with big females. That in turn means that the normal conservationist approach to fishing — taking only the big ones and throwing small ones back — does not secure the future of this most prized eating fish.

Giant barramundi

The species has vanished or become rare over much of its natural range, in coastal regions from northern Australia and New Guinea to the Red Sea and Japan. Overseas in times past, some barramundi were reported to exceed a hundred kilograms. Australians used to boast of catching fish 1.8 metres long and weighing more than sixty kilos. Now, however remote the river reaches and billabongs that are fished, anglers consider themselves lucky to bring in a barramundi of over six kilos. Rigid policing of bag limits, as well as closed seasons and marketing controls, offer the only hope of preventing the further decline and possible extinction of the species.

Authorities differ on how old and how big barramundi need to be before they change sex. Findings vary from four years to seven, and from fifty to ninety centimetres in length. The fish probably spend a season or two as sexually active males.

Growth rates are in any case highly variable because feeding opportunities are different. Barramundi in permanent waterways enjoy good nutrition year-round. Those whose seasonal rivers turn into chains of landlocked, shrinking billabongs may endure hard times as they wait for the return of the Wet.

A barramundi Lates calcarifer *stalking an unsuspecting rainbow fish*

The cobbler Tandanus bostocki *lives in fresh water in southern Western Australia*

feed independently, stay close enough to be gulped in again by their mothers if danger threatens.

These two mouth-breeders are Australia's only representatives of an ancient family of 'bony-tongued' fishes. They are also thought to be the only Australian fishes apart from the salamanderfish (see September, page 191) to have evolved entirely in fresh water. All others had a marine origin, or were introduced.

Eel-tailed catfishes

Freshwater eel-tailed catfishes start spawning around the end of October in most regions where rivers are rising. Well-known types such as the jewfish *Tandanus tandanus* in the east and southeast and the cobbler *Tandanus bostocki* in the southwest are nest builders. Males collect riverbed gravel in their mouths and spread it in low circles or ovals up to two metres across. Females spawn tens of thousands of heavy eggs that sink down between the pebbles, safe from predators. The males stay on guard, fanning their nests, during the week that it takes for the eggs to hatch.

The eggs of gudgeons and gobies are also guarded and fanned by the males. Rising, warming waters in the east and southeast trigger a long breeding season during which pairs spawn every few weeks. They mark their coming into condition by taking on striking coloration, especially the males. Eggs are attached by threads or stems to stones, aquatic plants and all kinds of underwater debris. Some species seek hollow objects such as empty snail shells, fastening their eggs out of sight.

Off far northern Queensland, October is the peak month of the marlin fishing season. Big black marlin *Makaira indica*,

Spawning times vary for the same reason. Barramundi in permanent rivers move downstream in response to rising water levels and increasing silt loads as early as October. Those holding out in billabongs have to wait until the floods of the full Wet transform their habitats, probably around January.

Barramundi in the upstream phase of their cycle tend to a creamy colour. Juveniles have chocolate markings along their backs. As spawning adults move into brackish tidal waters they start to take on a silvery hue that intensifies in brilliance during their time in estuaries or nearshore coastal waters.

Spawned and fertilised in abundance, the eggs drift away in saltwater plankton. A few hatchlings survive to complete their larval stages during the following year and enter estuaries as juveniles. They work their way upstream in the same rain-boosted waters that carry down adults, relying on the silt suspended in the water to hide them from predators. If they should enter rivers that are dammed or otherwise engineered for flood control, they face a bleak future. So do adults, returning later from their spawning.

Two species of an unrelated genus are also often called barramundi. The name was taken from a southeastern Queensland Aboriginal word that may have been applied indiscriminately to all big river fish that were good to eat — including the Queensland lungfish.

The name saratoga is now preferred for the other 'barramundi', the most widespread species of which is *Scleropages jardini*. It is found well upstream in rivers that flow into the Gulf of Carpentaria and the Arafura and Timor Seas. The 'spotted barramundi' *Scleropages leichhardti* occurs naturally only in the Fitzroy River and its tributaries, near Rockhampton. Stocks have been introduced to rivers nearer Brisbane.

Females of both *Scleropages* species, mature at four years, produce fewer than 200 eggs. They can be so sparing because they incubate the eggs and brood the small fry in their mouths. Fingerlings about four centimetres long, emerging to

Most adult Gulf saratogas Scleropages jardini *are about sixty centimetres long*

Male and female empire gudgeons Hypseleotris compressa *turn red when breeding*

frequently weighing more than 400 kilos, gather to spawn between August and December, just beyond the main structures of the Great Barrier Reef. Capable of fighting for hours, leaping, 'tailwalking' and running at speeds perhaps exceeding eighty kilometres an hour, they are the most prized of gamefishes.

Only likely record-breakers are brought in for weighing, however. The ethics of modern gamefishing call for other catches to be tagged and released. The recapture of tagged marlin indicates that they cover thousands of kilometres in their travels, but return to the same areas each year.

The biggest black marlin apparently disperse to oceanic feeding grounds after spawning. Juveniles occur inside the Barrier Reef at most times of year. Fish of intermediate size move south at the end of summer, following prey species taking advantage of the East Australian Current.

Black marlin pursue schooling surface fish such as tuna and Spanish mackerel. When they charge at packed schools some prey may be impaled on their beaked upper jaws, but this seems to be accidental. The bills are more often jerked from side to side to stun prey.

Marlin and swordfish

Blue marlin *Makaira nigricans* reach a similar size but the very biggest are not often seen in Australian waters. The species can be caught in summer and autumn off most mainland coasts but is more common outside the tropics. Fish weighing up to 300 kilos are caught fairly consistently in late summer off Fremantle.

Striped marlin *Tetrapturus audax* range to southern Tasmania, though they are also seen in tropical waters. Longline fishing by Japanese and Russian crews is blamed for declining catches during the southeastern offshore season, which usually starts in October. Striped marlin weighing more than 200 kilos are few and far between, but as fighting fish they are especially fast and agile.

Broadbill swordfish of a single worldwide species, *Xiphias gladius*, occur all around Australia but are relatively rare. They can exceed 400 kilos in weight and five metres in length — including a flat bill more than a metre long — and estimates of their speed through the water range up to ninety kilometres an hour.

Swordfish feed on small fish and squid, gulping them down whole because they lose their teeth on reaching maturity. Solitary at most times, they spawn in small groups in open tropical waters. On dispersal the males seem to stay in warm water while females go south. People out gamefishing make rare catches, usually when they are after big marlin, but most swordfish are taken in the south in winter by longline fishing.

One of the mainstays of tropical commercial fisheries and also a popular sporting fish, the Spanish or narrow-barred mackerel *Scomberomorus commerson* starts spawning in October off the northern section of the Barrier Reef. Around the Monte Bello Islands in the northwest its season comes in summer.

These are the biggest Australian members of the mackerel family, sometimes

UNUSUAL MARSUPIALS
An imported fish with a pouch

Mosquito fish *Gambusia affinis* give birth to live young. Males have a most unusual development of the anal fin that allows copulation rather than spawning. The females are fertilised internally, several times a season while water temperatures are high. Eggs pass into a brood pouch where up to eighty hatchlings grow to a stage at which they can be independent before being expelled.

The fish are common in slow-flowing eastern streams but are seldom noticed because they are small — females reach only five centimetres and males half that size. Their ancestors were introduced from Central America in a futile effort to prevent the larval growth of disease-bearing mosquitoes. Related species in some Queensland streams, the guppy *Poecilia reticulata* and swordtails *Xiphophorus*, were probably released by aquarium owners. They too are pouched and bear live young.

Male and female mosquito fish; they breed rapidly and are now a threat to native species

Yellowtail kingfish Seriola lalandi *are common around the southern half of Australia*

exceeding fifty kilos. They are far-ranging travellers in coastal waters at other times of year. Big schools take advantage of both the East Australian and Leeuwin Currents, reaching the New South Wales south coast in autumn and remaining off the southwest as late as June.

Yellowtail kingfish *Seriola lalandi* are among the most admired sporting fish of

Snapper Chrysophrys auratus *live off a diet of molluscs, crustaceans and fish*

temperate waters, also ranking high in commercial importance. Some giants are said to exceed sixty kilos, though weights of less than ten kilos are more usual. Off the southeastern coast, where the best catches are made, they spawn in October and November.

Kingfish are brought closest to shore by runs of their favourite prey, garfish. The eastern sea garfish or 'beakie' *Hyporhamphus australis* moves from open waters into bays and estuaries in spring and summer to spawn in seagrass beds, first feeding up on small crustaceans and algae. The southern sea garfish *Hyporhamphus melanochir* stays close inshore year-round, providing a significant fisheries resource all along the Southern Ocean coast.

In the same regions around October, the movement inshore of spawning snapper *Chrysophrys auratus* signals the start of a rich season of reef fishing. On the east

coast they may come in earlier in pursuit of spawning cuttlefish. The biggest are about a metre long and weigh more than twenty kilos, though anglers are delighted with catches half that size.

Fishermen generally use the name snapper only for specimens over about 1.5 kilos, with blue-spotted pink scales that show their maturity. Juvenile fish, living year-round in estuaries, are known first as 'cockney' and then as 'red bream'. Fish in their first year in deep water, while still not mature, are called 'squire'. Even the adult name has an alternative spelling. The Dutch version, 'schnapper', is sometimes used to distinguish *Chrysophrys* from unrelated fish also called snappers that frequent tropical reefs.

Mature snapper, four years old or more, make seasonal movements to and from waters as deep as 200 metres. Tagging shows that some at least also make lengthy migrations along the coast. But the five different population groups keep themselves to themselves. Some authorities believe they should be classified as separate subspecies.

Four groups are distributed between the southern Indian Ocean coast of Western Australia and Wilsons Promontory, Victoria. The fifth ranges between eastern Victoria and southern Queensland. It is intriguing that the two groups whose feeding grounds almost meet at the promontory do not mix. On migration one goes west and the other northeast — as if the Bass Strait land barrier of 10 000 years ago still existed.□

SHOOTING STARS
A fish that squirts for its supper

Swimming or floating creatures are the principal prey of archer fish *Toxotes*, but they are celebrated for their skill in bringing down hovering insects and those resting on foliage above the water by spitting at them. A sudden shutting of the gill covers forces water along a groove in the roof of the mouth and out through a notch at the front of the upper jaw.

Targets can be hit at ranges of up to 1.5 metres. Such accuracy is all the more astonishing because the fish's head stays below the surface. Somehow it calculates and corrects for the refractive bending of light through the water.

One archer fish, *Toxotes jaculator*, frequents saltwater mudflats along the tropical east coast and probably spawns in spring. *Toxotes chatareus*, common in rivers across the monsoonal north, presumably waits for summer flooding. Some are found so far inland that the sea can play no part in their life cycle.

The common archer fish Toxotes chatareus *grows up to forty centimetres long*

Two male green tree frogs Litoria caerulea *at Springbrook in Queensland*

NOVEMBER

THIS MONTH'S WEATHER

Average temperatures rise quickly in most regions, and spring comes at last to the southeastern highlands. Storms increase in the far north, where the Top End has its hottest month. The southwest and the southern mainland enter their driest periods, though good rains are maintained in Tasmania.

AROUND THE COUNTRY	RAIN (mm)	MAX. (°C)	MIN. (°C)	SUN hrs/day
Adelaide	33	25	14	8.5
Alice Springs	27	33	18	10.2
Brisbane	98	27	18	8.2
Canberra	62	22	8	8.9
Darwin	141	33	25	8.4
Hobart	56	18	9	6.9
Melbourne	59	22	11	7.3
Perth	21	25	14	9.9
Port Hedland	4	36	21	11.8
Sydney	81	24	15	7.7
Townsville	53	31	23	9.4
Weipa	103	35	23	9.3

Out of their element

November is the time of year when many water-based animals produce their young on land, often exposing themselves and their offspring to all kinds of risks

They roam the oceans for perhaps ten years before reaching sexual maturity, then in one night, female sea turtles risk everything when they come ashore to lay their eggs. Painfully slow-moving and temporarily obsessed with their task, they make ridiculously easy prey for hunters. Giants one metre long or more are made defenceless simply by flipping them onto their backs.

Factory ruins on a deserted coral cay near Heron Island in Queensland attest to Australia's part in a slaughter that went on in all tropical regions of the world. Late last century, European gourmets would pay any price for turtle soup.

Green turtles *Chelonia mydas* made the best eating. Soon they were all but wiped out from accessible breeding grounds. So canneries substituted the meat of the hawksbill *Eretmochelys imbricata*. This species was already hunted for its carapace, from which 'tortoiseshell' spectacle frames and ornaments were cut.

Adult green turtles are vegetarian, grazing sea grasses and algae. But the hawksbill, like all other sea turtles, is carnivorous. Something in its diet of fish, crustaceans, jellyfishes and molluscs occasionally makes its flesh highly toxic. Poisoning scandals put a quick end to the soup trade, and decorative plastics eventually supplanted shell.

One species of sea turtle, the flatback *Chelonia depressa*, is peculiar to Australian waters. Six other species are widely distributed in the tropics, and five of these visit our shores. All are legally protected — in or out of the water — though in the far north they may be taken by tribal Aboriginals and Torres Strait islanders for whom they are part of a traditional diet. Attempts to farm them as a Torres Strait industry have failed.

Turtles originated as land animals, far back in the age of dinosaurs. Having perfected the defence of an impenetrable shell, they took to living in water where the great weight of their carapaces was more easily supported. Their legs were modified as flippers. When some cataclysm or climatic change killed off dinosaurs, the turtles — like crocodiles — were saved by their watery environment.

But the adaptation was not complete. Again like crocodiles, the turtles continued to nest on land. Their eggs remained characteristic of a terrestrial reptile, parchment-shelled and porous so that the embryos could breathe. Even if the eggs had been waterproof, they were safer buried ashore than deposited where fish would gobble them up.

Millions of years before human hunter-gatherers came along to interfere, the strategy already had fatal flaws. On mainland beaches goannas often raid the nests. And the tiny, soft-shelled hatchlings have to get back to the sea. If they emerge by day they are snapped up by gulls and

At Raine Island on the outer Barrier Reef,

other birds. At night near the water's edge, predatory ghost crabs ambush them. Fish also exact their toll as young turtles enter the water, and for a long time after.

The turtles' answer has been to overbreed. When a female is mated — apparently not every year — she lays hundreds of eggs. She deposits three to five clutches in separate nests, but always on the same beach, during fortnightly visits over a period of up to ten weeks.

While her mate loiters in the water, the female drags herself up a dark, sandy beach and embarks on a ponderous exploration above the high-water mark. After frequent hesitations and changes of mind — at this stage she is easily disturbed — she decides on a site and starts

A brood of flatback hatchlings; they emerge seven weeks after eggs are laid

256

the beach becomes crowded with female green turtles surging from the sea to lay their eggs

to excavate it. Squirming her body and flailing her front flippers, she flings sand in all directions. When a hollow is made big enough to take her, she settles into it.

Nothing will distract a laying turtle
Next the hind flippers are put to work digging a pit about forty centimetres deep and half as wide. At this stage the turtle becomes totally preoccupied. Lights and noise will not distract her, not even researchers clipping a tag on one of her flippers to monitor her nesting visits and track her subsequent ocean voyages.

Between fifty and 150 eggs, looking much like table tennis balls, are laid in half an hour or so. Their number and size vary with the type of turtle. Then the

mother heaves herself out of the nest and fills it in. More sand is scattered about in an effort to conceal the site — a futile exercise, for deeply furrowed tracks mark her progress to and from the nest.

In about seven weeks the young hatch almost simultaneously. The proportion of females to males is determined by the average temperature inside the nest — another characteristic shared with crocodiles. At about 30°C, the sexes are equally represented. Males predominate in a cooler nest and females in a warmer one.

What instinct guides the hatchlings in their hazardous journey to the sea is a mystery to scientists. Vision seems to come into it, because they become confused by navigation beacons and other

lights. Yet they find the water even when it is hidden behind a ridge.

Turtles breed on remote and undisturbed beaches all around the tropical coast, and especially on offshore islands and cays. On Raine Island, at the northernmost and outermost part of the Great Barrier Reef, nightly counts of females coming ashore at the peak of a good season have exceeded 10 000. The competition for sites is so intense that latecomers may dig up existing nests.

Breeding times vary between regions, but are fixed for each locality. November and December are unfailingly nesting months on southern Barrier Reef cays and at the best-known mainland site, Mon Repos Beach near Bundaberg.

Relatively few turtles come to Mon Repos — it is south of the Tropic of Capricorn — but most research has been done there. Breeding females are weighed, and hatchlings as well as their mothers are tagged. It is known already that some turtles travel thousands of kilometres, and that they may live for 100 years. It is also known that the females, once they have started breeding, return to the same beaches in later seasons. What is of greatest importance to future conservation efforts, but will take many more years to prove, is whether turtles come back to their birthplaces to breed.

Flatbacks are the first to arrive at Mon Repos. Growing to 1.2 metres, they lay about fifty eggs in a clutch. Some green turtles also turn up, though they have become increasingly rare in this region. They reach one metre in length and lay about 100 eggs at a time. But the dominant and most prolific species here is the loggerhead turtle *Caretta caretta*. It lays more than 100 eggs and can grow up to 1.5 metres in length.

The Pacific ridley *Lepidochelys olivacea*, similar in size and productivity, visits the northernmost shores of the Northern Territory and Cape York Peninsula. The hawksbill — the flesh of which can be extremely toxic — abounds in all our tropical waters and is frequently seen over submerged coral. But its nesting sites are obscure and may also be limited to the far north. Reaching one metre in length, it lays clutches of about fifty eggs.

By far the biggest of its kind is the leathery turtle or luth *Dermochelys coriacea*. It can grow to well over two metres. Though it rarely nests in Australia it is the turtle most likely to be seen in

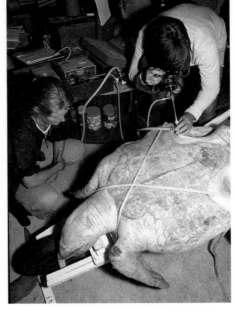

At Mon Repos a loggerhead turtle has her reproductive organs photographed

subtropical waters — as far south as Perth on the west coast and beyond Sydney in the east. The luth's southern ventures are no accident of warm summer currents, for it stays in some cool bays and estuaries year-round. It is said to gorge itself on jellyfish swarms.

The arrival of pregnant seals

Seals face problems even greater than those of turtles. Though well adapted for swimming and diving, and unable to get food anywhere but in the sea, they must breed on land and rest and moult there as well. Their young are totally shorebound for months — safe from sharks, but not from man. Within ten years of European colonisation, commercial exploitation of fur-bearing species was in full swing.

Fur seals ashore live communally, under the leadership of massive bulls that can protect the cows and pups from any natural danger. But their strategy of safety in numbers worked against them when sealing gangs invaded their breeding grounds on mainland beaches and islands along the southern coast and around Tasmania.

Parties were put ashore on even the most remote islands. From the proceeds of a few seasons of shooting or clubbing every fur seal they found, desperate men could set themselves up for life. As early as 1820, their quarry was scarce. Yet the slaughter continued until the 1890s in Victoria and the 1920s in Tasmania.

Fur seals of two species breed in Australia. Though they have not returned to all their old grounds, numbers have recovered well enough for legal protection to be relaxed to some extent. Seals can be destroyed with permission if they interfere seriously with commercial fishing.

The Australia fur seal *Arctocephalus pusillus* is restricted to Tasmania, Victoria and New South Wales as far north as Port Stephens. Mature males average more than two metres in length and nearly 300 kilos in weight. Females are shorter and weigh only about one-third as much. The generally smaller New Zealand fur seal *Arctocephalus forsteri* also has resident representatives here, breeding in South and Western Australia.

Non-breeding seals may choose any rocky shore as a resting area. Breeding grounds, called rookeries, are on boulder-strewn island beaches where there is sheltering vegetation not too far from the water. Rookeries may be occupied throughout the year. But at breeding time — six weeks in November and December — a strict social order is imposed.

Mature bulls — called 'wigs' in the old days because of their prominent manes — assemble in October. Territories are claimed and contested in rituals of aggressive posturing, growling and barking. Deliberate intrusions lead to chest-to-chest bouts of shoving and biting, sometimes resulting in severe injury. Vigilance and endurance are demanded as well as strength — the combatants may go a month or more without food or water. Defeated bulls eventually accept relegation to the outskirts of the rookery or to offshore rocks, along with immature members of the community.

Pregnant females, arriving in November, are herded onto the bulls' breeding territories in groups of about six or eight. Some sites are so crowded that the cows — called 'clapmatches' by the sealers, from a Dutch word — are almost touching. But unlike sea-lions, the bulls do not keep harems. The cows are free to move between territories.

Her back and head covered with sand from vigorous digging, a loggerhead settles down to laying eggs in the pit she has made

It takes about 30 minutes to lay 50 to 150 eggs, about the size of table tennis balls

pups take to mixing and playing with others of their age group. At about eight months they start to accompany their mothers on hunting expeditions, sampling a diet of fish, squid, octopus and crayfish. But they will not be weaned until they are ten or eleven months old.

The annual mating of seals, so quickly after the females have given birth, is designed to keep the adults' period of shore dependency to a minimum. It has nothing to do with the gestation period, which is less than eight months. The discrepancy is covered, and females are given time to regain prime condition, by delayed implantation. A fertilised ovum remains quiescent for about four months before it is fixed to the uterus wall and receives nutrition.

Fur seals of both sexes are ready to breed at four to five years. Females may live for more than ten years and males as long as twenty. But the competition among bulls is so rigorous that most have to wait until they are about ten before they can succeed in claiming breeding territories, and few are able to hold them for more than three seasons.

How seals have evolved

The ancestors of seals are thought to have started adapting to water about twenty-five million years ago. Their limb bones became so short that only their paws project from their bodies, with the toes webbed to form fins. Like whales, they have developed thick layers of blubber below their skins to insulate them in very cold water.

Other modifications enable seals to make prolonged, deep dives in search of their prey or to escape from sharks. Their bodies contain a much greater volume of blood than those of land mammals of equivalent size, giving them a greater quantity of oxygen. When a seal dives, its heart rate slows by about ninety per cent. And many of its blood vessels are constricted, reserving a maximum supply of oxygen for the heart and brain.

The front surfaces of a seal's eyes are flat instead of curved — a better shape for focusing underwater vision. In the darkest depths it may also echo-locate, emitting sounds that are reflected off shoals of fish and big bottom-dwelling prey.

Two groups of seals have evolved in much the same way, though they are descended from different types of land animals. The ancestors of fur seals and sea-lions seem to have been bear-like. So-called 'true' seals, which spend more time in the water and migrate, probably originated as otter-like animals.

Fur seals and sea-lions have external ears; 'true' seals do not. That is the easiest way to tell them apart. But another distinction is more important to the animals

About five days after coming ashore, the cows give birth. Each has a single pup, and suckles no other. Affectionate bonds are formed quickly, through the recognition of odours and a constant exchange of calls. The pups mew like kittens and are answered with soft moanings.

A mother stays ashore for the next ten days, eating nothing. She loses weight as rapidly as her pup gains it — about a kilo a day — for her milk is about fifty per cent fat, converted from her own blubber.

A week or even sooner after giving birth, the mother parks her pup in the shelter of a boulder and turns her attention to the bull whose territory she occupies. After a perfunctory courtship of nuzzlings and rubbings they mate, and the starved female promptly departs for the sea. Throughout the rest of the summer and autumn, and well into the winter, she will return at intervals of a few days to suckle her pup.

When all cows have been mated the breeding bulls go their own way and discipline is relaxed. Immature seals and bachelor bulls are free to come and go. In between their mothers' feeding visits, the

themselves. Fur seals and sea-lions can turn their hind flippers forward, and have front flippers long enough to prop up their bodies. They can walk on land in a clumsy fashion — even raising a gallop in emergencies. Earless seals gain little help from their flippers on land, and have to get about by laboriously squirming or humping their bodies.

In the water, however, the earless seal is the more effortless and energy-efficient swimmer. It propels itself by beating its hind flippers like the tail of a fish, using the front flippers only for steering. Fur seals and sea-lions draw themselves along by using their front flippers like oars.

Sadly, Australia no longer gives a home to the most impressive of the earless seals, the enormous southern elephant seal *Mirounga leonina*. Bulls can exceed four metres and weigh nearly four tonnes. The species used to breed along the northern coast of Tasmania, where it provided food for Aboriginals. The last community, on King Island in Bass Strait, was wiped out by Europeans in the nineteenth century.

Strays and stragglers from elephant seal migrations occasionally beach themselves on our shores. But Australia's claim to these magnificent creatures can be sustained only on the subantarctic territories of Macquarie and Heard Islands, where pups are born in September or October. They are suckled for only three weeks, fasting for another seven while they learn to swim and hunt.

Earless seals that breed in Antarctica sometimes strand themselves in Australia during their migrations. The most common of these accidental arrivals — usually in poor condition — is the leopard seal *Hydrurga leptonyx*, easily distinguished by its spotted coat. The crab-eater seal *Lobodon carcinophagus* has turned up on the east coast as far north as the New South Wales-Queensland border. Very rare finds have been made of Weddell and Ross seals.

Shearwaters arrive on schedule
Sealers at the end of the eighteenth century, sickened of a constant diet of the animals they skinned, were the first Europeans to put the flesh and eggs of Australian 'muttonbirds' on their summertime menu. They followed a custom of southern Aboriginal tribes. The inroads made by genuinely hungry people of either race were slight, considering the millions of muttonbirds — shearwaters —

This group of Australian fur seals is resting on Tasmania's east coast

that came to Australia every year.

Commercial exploitation was another matter. In the late 1880s and early 1900s eggs were collected in scores of thousands from easily accessible breeding grounds, simply to boost profits from cake and confectionery manufacturing. Eggs were also sold to racehorse trainers, who mixed them in stamina-building potions. Though the fatty, fishy meat never gained wide popularity, many a quilt was stuffed with the feathers and down of chicks.

Of all the free-ranging, ocean-loving creatures obliged to come ashore for part of the year, shearwaters place themselves in greatest jeopardy. They adopt a humble existence in dead-end burrows. Although

Like a whale, the fur seal has a thick layer of blubber beneath its skin

REBIRTH OF THE BUNYIP LEGEND

It is likely that hungry seals have inspired stories of water-dwelling monsters

Seals chasing shoals of fish travel surprisingly distances up the tidal reaches of rivers. Last century, unexpected glimpses prompted most of the southeast's stories of bunyips — roaring monsters rising out of waterways. Often the scariness was reinforced by the booming night-time calls of bitterns frequenting the same areas.

Tales of some sort of aquatic monster were too widespread in Aboriginal lore not to have a basis in fact. But the Aboriginals' bunyips were nothing like seals. They were aggressive, fast-moving giants that ate people. Perhaps southern tribes shared a fearful memory of their tropical heritage and bunyips do exist, after all, but only in the north, in the shape of estuarine crocodiles.

gulls cannot get at their eggs or their chicks, which remain there helpless for three months after hatching, snakes and goannas dine richly.

Shearwaters are even more vulnerable to human harvesting because of the regularity of their breeding cycle. In the case of the most abundant species, the short-tailed shearwater *Puffinus tenuirostris*, the times of egglaying, hatching and the fledging of chicks can be narrowed down to less than a fortnight.

Wherever short-tailed shearwaters breed — from the eastern end of the Bight to mid-New South Wales — they start laying about 20 November and finish by 2 December, with a peak of production around 25 November. Such precise timing — the most predictable known among animals in Australia — is all the more

surprising because these birds have come from waters off Siberia or Alaska.

From October to January in some years, if the migrants are betrayed by fickle winds, east coast shores are strewn with starved birds dead or dying. Most are immature. Vigorous adults have reached their nesting grounds by September. If they have bred before, they go back to the same burrows or ones close by, and renew the partnerships of previous seasons.

Traditional sites on headlands or nearshore islands accommodate thousands of birds to the hectare. Under a cover of low vegetation, gritty soils are riddled with holes leading as far as two metres into leaf-lined nests that are refurbished each year.

No sooner have the colonies formed than the birds are back at sea, cramming

themselves with surface plankton, small fish and occasionally squid. They have to regain condition after their long migration. Roving as far as 150 kilometres from their nests on favourable winds, they spend all the hours of daylight on or over the water — solitary for most of the time.

Towards sunset the birds come inshore, often gathering quietly in floating groups. They make no move towards their burrows until darkness is complete. Then they wing silently in, skimming far past the nesting ground and turning back into the sea breeze to get their final lift.

An observer expecting huge flocks to fly straight in is unlikely to be aware of their arrival until suddenly the ground comes alive with rustling noises. Soon the night air is filled with greeting and courtship calls — croonings repeated more and

more rapidly and rising to an excited pitch
— or the raucous cries of disputes over
burrow ownership. Non-breeding birds
may be joining the colony by now.

Paired breeders court by performing a
duet of head and neck movements and by
bill-touching and mutual preening. They
copulate around the end of October and
return to the sea, staying out day and
night for three more weeks of intensive
feeding before the eggs are laid.

The male stays in constant attendance
to incubate the single egg — a long oval
the size of a duck egg — for the first twelve
to fourteen days. Then the female takes
over for a similar spell. They continue to
change places until hatching occurs after
seven to eight weeks, in mid-January.

Chicks remain in the burrows for more
than three months. They are visited and
fed by a parent nightly for the first week,
but less frequently after that. Even so they
fatten with remarkable speed. By the time
their down is replaced by flight feathers
they weigh about a kilo — much heavier
than they will ever be once they begin
their lives of energy-sapping flight.

Adults form loose flocks of thousands
to migrate to their winter quarters in
March or April. After being abandoned for
about a fortnight, chicks hop to the sea
and learn to fly there. The fledglings
migrate in late April or early May, finding
their own way to the north Pacific.

Another species that is abundant is
the wedge-tailed shearwater *Puffinus
pacificus*, which favours tropical and subtropical coasts. It makes shorter winter
migrations to the corresponding zones of
the northern hemisphere. Colonies of
wedge-tailed shearwaters are found on the
west coast from Perth to Port Hedland,
and along the whole length of the east

*From the waters off Siberia and
Alaska to southern Australia*

HOME RUN

*Every year, shearwaters
undertake an enormous 30 000-
kilometre round-trip*

Navigational skills of shearwaters,
crossing between hemispheres and
returning not merely to their countries of origin but to the very same
burrows, are among the most impressive in the avian world. Scientists can only guess what senses and
indicators are used. In a celebrated
experiment a European shearwater
was taken from its nest on a Welsh
island and air-freighted 5000 kilometres across the Atlantic to Boston
in the United States. Released there,
it re-entered its Welsh burrow just
twelve and a half days later.

coast. In southern New South Wales it
shares breeding grounds with the short-
tailed species, but can be distinguished by
the eerie wailing of its greeting and courtship calls. Two competing birds sound just
like cats preparing to fight.

A third important species occurs in
smaller numbers, and nests only where it
can share breeding grounds with either or
both of the other two. This is the sooty
shearwater or ghostbird *Puffinus
griseus*. It is the dominant species of southern New
Zealand, where it remains a staple of
Maori diet.

'Birding' — the harvesting of short-
tailed shearwater chicks — is permitted
on some Bass Strait islands for about five
weeks each year, from late March to the
end of April. Down, feathers and meat
fetch fair prices, but perhaps the most
significant product is an oil refined from
the stomach contents, which is put to
medicinal use.

Seasonal catch limits are set to ensure
that population levels are maintained
from year to year. The trade is defended
on the ground that if there had been no
commercial interest in the nesting areas,
they would have been trampled by grazing
livestock. And without secure burrows,
there would be no muttonbirds at all.

A time of peril for crocodiles
No destruction of Australian wildlife in
pursuit of profit has been more pitiless
and shameful than the slaughter of freshwater crocodiles. The traffic in their skins
was not born of pioneering necessity, or
fostered in ignorance of the consequences. People did not start wiping out

*The single chick remains helpless for
three months after it is born*

*Short-tailed
shearwaters at dawn
as they prepare to take
off over the sea from
Big Dog Island in Bass
Strait*

*A freshwater crocodile
(below) can easily find
herself trapped in a
shrinking billabong
before the wet season
starts. She depends on
good rains at the right
time to provide her
young with plenty of
territory to claim*

small, harmless freshwater crocodiles until the 1960s, when — and because — they had brought the big estuarine species to the brink of extinction.

Skins taken from the narrow-snouted *Crocodylus johnstoni* contain bony lumps under the belly scales. This caused difficulties in their tanning. No one bothered with them while there was a ready supply of skins from estuarine crocodiles.

When the latter were shot out of all accessible areas, the tanning industry quickly solved its problems and hunters had a new, defenceless quarry. They did not even need rifles. Most streams and billabongs could be emptied of 'freshies' with simple dragnets. Even juveniles were taken, to be stuffed as mantelpiece ornaments. In ten years or so until legal protection and an export ban were enforced, populations were drastically depleted. In settled parts of Queensland they are unlikely ever to recover.

November is a time of great peril for freshwater crocodiles. Though isolated storms are frequent, the wet season is not advanced enough for smaller streams to flow. Many female crocodiles are confined to shrunken billabongs. They do not attempt to escape to bigger waterways because they have been tending their nests.

Two months or so earlier, each breeding female scratched a hole in a sandbank and laid about twenty eggs. Now the young are about to hatch. Their fate depends largely on the weather. If floods come a little too soon, the eggs are swept away and destroyed. Too late, and the hatchlings are trapped in shallow pools at the mercy of many kinds of predators — including cannibalistic adults.

A good flow of water must come at just the right time to disperse the newly-hatched young to places where they can find ample food and grow in safety. The lucky ones will eat insects at first, then tiny fish and frogs. Adult freshwater crocodiles are principally fish-eaters, but not averse to dogs or piglets. They present no danger to humans — Aboriginal children sometimes swim with them in waterholes — unless they are wounded and cornered. Then their snapping jaws could amputate fingers or toes. □

The dingo's debut

Various mammals take advantage of settled conditions to bring out their spring-born young and teach them survival techniques

Romping bumble-footed in pursuit of their mother, four-month-old dingoes are typical puppies — excitable, inquisitive, playful. But life is about to become deadly earnest. Around November, not long after their first outings away from the den where they were born, they must quickly learn the arts of hunting and killing. Before long they may have to fend for themselves.

Dingo pups — averaging five to the litter, though as many as twelve have been seen — are weaned at five months. In some years they are abandoned almost immediately. Few at that age can survive. In other years they get parental help until the next breeding season, then depart of their own accord. The parents' inconsistency, for no obvious reason, results in periods of population stability interspersed with sharp increases.

Unlike domestic dogs, which have two seasons, the dingo *Canis familiaris dingo* breeds only once a year. Bitches come on heat for just a few days in autumn or early winter, mostly in May. They whelp nine weeks after mating but the pups stay in their den — a hollow log, a cave or a crevice — until late in spring.

Before then the pups are well accustomed to solid food. The mother carries prey of manageable size back to the den, or regurgitates some of what she has eaten from bigger kills. Her mate sometimes assists in feeding. Medium to large native mammals — especially wallabies — contribute most to a dingo diet. Reptiles and birds make up the remainder.

Bitches use the same breeding dens each year. But the family has other dens for resting, spread out over hunting ranges that cover thousands of hectares. Adults move around day and night, for about sixteen hours out of each twenty-four, alternating bursts of activity of an hour or less with rests that are even shorter.

When pups are to be educated, the mother takes them out to watch and then participate in kills. Day by day they are also taken to lie up in different dens, gradually mastering the geography of the range until they are capable of finding their own way about. As they grow older they hunt independently.

Dingoes are essentially solitary crea-

These pups were born early in spring and are three months old. Their mother teaches

tures, without the strong social instinct of domestic dogs. Beyond their temporary family groupings, they do not normally hunt together. But adults maintain contact, meeting at regular intervals during their daily comings and goings. They communicate by facial expressions and body language, and over long distances by howling — they cannot bark. When bigger prey such as a kangaroo is available, they join forces to kill it and eat it.

Pack attacks on livestock — especially those incidents in which large numbers of sheep are wantonly killed and not eaten — are likely to be the work of feral dogs of domestic breeds or hybrids, rather than dingoes. Nevertheless sheep farming and dingoes do not mix. Once distributed all over the mainland wherever there were reliable supplies of water, dingoes have been virtually eliminated from woolgrowing country by campaigns of fencing and trapping. Not classified as native animals, they receive protection only in national parks and other designated reserves.

Remaining strongholds of the dingo are in central Australia, Arnhem Land, the Kimberley and in steep, broken country east of the Great Divide. In the east it is a disappearing breed because it is increasingly hybridised with feral dogs.

Dingoes interbreed freely with domestic dogs, and may themselves have been domesticated at one time. They bear

resemblances to a semi-wild type of dog, possibly a descendant of the Asiatic wolf, that used to be distributed widely from the eastern Mediterranean through southern Asia to the western Pacific.

One theory has it that dingoes were brought into our region by Indian voyagers. Sheep, goats and similar dogs were taken to Timor 3500 years ago or more. The oldest dingo fossil to be found in Australia dates back little more than 3000 years — to the time when the only comparable native predator, the thylacine or Tasmanian tiger, was disappearing from the mainland.

Aboriginals were followed about by dingoes, which in the Sydney region they called warrigals. 'Dingo' was a word the Aboriginals used in contempt of the outlandish dogs that colonisers brought ashore. When they saw how tractable the European breeds were, and how useful some were in hunting, they quickly sought to own them.

The dingo's place in pre-European Aboriginal society is unclear. It seems that the dogs were encouraged to be tame but were not fed — except for orphaned pups, which were suckled by women. It is doubtful whether they were much help in hunting. Most authorities agree that the principal roles of the tamest dingoes were as wintertime bedwarmers and portable food supplies.

them to hunt prey such as wallabies

Predation and competition by dingoes were presumably factors in the elimination from the mainland of Tasmanian devils. Once widespread, they survived in Victoria as recently as 600 years ago. In spite of their fierce screaming and posturing when cornered, and their possession of sharp teeth and massive jaws that can crunch a kangaroo's skull, these slow-moving scavengers are no match for a determined dog.

A marsupial version of the hyena
The Tasmanian devil *Sarcophilus harrisii* is the marsupial equivalent of Africa's hyena — more a disposer of carrion than a predator. Though the size of a stout spaniel or corgi, it can be outrun and outfought by even a rat. Some insects, reptiles and nesting birds are taken live, the latter mostly by juvenile devils which are more agile than their elders and can climb trees.

Active only at night, when they forage continuously, devils make their homes in hollow logs and caves. Open forests and coastal heathlands are the most favoured environments, but in Tasmania they have adapted to all kinds of habitats, including farms and bushland suburbs. Their numbers fell alarmingly early this century — probably because of an epidemic disease — and again in the 1950s, but have since returned to abundance.

Devils mate in March or April. To the mystification of scientists the female produces up to 100 ova, though she will rear only two cubs if she is breeding for the first time and four in later seasons. Embryos creep into her backward-opening pouch after a month's gestation.

Cubs leave the pouch at about fifteen weeks but continue to suckle for fifteen more, remaining in the den all the time. When they first appear outside, usually in November, they ride on the mother's back. They follow at heel for a few more outings — loping along with a rocking, lurching gait that is unique — before taking up a search for dens of their own.

Their lives will be mostly solitary, but they do not claim individual territories. Foraging grounds overlap, and groups of devils feed together on big carcasses. If a feast takes more than one night to eat, they may camp out nearby. Dr Eric Guiler, a leading authority on the habits of devils, tells of a pair that took up temporary residence inside the rib cage of a dead cow for two days, while they devoured the rest of the corpse.

Blood-curdling screeches, frequently piercing the night in the Tasmanian bush, come from devils disputing over food. Incautious youngsters may be killed in some of these arguments. The birthrate is not reflected in the makeup of the general population, which shows a preponderance of old males, living as long as eight years. Deliberate cannibalism of very young cubs is known to occur.

Screaming matches between devils of equal size rarely lead to physical combat, however. They are ritual displays of ferocity, conducted chin-to-chin, to establish rights to a share of food. Devils seem unable to fight at all without first issuing a standing threat — making them easy meat for hunting dogs.

In the early days of Tasmanian settlement devils were persecuted because of a scarcely-deserved reputation for attacking livestock. They are not capable of bringing down healthy, mobile stock. But they may victimise animals giving birth, or start to feed on ailing beasts before they are dead. On the whole, devils are beneficial to agriculture because they clean up carrion in which blowflies would breed.

Quokkas begin their yearly ordeal
On another island, almost as far west as one can go in Australia, November brings on an annual climatic crisis for the quokka *Setonix brachyurus*. This tree-climbing, browsing wallaby seems always to have been limited to southwestern Western Australia. Now its main stronghold is Rottnest Island, off Perth.

With salty lakes and a virtual certainty of five months' drought every year, there could hardly be a less suitable place. The stress on the animals is enormous. But somehow the numbers are maintained, and to holidaymakers the island seems overrun by the cat-sized creatures which were responsible for its name — Dutch for rats' nest. The navigator Willem de Vlamingh observed their numbers there in 1696.

Quokkas disperse as widely as possible during the moister months. With the onset of summer heat and dryness they are forced to congregate around a few freshwater soaks — sometimes so crowded that they fight for shaded resting places. Their normal food plants start to decline in water and nitrogen content.

November is usually the first time that Tasmanian devil young can be seen

Quokkas on Rottnest Island enjoy their last stress-free days before hot, dry weather

Alternative vegetation is more succulent but lacking in nutrients. By March, many quokkas will have died of the combined effects of thirst and malnutrition.

One of the keys to the surprising survival of Rottnest's quokkas is a weather-adapted breeding cycle. In their few mainland habitats, well-watered and forested, they seem able to breed at any time of year. But on the island, females do not come into season until the summer ordeal is almost over — January if it is cool, or as late as March.

This narrowing of the season ensures that a breeding female will be eating well throughout the time she is nursing her single joey. Young quokkas emerge from their mothers' pouches in August but continue to be suckled for about two months more.

In isolated patches of the Victorian highlands, November's rising temperatures signal the annual salvation of a rare species of native rodent, the smoky mouse *Pseudomys fumeus*. It endures a severe climate by completely changing its diet according to the time of year, and now is the time of its richest dining.

In summer and autumn the smoky mouse eats the seeds of heaths and legumes — the nitrogen-fixing plants that typically thrive in the aftermath of bushfires. In winter and early spring it scratches up an underground fungus. Its hardest times are faced in late spring, when the fungus shrivels in drying soils and few plants are ready to seed.

To save the day, with almost clockwork regularity, along come bogong moths. The tiny mice feast voraciously on the insects' fat bodies. The contrast in diet may trigger sexual responses, for breeding starts almost immediately. □

A BAT THAT ACTS LIKE A SEA-EAGLE

The large-footed mouse-eared bat is now breeding in Victoria and New South Wales

In all the diversity of bats that Australia has to offer, only one hunts in the manner of *Myotis adversus*. Equipped with oversized feet and sharp, curved claws, it makes swooping flights across the surface of rivers or lakes, raking up fish and aquatic insects in the same way that sea-eagles and ospreys catch fish. The technique is common among mouse-eared bats, which are distributed worldwide in more than sixty species. Australia has only this species, and it is limited to mainland districts of high rainfall.

November is the peak month for breeding in Victoria and New South Wales, where the large-footed mouse-eared bat gives birth to just one offspring a year. There are two seasons in southeastern Queensland, October and January, and three in the tropical zone. Breeding bats form small colonies in caves and mine shafts. In addition to a highly individual style of hunting, male bats also have a most unusual habit of controlling harems of females in tiny territories from which any other males are excluded.

A freshly caught fish is proof of the large-footed mouse-eared bat's skill

The smoky mouse will feast on moths

Australia's largest and deadliest snake needs warm, humid weather before it lays its eggs, preferably in a rotting log

An independent start in life for taipans

Slithering through forest litter, the pregnant taipan searches tirelessly for the ideal rotting log in which to lay her eggs. Rats and mice are ignored — she will not eat during the days or weeks that her quest may take. A site must be found that offers maximum protection and the right combination of warmth and moisture. This determined selection of an appropriate birthplace is all the maternal care the eggs and young will get.

The task of laying can take up to about twelve hours, after which the mother shows no interest in the eggs. She sets out immediately to hunt, loaded after her fast with a huge volume of extremely toxic venom. Researchers have 'milked' an enormous amount of venom — more than a cupful and enough to kill tens of thousands of mice — from a well-grown but hungry taipan.

The taipan mother does not look after her young. The eggs hatch several months after she has laid and left them

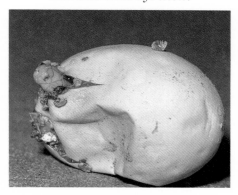

A taipan is already long at birth

Though they may hunt at night in extremely hot weather, taipans are active by day normally, and are more tolerant of high temperatures than most other snakes. November's storms and rising humidity at the Top End and on Cape York herald the start of egg-laying there. At the southern limit of the taipan's range, around the Queensland-New South Wales border, eggs are not laid until January.

Soft and rubbery, they are about as long as hens' eggs but not as wide. They are white at first, turning beige as the embryos take in moisture. Clutches of ten to fifteen are common. Twenty or even more are sometimes laid, but in a clutch of that size many are likely to be under-developed and infertile.

Incubation is slow, taking at least ten weeks in the tropics and as many as fourteen in cooler climates. Emerging hatchlings unwind to an astonishing length, some exceeding half a metre. Fully formed and armed, they seek their first kill in a day or so. They pose little threat to people — their heads are too small for a successful strike at a big target.

Adult taipans, however, are Australia's most dangerous snakes. For one thing they are the longest of all the venomous species. Growing throughout a lifetime that may span more than twenty years, they can exceed three metres. Average specimens measure more than two.

Taipans strike repeatedly

More importantly, taipans have fangs far longer than those of other snakes, so their ample volumes of venom are injected most deeply into the tissues of their victims. And instead of striking once and gripping, as some snakes do, taipans strike repeatedly. They do not bother to grip or coil round their normal prey — some birds, as well as small mammals — since death will be almost instantaneous.

Fortunately taipans are relatively uncommon and extremely shy, aggressive only if they are interfered with while cornered. Then they will hurl themselves at a tormentor with a speed that is too fast for the eye to follow. But they cannot jump off the ground. No snake can. And in spite of many tall stories from the Queensland bush, taipans do not chase people.

Rainforests, open forests and grassy woodlands all provide habitats for taipans.

They generally shelter in or under fallen, decaying trees. Where settlements are close by, the snakes' appetite for rats and mice may bring them close to outbuildings and rubbish dumps. The same appetite takes them into canefields. But they have no taste for the giant toads that infest cane. In that respect they are lucky, for the toads are lethally poisonous. Mulga snakes, less discriminating in their diet, are frequently killed.

Egg-laying is fairly common among Australian snakes as a whole, and this characteristic of the taipan *Oxyuranus scutellatus* is shared by about half of the dangerously venomous species. The mulga snake *Pseudechis australis* is the most widespread of the other egg-layers, occurring all over the mainland except in the southeast and the extreme southwest. More heavily built than the taipan and nearly as long, it too has a prodigious output of venom.

Black snakes and brown snakes

The mulga snake is a nocturnal hunter in the tropics but elsewhere is most active by day. It eats rodents, lizards, frogs and smaller snakes. Though its skin is brown, it belongs in the group called black snakes. The spotted or blue-bellied black snake of southern Queensland and northern New South Wales, *Pseudechis guttatus*, is a close relative. So is the red-bellied black snake *Pseudechis porphyriacus*, common in the east and

southeast. Strangely, the latter species does not lay eggs but bears its young live.

Various species of venomous brown snakes *Pseudonaja*, between them occupying the entire mainland, are egg-layers with habits not unlike the taipan's. The eastern brown *Pseudonaja textilis* causes most trouble because its range coincides with the greatest rural populations. It outdoes the taipan as the leading cause of life-threatening bites in Queensland. Though the venom output is low, the mixture includes the most potent neurotoxin known in land snakes.

Related brown snakes of the west are causing mounting concern as populations increase. The southwest corner, including Perth, has the dugite *Pseudonaja affinis*. To the north, and all across the continent except for the far south and east, the gwardar or western brown *Pseudonaja nuchalis* is a potential threat.

Among other egg-laying species, venomous but not big enough to present much danger to people, are the slender, fast-moving whip snakes *Demansia* and the naped snakes *Furina*. Both types are likely to be seen by day. Others, nocturnal and secretive, include crowned snakes *Cacophis* and the burrowing bandy-bandies *Vermicella*.□

The mulga snake is shown here in desert conditions, but it can live anywhere except the southeast and southwest corners of the continent

Jungle drums

Many birds are breeding now, in late spring. They include both natives and migrants, and their various courtship displays involve some fascinating behaviour. These are just a few of the myriad signs that summer is on its way

Mysterious, regular knocking sounds, punctuating the dawn chorus of birdsong at the onset of the wet season near Cape York, led North Queensland naturalist Graham Wood to an astounding discovery. Around the vine-tangled monsoon forests of Iron Range National Park, he watched birds that were making and using implements.

Few animals employ tools, let alone manufacture them. But Wood, who camped for months near the nesting sites of palm cockatoos, saw the males engaged in a skilled, systematic craft.

Locking the notched mandibles of their massive bills onto branches, the big birds chopped off sections short enough to wield with one foot. Minutes were spent chewing them to strip off the bark. The finished products were drumsticks — made so that adults of both sexes could beat them against hollow tree trunks.

Reporting his findings in *Australian Natural History* magazine in 1987, Wood pointed out that the only comparable examples of non-human toolmaking, by primates such as apes, were for obtaining food. The palm cockatoo's production of an acoustic device, to proclaim territories and perhaps also to reinforce bonds between paired birds, is unique.

In more open areas of their range, which reaches only a few hundred kilometres south of Cape York, palm cockatoos find big wooden seed cases shed by a tropical grevillea. They hammer with the capsules, seldom bothering to make drumsticks. It seems likely that their impulse to advertise themselves by creating artificial noise began in this more simple way.

Drumming is always performed on or near hollows that could be used for nesting, according to Wood. He observed pairs of birds doing their rounds of possible sites every day at dawn and again at dusk. They drummed most often when they were preparing to nest, and when the young were about to fly for the first time.

Breeding starts late in spring when heavy rains have set in at the Cape. Each pair readies several nesting hollows, installing porous platforms of splintered sticks. But only one egg is laid. It is

A male palm cockatoo strips branches to make drumsticks, like the ones shown left. Grevillea seed cases are also used as instruments for beating out territorial messages

A male superb fruit dove, probably close to its nest in the rainforest

incubated by the female alone in just over a month. The young cockatoo is fledged fourteen to sixteen weeks later, but the parents continue to feed it for some weeks after it has been drummed out of the nest. It may have thirty years or more of life ahead of it.

Cape York's drumming palm cockatoos *Probosciger aterrimus* are an outlying race of what is essentially a New Guinea bird. They gain their common name from a liking for pandanus seeds. But they eat a wide range of other seeds, nuts, berries and buds, taken from the crowns of trees along forest edges or in nearby woodlands.

The arrival of paradise kingfishers
Every year in early November, the same forests are suddenly filled with the clucking calls of paradise kingfishers. At this time, in fresh breeding plumage, they rank among the most beautiful of our migratory birds. Having wintered in New Guinea, they come now to nest in lowland rainforests from the Cape south to about Townsville.

The annual invasion of *Tanysiptera sylvia* is bad news for young termite colonies. Choosing mounds jutting less than half a metre from the forest floor, paired birds use their bills to drill holes just big enough to admit their bodies. Up to a month is spent excavating an inner chamber where three or four eggs are laid.

Incubated by both parents, the eggs hatch between Christmas and mid-January. Chicks squabble incessantly for a share of the adults' prey — insects, snails, small lizards and frogs. Fledged young tumble out of the termite mound three or four weeks after hatching. By then the adults' plumage is stained and tattered by the crowding inside.

Early-breeding paradise kingfishers start their return trip to New Guinea before the end of March. Most birds go in April, the short-tailed, dull-coloured younger generation departing last.

Superb fruit doves nesting
On rainforest edges of the northeast, November is also the peak nesting month for fruit doves. Single eggs are laid on absurdly flimsy platforms of twigs, in tree forks and tangles of vines, or sometimes on flat palm leaves.

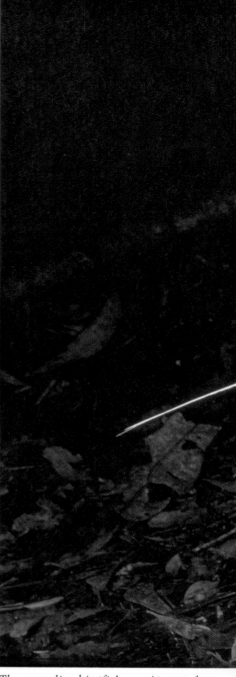

The paradise kingfisher migrates from

The most colourful of the family, the superb fruit dove *Ptilinopus superbus*, often nests within a metre or two of the ground. The male, which takes the day shift while the egg is being incubated, avoids detection by keeping his back turned to an intruder, showing cream and dull green plumage instead of his brilliant head and neck colours.

Laurels and more than fifty other kinds of trees and vines provide food for the superb fruit dove. The irregular timing of their fruiting in Queensland rainforests obliges the doves to become at least partly nomadic when not breeding. Patterns of movement are poorly understood because the longest flights seem to be made at

In their search for eucalypt blossoms, and for cicadas during the monsoon months, rufous-throated honeyeaters travel to the far north of the country

New Guinea in early November to build its nest in a termite mound. It drills a hole with its beak

night. The species has been seen as far south as Tasmania.

November sees a northwestward movement of rufous-throated honeyeaters *Conopophila rufogularis*. They are nomads who seek out blossoming eucalypts over most of northern Australia. Earlier in spring their greatest concentrations were in Queensland. Now, in loose flocks sometimes numbering hundreds, they become prominent from coastal Arnhem Land to the Kimberley.

Though called honey-eaters, members of the *Conopophila* group are also avid hunters of insects. The rufous-throated species pursues them on the wing, or may hover just above the ground to prey on ants and spiders. At this time in the north, cicadas may provide its richest pickings.

Flocks break up at breeding time, pairs nesting as far apart as possible but usually staying close to water. The nest is a lopsided cup of plant material and cobweb, hung from the end of a leafy branch.

In Tasmania, courting finches

Far away in Tasmania, the male of a small but eye-catching finch, the beautiful firetail *Emblema bella*, is starting a comical courtship. Grasping a long blade of grass in his bill, he nods three times, pauses, nods three more times and continues in this manner until his mate — they are permanently paired —

approaches. That prompts him to fan his tail and display his crimson rump. Then he bounces up and down, making a noise like a cricket, until she presents her tail.

Four or five eggs are laid under a big dome of plant stems and slender twigs, gathered and woven by both parents. They share incubation and both sleep in the nest. The off-duty one occupies a special recess in the entrance tunnel.

Beautiful firetails reside permanently among dense growths of heaths with water and grasses near by. They forage in pairs, on the ground but under cover, for seeds and sap-sucking insects. Fairly numerous in Tasmania, they also may be found on the southeastern mainland.

The great crested grebe is nesting now on a floating mat of vegetation

The great crested grebe *Podiceps cristatus* also starts to breed in November, wherever there are extensive sheets of fresh or brackish water with good growths of reeds or aquatic weeds. Both sexes take part in a complicated routine of courtship displays, many of them underwater.

Nests are floating mats of vegetation, anchored to growing plants. Sometimes several pairs build their nests close together. About five eggs are laid. Incubation, by both parents, takes four or five weeks. Newly hatched chicks ride on a parent's back, or occasionally are tucked under the wings.

Grebes are awkward on land and reluctant fliers, except when drought forces them to find new feeding grounds. All food is captured underwater, in dives that can last almost a minute. The diet is mainly fish but insects, crustaceans, tadpoles and snails are also taken.

Migrating terns signal summer
All across the north coast, white-winged terns *Chlidonias leucoptera* are flocking in now from their breeding grounds in central Asia. They take up summer occupation of swamps and lagoons where they feed on insects. Favoured by monsoon conditions, most remain in the north but a few travel down the west and east coasts. This species leaves at about the end of March. Smaller numbers of the common tern *Sterna hirundo* of Europe and Asia also arrive now, staying on until May.

Our other migratory tern, the white-fronted tern *Sterna striata*, is leaving as the others arrive. A fish-eater that breeds in New Zealand, it has wintered on southeastern and subtropical eastern estuaries since May. Most of the birds that come over the Tasman are immature — less than a year old. A few may stay behind in Australia until they are ready to breed, a year later. □

Red-eyed tree frogs Litoria chloris, (above) in southeast Queensland. Their call is a loud moan followed by a chirping

The large — it can grow to ten centimetres — green tree frog Litoria caerulea (right). It is often found in and around houses. Next right, the slender tree frog L. gracilenta; this is a calling male

GETTING DOWN TO BUSINESS

Australia has about fifty species of tree frogs, some of which may live in swamps or streams in spite of their common name

Wherever trees grow in Australia, there are tree frogs. Mostly species of *Litoria*, they are adapted for climbing. Enlarged pads on their fingers and toes are coated with a sticky secretion. Varying widely in colour and size — from two centimetres to well over ten centimetres in length — they all have the advantage of being able to conserve their body moisture by sheltering in plants. Their diet, mainly of insects, comes to them.

But all tree frogs have to breed in water. For most of them, good rains around November will trigger the start of their season. Tree-dwelling tree frogs descend from their hideouts and begin to assemble around pools or swamps, calling constantly in voices that are exclusive to their species. Vast, clamorous congregations may build up before spawning takes place.

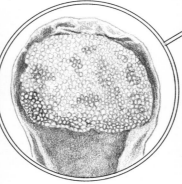

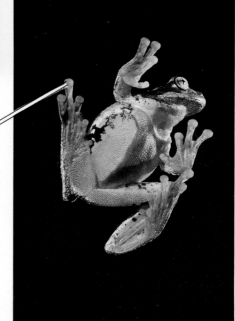

Peron's tree frog L. peronii on a window pane (right). Tree frogs' toe discs include glands that secrete an adhesive

Bogong moths clustering in crevices in alpine caves. Their colour lightens in autumn, as they prepare to return to Queensland

ROUTE OF BOGONG MOTH MIGRATION

Mountaineering moths

In November billions of migrating bogong moths arrive in the Victorian Alps and Snowy Mountains at the end of a perilous journey from Queensland. Other moths and insects are breeding now, or their larvae are feeding and growing rapidly

Frosty night air, high in the Snowy Mountains and Victorian Alps, is suddenly thick with small, plump moths. The invasion of the bogongs has begun. During November they will arrive in billions.

Alighting among rocks, the moths fold their wings and creep into crevices and caves that will be their homes for the next five months. Clustered together, they will not eat and will scarcely breathe in all this time. When they stir in April, it is to start a return journey to their birthplace.

Aboriginals used to climb to the alpine summits every summer to feast on bogongs. Their name, a tribal word for this bountiful food source, was also bestowed on the Bogong High Plains of Victoria, now better known as skifields. To the Aboriginals the dependable arrival of the moths would have been accepted as one of nature's more mysterious gifts. Now that the life history of bogongs is known, their two way migration ranks among the greatest feats of insect travelling.

Bogong eggs are laid early in winter in grassland soils of northwestern New South Wales and southwestern Queensland. Throughout the winter, larvae feed at ground level on annual plants. In early spring they rest underground to await their transformation from pupae into moths. When they emerge, temperatures are already climbing and food plants are dying off.

Instead of mating as soon as possible, as most moths do, the bogongs head south for cooler air. Night after night they press on, sheltering by day in whatever foliage they can find. Eventually confronted by the inland slopes of the great Dividing Range, they ascend higher and higher.

Urban areas may be visited on the way — especially in the Australian Capital Territory, near the end of the journey. Clouds of moths temporarily infest Canberra in some years, blotting out street lighting and swarming into homes. In higher buildings, possibly mistaken for alpine destinations, unguarded lift machinery and air conditioning ducts have become clogged with the insects' bodies.

A strong westerly wind can bring millions of bogongs to grief, sweeping them clear over the lower parts of the Great Divide and all the way to the Tasman Sea. Sydney and other New South Wales coastal centres are invaded. The moths blunder about, disoriented by lights; these days countless numbers are 'zapped' by electrical anti-insect devices. Some may struggle westward on a change of wind, reaching havens such as the Blue Mountains. More perish in the ocean, their corpses washing in to collect along the high-water lines of beaches.

Similar detours may be forced on the bogongs in autumn, during their northbound flight. Sufficient numbers always make it home to found the next generation. Mating takes place only after the moths have arrived and dispersed widely. Once eggs have been laid, all of the travellers die.

The bogong *Agrotis infusa* belongs to a big family known as owlet moths. Its larvae and those of many of its relatives are called cutworms, because they topple plants by chewing through stems at the soil surface. Farmers growing winter crops regard cutworms as a major pest.

Moth caterpillars and their defences

For countless other moths in warm and temperate regions, November is a peak month either for their breeding or for larvae to feed. Australia's moth species are numbered in the thousands, with thousands more still to be studied. Some in their adult form are no bigger than mosquitoes. A few have wing areas as great as a handspan.

Moths are classified in the same insect order as butterflies. Structural differences are few. The fore and hind wings of most moths are coupled on each side; in butterflies they work independently. Moths usually rest with their wings spread, while butterflies close their wings vertically over their backs. Most moths have short, thick antennae, in contrast to the slender but club-tipped antennae of butterflies.

Nearly all moths are nocturnal, gaining most notice as nuisances when they are drawn to artificial lights. Their colours, with a few spectacular exceptions, are more sombre than those of butterflies. In their general habits the difference is little. Species of both groups home in on particular plants, around which they find mates and on which their young will feed, though many of the adults themselves eat nothing at all.

Moth larvae — caterpillars — command more of our attention. Usually growing to a body size far greater than that of their parents, they can destroy plant foliage at a prodigious rate. Some stay

---

TOP TUCKER
Moths that make a tasty treat

Well-cooked bogongs are said to taste very like walnuts. The recommended method is to make a fire in a small pit of sandy soil. After every trace of embers or ash is removed, stir the moths in the hot soil until the wings and legs fall off. Take them out and sift them to remove the heads and any clinging dirt.

Bogongs can be eaten one by one. Aboriginals more often used to mash the bodies into a paste. Either way it is important that they are not scorched by contact with burning material. Burning ruins the flavour — and according to Aboriginal lore, brings on a mountaintop storm.

---

covered or camouflaged, but many are show-offs that dissuade predators such as birds, by means of their shapes and gaudy colour patterns. For the same reason, some caterpillars that feed in exposed situations have venomous probes or are covered with brittle, irritant bristles.

The worst rashes are inflicted by the gumleaf skeletoniser — the venomous larva of *Uraba lugens*, an insignificant grey moth that flies to taller eucalypts all over the country. Two generations are bred each year, so the caterpillars can be about from early summer until late winter. Older caterpillars distinguish themselves by wearing an absurd stack of 'hats'. These are head casings kept from the successive skin moults that the caterpillars undergo as they grow.

Also amusing to see but potentially troublesome are processionary caterpillars. They feed on acacias and travel in long files, head-to-tail. The larvae of *Ochrogaster contraria*, active around November, have bristles that affect some people worse than stinging nettles.

Among the most eye-catching of common caterpillars are the saddlebacks or Chinese junks, so called because their bodies are raised at both ends. These are larvae of cup moths *Doratifera*. Their vivid colour combinations change with each moult. Lumps on the front and rear superstructures contain bunches of venomous spikes that push out if the caterpillar is disturbed.

All moth caterpillars spin a coating of silk round their cocoons before they go into their pupal stage to become adults. The hairymary *Anthela nicothoe*, another feeder on acacias, provides itself with extra protection. It sheds its bristles, barbed at both ends, and embeds them in the silk. In the summer when the disused cocoons disintegrate, windblown bristles are a frequent cause of eye complaints.

Gum emperor moths *Antheraea*, also cover their pupal cases with irritant bristles. The caterpillars feed on eucalypt leaves and attach their oval grey cocoons to the bark. They belong to a family of big, heavily-built moths that have eye-like markings on their wings to confuse predators. The group includes northern Queensland's giant *Coscinocera hercules*. Its hind wings extended in exaggerated tails, the male has a fore-to-aft wing measurement of more than twenty centimetres; the female grows the biggest moth wings in the world.

Huge wingspan widths are found among goat moths *Xyleutes*. Females of two species span twenty-three centimetres and have abdomens seven centimetres long. They lay thousands of eggs. The larvae lower themselves from eucalypt foliage on strands of silk and bore into the trunks. Caterpillars take two or three years to reach maturity, growing eighteen centimetres long.

Surprising butterfly habits

Butterflies are abundant throughout Australia's temperate zone in November. In Melbourne and other southern centres, the big, lazy-fluttering wanderer or monarch *Danaus plexippus* is welcomed as a harbinger of summer. A long-living species, it will stay around during the warmer months and then move north, perhaps surviving the whole of winter in a milder climate.

The wanderer is common all along the east coast and is seen as far away as Alice Springs, Perth and Tasmania. Surprisingly, this most widely known and hardy of our butterflies did not originate here. It introduced itself from North America in the 1870s after its food plants, cottonbushes and milkweeds, were established in Australia.

Crossing the Pacific by island-hopping is well within the capacity of the wanderer. Flights of 3000 kilometres have been recorded in North America. There this butterfly is famous for mass migrations. In Australia its movements are apparently less systematic.

The wanderer and many of its endemic Australian relatives in the nymphalid family specialise in eating highly toxic plants. The poisons, absorbed into the bodies of the caterpillars and retained in the pupae and the flying adults, deter birds from attacking them.

One of the better-known native examples is *Euploea core*. It has taken to laying its eggs on *Nerium oleander*, a popular but notoriously toxic ornamental tree introduced from the Mediterranean. Formerly called the common crow, this butterfly is so attracted to the nectar of oleander flowers that a new name has taken over, the oleander butterfly.

North Queensland has an extraordinary butterfly that eats ant larvae. The moth butterfly *Liphyra brassolis*, because of its subdued colours and habit of flying at dawn and dusk, is usually mistaken for a dullish moth. But the discovery of its diet raised scientific eyebrows.

Caterpillars of the moth butterfly have unusually hard skins. They take up residence near the nests of green tree ants and gorge on ant larvae with impunity. They do not make cocoons but pupate inside their last larval shells. New, soft-bodied adults emerge covered in loose scales. The outraged ants attack but are shaken off along with the scales, and the butterflies escape unscathed.

Ants that farm aphids

The moth butterfly is the biggest and most primitive member of the lycaenid family. Many of its relatives — usually called 'blue' butterflies, though that may not be their main colour — spend their early lives in close association with ants. But in

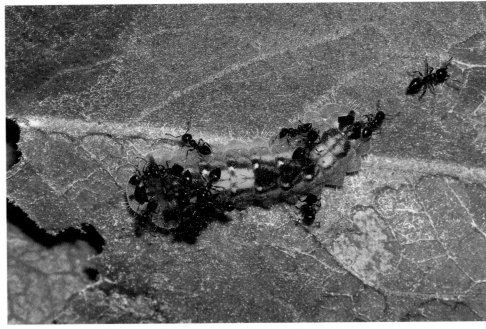

A fiery jewel butterfly caterpillar being taken out to feed by its ant attendants

these cases the ants are in control.

The attraction for the ants is a nourishing fluid exuding from a gland towards the rear of a lycaenid caterpillar's back. The ants seem to know what to expect, because some have been known to guard the butterfly's eggs long before any reward is available, and continue to care for the pupa although the food source may be cut off. Caterpillars are constantly attended by ants wherever they feed. Some ant species shelter the caterpillars in their nests by day, leading them out to suitable food plants only at night.

Colourful and widespread species that enjoy an ant-assisted upbringing include the common imperial blue *Jalmenus evagoras*, on shrubby acacias, the amaryllis azure *Ogyris amaryllis*, on the mistletoes that drape casuarinas, and the fiery jewel *Hypochrysops ignita*, on many native trees.

Ants are better known for their husbandry of sap-sucking insects. This is their time of busiest dedication. Again the attraction is a digestible secretion, a sugary liquid called honeydew. Aphids are stroked to stimulate its production. Some species are tended with as much care as a farmer gives his livestock. Eggs may be collected and guarded, shelters are built, aphids are carried from one prime feeding spot to another.

In return, the aphids receive protection. Soft-bodied and slow-moving, they would otherwise make easy prey for birds,

A wanderer (above) and its larva (right), coloured to warn of its poison

Painted cup moth caterpillar Doratifera oxleyi. *These larvae are also called saddlebacks*

Another cup moth caterpillar, Doratifera vulnerans. *Its hairs sting on contact*

Processionary caterpillars emerge from acacias at night to feed. They travel in a long line, head to tail, and each spins a silken thread, which marks their route along the ground

spiders and any number of predatory insects. Their only independent defence, a feeble one, is in fact the honeydew secretion. They make it into pellets coated with wax and flick them at threatening insects.

Most aphid species were introduced to this country. The closeness of their association with ants varies among species. And sometimes it is seasonal. The ants farm their aphids energetically in spring and early summer, then lose interest.

This behaviour may be connected with the strange life cycle of aphids. Among the seven or more generations born during a

A shelter for honeydew-secreting aphids has been built by ants on a stalk of spinifex

year, clear variations occur in size, structure and reproductive abilities. Different generations can be virtually different animals. Polymorphism, as it is called, seems to have evolved as a response to climatic extremes, enabling aphids to adapt to completely different types of food plants according to the season.

Methods of reproduction also vary seasonally. Males and egg-laying females are born only in autumn. They mate and the eggs over-winter. Winged females are produced. These and the following generations bear their young live, without mating. Generations usually alternate between winged and flightless forms, with mouthparts, legs and other anatomical features modified to suit the plants they are on. Sexual reproduction cannot occur again until some males are produced during the next autumn.

In northern hemisphere aphids, male births are triggered by sharper falls in temperature than the introduced species are likely to experience here. These species probably have no sex life at all in Australia, the females reproducing of their own accord all year round.

The complexity of ant communities
Ants of many species are likely to take to the air on mating flights in November. When flying ants make a nuisance of themselves by swarming into houses on warm nights, they are not the ants we normally see, suddenly having sprouted wings. The invading insects are short-lived males, born for these annual flights.

Except at the time of mating, ant communities are made up entirely of females and female-neuters, differing in form according to their social class and function. There may be more than one

winged, sexually-complete queen in a big nest, but seldom many. In some species there is an intermediate form, capable of reproduction but wingless and not destined to mate.

Workers, the wingless female-neuters that make up the bulk of the population, gather food and feed the queens and larvae. They are graded in two or three sizes. The biggest, known as soldiers, have the additional role of defending the nest. Caste numbers are adjusted when necessary through alterations in the diet of the egg-laying queens and the larvae.

At mating time, males and young queens swarm out of the nest together. After copulating, the males wander aimlessly and soon die. Females seek sites for new colonies, shedding their wings as soon as a place is chosen. In the more advanced species the wing muscles are converted into a food supply to tide queens over until they have raised workers to attend to their needs.

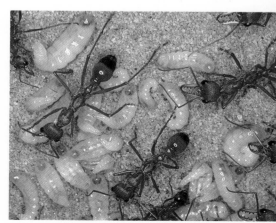

Bulldog ants taking care of larvae

Green tree ants are quite amazing. They form work chains, (left), to build new nests close to existing ones by pulling together a number of leaves. Some of the workers collect larvae from the nest and squeeze the grubs so that they exude a silk which is then used to bind together the leaves making the nest (above)

Most Australian ants excavate nests deep in soil, or more shallowly under rocks and buildings. Forest species often favour rotting logs, and there are some tree-dwellers that build nests on leaves and twigs, or take over beetle burrows.

Leaf-nesting green tree ants *Oecophylla smaragdina* expand their communities by splitting off into neighbouring colonies rather than flying to new sites. Their building method, easily observed in tropical woodlands, is a remarkable example of ingenuity.

Parties of workers form living chains to draw together leaves not far from an existing nest. Then they have to bind them together with silk. But the adult workers cannot make silk. While some keep a grip on the leaves, others disappear into the nest and return with larvae. They hold the grubs in their jaws and squeeze them to force out silk, dabbing the rear ends on the leaf edges as if their young relatives were glue applicators.

Some ants, especially in arid but flood-prone areas, raise mounds of excavated soil around the entrances to their nests, or protect them with heaps of leaves, twigs or pebbles. But the tall, rocklike structures that stud northern grasslands and woodlands are not ant-hills, as many people call them, but termite mounds.

Termites too are likely to take mating flights around November, though some species have an autumn season. Termite communities have social castes and cooperative objectives much like those of ants. Although they are often called 'white ants', they are not even distantly related.

A landscape created by insects
Male termites are few, but those that succeed in mating have a permanent role in society. A chosen male, wings already shed, accompanies his young queen to a new nesting site where they seal themselves in and copulate. The bridegroom becomes king of the colony, fertilising the queen at regular intervals for decades to come, perhaps as long as fifty years. For much of this time the royal couple produces only workers and soldiers, at a rate of thousands of eggs a day in some species.

Virtually any kind of vegetable matter is eaten by termites, according to their type. Australia has more than 200 species. The ones of greatest economic importance are those that eat trees, building materials, crops, electrical cables and plastic pipes. In the north, mound-building species — usually grass-eaters — have an impact on the scenery that no other animal can rival. They remodel the landscape with their constructions.

Shapes and sizes of termite mounds vary with the species. Some are seven metres high or more. Their outer parts are of solid clay or compacted earth, protecting inner labyrinths where a constant humidity is maintained regardless of the season. Underground galleries or covered runways leading out from each mound give the workers access to as much as a hectare of food supplies.

Termites are food for many other animals, and they are the sole diet of the echidna and the numbat. When termites take flight, they make a rare feast for frogs, lizards, snakes, birds and predatory insects. Termite mounds also provide lodgings — goannas, kingfishers and some parrots make their nests in them. □

TERMITES SHOW THE WAY

North-pointing mounds deflect the sun

Some termite mounds on grasslands near Darwin and on Cape York Peninsula are narrowly wedge-shaped. The long axis from the base to the sharp end always points due north. Once it was thought that the builders, *Amitermes meridionalis*, sensed the earth's magnetic field. But the explanation is simpler. The termites build to avoid overheating. They present the least surface area to the direction of the midday sun during a hot, dry winter.

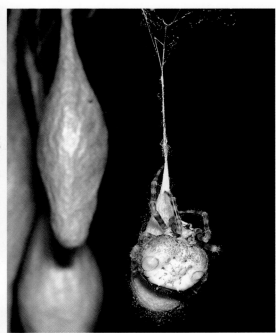

A magnificent spider with its cocoons (right), and sending out a line of silk (above) to trap a male moth in the sticky globule dangling on the end

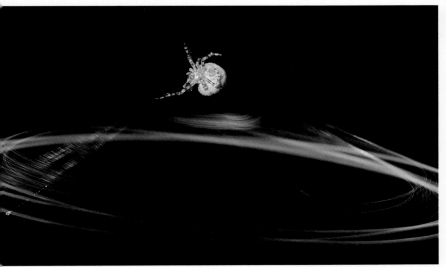

Its ability to whirl its thread has given the bolas spider its name

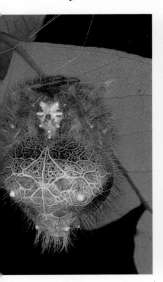

Another bolas spider, the hairy imperial

Doing its best to live up to its common name, the bird-dropping or orchard spider rests on a twig

Night fliers come to a sticky end

Spiders that specialise in moth-trapping

Bolas spiders wield an ingenious weapon to catch moths in mid-air. They secrete a single strand of silk held with one leg. A big sticky globule forms and falls along the thread to dangle at the end. The globule lures male moths, probably with an odour resembling their sex-attractant emissions. When a moth flies near, the spider detects the wing vibrations. With a slight movement of its leg it sets the heavy globule twirling, faster and faster. As soon as the moth gets within range it is clobbered by the gluey mass, immobilised, hauled up and wrapped in silk, to be devoured at leisure.

Eastern Australia has two species of bolas or angler spiders. They are the hairy imperial *Dicrostichus furcatus* and the magnificent spider *D. magnificus*. Both are best known for the 'cow's teat' egg cocoons that the big females spin later in the summer.

Camouflaged as bird-dropping

Another specialist predator of moths is the bird-dropping or orchard spider *Celaenia*, common in the southwest and southeast. It almost certainly fakes a sex-attractant, and a female one at that, because all the moths that approach it are males. The spider simply waits, for hours if necessary, with its forelegs bent mantis-fashion until a moth comes within grasping distance.

The bird-dropping spider earns its common name by a convincing daytime camouflage. It can rest in the open on a leaf or twig, the blotched, lumpy body of the female looking like a big blob of excrement. Spherical eggs are hung in bunches under foliage late in summer, and guarded by the female until the spiderlings emerge.□

Warming waters give fish a message

In the rivers of the southeast, November sees fish migrating upstream to spawn

Old records are claimed of Murray cod nearly two metres long, weighing over 110 kilos. There are none like that around any more. An average weight now is four kilos and a specimen tipping the scales at more than thirty kilos is a rare whopper. The decline is due partly to silting in some rivers, but more to the inroads made by generations of anglers. The fish simply have not been allowed to live long enough.

The Murray cod *Maccullochella peeli* is quite easily caught because it is not a fighter and its seasonal movements are predictable. Mature fish, four years old or more, go upstream to spawn in late spring. Their migration is triggered when the water temperature reaches 20°C, in combination with the rising water levels that are usual in the Darling-Murray system and other rivers of the southeast.

Females produce up to 50 000 eggs in a spawning. Eggs are attached to unmoving submerged objects such as boulders, and hatch within a fortnight. Adults and fry go downstream in autumn, many of the young falling victims to cannibalism. The usual diet is fish, yabbies, shrimps and mussels. But waterfowl, rats and lizards may also be taken.

In spite of some resemblance to marine cods and gropers, the Murray cod is a member of the bass family. Its Australian freshwater relatives include the 'trout cod' *Maccullochella macquariensis* and the so-called perches that also migrate upstream in flooding rivers at this time.

Most abundant of these is the golden perch or callop *Macquaria ambigua*. Well-grown females may carry hundreds of thousands of eggs, and are capable of holding them until conditions are just right, or reabsorbing them if not. The spawning trigger is a water temperature of 23°C in floodplain shallows where the eggs hatch in two days and the fry can develop fairly safely.

Less common are the silver perch *Bidyanus bidyanus* (which does not belong to the bass family), and the Macquarie or mountain perch *Macquaria australasica*. Both of these species frequent smaller rivers and their populations are vulnerable to damming. □

A female Murray cod is usually about four years old and nearly sixty centimetres long when she first spawns

The silver perch (above) is one of the few freshwater fish to let its eggs float or drift near the surface, instead of attaching them to some submerged object

Although it is a close relative of the Murray cod, the trout cod (left) grows to only about sixteen kilos. It generally prefers to stay in the cooler upper reaches of the Murray system

OFF THE SOUTH COASTS ...

Bream and tuna are on the move

Fishermen welcome November as the month when bream *Acanthopagrus* are most likely to be spawning. Bream move out from the inner reaches of southern estuaries, but do not go into the open sea unless they are forced there by floods.

In deep waters near the edge of the continental shelf, schools of tuna are on the move around southern Australia. The commercial fishing season for the southern bluefin *Thunnus maccoyii* opens at Port Lincoln, South Australia, and yellowtail *Thunnus albacares* are biting off southern New South Wales.

Closer in, off both the east and the west coasts, there may be an even more thrilling sight than leaping tuna — the return passage southward of families of humpback whales.

The golden perch, also known as yellowbelly, likes to breed during warm floods

DECEMBER

THIS MONTH'S WEATHER

Substantial rains are combined with oppressive heat along the Queensland coast. At the Top End, however, buildup of cloud cover preceding the monsoon is so extensive that temperatures fall slightly. Towards the end of the month the first tropical cyclones of the season may brew up. The south and southwest become hot and parched, and the southeast is also generally short of rain, with an increasing risk of bushfires.

AROUND THE COUNTRY	RAIN (mm)	MAX. (°C)	MIN. (°C)	SUN hrs/day
Adelaide	28	27	15	9.4
Alice Springs	36	35	20	10.3
Brisbane	122	29	20	8.7
Canberra	50	26	11	9.4
Darwin	222	33	25	7.2
Hobart	57	20	11	7.3
Melbourne	58	24	13	8.2
Perth	14	27	16	10.7
Port Hedland	18	37	24	11.5
Sydney	77	25	17	7.6
Townsville	114	31	24	8.9
Weipa	251	33	24	7.3

Cicada nymphs at the moment of transformation into adults

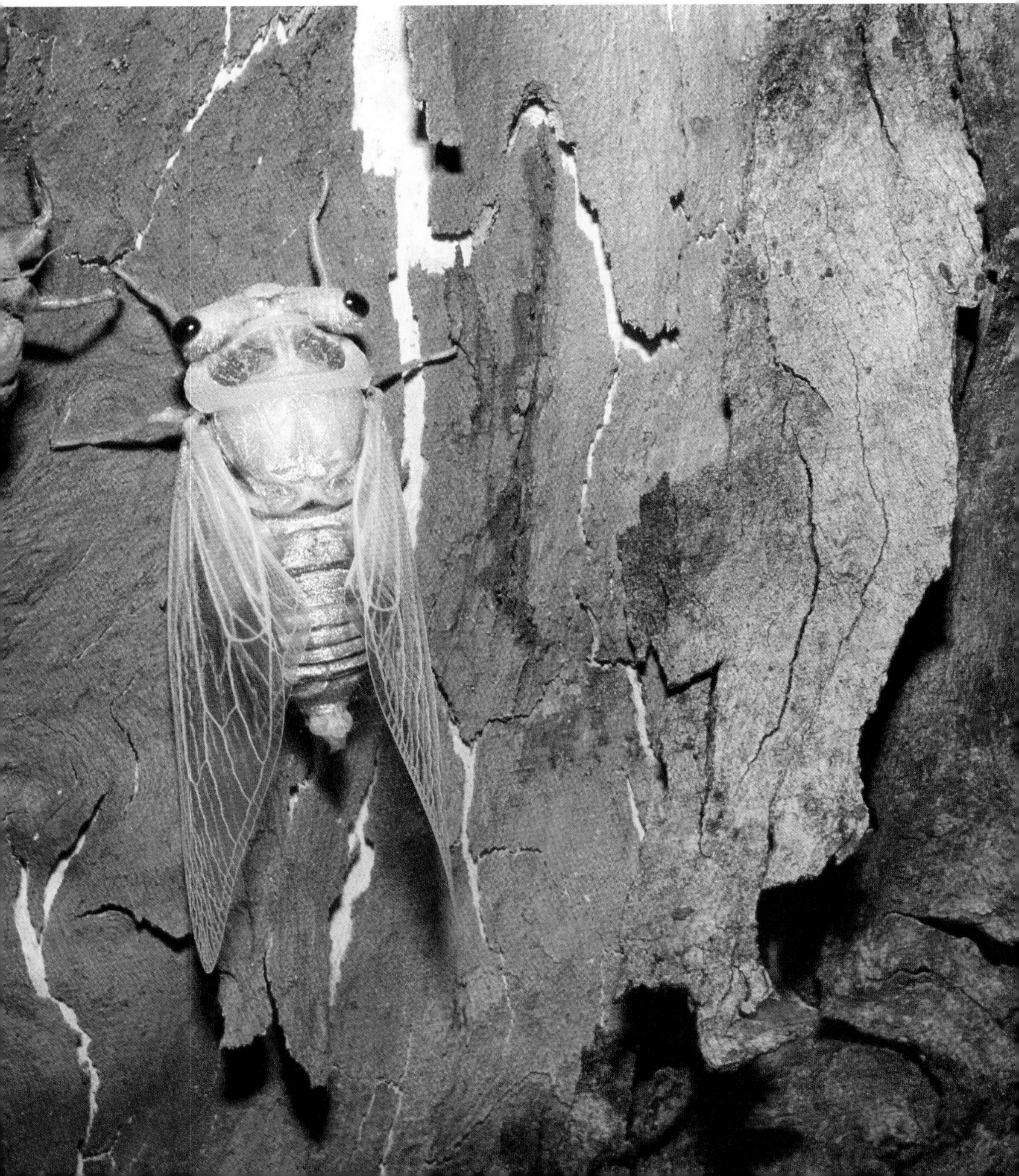

Koalas in the wild are loners, shunning companionship even though they have to share feeding areas. Vocal communication consists mainly of belligerent bellows and snarled threats. Mating is a brutish assault, without the least niceties of courtship, and like most other close encounters it usually leads to fighting.

Studies of captive koalas, their behaviour modified by enforced familiarity, gave rise to some misconceptions. Their unfriendly society appeared to have no structure. But years of field work by Monash University zoologist Peter Mitchell have changed that view. His findings, published in 1988, indicate that wild koalas of both sexes form clusters, each under the tyranny of one big and powerful male. He seizes most, perhaps all, of the breeding opportunities.

Mitchell fitted radio-transmitter collars to koalas on French Island, in Westernport Bay, Victoria, and traced the movements of individuals within their groups. He discovered that certain males had wider ranges than the others, and that these more often overlapped the ranges of the females.

Fighting over females

The 'alpha' males, as he calls them, choose whatever trees they like, often attacking and evicting other males. Deep bite wounds are sometimes inflicted in the process. This bullying continues even

Bullies rule a violent society

December is peak breeding time for koalas, but these amiable-looking creatures are far from affectionate

when 'alpha' males wander outside their home range and meet subordinate males of other groups.

Fighting increases during a breeding season of six months or more. Breeding reaches its peak in December in the southeast and November in Queensland. When females have weaned their young of the previous year, they start a cycle of ovulation that brings them into heat for just a few hours every thirty-five days. Regardless of that, males attempt to mate at any time during the season.

Snarling in protest, females are pounced upon, seized by the neck and pinned against tree trunks. But copulation is impossible unless a female voluntarily raises her rump. Most often the outcome is a fierce bout of screaming, scratching, biting and bellowing. The din is likely to fetch the group's 'alpha' male, hurrying to enforce his monopoly against a subordi-

nate. The only successful matings that Mitchell saw were by 'alpha' males.

The koala *Phascolarctos cinereus* is sexually capable at two years. But a male is unlikely to be able to assert 'alpha' dominance until he gains maximum size and strength at about five. Animals that escape disease and the effects of drought and bushfires live for ten years or more before their teeth wear out.

Males signify their maturity by a regular bellowing, increasing in frequency during the breeding season. On waking, the koala points his nose skywards and makes a long, quavering inhalation. Then the air is forced out as a low, sharp belch. A series of these two-note calls, which sound like a pig trying to imitate a donkey, usually lasts about fifteen seconds. On still nights the noise can carry more than half a kilometre. Other males answer, setting up a reverberating clamour.

Bellows are also uttered in victory after a fight, or in annoyance at a sexual rejection. Females in heat sometimes make a similar noise, though seldom as loudly as males. While not apparently a mating call in the usual sense — it seems chiefly to be an indicator of position — the bellow may attract a partner from outside an animal's normal range.

Self-advertisement by bellowing averts some accidental encounters and their violent consequences. So does scent-marking. Both sexes sometimes urinate

Male koalas attempt to mate at any time during the six-month breeding season, although females are seldom in heat. The male showing an interest in the female (left) will not be allowed to mate with her unless he is a dominant or 'alpha' male. He will try to force the issue, but the female's noisy rejection of his advances (right) will bring the dominant male hurrying to the scene to see off the attempted rapist. In the ensuing fight, deep bites and scratches may be inflicted, but the injuries are rarely fatal, unless one of the protagonists loses his grip and falls out of the tree

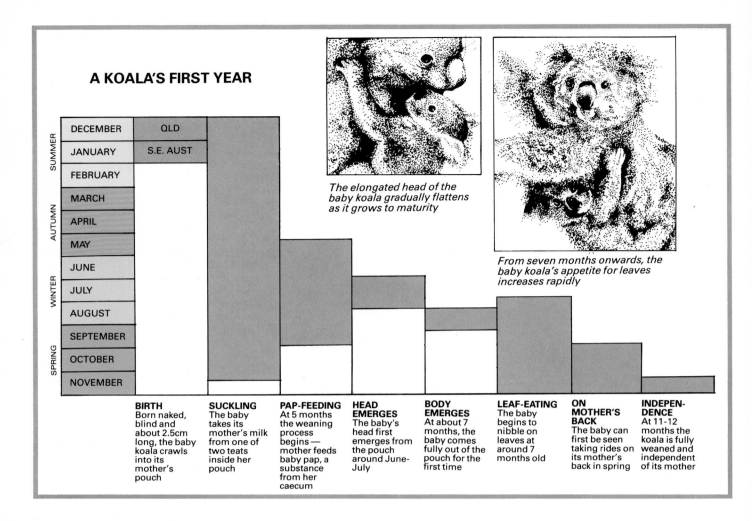

A KOALA'S FIRST YEAR

		BIRTH	SUCKLING	PAP-FEEDING	HEAD EMERGES	BODY EMERGES	LEAF-EATING	ON MOTHER'S BACK	INDEPEN-DENCE
SUMMER	DECEMBER	QLD							
	JANUARY	S.E. AUST							
	FEBRUARY								
AUTUMN	MARCH								
	APRIL								
	MAY								
WINTER	JUNE								
	JULY								
	AUGUST								
SPRING	SEPTEMBER								
	OCTOBER								
	NOVEMBER								

The elongated head of the baby koala gradually flattens as it grows to maturity

From seven months onwards, the baby koala's appetite for leaves increases rapidly

BIRTH
Born naked, blind and about 2.5cm long, the baby koala crawls into its mother's pouch

SUCKLING
The baby takes its mother's milk from one of two teats inside her pouch

PAP-FEEDING
At 5 months the weaning process begins — mother feeds baby pap, a substance from her caecum

HEAD EMERGES
The baby's head first emerges from the pouch around June-July

BODY EMERGES
At about 7 months, the baby comes fully out of the pouch for the first time

LEAF-EATING
The baby begins to nibble on leaves at around 7 months old

ON MOTHER'S BACK
The baby can first be seen taking rides on its mother's back in spring

INDEPEN-DENCE
At 11-12 months the koala is fully weaned and independent of its mother

The bond between mother and cub is severed as soon as a new baby is born

on the trunk of a chosen tree or around its base. During the breeding season the male also uses a scent gland, located in a strip of bare skin down the middle of his chest. He activates it by flattening his chest against a tree trunk and rubbing up and down. The oily fluid exuded makes a vertical orange stain on his chest fur.

Koalas are heavy for tree-dwelling mammals. Some males in Victoria weigh more than thirteen kilos, and females reach eleven kilos. Long, dense fur contributes to their bulk. At the north of their geographical range, on the Atherton Tableland near Cairns in Queensland, koalas are considerably smaller, with short hair giving them a scrawnier look.

Infancy lasts for a year

A mated female gives birth about thirty-five days later to a single offspring — twins are a rare event — about the size of a peanut and weighing only half a gram. It crawls into her backward-opening pouch and attaches its mouth to one of two teats, never letting go for the next thirteen weeks.

At five to six months the cub's eyes open and it starts to put its head out of the pouch. Now a remarkable development takes place in the mother. As well as excreting normal faeces, at times she discharges pap, a runny substance that is eaten by the cub. This material is thought to come from the caecum, a blind offshoot of the gut.

Most mammals including humans have a caecum, but in the koala it is of extraordinary size — about two metres long. It is thought to contain bacteria that aid digestion by fermentation, and may also destroy poisons and build nutrient proteins. Whatever the functions of this huge organ, the cub obviously needs some of its contents to prime its own system in readiness for a grown-up diet.

Leaves are first eaten at seven or eight months of age, while the cub clings to the belly fur of its feeding mother. A little later it takes to resting on the mother's back. Though out of the pouch, it sometimes suckles, on a teat so stretched that it may poke out of the pouch.

At about nine months the cub starts to feed independently of its mother, but stays very close and returns frequently to her back. Their association continues until the cub is about a year old, when a new birth abruptly breaks up the relationship. From then on, attempts to suckle or ride are rebuffed. A cub may climb onto another adult female or even a male, but this sometimes leads to a fatal attack.

The young remain near their birthplace for a further year. Males disperse at two, roaming in search of new feeding and breeding areas. Females take up residence on ranges close to those of their mothers. There they are soon mated, presumably with their fathers.

Throughout the long upbringing of cubs, mothers show a passive tolerance rather than any affection. Cubs are not groomed, tended, played with or trained. The only active response by a mother comes when a young cub is separated from her and makes a squeaking noise. Then she will begin to search for the source of the sound.

A varied and finicky diet
Koalas show strong preferences in their diet, but their choice is not as narrow as experience with captive animals used to suggest. In various areas the leaves of more than thirty eucalypt species, and occasionally those of unrelated plants, are known to be eaten.

Typically, where there may be two or three suitable eucalypt species in one locality, preferences vary among members of a koala community. And whichever they favour for most of the year, they go off it for a time. Presumably this has to do with changes in the chemical composition of gumleaf oils, but the reasons are not understood.

ACQUIRED TASTE
Eucalyptus leaves are not their only food

Popular myth has it that koalas eat only gumleaves. Given the opportunity, wild populations vary their diet occasionally. Leaves of acacias, boxes, native cherry, coastal teatree, native kapok and swamp paperbark are taken.

Some koalas have been seen feeding on introduced apple trees. Even more oddly, two that kept disappearing from their manna gum grove on French Island, Victoria, were found to have taken a liking to pine needles.

Koalas feed mainly in the evening

Most eating is done just before sundown and between dusk and midnight. There are usually two to four other short sessions of feeding, some during the day. But about nineteen hours out of every twenty-four are spent sleeping or resting. Movements from tree to tree are made mostly in the dark, soon after midnight.

On the ground, the koala walks with a slow, ambling gait. But it is capable of a bounding run. Its dedication to life in the treetops is puzzling. Though its paws are well adapted for climbing, in other respects its anatomy is much more suited to living on the ground.

For one thing the koala has only a rudimentary tail, hidden by its fur. And the backward-opening pouch of the female is characteristic of a burrowing marsupial, not a climber. Tail and foot structure and some internal features of the koala resemble those of wombats.

Recent genetic studies tend to support a view that wombats and the koala had the same terrestrial ancestor, scores of millions of years ago. If so they have diverged in one particularly curious way. A wombat's brain is relatively big for its body size. A koala's is very small, weighing only about sixty per cent of what could be expected. And its structure is much simpler, perhaps accounting for the koala's uncomplicated social behaviour.

Their range has long been shrinking
Fossil finds show that koalas were widespread across the mainland in pre-human times. Climatic change and the shrinkage of forests reduced their range, but a greater menace seems to have come from Aboriginal hunting and the depredations of dingoes. When the New South Wales colony was founded koalas were so scarce that they went unnoticed for ten years.

Clearance of wooded country for agriculture limited the habitats of koalas still further. But where koalas remained, they thrived in remarkable abundance. In the latter part of the nineteenth century koalas were counted in thousands in districts where they had been unknown at the time of European settlement. A fur trade prospered on their easy slaughter.

Protected in Victoria since 1898, New South Wales since 1909 and Queensland since 1927, koalas have regained their numbers in limited areas of the southeast. In a few places there are too many for their own good, and surplus animals have been taken to areas where the species had been wiped out by hunting or fires. Some national parks in South and Western Australia were stocked in this way.

A peculiarity of koala anatomy makes the females unusually prone to diseases of the reproductive tract. In particular they are vulnerable to infection by one of the Chlamydias — tiny germs that multiply in nearly all species of native birds and many mammals. They are the cause of psittacosis, which can damage human lungs, and is caught from pet birds.

Chlamydiosis in koalas is sexually transmitted. In its most severe form it causes kidney damage and infertility. Zoologists in the mid-1980s found infection so prevalent that they forecast doom for most koala populations. Studies since then have shown that communities long exposed to the disease cope with it. Many infected females go on breeding, and populations continue to grow.

Where koalas thrive, it is in their nature to spread out. Nothing regulates their numbers. If they cannot expand their range, they kill their food trees by complete defoliation and starve themselves to death. In protected conditions the chief modern danger to koalas, apart from bushfires, is their own success. □

Baby bats fill the caves

No matter whether this scourge of insects mates in autumn or waits until spring, the young all arrive for Christmas

Nursery caves of bent-wing bats are scattered in forests and woodlands from the Kimberley, Arnhem Land and Cape York to the Victorian shores of Bass Strait. Throughout this vast geographical and climatic range, all their young are born in December. What makes such timing even more surprising is that northern and southern mating seasons are four months apart.

Tropical populations of the common bent-wing bat *Miniopterus schreibersii* enjoy a year-round abundance of insect prey. They mate in September and embryos develop rapidly. Outside the tropics, identical bats have a different breeding biology.

Because food is scarce in winter, the southerners are conditioned to hibernation. But first, around May, the adults mate. A single egg is fertilised in each female. Her body temperature falls so low during hibernation that the egg scarcely develops. It is not implanted until just before she emerges in August or September. After that, higher temperatures and renewed nourishment trigger normal embryonic growth.

Traditional nursery sites are used summer after summer by bats flying in from hundreds of kilometres around. In Queensland and northern New South Wales they are often shared with the little bent-wing bat *Miniopterus australis*. Suitable caves are scarce because they must be the right shape to retain air that is heated by the crowding together of thousands of adult females.

In the fetid, dung-heaped inner reaches of a cave, where the constant temperature may approach 40°C, naked young are born and placed against ceilings and high walls. They are so tightly packed, more than a thousand to a square metre, that they form a solid pink mass.

Mothers, barely able to tolerate the stifling heat, visit their offspring and suckle them only around dawn. During the day they withdraw to resting places nearer the cave entrance. At night the young stay in the cave while the mothers go out to patrol above the canopies of trees, hunting for flying insects.

Baby bats are fully furred after a month or so, and soon weaned. Their early flights seldom take them far from the birth cave, but by late February or early March they are ready to disperse. The mothers return to old, habitual hunting grounds and the juveniles go their own way. Sexually mature in their second season, they may live for more than fifteen years.

Males, and females free of maternal duties, choose cooler caves as daytime roosts. Many human structures serve just as well: disused mine diggings, tunnels, stormwater drains and sometimes neglected buildings. Big off-season colonies are formed if roosting areas are spacious enough.

Wired for sound

Bent-wing bats are prominent among a large family of insectivorous bats called vespertilionids. It embraces nearly half of the bat species in Australia and also includes such well-known types as the long-eared bats, wattled bats, broad-nosed bats and eptesicuses. Vespertilionids share a capacity for hibernation in cooler regions. But the common bent-wing's delayed implantation is unique among hiber-

nating species. Other females, after mating in autumn, store the male sperm.

All insect-eating bats hunt their prey and find their way about at night by echolocation. They emit extremely high-pitched sounds in short bursts and judge shapes and distances by how long it takes the signals to return. Such bats, always tiny in comparison with fruit bats, are characteristically small-eyed and big-eared. Some unrelated types such as the ghost bat and horseshoe bats, but not our vespertilionids, have grotesque facial formations to direct the sounds.

Flying prey is not usually caught in the mouth; that would interfere with sound emission. Insects are trapped in the flexible hand membranes or 'wings' and transferred to the mouth in flight, or taken to a tree. These bats often alight on branches to capture crawling insects, and some occasionally hunt on the ground.

Mothers that take baby on the hunt

In the air or at rest, many insect-eating bats fall prey to owls, feral cats and pythons, which strike quickly enough to snap them up in midflight. Even domestic cats may supplement their diet by catching Australia's most widespread and abundant bat, the lesser long-eared *Nyctophilus geoffroyi*, which hunts on or very close to the ground and takes readily to urban surroundings.

The lesser long-eared bat may choose daytime roosts in the ceilings of buildings or hide among clothing or other fabrics left hanging outside. In a bushland environment it may roost in caves, but more often shelters under loose bark, in tree hollows, or on the ground under rocks.

December is again the month when most young are born. Maternity colonies are usually made up of scores of mothers, rather than the tens of thousands in which bent-wing bats gather. Twin offspring are fairly common.

Tucked into their mother's 'armpits', young long-eared bats can be carried in flight while they are suckling. More often they are left in the maternity roost. In the other main groups of vespertilionids, the broad-nosed bats *Nycticeius*, the wattled bats *Chalinobus* and the forest eptesicuses *Eptesicus*, carriage of newborn young by foraging mothers seems to be the rule. □

Bat breeding caves get very hot; adult females return from hunting to suckle their young only in the cool of the dawn

The fork-tailed swift flies over Australia in the summer — but rarely lands

Reunion of the air aces

Two champion long-distance fliers, neighbours in northern Asia, cross Australia by different routes but join forces at journey's end

Back in October, high over lonely northwestern shores, a huge aerial force began an unseen invasion of Australia. At the same time other formations streamed into the northeast, over Cape York Peninsula. The invaders are two types of swifts whose breeding grounds are in northern China, Mongolia and Japan. By December a vast pincer movement will have brought most of them together in Victoria and southern New South Wales.

Swifts are non-stop travellers. The vast distances covered when they migrate are equalled only by some seabirds that rest on the water. Their flight is not notably fast — contrary to the popular belief that gave them their name — but it is economical. Bursts of flapping with sickle-shaped wings are mere punctuations to long spells of relaxed gliding. Strong high-altitude winds push the birds along. And they can sleep on the wing, in flocks of hundreds forming tightly packed rafts.

In Australia over summer the swifts stay aloft night and day. They eat in flight, scooping insects into their short, gaping bills, and drink while skimming over waterholes and puddles. At home in Asia they even mate in mid-air.

We generally see swifts only early and late in the day, when they hawk for insects at heights below a hundred metres, often just a few centimetres from the ground. Sometimes they deliberately brush tree foliage to flush out prey. All kinds of flies, bugs, beetles and moths are taken, together with feasts of ants and termites on their mating flights.

Swooping into insect swarms, swifts face a problem similar to that of a high-speed motorist whose windscreen is soon spattered and smeared with corpses and their juices. A swift copes with the help of protective feathers projecting around its eyes, and its own version of windscreen wipers — transparent membranes that it can blink to clear away obstructions.

The black, white-rumped birds that come in from the northwest are fork-tailed swifts *Apus pacificus*. In the summer they can turn up anywhere on the mainland and in Tasmania. But the general course is south or southeastward over semi-arid regions.

They move across the continent in waves every four or five days, assisted by the rising air in travelling low-pressure systems that interrupt the usual chain of anticyclones. If they see a column of scrubfire smoke they make straight for it. They gain lift from the heated air — and a bonus of insects caught in the updraft.

Meanwhile the other force of bigger, brownish swifts is making a more leisurely progress south from Cape York and the Gulf of Carpentaria, keeping mostly to the forested slopes of the Great Dividing Range. These are the white-throated

A flock of galahs; a common sight despite their harsh rearing

Welcome swallows settle near water because they need mud for nest-building

needletails *Hirundapus caudacutus*. Their main movements exploit the wind shifts of changing weather and the buildup of thunderstorms. They too are drawn to smoke columns. Some birds will travel as far as Tasmania or the South Australian gulfs, but the main summer concentration will be on the southeastern mainland.

Meeting and parting
Where their routes converge, the two types of swifts often associate. They may be seen hawking together. Towards autumn both species begin a parallel northward journey. The needletails again keep to the Great Divide while the fork-tailed swifts follow the drier western flanks. By April most will have left the country, though a few immature birds may well spend the winter in the Northern Territory.

Swifts never land on the ground if they can help it, and although their hawk-like toes enable them to cling easily to tree trunks they rarely alight on branches. Not so another summer visitor from Asia, the oriental cuckoo *Cuculus saturatus*. It does all its hunting kingfisher-fashion, from a perch on a high, open branch where it can spot insects below. Caterpillars, stick insects, beetles and bigger ants are its principal prey.

Oriental cuckoos start arriving on the north coast in November. By December the leaders are making their way south through forests close to the eastern seaboard. They may divert to hunt in mangrove stands and paperbark swamps. Few birds travel beyond Sydney. Ahead of them a potentially competitive native, the pallid cuckoo, has already pushed farther south to find nurses for its young.

In Australia the oriental cuckoo sports a confusing variety of mature and immature plumage in colours ranging from dove grey to brown. But it can always be distinguished from the pallid cuckoo by the bars on its underparts.

Visitors from Indonesia
Around December the barn swallow *Hirundo rustica* appears on the north coast in small numbers. It is one of the best-known birds in the northern hemisphere, breeding in all regions of the temperate zone. Annual migrations of the Asian population take most birds only as far as Indonesia. That is a matter of regret to people enduring tropical wet seasons in Australia because barn swallows enjoy roosting on or close to buildings, and feast on flies, mosquitoes and midges.

A few barn swallows may appear at scattered localities along the east coast as far south as Sydney. The main concentration is between Broome and Darwin, where the welcome swallow, a very similar native bird, is not likely to venture. Much the same range is occupied during the Wet by sparse scatterings of yellow wagtails *Motacilla flava*. They breed from eastern Europe to Alaska, and again the visitors reaching Australia are merely the overspill of vast numbers wintering in Indonesia. They feed on the ground in the

A GRIM TIME FOR GALAHS
The young birds are abandoned to fend for themselves

In open woodlands and grasslands throughout the country, young galahs have been thriving in abundance since their hatching in spring. For six to eight weeks the fledglings have been in creches of up to a hundred birds, fed daily by foraging adults. Now it is time for the parents to moult, and the young are abandoned. Most die. Only about one in ten of the nestlings that are successfully fledged survives to breeding age.

More survive because of agriculture
Flocks of immature birds will wander for two or three years, but are unlikely to go more than fifty kilometres from their birthplace. Once they start to breed they stick to permanent home ranges with nesting sites that are used season after season. Their feeding areas are wide, however, thanks to a powerful flying action that can carry them at over fifty kilometres an hour. Outside the breeding season, flocks of up to a thousand galahs are commonly seen foraging for grass seeds or raiding wheat crops. Agriculture has been a boon, providing not only a more reliable food supply but also permanent stores of water. The galah *Cacatua roseicapilla* drinks every day, late in the afternoon. Then flocks put on one of the great spectacles of the outback, flashing their pink and grey plumage in unison as they perform group aerobatics before flying home to communal roosts.

Breeding is territorial but crowding is tolerated. Paired birds, probably mated for life, guard a single tree containing a nesting hole. A patch of bark is stripped from the tree and both birds frequently rub their faces on the bare patch, apparently to signify their occupancy. A nest of twigs is lined with fresh leaves on which at least two and sometimes as many as six eggs are laid. Incubated by both parents, they hatch in about a month.

A view of the oriental cuckoo's barred underparts

Most yellow wagtails winter in Indonesia, but a few visit the north of Australia during the Wet

All wander locally to some extent. Most are also migratory, shifting north in winter. The most widespread is the black-faced cuckoo-shrike *Coracina novaehollandiae*. Its comings and goings in Tasmania and the higher country of the southeastern mainland are so noticeable that many people call it the summerbird.

Nests of cuckoo-shrikes are shallow saucers of twigs and bark, bound with cobweb. All lay two or three green eggs except for the canopy-feeding cicadabird *Coracina tenuirostris*, which produces only one. The cicadabird's egg may be more of a blueish colour — and it is said to be laid always at sunrise.

Ground cuckoo-shrikes are spring breeders over most of their semi-arid inland range, and their nesting season is ending now. *Coracina maxima* stands out from the rest of its family in other ways too. It is the only one to walk and feed on the ground, taking grassland insects. It also has vivid markings on its back — perhaps so that its own kind, in flight, can recognise it from above. And it has a

same fashion and with the same mannerisms as our familiar willie wagtail, though the two birds are unrelated.

December is a peak breeding month for tree-feeding native cuckoo-shrikes, which live on insects but sometimes eat fruits.

Young black-faced cuckoo-shrikes call for food (above); ground cuckoo-shrike parents feed a fledgling (below)

The great egret abandons its solitary lifestyle during the breeding season — note the nuptial plumes on this bird's back

communal spirit which even extends to neighbours helping one another with nest-building and the feeding of the young.

Similar cooperation is shown among figbirds *Sphecotheres viridis*, most of which are breeding now. Unattached males make donations of regurgitated soft fruits to the young of other birds, and may baby-sit while both parents are away feeding. Figbirds live in and around forests in the best-watered districts of the north and east coasts. Noisy flocks sometimes raid parks and gardens for the fruits of native trees and crops.

In the southeast, December is the peak month in an unusually late breeding season for a honeyeater, the yellow-faced *Lichenostomus chrysops*. Some pairs may not nest until February. As well as brushing nectar and pollen from the blossoms of eucalypts and a variety of shrubs and heaths, this honeyeater is an active hunter of tree-dwelling insects. Flocks move north between March and May, one bunch following another on traditional flight paths. Some birds work their way as far as tropical Queensland.

Egrets in courting dress
Delicate nuptial plumes are most likely to be seen in December on the biggest of the white herons, the great egret *Ardea alba*.

They sprout from the back and extend beyond the tail. The bills of both sexes, yellow for most of the year, turn black when they are ready to breed. Yellow eyes go red and the blue-green facial skin turns to yellow.

Egrets that usually stalk about alone, or more often stand motionless as they watch for fish, will now court the opposite sex with displays of bill-snapping and neck-stretching. Nesting platforms of sticks are built high up in trees, or occasionally in beds of reeds. As many as six eggs are laid, to be incubated by both parents, though it is rare for more than two chicks to be raised. □

The yellow-faced honeyeater breeds late, in December in the southeast

A female estuarine crocodile guards her nest against predators; she will stay near it for the entire incubation period — which is

Crocodiles have to be lucky to reach adulthood

The monarch of tropical waterways must beat long odds to reach maturity and win the right to breed. Then its only threat is from people

Thunder rumbles along the northern coast and leaden skies threaten yet another dumping of rain. Dusty red soils have turned to mud. Beside spreading swamps and swelling waterways, big female estuarine crocodiles are toiling to found a new generation. Many will be wasting their time.

Arduous hours are spent scraping up dead leaves, twigs and sand or mud from a wide area around a chosen nesting site. The material is pushed into a pile as much as a metre high and two metres in diameter at the base. The crocodile sprawls over it and in the course of a night lays fifty or more pliable, leathery-skinned eggs, about the size of a goose's. More scraping adds a covering layer some thirty centimetres deep. Until about March the mother will spend much of her time on or

close to the nest mound. Heat from the rotting of the plant matter provides a consistently high temperature for incubation. But the nest must not get excessively hot. If the overcast skies of the wet season should give way to strong sunshine, the mother cools the nest by soaking the surface with sprays of urine.

She is also ready, and fearsomely able, to ward off interference to the nest. At this stage the main natural enemies are big goannas. They probably do not steal viable eggs, as was once supposed, but are attracted to rotting ones. If allowed to dig these out they endanger the whole clutch.

One thing the mother is powerless against, however, is destruction of the nest by floodwaters. Mounds are never more than twenty metres from major watercourses, and seldom far above their

around three months

surface level. In summers when the monsoonal rains are unusually intense and persistent, egg losses are enormous.

If her nest survives until hatching time, the mother must also be on hand to open it. The young would suffocate if they broke out of their shells while still buried. When almost ready to hatch they set up a chorus of squeaking to alert the mother.

Heavy losses are no problem
At the best of times, only a small minority of embryos develop to hatching. The young wriggle out as perfect miniatures of the adult form, not much more than twenty centimetres long. The mother soon guides them to the water.

Though fully equipped with snapping jaws and needle-sharp teeth, newborn crocodiles are no match for the predators that beset them once they lose maternal protection. They make tasty eating for fishes, waterfowl and older crocodiles.

Survivors live at first on aquatic insects, tadpoles, crustaceans and tiny fishes. Later they can manage birds, bigger fishes, frogs and lizards. But it will be years before they show an adult's preference for mammals. They grow about forty-five centimetres a year until they reach sexual maturity — females at about six, males at eight. Growth is slower after that, but goes on for the rest of a crocodile's life.

With the onset of sexual impulses, signalled by a glandular secretion detectable in the water, males face a further process of merciless weeding out. They must establish territories in order to breed. For most there is no room, and no chance of evicting older occupants that may be twice their length and ten times their weight. They are condemned to a roaming exile, always under the threat of death if they happen to trespass.

A heavy wastage of the young is acceptable in a crocodile community because so few are needed to maintain a stable population. *Crocodylus porosus* may live and breed for seventy years or more. Forcing junior males to wander in search of territory ensures two things: the community is always ready to expand its range if the chance arises, and replacement candidates are on hand immediately in the rare event of a veteran's death.

Back from the brink of extinction
That is the situation that applied for about sixty-five million years, after crocodiles found themselves rid of the competition of dinosaurs. Big crocodiles were invulnerable to any other creature in their natural environment. But human ingenuity with traps, and lately with firearms, brought about their decline in every tropical region of the world.

How easily and suddenly that could happen was demonstrated all too clearly in northern Australia. Estuarine crocodiles were in fair abundance before the Second World War. Shot for sport and then for the value of their skins, they were on the brink of extinction by 1970.

Conversely, since crocodiles were given legal protection, Australia has had the most graphic proof of their ability to recolonise their habitat and rebuild their numbers. The Northern Territory population is now counted in scores of thousands, and seems to have been growing at a rate approaching ten per cent a year. At predictable spots on rivers and billabongs south and east of Darwin, tourists can be guaranteed a sight of crocodiles in the wild. And they are of increasingly imposing size.

Because we can only guess how long estuarine crocodiles live, we cannot put a limit on their size. A dubious record of 9.6 metres is claimed for an animal shot long ago near Mackay, Queensland. Tales from the old days of specimens around eight metres do not seem too far-fetched. In any case a crocodile four metres long, which is common enough now, is awe-inspiring and highly dangerous. It is fast both on its feet and in the water, and because it was born after shooting was banned, it may not be wary of human beings.

Light eaters for their size
No crocodile is especially interested in people as food, however. Unless we foolishly offer ourselves, it is most unlikely to make the first move. Nor are crocodiles, in spite of their size, greedy eaters of anything else. They need only a tenth of the nourishment of an equivalent mammal, which would have to spend energy on maintaining a steady body temperature. A crocodile gains heat from the sun by daytime basking, and holds much of it by spending more time in the water at night.

Adaptation to hunting in or from the water is superb. The eyes, nostrils and ears are placed so that a crocodile can cruise or drift with nothing else showing above the surface. Propulsion and steering come solely from a waving of the huge tail, which is vertically flattened like a sea snake's. If a crocodile chooses to submerge completely, valves seal the nostrils and ears and transparent membranes protect the eyes. It can slow its rate of oxygen use to remain under water for an hour. Crocodiles can also feed under water, thanks to a flap that shuts off their windpipe from their gullet. But contrary to a common belief, they do not store food down below and wait for it to rot. Prey is eaten fresh. It is gulped down whole if that can be managed, or alternatively torn into pieces by wrenching bites.

The natural range of estuarine crocodiles is from around Broome, Western Australia, to Maryborough, Queensland, including the big islands near Darwin and in the Gulf of Carpentaria. Bachelor males go to sea, leaving one river mouth in search of another. They cross between Australia and Papua New Guinea, and reports of sightings off northern New South Wales are not beyond belief.

More to the point when human safety is to be considered, estuarine crocodiles can be found in rivers, floodplain billabongs and swamps scores of kilometres inland. Signs warning against bathing or fishing, placed where people are likely to encounter animals of dangerous size, are meant most seriously.

After a woman was taken at the end of 1985 there was a widespread slaughter of estuarine crocodiles in Queensland. Now, under a state government edict, wildlife officers must capture any living near

Crocodile eggs being sorted

These young have been farmed from eggs taken under licence in the wild

settled areas and remove them to farms or fauna parks. Officers of the Northern Territory Conservation Commission have discretion to remove troublesome individual crocodiles. But unless some outrage reverses public opinion in the Territory, ample wild populations will remain there, especially in Kakadu National Park.

Captive-bred crocodiles provide skins for a Canberra-controlled export trade from both Queensland and the Northern Territory. Juveniles, farmed in thousands, are culled at four years of age. Many of the Top End crop were raised from flood-threatened eggs collected in the wild. □

The freshwater crocodile (left) is generally smaller than the estuarine crocodile (below). Freshwater males start breeding at around 1.7 metres and 'salties' at 3.3 metres. The estuarine crocodile gets bigger by eating larger prey

EASY TO TELL APART

Although close inspection is not advised

The most obvious difference between estuarine crocodiles and their inoffensive relatives, the so-called freshwater crocodiles *Crocodylus johnstoni*, is in their snouts. The potentially dangerous species' is short, broad and lumpy; the other's is long, narrow and smooth.

People can be misled by the old-fashioned common names, saltwater crocodile and 'saltie'. *Crocodylus porosus* may be found in salty tidal reaches of rivers and it sometimes goes out to sea. But it is just as much at home in fresh water.

In fact nest mounds are built only beside fresh-flowing watercourses or, nearer the coast, in freshwater swamps.

Last of the buffaloes

Herds reunite in time for the mating season

Rains reaching spasmodically into southeastern Arnhem Land, usually towards Christmas, end a long segregation for the Northern Territory's remaining free herds of water buffaloes. During the dry season the bulls have kept to themselves, withstanding the fierce heat of open plains near a few permanent sources of water. Cows and juveniles sought shelter in woodlands. Now the herds reunite for their mating season, which will reach its peak in autumn.

In the early 1980s the Northern Territory had an estimated 300 000 buffaloes, most of them grazing floodplains nearer the coast. Their habit of making wallows, to cool off and to coat themselves with mud to ward off flies and ticks, was blamed for the degradation of many wetlands wildlife habitats. The buffaloes also provided a reservoir of bovine tuberculosis and brucellosis, threats to the beef cattle industry and to human health.

About 30 000 animals, certified disease-free,

Buffaloes wallow in mud (above) not just to avoid the heat of the Top End summer, but also to rid themselves of parasites. The mud dries, cakes, and flakes off, taking the irritating ticks with it

Buffaloes herd together for the mating season — this small group of adults and young (below) is stampeding across typical Northern Territory tropical wetlands terrain

have been rounded up for controlled farming. Under a government programme of eradication, more than 200 000 had been destroyed by the end of 1988, most shot in helicopter operations that drew hostile publicity in Europe and North America. Some 50 000, showing low rates of infection, were left scattered in remote country where no cattle are run.

Time spent drinking and wallowing

The water buffalo *Bubalus bubalis* is an ox of Asiatic origin, domesticated for thousands of years. It resists many tropical diseases that debilitate European cattle breeds, and can survive on plants that they cannot eat. Northern Australia's population descended from herds imported from Indonesia to support early coastal settlements, and from the wreck of a ship carrying stock to supply meat to southern goldfields. Buffalo hunting, for hides and trophy horns, used to have a frontiersman image to rival that of crocodile shooting. In fact the slaughter of buffaloes, by adventurers and more recently by contractors, was made ridiculously easy by the animals' habits. Their movements are highly predictable.

Unless the Wet fails and buffaloes are forced to wander in search of food — they can even eat the leaves of pandanus palm — family groups confine themselves to home ranges as small as 200 hectares. There they wear tracks between their sleeping camps and the separate areas that they establish for grazing, drinking and wallowing.

Feeding in the wild is by day for most of the year, in the first half of the morning and the second half of the afternoon. The intervening time is spent drinking and wallowing. When dry season heat is fiercest, buffaloes switch to night-time grazing and spend nearly all day in their wallow. Animals that escape prolonged, killing droughts may live for about twenty years. □

Ear-splitting end to a secret life

Vying to attract mates, male cicadas are the world's rowdiest insects. But their summertime din is a mere footnote to long lives spent in silence and in darkness

When all else is quiet, the call of a solitary male cicada can be heard about half a kilometre away. Measured at a range of one metre, the noise may reach 120 decibels — approaching the threshold of human pain. Cicadas calling in a group can blot out most other sounds.

No insects are more insistent in drawing attention to themselves. And few animals of any kind are as widely collected and examined, especially by children Various species, recognised and nicknamed, are traded in school playgrounds at exchange rates based on their availability: six 'greengrocers' or 'yellow Mondays' for a 'black prince', for example. Yet for all our familiarity with cicadas, we know only a fraction of their life history.

Adult cicadas seen and heard in early summer have three or four weeks to live.

In this time they must mate and the females must produce and lay eggs. It is a sudden and hectic culmination of a life largely spent in obscurity, deep underground. This hidden development takes years. Just how many is anyone's guess.

Two North American species, the only ones thoroughly studied, have lifespans of thirteen and seventeen years. In frost-free Australian soils, it is conjectured that some of the common species, out of more than two hundred in this country, may spend four to eight years underground.

The cycle starts when mated females cut slits in plant stems or in the bark of trees. Each deposits hundreds of tiny eggs and dies soon after. After a few weeks shrimp-like young hatch and fall to the ground. They quickly burrow to the roots, where they will cling most of their lives.

Typical of their order of Hemiptera — bugs, leaf-hoppers and aphids — cicadas suck sap. Some small species are associa-

A red eye cicada struggles to emerge from its nymph case; soon the limp wings will swell with body fluids and straighten out

ted with grasses; those we know better feed on trees and shrubs. The nymphs, as they are called in their underground form, differ little from adults except in having no wings. They probably moult their skins at least four times as they grow.

In its last nymphal stage, an already-elderly cicada tunnels to the surface. Strong, hooked forelimbs enable it to clamber up a tree trunk or a fence, usually at night. Firmly attached, it undergoes a final moult. The shell splits down the back and a soft-winged adult crawls out. By morning the wings have hardened and it flies up to a leafy branch to congregate with others of its species.

Every male has his own song

Cicadas may emerge as early as October in the warmest regions, or November in mid-coastal climates farther south. Congregations are generally biggest and loudest by December. But populations and the proportions of different species vary from summer to summer. These fluctuations do not reflect present conditions so much as the success or failure of parent generations years before.

Individual males may call at any time of day, and some species at night. On calm, warm evenings groups often join in deafening sessions that start and stop abruptly. Their cue is probably a subtle variation in atmospheric pressure.

What we hear then is not a chorus but a contest. Each male is doing his utmost to summon females, and at the same time urging other males to keep their distance. Both sexes hear the noise through membranes under their abdomens, the most complex auditory organs in the insect world. But a male is spared his own din: the membranes slacken automatically when his sound-producing mechanism is in use.

Only the males are equipped to make a loud noise. Also on their abdomens are two drumlike chambers, each containing a muscle attached to a stiff covering. The covering clicks as it is pulled in and again as it is released. The effect is much like that of a tin lid being pushed and let go. A cicada can do it as often as six hundred times a second.

Flaps are used to vary the volume, while the pulsing slows and quickens in rhythmical patterns that give each species a characteristic 'song' identifiable by its own kind. Intervals are too short for the human ear to discern the intricacies of these rhythms. We notice only the strongest beats and differences of pitch that make some cicadas seem to screech while others clatter or sizzle.

Not all cicadas are loud. Two species of hairy cicada *Tettigarcta*, confined to alpine regions of Tasmania and the southeastern mainland, call so discreetly that

The underside of a large click beetle Paracalais macleayi

they were thought until recently to be noiseless. These species are peculiar to Australia. Related types are found elsewhere only as fossils.

Some beetles click...

Among the most disconcerting sounds to come from insects is the sharp cracking of click beetles or skipjacks. On warm summer evenings, they are attracted to light and sometimes stray into houses. In the dead of night their sudden noise can alarm nervous people.

The sound is made accidentally by a surprising mechanical device. Narrow-bodied beetles of the elaterid family have pegs on their thoraxes which they can fit into cavities in their abdomens. When such a beetle lands on its back or is threatened by a predator it locks in the

The glow of fireflies is caused by a chemical reaction in the abdomen

peg and pulls, bending itself double. Then it disengages the peg and the release of tension hurls the insect into the air for instant flight.

Species of *Paracalais*, the biggest click beetles at five centimetres in length, can fling themselves to a height of twenty centimetres. Their larvae are carnivorous, preying on wood-boring weevils and longhorn beetles. Most other elaterids, some as small as three millimetres, are planteaters. Their larvae include the crop pests known as wireworms.

Others flash lights

Elaterid beetles in South America and on some Pacific islands emit light at night. Australia has none of these. Our 'fireflies' are small lampyrid beetles, species of *Luciola* and *Atyphella*. Their season is short — just a week or two in December — and their mating displays are seen by few people. The insects are mostly confined to tropical and subtropical rainforests and mangrove stands.

Adult lampyrids of both sexes have transparent panels towards the rear undersides of their abdomens. Inside these are cells containing crystals. At short intervals an enzyme destroys some of the crystals. Energy from the chemical reaction is transmitted as a greenish light, which is intensified by reflecting cells deeper in the body. Lights flash every second or two, but the exact interval varies according to the species. It is an exclusive sexual signal, reinforced by special dancing patterns made by the male in flight. Females, though they have wings, do not seem to fly. A fainter light is given off by the pupae, larvae and even the eggs of fireflies, for no apparent reason.

A firefly may eat little during its adult phase. Larvae on the other hand are aggressive carnivores, tackling snails and slugs many times their own size with the aid of a paralysing, tissue-destroying chemical that is injected into their prey.

Christmas beetles bring little joy

In open forests and woodlands, or wherever eucalypts are planted in gardens, emerging Christmas beetles *Anoplognathus* appear, inevitably on December nights. Though many people welcome them as heralds of the festive season, these metallic-coloured scarabs have a damaging appetite.

Swarming in sufficient numbers, Christmas beetles that do not blunder into houses or drown in pools are capable of defoliating a young gumtree in a single night. Their larvae are also highly destructive, feeding on the roots of lawn and pasture grasses. If there is a benefit to be found in their presence, it is in the amount of food they provide for birds and other insect eaters.

The bronze orange bug has become a serious pest to citrus trees

Among the most persistent and unwelcome plant pests emerging in December are shield bugs. Out of more than four hundred Australian species, the best known is probably the bronze orange bug *Musgraveia sulciventris*. Originally favouring the saps of native shrubs such as boronias and correas, it has taken determinedly to introduced citrus trees. Big congregations can leave young foliage shrivelled and dying.

Insects with defensive devices

Shield bugs are often called stink bugs, because of the foul-smelling secretions that they spray from anal glands if they are disturbed. But the smell is not the worst part. These acrid chemical compounds burn painfully in the mouths of children or pets, and if they are sprayed in the eyes can cause temporary blindness.

Corrosive secretions are also used in defence by many species of rove beetles *Paederus*. These slender insects, five to ten millimetres long, are carnivores that dash about in moist sand or gravel beside rivers and lakes. The rashes that some of them can cause if brushed against the skin have earned them the nickname of whiplash beetles. A bigger and more familiar rove beetle, the devil's coach horse *Creophilus erythrocephalus*, preys on other insects in rotting carcasses. It adopts a threatening attitude if disturbed, but is harmless.

An intriguing defensive system has been developed by the bombardier beetle *Pheropsophus verticalis*, which lives under stones in damp areas. Glands produce different chemicals that are suddenly mixed if the insect is alarmed. The result is an audible explosion and a cloud of hot, corrosive gases.

Most eye-catching of the beetles and bugs emerging in early summer are the jewel beetles, especially the many species of *Stigmodera*. Gaily coloured and ranging in length from one to six centimetres, they gained their common name because specimens used to be set in jewellery.

The bigger jewel beetles are active in the full heat of summer days. Though they live for no more than a week or two in their adult form, they are strong fliers and resolute wanderers, travelling up to fifty kilometres in a day to obtain nectar from blossoming native trees. Their larvae are wood borers. On the evidence of adults emerging from the timbers of houses, the larval lives of some species span decades.

Ladybirds make welcome garden guests

To gardeners and orchardists, the most beneficial beetles attracting attention in early summer are vividly coloured ladybirds. The larvae and adults of more than two hundred Australian species prey heavily on pests such as aphids, scale insects and mealy bugs. Our *Rodolia cardinalis* won international fame late last century when an exported supply rescued California's orange industry from a disastrous scale plague.

Ladybird larvae are active grubs, crawl-

Stigmodera regia jewel beetles occur only in tropical areas of Australia

ing about in the open. With narrow bodies and spiny or lumpy segmented skins, they look nothing like the round, compact adults. Many gardeners, failing to recognise the immature form, destroy the insects when they are doing most good.

Frightened adult ladybirds play dead. In defence they force blood, toxic to birds and other vertebrates, from their leg

Australia is home to no less than 800 species of jewel beetle

The larvae of most ladybird species are predatory; many feed on aphids

joints. They are capable of surviving in dormancy if food is scarce or if they fail to mate. But among the aphid-eating species at least, chances of mating are increased by a habit of assembling in vast numbers. Gatherings occur because all of the ladybirds in one area follow an instinct to move towards the most prominent shape on their horizon.

The solitary praying mantid

Praying mantids, also active at this time, are by contrast among the most antisocial of insects. They behave more like spiders, claiming individual feeding territories and often eating their own kind — including males devoured as they are mating.

Mantids seldom hunt, preferring to wait with their grasping forelegs poised until other insects are within reach. As a camouflage against birds, mantids that live on foliage are green while those found on bark or on the ground are brown. Some types may be capable of changing colour. Males of most species can fly, but rarely the females. Masses of eggs are laid in a frothy secretion that dries into horny cases. Wasps penetrate these to lay their own eggs, keeping mantid populations generally low.

Some assassin bugs may be mistaken for mantids because of their long bodies and similar habit of waiting motionless with their forelegs raised. Of species active by day, the most familiar is probably the 'bee-killer' *Pristhesancus papuensis*. Very common but seldom seen, because most live in forests and are active at night, are 'pirate bugs' *Pirates* and *Ectomocoris*. The mouthparts of assassin bugs are modified as sharp beaks to pierce the shells of prey insects. They inject salivary secretions that paralyse the prey and liquefy tissues.

The 'bee-killer' assassin bug stalks its prey on flowering plants

Lethocerus insulanus *is one of the two biggest species of giant water bugs*

Supreme among predatory bugs are belostomatids, or giant water bugs. They feed mainly on aquatic insects. But two species of *Lethocerus*, growing as long as seven centimetres in the tropics, also kill small fish and tadpoles. They too have heavy beaks to impale their prey. If interfered with, such bugs are formidable in their own defence. And they are not confined to water — the adults in summer are night fliers, attracted to light. □

A LACEWING'S MURKY PAST
*Fragile parents
produce formidable offspring*

Lacewings fly feebly on warm nights early in summer, usually just before rain. Nothing about their appearance, delicate and vulnerable, gives a hint of aggressiveness. Yet many of them, until just a few weeks ago, were squat, massive-jawed killing machines called ant-lions.

Two families of big lacewings have ant-lion larvae. Strong and highly mobile, the grubs dig pits in sand or loose soil and bury themselves at the bottom with only their jaws exposed. Ants falling in are crushed and devoured. Any trying to escape are pelted with sand until they fall again or the pit walls collapse.

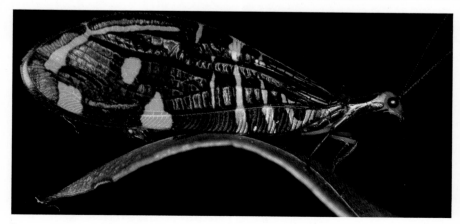

Porismus strigatus, *like most lacewings, helps gardeners by eating pests*

The redback spider weaves a strong and complex web to trap its prey, and then subdues it by trussing it up in fine silk and

A snare
that plucks
up prey

*The redback heads a group of
artful spiders that set traps to
hoist small insects off their feet
and leave them dangling*

Haphazard tangles of dry cobweb thrown together by redback spiders and their relatives are merely dining areas. The danger to prey is below, in a few stout threads of silk fixed to surfaces where insects walk. At the base these lines are beaded with adhesive globules.

An insect blundering into a trapline is quickly stuck. Its struggles dislodge the thread from its attachment. With tension released the strand coils like a broken watch spring, jerking a small victim off its feet and leaving it dangling in mid-air. Big beetles and cockroaches do not leave the

ground but remain entangled. The traplines are so strong that occasionally skinks and mice are caught.

Vibrations tell the spider that the trap has been sprung. It scurries to the top end of the line and hauls its prisoner to the outskirts of the cobweb. Then, to over-power an animal that may be many times its own size, the spider displays another remarkable skill. Throwing out bands of silk at a phenomenal rate, it systematically trusses the victim, deftly turning it until it is completely enswathed. Before or during this process, the spider pauses to

delivering paralysing bites

deliver paralysing bites. Finally the parcelled prey is levered into the cobweb to be sucked dry.

December is the peak of a long breeding season in many localities. Now the insignificant males are most likely to be seen, perhaps loitering on the fringes of a female's web. Creamy-coloured with brown markings, a mature male is only about a third of the size of the glossy black adult female with her unmistakable red or orange back markings.

A courting male plucks gingerly at the web, setting up rhythmical vibrations that the female recognises as the signal of her own species. Temporarily pacified, she adopts a submissive pose and allows the male to approach. In characteristic spider fashion he inserts his sperm-loaded palps and hurriedly retreats.

Some males are killed while mating, earning spiders of the worldwide genus *Latrodectus* the nickname of 'widow' spiders. But such behaviour is not more marked in this group than in many others. In any case the males are destined to die soon after mating. They live for four to seven months. This short span means that breeding has to be spread from early spring to autumn, with some slow-developing eggs and spiderlings wintering over in warm, sheltered situations.

Females, living for a year or slightly more, build tubular nesting chambers. In a confined space the nest leads directly off the cobweb feeding area. Where shelter is found high up — in a shed or under the eaves of a building, for example — the chamber is built there and long threads connect it with the web and snare.

Spiderlings are cannibals

Thousands of eggs may be produced during a female redback's breeding career. As many as six sacs are made at a time, each containing scores or hundreds of eggs. They take two weeks to hatch in midsummer temperatures, but longer than ten weeks in cooler weather.

The young show a degree of sociability that is fairly unusual among spiders. They are slow to disperse, sharing their mother's web and some of her prey for a long time. But their communal spirit goes hand-in-hand with cannibalism. A hungry mother may devour some of her young. Stronger spiderlings eat the weak. And when an elderly female dies, her last crop of progeny may enjoy a final feast on her body juices before they lower themselves on single threads to seek territories of their own.

The redback *Latrodectus hasselti* is a semi-domestic spider where shelter is made available, though it will not settle in busy rooms or where lights are on at night. But it does equally well in bush habitats: among foliage, in hollow logs, in cave entrances or in spaces under rocks.

It is hard to say where this spider is most at home. It is closely associated with human habitations in southern Asia and the southwestern Pacific. Some scientists conjecture that it is a relative newcomer to Australia, perhaps introduced by Asian or Polynesian voyagers.

New Zealand's katipo — a seashore species — and North America's black widow are very like the redback. Similar widow spiders are found around the Mediterranean, in southern regions of the Soviet Union, in southern Africa and in South America. All are notorious for the agonising and potentially lethal bites that the females can inflict on people. They are not aggressive spiders, however. They bite only in retaliation if they are squeezed or if their egg sacs are interfered with.

Two other types of theridiid spiders, with similar snare-building and prey-wrapping skills, live in even more intimate association with people. These are the grey house spider *Achaearanea tepidariorum* and species of cupboard spiders *Steatoda*. They give no cause for worry, but the messiness of their cobwebs may be annoying.

Also harmless, but even untidier, is the thoroughly domesticated daddy longlegs *Pholcus phalangioides*. Voluminous webs, doubling as snares as well as residences, are maintained for years by these long-living spiders. Beneath them is always a litter of small prey parcels, sucked dry and discarded from the web. □

COMBS TO SPIN A SHROUD

Some spiders enjoy their meal only after it is gift-wrapped

Redbacks and many other spiders are classed as theridiids: comb-footed spiders. They all wrap their prey in shrouds of fine silk. Rapid production is made possible by combs of serrated bristles at the ends of the hindmost pair of legs.

While a victim dangles on a 'gum-foot' trapline, the spider turns its back and exudes fine strands of liquid silk. Pulled by the combs, these harden into a continuous band swathed round the prey, which is rotated by the spider's other legs.

A female redback in the act of trussing its prey; the white, spherical object is an egg cocoon

Hot winds inflict bushflies on the south

All across southern Australia as Christmas approaches, bushfly populations soar. On sunny days in cities such as Melbourne and Canberra, pedestrians' backs are blackened. The flies are the descendants of migrants, travelling south on warm northerly winds late in spring

Bushflies are year-round pests in warmer parts of the outback, especially where livestock graze. They cannot breed in colder climates; nor are they or their eggs able to winter over in dormancy. The mystery of their annual infestations of the south was not solved until 1969, when CSIRO entomologists began tracing their migration routes.

These can span 1000 kilometres or more. When the winds are right some bushflies manage to make the whole journey. More importantly they mate and lay eggs on the way, so reinforcements soon follow. Huge breeding populations are established in southern agricultural areas by November. They will thrive, generation after generation, until autumn brings a night-time chill.

The eggs of the bushfly *Musca vetustissima* are invariably laid in moist dung, which provides the protein for larval development. In average summer conditions they hatch in a few hours and the maggots complete their development in about three days. Then they burrow into the soil to pupate in little barrel-shaped cases, emerging as adult flies after four or five more days. During heat waves, females can be laying eggs a little over a week after their own birth.

Bushflies can live for about three months, breeding continuously. Males sustain themselves on sugars from flower nectar and insect secretions. But the females need protein for egg production. Most of it nowadays is obtained from mucus dripping from the eyes and noses of cattle.

The bushfly is the outdoor counterpart of the closely related housefly *Musca domestica*, and has had an even longer human association. It probably travelled with the first people to come to Australia, relying entirely on their droppings of

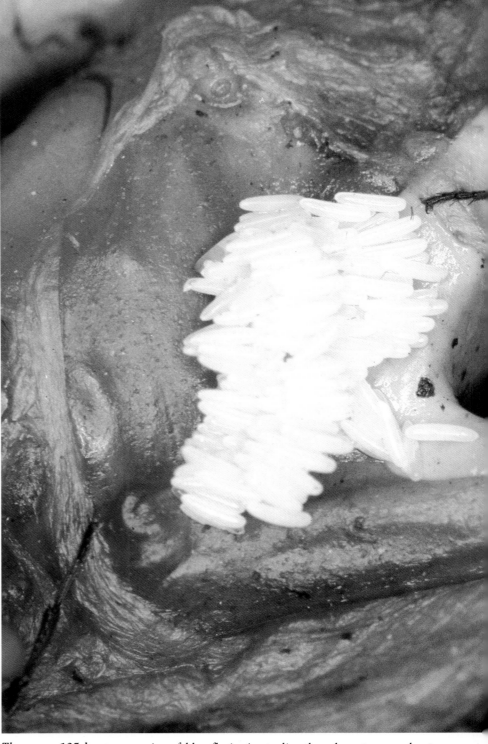

There are 135 known species of blowfly in Australia; they do not carry dangerous

faeces. It is unlikely to have been here before humans arrived, because the dry, hard dung pellets of marsupials do not favour its breeding. Emu droppings would have been about its only hope.

Fly breeding must have been given a fillip by the later spread of dingoes. But today's enormous populations were founded on the European introduction of livestock. Most maggots develop in cow pats and sheep droppings, which more

than make up for the human help lost through improved hygiene and sanitation.

Females hungry for protein

Tens of thousands of years of conditioning cannot be broken in a mere century or two, however. Bushflies are drawn irresistibly to people, probably by our body odours. Those that cluster on our backs are not there primarily to feed on sweat, though they may take some refreshment.

diseases, and only their habit of laying eggs in exposed meat or flesh brings them into conflict with man

They are nearly all females ready to lay eggs, waiting for us to defecate. The flies that keep trying to alight on our faces are malnourished females, seeking protein from mucus or tears.

Bushflies leave us alone if we retreat into deep shade, and rarely go into any building. The same cannot be said for another cosmopolitan group, the 'blue-bottle' blowflies *Calliphora*. Natural breeders in animal carrion, they too may come into settled areas on warm winds in late spring and early summer. They readily invade houses and lay their eggs in raw meat or sometimes woollen fabrics.

In rural areas, if spring has been warm but persistently wet, blowflies are likely to be wreaking havoc among sheep flocks. The primary culprits are the 'greenbottle' *Lucilia cuprina*, an introduced species, and to a much lesser extent *Calliphora augur*. Eggs are laid on infected skin under fleeces that have been damp for too long. The maggots burrow into the skin, opening the way for potentially deadly 'strikes' by other species.

Blowflies breed even more quickly than bushflies and houseflies. If laying is delayed in hot weather the eggs hatch inside the female and maggots are laid. Sometimes they are even air-dropped — meat can be strewn with already-active maggots from a female in mid-flight. □

In December bright-coloured dragonflies fly courtship displays over the water

The red-winged fairy wren lives in small groups in creeks and gullies near water

The white-browed scrubwren is one of the most widespread of Australia's small ground-feeding birds

The water rat Hydromys chrysogaster grows to a length of sixty centimetres, including tail

Beedelup National Park, Western Australia

The mayfly has a short life as an adult, and is unable to eat

While the going is good

Short-lived aquatic insects start a forest food chain

Rushing now over a bed of ancient granite, this stream will soon dwindle in the fierce heat and drought of a Western Australian summer. Yet only in the past few weeks have its waters been warm enough to trigger the hatching of myriad aquatic insects. Their life cycles are completed at a frenzied pace, many of these creatures producing generation after generation in the one short season. In their larval and adult forms they provide a sudden abundance of food for fishes, crustaceans and frogs. In turn the reptiles, mammals and birds of the forest enjoy a nutritional bonanza — all based on fallen leaves. At the bottom of the chain are the least noticed but most important animals of all, the shredders. Larvae of caddisflies and stoneflies trap drifting leaf fragments from stately western eucalypts — karri, jarrah and marri — and break them down into microscopic particles on which edible bacteria and fungi grow.

The sacred kingfisher is a solitary bird, pairing only for breeding

Australia is home to fourteen species of Dobson fly. They are an important source of food for fish

Whirligig beetles swim on the surface, using their short middle and hind legs as paddles

Water striders glide on the surface; there are both winged and flightless species

Water boatmen, unlike the predatory backswimmers, feed mainly by sucking on plants

Backswimmers swim upside down, storing air in hair-covered cavities in the abdomen

The fiercely predatory water tiger propels itself underwater by means of its hair-fringed hind legs, which kick together

Crane flies are commonly, and incorrectly, known as 'daddy long-legs'; Australia has 850 species

Water scavengers swim underwater with alternate strokes of the hind legs

The world's largest and smallest freshwater crayfish or 'yabbies' occur in Australia; they vary from 40 to 2.5 centimetres in length

True midges resemble mosquitoes but are smaller, with a wingspan up to seven millimetres

The nocturnal Litoria bicolor is, at three centimetres, one of Australia's smallest frogs

There are ten main families of gastropods or snails occurring in Australian inland waters

The freshwater worm, Oligochaetes, feeds on organic material and bacteria in the riverbed

Fireworks on the Barrier Reef

Corals spawn in synchronised, multi-coloured explosions. Other marine animals contribute to the display, creating drifting masses of life that trust their future to random currents

Reef corals reproduce in two ways. At any time, mature polyps form buds that eventually divide from the parents and start lives of their own. That is how existing reefs keep on growing upwards and outwards. But new colonies can be founded only by a sexual process. The annual spawning on the Great Barrier Reef, just after the first full moon of summer, provides an unforgettable spectacle for those lucky enough to witness it.

Some corals are hermaphrodites, possessing both male and female reproductive organs. Other species are single-sexed, so the clones that have budded in one colony may all be male, and those of another colony female. The regular occurrence of a generation of mobile offspring — helped by ocean currents and tides — is especially important to these latter species.

Egg cells begin a slow development in midwinter. It accelerates as water temperatures rise in spring. Tiny but brightly coloured organisms form inside female or hermaphrodite polyps. Well into spring, male cells start to produce sperm. The microscopic spermatozoa, tadpole-like at first, develop strongly beating tails that will allow a wide dispersal.

At nightfall when it is ready to spawn, a polyp assembles its eggs, sperm, or a combination of both, into one mass. It is held in or below the polyp's upturned mouth. About a quarter of an hour later, the mass is expelled in a jet of water.

Five nights after the full moon

In one area, for no clear reason, millions of polyps of dozens of species will all spawn in the same few minutes — sometimes in only seconds. The phenomenon may occur in some locations as early as the first or second night after the full moon, but the biggest and most widespread displays have been observed on or about the fifth night. Torches shone from boats or carried by divers reveal a multi-coloured storm of pinhead-sized balls shooting to the surface.

The annual spawning of coral on the Great Barrier Reef has been likened to an

underwater firework display; this is a large table coral Acropora tenuis *at the moment of release*

A dramatic photograph of the Great Barrier Reef taken from the air on the morning after spawning; it shows a pink slick of eggs

Fertilised eggs develop into larvae that look much like minuscule jellyfishes — the closest relatives of corals. They can swim, but largely allow themselves to drift. Some species float for just a few days, others for weeks or months, before settling to the bottom and finding points of attachment for lives that will be forever after sedentary.

Astronomical numbers of coral eggs and larvae are eaten by predators. But the parent polyps overbreed to allow for this.

And the coral offspring comprise just one component of the drifting masses of small creatures that thicken Barrier Reef waters at this time of year, providing an abundance of food for animals of greater size.

The countless micro-organisms that spend their whole lives as plankton are joined now by the eggs or immature forms of other marine animals. Later in life — if they survive — many may never go near the surface again. The larvae of crabs, shrimps, prawns and the like live on and

in the plankton. So do those of snails and shellfishes, along with starfishes, sea anemones, sea slugs, sea cucumbers, sea urchins and so on. The eggs of reef eels such as the moray are also sent to the surface among the rest.

Fish are spawning too

Many prominent species of reef fishes engage in surface spawning, usually in December or just before. They move to outer reefs where strong currents ensure

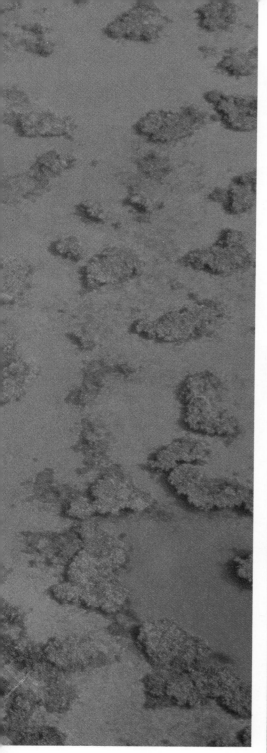

drifting on the sea surface

the eggs are dispersed into deeper water. Predation is less likely there.

Orgies of mass spawning by parrotfish, wrasses and goatfish are often seen by divers. Big gropers including some species of 'coral trout' also congregate to breed. They move out to sites around the breaks in ribbon reefs. There may be places where they breed in thousands. While scientists regret that their knowledge is scanty, the gropers' elusiveness prevents a possible fishing massacre. □

A colony of brain coral Favites flexuosa *producing balls of eggs and sperm*

Observing and photographing eastern grey kangaroos in the McPherson Range on the Queensland–New South Wales border

Part Four

AN OBSERVER'S GUIDE

From the backyard to the back of beyond, opportunities abound to study animals and to make discoveries that may surprise even the experts. This section includes some practical tips to make your wildlife-watching as rewarding as possible

Reward for an early riser: this common wombat building a large burrow in a sheep paddock was photographed just after dawn

Rise early, rest easy, take notes

Timing and planning increase the chances of interesting wildlife sightings. And making the most of the experience involves plenty of paperwork

Wildlife observation need not demand great exertion or expense. But it does take time and patience. Dedicated watchers have to adjust their living schedules to the daily and seasonal cycles of the animals they study. Very often that means being up before the sun.

Birds start their chorusing and bats return to their roosts well before dawn. Kangaroos and other grazing marsupials have a major feeding session in half-light, as do koalas and platypuses. Usually elusive flying insects can be found at rest, torpid and sluggish in the cool of the morning, or climbing plants to seek the warmth of the rising sun. As it gains strength, snakes and lizards emerge to bask. Fish in streams are most actively hungry early in the morning, sometimes leaping out of the water. Beaches are least trodden and picked over.

Another peak of activity among nesting or roosting birds and many mammals occurs around dusk. Keeping watch then is all too often frustrating: just as a momentous sighting is made, the light fails. A further wait for full darkness in bushland is rewarded by the sounds of nocturnal animals — possums and gliders, owls, frogs and various scurrying creatures. But moving about becomes tricky for us, and few of the animals are seen without spotlighting.

Time spent in the middle of the day, especially in hot weather, is least fruitful unless your interest is in butterflies, dragonflies and the like. Even the reptiles that seek morning warmth cannot stand an excess of it, and take shelter.

Opportunities to study shoreline marine life are ruled by the rhythms of the tides. To give yourself maximum time, don't start at low water but when the tide is high — then follow it out. The greatest range for exploration is exposed by the ebb of 'spring' tides (so-called because they leap high) immediately after full moon and new moon in any month. The farthest ebbs of all come in the second half of March and September around most of Australia, on the spring tides closest to the equinoxes. In the far north they are concentrated in the summer months.

In any region summer's longer days offer the greatest scope to find time for wildlife observation outside school or working hours. Generally speaking, however, in the temperate and subtropical zones the most intensive and varied activity may be seen in spring. For chances to watch many animals that are nocturnal in warmer weather, dull winter days are best of all. And there are fewer troublesome pests then.

Pick the right weather

Weather that is unsuitable for one field of study can be ideal for another. You can't see far in early-morning mist, but there is nothing better to highlight spiders' webs and to bring out frogs, snails and many insects. After severe storms, when bushland routes may be impassable, beachcombers make their richest finds. Inland drought dries up or impoverishes streams, but it means that birds and mammals will be concentrated on and around remaining bodies of water.

Wherever you look for wildlife, prepare to stay put. Bushwalkers catch glimpses of fleeing animals and hear the alarm calls of birds, but rarely make worthwhile sightings — until they stop to rest or make camp. The first art of wildlife observation is in picking the best vantage point. That requires as much advance information as you can get.

If your interest is in the general fauna of a particular area, obtain a survey map detailing contours, vegetation and watercourses as well as safe and permissible access ways. Seek out local knowledge of animal habitats and movements. In national parks and other reserves, talk to rangers and read the relevant leaflets.

If you are specially interested in animals of a certain type, you need to know not only their likely location but also as much as you can of their habits — especially their food preferences and feeding times. Good reference books provide general information, but again the most useful advice always comes from rangers and other knowledgeable locals.

When you establish your observation position there is generally no need to conceal yourself, as long as you keep quiet and fairly still. Once animals are used to your presence, they may come surprisingly close. If you have a good view from a car, stay in it — most animals are even less suspicious of stationary or slow-moving vehicles than of a human figure. But keep to formed roads and parking

A NATURALIST'S NOTEBOOK

This specimen page of field notes includes a sketch and all the details necessary to identify the bird as a rufous songlark – a male in breeding condition

A DISTRIBUTION MAP

● LORIKEET   ● POSSUM

This simple distribution map shows sightings of two common backyard creatures. More complex maps could show nesting-sites, direction of travel, feeding areas and seasonal variations for a whole range of animals

areas: driving off-road vehicles through the bush destroys wildlife habitats.

If your quest is going to take you closer to nature than a car seat, carry whatever is manageable to make waiting comfortable. Aches, cramps and itches may keep you alert, but are more likely to be distracting. An inflatable cushion, a camp stool or a ground sheet could become your second most valuable possession — next to an ample supply of insect repellent.

Dress protectively in bushland, especially if you are going off the beaten track into thickets and swamps. Carry disinfectant and dressings for scratches and a pressure bandage in case of snakebite. Serious snake envenomation is a rare occurrence, but it is unwise to be alone and beyond calling range of help.

Leeches are harmless — they drop off in a few minutes, fully fed — and ticks can be removed with care. Potentially more menacing to people sitting or lying in the bush are the stings of venomous bulldog ants (see September, page 200). If repeated on later occasions, they can arouse life-threatening allergic reactions similar to those arising from bee-stings.

Special equipment

Binoculars are invaluable aids to observation. But biggest may not mean best. The most burdensome and costly products, letting you see objects hundreds of metres away, do not focus down to show the distinguishing features of animals you are watching closely — a bird in a tree above you, for example. Binoculars of moderate power, light enough to be used with one hand, are usually preferable.

A magnifying glass is always worth carrying, not only for examining insects and spiders but also for the fine detective work that sometimes helps identify bigger animals from their tracks. Even in the daytime, a powerful torch is useful for inspecting caves and crevices.

Plastic bags in various sizes are the most convenient containers for droppings, skins, feathers, bones, eggshells and other animal remains that you may wish to examine thoroughly later. But living animals must not be killed or captured, and viable eggs must not be touched or taken. All species are protected in national parks, and many wherever they are found.

Of all the gear carried by amateur naturalists, the most important in the long run may prove to be a notebook (or tape recorder) and a sketching pad. Observations should be noted immediately, and as fully as possible. The most vivid impressions fade in the memory as they are superseded by others.

If you make an interesting sighting, note the location, date, time of day and weather. Describe the terrain and vegetation. Note what you saw the animal doing,

MASTERS OF CAMOUFLAGE
Now you see it, now you don't

Rocks, tree trunks, foliage, streams, beach sands and ocean waters all offer an entertaining challenge to wildlife observers — the discovery of camouflaged creatures. Merging into a background by matching its colours, or breaking up a body outline with boldly contrasting patterns, are among the most widespread of animal defences. They go hand-in-hand, of course, with a stolid determination to stay motionless, even under threat.

Clockwise from right: a praying mantis lurking among grass stems; a bearded dragon Pogona barbata *'freezes' on a tree stump; a hawk moth* Psilogramma *on the bark of a tree; two white-throated nightjars* Caprimulgus mystacalis *resting during the day on the ground near their nest; Lesueur's velvet gecko* Oedura lesueurii *moulding its shape into that of a banksia cone; and a caterpillar under threat quickly succeeds in transforming itself into a part of the branch it was climbing*

including any peculiarities of posture or movement. If it was eating, say what sort of food if you can.

When an animal is unknown to you, make an on-the-spot sketch pointing out markings, colours and whatever other details you can discern. Try to establish its size and the relative proportions of the main parts of its body. (In the case of an inert insect or other small creature, mark its dimensions along the edge of your

notepaper and measure them later.) Put down your version of any noises that the animal made.

Such information should enable you later to clear up most mysteries of identification. Compiled for species that you already know, it builds up a picture of habits and behaviour. If such a technique is applied to all the different types of animals that you can see in a given area — including your own backyard — a picture

emerges of the overall ecology. It can add a new dimension to your enjoyment of nature.

Children and adults too can have fun building up animal distribution maps of their neighbourhood. The locations of prominent territorial species such as possums and nesting birds can be marked, along with the directions of movement of visiting feeders. By using tracing-paper overlays at seasonal intervals, changing patterns can be seen, and the significance of various plant and insect food supplies is better understood.

Don't disbelieve your own eyes if you see an animal where the books say it does not occur, or behaving in an unexpected way. No book is perfect. Report your finding, with all the details, to a professional society, to your state wildlife authority or to the relevant department of a major museum, a university or the CSIRO.

Zoologists make no claim to know everything about animals that they have studied, let alone about many that have never been investigated. Among insects, spiders and other small invertebrates, and probably also among frogs and small lizards, thousands of species in Australia are thought to have escaped scientific discovery. Your observations, particularly in remote or densely forested areas, could break new ground.□

The snakeskin chiton Chiton pelliserpentis *is common from the central coast of New South Wales to Victoria and eastern Tasmania*

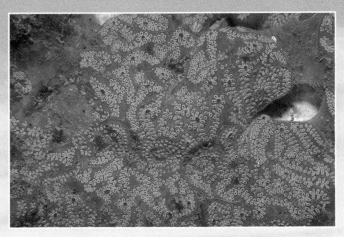

A colony of sea-squirts Botrylloides leachi, *found encrusting boulders on rocky shores all around Australia*

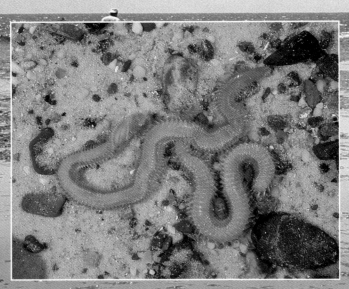

Salmon-pink bristle worms Eurythoe complanata *of the type found in temperate waters; there is also a tropical large dark grey form. Both sting and should not be handled*

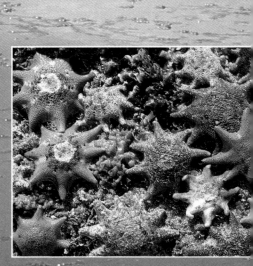

A typical rock platform shoreline in Sydney's northern suburbs (main picture)

Waratah anemones Actinia tenebrosa *are often seen in clusters*

One of the more common sea-star species Patiriella calcar, *usually found in rock-pools near the low-water mark*

Sea creatures claim the land

Marine animals, confined to pools or tolerating exposure, dominate the intertidal zones

On any seashore, tidal movement creates a zone of alternating inundation and evaporation that land animals cannot colonise. Birds exploit it, feeding as the tide recedes, but they cannot live there. The intertidal zone is the realm of marine life, much of it adapted to exposure to air and strong sunlight. Corals attract most attention, but the animals that occupy wave-carved rock platforms are every bit as fascinating and far more diverse.

Many take a lifetime grip on the rock — oysters, barnacles, tubeworms, sea-squirts and so on. Some that are able to move slowly, such as sea anemones, mussels and limpets, prefer not to. Starfishes, crabs, sea-urchins and snails, freely mobile, stay in their favourite pools when the tide goes out. Their habitat is best explored when a low tide occurs early in the morning. Move rocks and shells as little as possible and take nothing away. The sea does its own cleaning up.

These sea-urchins Tripneustes gratilla *cover themselves with shells or seaweed at low tide, possibly as protection from the sun*

'Neptune's necklace' Hormosira banksii *is a distinctive member of the brown algae group; it looks like thick strings of beads*

Photography and sound recording

They're hard on the back muscles — and on the pocket

Photographing animals in the wild is a difficult undertaking, full of disappointments and frustrations. Successful results can seldom be obtained without advanced equipment and accessories — not only expensive but also heavy to carry about. Even then there is much to learn by trial and error.

Cameras using 35mm film are virtually standard for general purposes. For wildlife photography you need one with a single-lens reflex action that gives through-the-lens viewfinding, so that what you see is what you get. A built-in light meter is desirable, along with an automatically compatible flash unit. A tripod and cable shutter-release mechanism are needed for many kinds of field work.

Such a camera probably offers fully automatic operation, but some situations, particularly those involving a moving subject, require overriding control of shutter speed and aperture size. The camera must have provision for removal and changing of lenses, if you are to exploit all your opportunities for long-range and close-up shots.

Standard lenses of 45mm are good for habitat scenes, medium-range shots of herds or flocks, and individual animals within about ten metres. But focusing down for a close-up of a small creature, the nearest you can get to your subject is seventy-five centimetres, at which distance an animal five centimetres long takes up only one-ninth of the frame.

More versatility can be gained with zoom lenses, speedily adjustable within a range that is typically from 35mm to 75mm. With a 'macro' facility, they take you significantly closer to small subjects, as well as extending your scope in distant shots. Perhaps the greatest advantage they offer in wildlife photography is the effect of instantly stepping back from your subject. With the barrel drawn in for maximum magnification you can take a detailed shot of an animal — a bird in a tree, say. Then by pushing the barrel right out, with no other adjustment, you shoot it surrounded by its setting — the whole tree.

The same 'pullback' effect can be achieved with telephoto zoom lenses. Usefully detailed pictures of distant animals can be obtained only with a telephoto lens of 200mm or more. Such a lens can be bulky, heavy and costly. It requires very fine focusing because its depth of field — the range within which the image is sharp — is shallow. Its weight makes it difficult to hold steady, and for best results a tripod is usually needed.

Shallowness of field is an even greater problem in close-up photography of insects, spiders and so on. Angles have to be chosen so that all parts of the animal are as nearly as possible at the same distance from the lens, otherwise some are blurred.

Standard lenses can be adapted for close-up work by screwing on 'step-up' lenses at the front. A better method, if the whole lens assembly can be removed from the camera body, is either to reverse the lens, or to fit an extension between it and the

This common brushtail possum Trichosurus vulpecula *is being photographed at night in Lamington National Park, Queensland. The best wildlife pictures are often taken in areas where animals have got used to humans approaching them*

body. Adjustable bellows may be favoured in studio work, but in the field extension rings are easier to fit and change. They are used in combinations to achieve various magnifications.

A flash unit is needed not only for night photography but also to permit faster shutter speeds. Then you can 'freeze' a bird in flight or overcome slight movements that mar close-up shots. Rarely is a live animal completely motionless. Your breath alone can cause a spider to sway in its web.

These three photographs are of the same subject, an enamelled spider Araneus bradleyi. They were taken early in the morning, not only to catch the dew on the web, but also because then there is least wind to make focusing difficult. For all three a 105mm 'macro' lens was used, with the addition of an extension ring for the close-up (below). This lens is ideal for photographing small creatures, as it gives good definition over close focusing distances. For more mobile animals, a zoom lens is useful

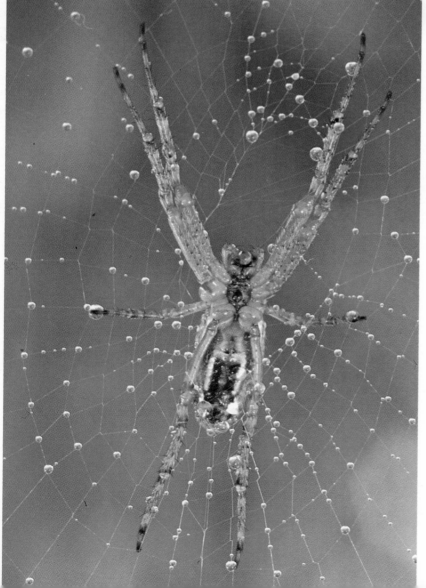

Where subjects are predictable in their movements, good results can be achieved by setting up a camera in advance and operating it from a distance by cable release. The method works well with birds attending nests, mammals using known dens, and various animals that can be enticed by trails of food or offerings of water.

Photographers have a responsibility to avoid disturbance, however. Too much fussing around nests or the entrances of dens may cause their abandonment and perhaps the loss of young. The greatest temptation that a photographer must resist is to remove foliage or other covering vegetation in order to get a clearer shot.

Tape recording birds and frogs

Sound recording brings added pleasure to a study of birds and can be a major aid to their identification. It is essential in any study of frogs — many are distinguishable only by their calls. Some fun can be had with an ordinary portable cassette player; but again, high-quality results can be achieved only with specialised equipment, including manual level controls and a bulky directional microphone. A normal microphone can be made directional, with fair results, by fitting it into an improvised reflecting dish. Chinese woks and reflectors from car headlights are popular for this purpose.

To make a faithful recording of an individual bird you need to set up your equipment in advance, close to where you know or hope it will alight, then stay out of sight. In your own garden, a mains-powered recorder can be set up more or less permanently near a nesting box or bird-table. Playing back the calls of birds often attracts them, but should not be overdone. Their curiosity and animation may develop into distress, perhaps disrupting their feeding or breeding.□

Wildlife in a natural garden

Many animals accept handouts and become semi-tame. For a more genuine effect use native plants to encourage them

Even in inner-city environments, dozens of bird species are easily enticed by regular offerings of food and water, placed out of the reach of dogs and cats. They and their descendants will become consistent visitors, trusting and almost domesticated. Some may pay you the compliment of nesting.

Near parks or bushland, possums can be similarly encouraged and turned into dole-dependants — at the risk of having them invade your house. Many birds will accustom themselves to unsuitable food. Kookaburras will become especially demanding, rapping on windows at ungodly hours on summer mornings. Parrots will loiter, whiling away their time by chewing at railings, guttering, cables and other perching places. Food left out, uneaten at the end of the day, will attract rats.

It is far better to provide, if you can, an authentic food supply from native trees and shrubs, thoughtfully planted to gain a maximum spread of flowering, fruiting and seeding seasons. Many more kinds of birds will come, perhaps along with fruit bats and climbing mammals. Lizards, beetles and butterflies will abound.

Australian painted ladies feeding on a native grasstree Xanthorrhoea

If you are content to let nature take its course, leaving fruits and seeds where they fall and permitting a buildup of leaf litter, twigs and fungi, you will promote the activities of insects, spiders, worms, snails and so on. These in turn will attract ground-feeding birds and mammals — if cats are discouraged. Safe repellents can be bought at garden shops, or you can make your own by soaking sawdust with kerosene and sprinkling it around the borders of your area. Mothballs and other camphor products are also fairly effective.

You may never see some of the more obscure forms of life that take up resi-

Crimson rosellas Platycercus elegans *flock to a bird-table. This simple and traditional method of attracting birds has several disadvantages*

A SIMPLE NESTING BOX

This is one of the best ways to attract birds into your backyard. A box is easily constructed from western red cedar using ordinary household tools. It should have a sloping roof, ventilation holes at the sides and back, and a removable front for ease of cleaning between seasons. The one illustrated is suitable for parrots, having a ladder for easy access and wooden reinforcement strips down the inside corners.

Place the box at least three metres above the ground, facing away from the prevailing wind, in a shady position on the edge of a clump of bushes or trees. Put it out in early spring, and be on the lookout for starlings, sparrows or common mynahs (see March, page 101), which may try to drive off native species. The entrance diameter is crucial in determining the species that may nest there, and the table on the right gives recommended dimensions for a variety of native birds. The depth of cavity is measured from the floor to the roof front, and the entrance height is from the floor to the centre of the hole

A red wattlebird feeding acrobatically on a bottlebrush Callistemon

Native plants to attract wildlife

The following species should entice all sorts of animals into your garden because they are sources of seeds (S), nectar (N) and/or insects (I)

Acacia species (wattle) **SNI**

Acmena species (lillypilly) **S**

Banksia species **SNI**

Boronia species **I**

Callistemon species (bottlebrush) **NI**

Cassia species **I**

Casuarina species (she-oak) **S**

Correa species **N**

Eucalyptus species **SNI**

Grevillea species **NI**

Hakea species **NI**

Helichrysum species (everlasting) **I**

Kennedia species (coral pea) **NI**

Kunzea species **NI**

Leptospermum species (tea tree) **I**

Melaleuca species (paperbark) **NI**

Pittosporum species **SN**

Prostanthera species (mint bush) **NI**

Telopea species (waratah) **N**

Xanthorrhoea species (grasstree) **I**

dence. Your garden will look unkempt — though the leaf mulch will keep it weed-free. The trees themselves will not be especially graceful or colourful. But you will have fostered an ecology of plants and animals interacting naturally. If wildlife is to have a chance in human environments, that is the way things should be.

If you have the space, eucalypts are the ideal trees. They have long flowering seasons and the greatest variety of birds is attracted to their blossoms, nectar, fruits, seed capsules and the sweet exudations from damaged bark. As they age and lose branches they provide nesting holes for all kinds of creatures.

Among other bigger trees, bottle-brushes *Callistemon,* wattles *Acacia,* and grevilleas are also recommended. Smaller plants suitable for the lower levels of foliage and for confined spaces include banksias, smaller grevilleas and hakeas. Some plants are strongly favoured by certain birds. This applies even more to butterflies: in order to attract types that you like, do some research and find out what their caterpillars eat.

Many local councils provide native seedlings to householders free of charge. Forestry authorities, parks and wildlife services and commercial native plant nurseries are all happy to suggest suitable species for your climate and soil type, and advise on spacing and planting.

Most native trees are fast-growing, and if the right species are chosen for local conditions they survive on rainfall alone. But regular access to water is important to birds. If it is not available for drinking and bathing, especially during hot weather or drought, they will desert you.

If you do not have a pool or pond safe from cats, install a birdbath. A pedestal type is best, preferably near an overhanging branch. The bowl should be at least half a metre across and a metre from the ground, but not so high that you cannot easily change the water. Keep it clean and fresh for your own sake, as well as the birds' — stale water breeds mosquitoes.

Ornamental birdbaths are fairly costly. You can improvise your own less elegant version. Erect a length of drainpipe, firmly bedded in the ground. Find a garbage-can lid with a central handle. Tie a weight to the handle and drop it down the pipe, inverting the lid. Then just add water.

In the context of a natural garden it may seem odd to include advice on building nesting boxes. But it may be the only way to encourage smaller birds to nest. Without special shelter they are likely to be bullied by bigger species. If they do manage to nest without your help, their squabs are exposed to predatory currawongs, kookaburras and owls. □

Species	Floor of cavity	Depth of cavity	Entrance height	Entrance diameter
Fairy and tree martins	100 × 100mm	250mm	200mm	38mm
Spotted pardalote	100 × 100mm	250mm	200mm	38mm
Striated pardalote	100 × 100mm	250mm	215mm	40mm
Dusky woodswallow	150 × 150mm	250mm	215mm	50mm
Eastern and western rosellas	180 × 180mm	270mm	220mm	60mm
Rainbow lorikeet	200 × 200mm	270mm	220mm	60mm
Boobook owl	215 × 215mm	460mm	360mm	100mm
Galah	250 × 250mm	610mm	510mm	100mm
Kookaburra	280 × 280mm	610mm	510mm	100mm
Wood duck (site near water)	280 × 300mm	300mm	170mm	130mm

ANIMAL TRACES
Clues to the presence of elusive wildlife

Zoologists working in the field do not rely on live sightings for their knowledge of what animals are where. They are trained to look for other evidence. Droppings — often called 'scats' — provide the richest information. They can be distinguished by size, shape, colour and consistency. Examined closely, they show the make-up of an animal's diet, and how it may vary through the year. Indigestible material such as fur, teeth and insect skeletons in the scats of predators reveals their impact on other wildlife in the area.

On soft surfaces ground-dwellers leave characteristic footprints. Some make recognisable trails through vegetation, or distinctive scrapes at feeding and drinking areas. Burrowers and some other diggers make identifiable holes. Various climbers leave different claw marks in the bark of trees. Higher up, the larvae of unseen insects carve their 'scribbles' under the bark, bore into the wood in special ways, or cause chemical reactions that deform leaves and twigs.

A snake trail at dawn in Yuraygir National Park, northern New South Wales

Koala droppings under a manna gum Eucalyptus viminalis (below)

The hole made by an echidna excavating a meat-ant nest

Dingo tracks on sun-baked mud (main picture)

324

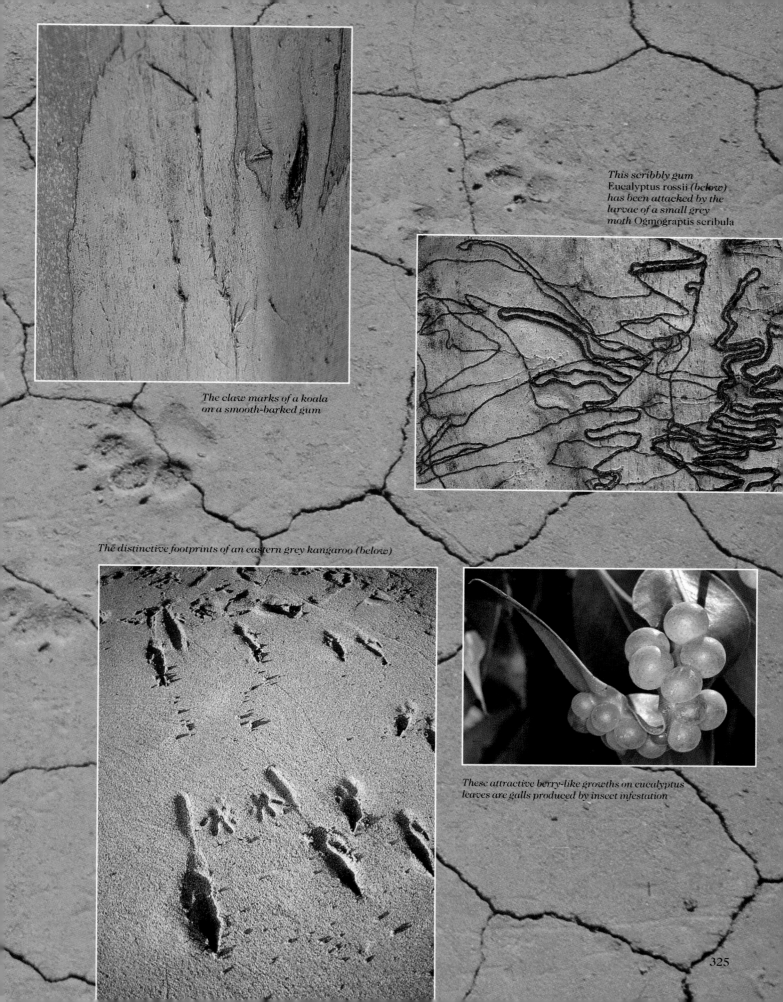

The claw marks of a koala
on a smooth-barked gum

This scribbly gum
Eucalyptus rossii (below)
has been attacked by the
larvae of a small grey
moth Ogmograptis scribula

The distinctive footprints of an eastern grey kangaroo (below)

These attractive berry-like growths on eucalyptus
leaves are galls produced by insect infestation

325

Appendix 1

WHAT'S HAPPENING NOW

JANUARY

In the wetlands of the far north, magpie geese, jacanas, brolgas and pied herons are nesting and laying eggs.

Midsummer is when young platypuses begin to emerge from their burrows. In alpine sphagnum bogs, tiny juvenile corroboree frogs feast on swarms of insects brought out by the mild temperatures. All across Australia, dragonflies are at their most plentiful.

Many eastern grey kangaroos give birth, though last year's joeys still suckle from time to time.

Lace monitors are laying eggs in termites' nests high in trees. The termites repair the damage and so create incubators for the lizards' eggs.

Southwestern Australia's oblong turtles leave evaporating streams and migrate overland to permanent watercourses.

Snakes avoid the heat by seeking refuge in crevices and hunting after dusk. Many that bear live young give birth now.

FEBRUARY

In the Kimberley and Arnhem Land, tiny nabarleks leave their rocky shelters to forage on grasses now plentiful on flooded plains. Agile wallabies graze floodplain margins on overcast days. Further south, wallaby births are reaching their peak. In the rainforests of north Queensland, musky rat-kangaroos are mating.

White cockatoos and long-billed corellas now form their largest flocks to strip feeding sites of seeds, fruits, bulbs and buds. Ravens also congregate in groups to hunt insects. Tropical finches are at the height of their breeding. As their mating season arrives, Gouldian finches change their diet from seeds to insects.

High country butterflies are emerging and breeding. In cool moist hiding-places from southeast Queensland to Tasmania, male funnelweb spiders cautiously approach the females to mate.

Off the east coast, warm waters flowing south bring dugongs to graze off northern New South Wales, also tiger sharks and several kinds of sea snake. Swarms of jelly blubbers, little mauve stingers, sea blubbers and Portuguese men o'war or blue-bottles appear on eastern seaboard beaches.

Black marlin, Spanish mackerel, wahoo and dolphin fish are migrating down the east and west coasts.

MARCH

In the forests and woodlands of the Great Dividing Range south of the Tropic of Capricorn, greater gliders scent-mark trees as courtship and territory signals. In the southeast, young sugar gliders are ejected from family nests. Ringtail possums may start to breed.

While many migratory birds are leaving for their breeding grounds in Asia, painted snipe, bar-shouldered doves, peaceful doves and red-tailed black cockatoos are breeding in the north. Silvereyes head north from Tasmania and Victoria as far as Queensland, flying at night and feeding by day. White-naped honeyeaters leave high country between Melbourne and Canberra for warmer areas inland.

On the southeast tablelands and in Tasmania wingless grasshoppers are breeding, attacking trees and crops as pastures dry off.

Fungi start to appear on damp ground and rotting wood.

APRIL

Black ducks begin courtship displays though they may not mate for several months. Bleak weather and scarcity of food force Tasmania's parrots – the orange-bellied, the blue-winged and the swift – to migrate to the mainland. Now the Wet is over in the far north, hooded and golden-shouldered parrots prepare nesting holes in rain-softened termite mounds. Also nesting are brown, masked and red-footed boobies, logrunners and brahminy kites.

Little red flying foxes are being born, while grey-headed, black and spectacled flying foxes are still mating – their young will be born six months from now.

Large numbers of fishes, such as sea mullet and Australian salmon, are migrating north to spawn.

Newly hatched wolf spiderlings ride on their mothers' backs in layers four deep. White-tailed spider females are brooding eggs in silk sacs.

After autumn rains in the southwest, turtle frogs emerge from burrows to breed. In the east, barred frogs lay their eggs on the banks of streams.

MAY

In Tasmania, eastern quoll males fight savagely before finding females and mating in an act that may last several hours. Mainland spotted-tailed quolls are breeding, while the western quoll or chuditch of the southwest waits for the rainfall at the end of this month before starting to breed.

High up in north Queensland's rainforest trees, white-tailed rats feed on the seeds of the silky oak.

In mallee and mulga scrub from the central West Australian coast to inland New South Wales, malleefowl cocks are beginning to renovate the mounds that will hold next season's eggs five or six months from now. Gang-gang cockatoos come down from highland forests to forage in the urban parks and gardens of the southeast. Pied currawongs, Tasmania's black currawongs, spotted and striated pardalotes, and Richard's pipits are all leaving the coldest areas. Among birds starting to breed now are pink cockatoos, red-winged parrots, the majority of black swans, and red-tailed tropicbirds.

JUNE

Lyrebird males are at their most vocal. Cassowaries court and mate, and female emus lay eggs for the males to incubate. Wedge-tailed eagles, paired for life, may be seen in pre-mating aerobatics. Fairy penguins return to their colonies after long absences feeding out at sea. Cape Barren geese are breeding, and wandering albatrosses and mollymawks may be seen off the southern and eastern coasts.

Huge numbers of blue sharks are brought by the currents to southeastern and southern waters, and shortfin makos move in from the Pacific. Great white sharks travel from the Great Australian Bight to the southwestern and southeastern coasts. Southern bluefin tuna, spawned in Indonesian waters, head south along the west coast.

Wombats and common planigales, nocturnal in summer, now appear by day. Mother wombats may have last year's cub at heel while this year's is in the pouch.

JULY

Echidnas are mating and laying eggs. Bandicoots are bearing young and antechinuses begin intense breeding activity. Swamp wallabies begin to congregate near settlements and forage for scraps as the food supply in their natural habitat dwindles.

Torres Strait imperial-pigeons are migrating south to breed on Cape York. Wompoo fruit-doves, tree martins and fairy martins are also nesting, as are scarlet, red-capped and yellow robins. Port Lincoln parrots are starting to breed, and Australian shelducks are incubating their eggs. Other birds breeding include wattlebirds, miners, friarbirds, scarlet honeyeaters, barking and rufous owls, and white-fronted chats. The hooting of boobook owls increases steadily as last year's young males compete with their elders for territory and mates.

The wallum froglet of southern Queensland is now spawning, and in the far southeast, Verreaux's frog is the only one to be heard calling at this time of year.

AUGUST

In woodland and forests, brushtail possum mothers reject their half-grown offspring before coming into season for the second time in the year. Pygmy-possums too are mating again, except in Tasmania where eastern pygmy-possums are entering their single breeding period. Many native mice are producing young.

Alpine brumbies are giving birth down in the foothills, and soon foals and adults will return to the high plains for summer.

Humpback whales bear calves off Queensland and West Australian coasts. Port Jackson sharks and various cuttlefishes come inshore to breed in the shallows.

Among birds of prey, peregrine falcons are incubating their eggs, and black-breasted buzzards are starting to breed. Ospreys show off to their mates in spectacular courtship flights.

Waders begin to arrive from Siberia – red-necked stints, curlews, sharp-tailed and terek sandpipers. Oystercatchers are one of the native waders starting to breed now.

Cuckoos are spying on prospective hosts so they can judge when to put their own eggs in their victims' nests. Willie wagtails, white-winged choughs, white-backed swallows and butcherbirds are breeding. Welcome swallows and dusky wood-swallows are on the way south to breed. Pink and red-breasted robins are leaving urban gardens for their high-country breeding areas. Fairy-wrens come into brilliant courtship plumage. Red-capped parrots in Western Australia and southern cockatiels are beginning to breed, as well as red-rumped parrots and elegant par-

rots. The booming of tawny frogmouths becomes persistent as they too enter their mating season.

SEPTEMBER

Swamp rats and many water rats begin to breed. Lungfish and salamanderfish are spawning. Near Sydney, juvenile long-finned eels travel by night up the Hawkesbury and Nepean rivers. Migratory lampreys are coming into rivers from the sea to spawn, and Australian bass are also travelling up southeastern rivers.

Pythons and tree snakes are laying their eggs. Gastric-brooding frogs are spawning in streams in Queensland. Also beginning to breed are brown-striped frogs and spotted grass frogs. Stick insect nymphs are emerging from capsules in leaf litter.

Satin bowerbird males rebuild and redecorate their bowers. Catbirds, paradise riflebirds, many lorikeets, rosellas and parrots are breeding. Many flycatchers are returning to southeastern forests and woodlands from wintering in the milder north. Kookaburras are mating and their previous years' offspring are ready to help raise the young. Sacred and collared kingfishers return to their southern breeding grounds. Pacific bazas are courting, and many ducks, spoonbills, egrets, gulls and native terns are also beginning to breed. Migratory birds arriving from the northern hemisphere include Mongolian plovers, ruddy turnstones, bar-tailed godwits and grey-tailed tattlers.

OCTOBER

Young numbats are now independent and brush wallaby joeys are beginning to leave the pouch. Ghost bats near Rockhampton return to the limestone caves they use as maternity ward and nursery. Eastern horseshoe bats are beginning to bear young, and Gould's wattled bats are at the peak of their birthing period.

Freshwater eel-tailed catfishes begin spawning, and jewfish and cobbler males are building their gravel nests. Gudgeon and goby males take on striking nuptial colouring. Black marlin gather to spawn just beyond the Great Barrier Reef. Yellowtail kingfish and snapper are beginning to spawn off the southeastern coast.

In mangrove swamps, fiddler crabs are active during their mating season. Mudcrabs and blue swimmers are also mating now. Chironex box jellyfish are growing fast in tropical coastal waters.

Wasps are pollinating wasp-imitating orchids. In Tasmania and the coldest parts

of Victoria, European and English wasp queens emerge to search for nectar and nesting sites. Worker honey bees are increasingly busy gathering food for the growing numbers of larvae.

Mistletoebirds and painted honeyeaters profit from the abundance of mistletoe berries and start to breed. Courtship peaks among white-headed pigeons and brown cuckoo-doves. Australian pratincoles and clamorous reed-warblers are returning southeast and south from wintering in the north. Other birds breeding include Australasian and little bitterns, little pied cormorants, chestnut teal and white-faced storm-petrels.

NOVEMBER

Dingo pups and Tasmanian devil cubs make their first excursions from their dens. In Western Australia, quokkas are forced to congregate around shrinking waterholes. Smoky mice in the highlands of Victoria change their diet from underground fungi to bogong moths which are arriving in billions. Large-footed mouse-eared bats are at their breeding peak.

On Cape York, palm cockatoos drum with sticks to proclaim territory before courting. Paradise kingfishers return from New Guinea to nest. Other birds breeding now include fruit-doves, beautiful firetails, great crested grebes and white-winged terns. All over Australia, short-tailed shearwaters start laying their eggs in the latter part of this month.

On Great Barrier Reef islands, flatback and loggerhead turtles come ashore to lay eggs. Inland freshwater crocodile eggs are beginning to hatch. In the south, fur seals are breeding.

DECEMBER

In the far north, estuarine crocodiles are laying their eggs.

Koalas of the southeast are at the height of their mating season.

Bent-wing bats across the country are giving birth though northern and southern mating seasons are four months apart.

Cicadas are at their most numerous and shrill. In the north, fireflies start their brief life as adults. Click beetles, jewel beetles and ladybirds appear. Bushfly populations soar. Squat ant-lions have transformed into delicate lacewings. Redback spiders are breeding.

On the Barrier Reef, coral polyps spawn in billions, and parrotfish, wrasse, goatfish and boxfish move to outer reefs to spawn.

Appendix 2
SCIENTIFIC TERMS

Zoologists the world over follow a unified system of naming animals, regardless of local common labels. The first part of a scientific name identifies a **genus** — a basic group of closely related animals. The second part indicates a particular **species**, which in most cases cannot interbreed successfully with any other to produce fertile offspring.

Sometimes a third part distinguishes a **subspecies** that is geographically separate from others and clearly different in appearance or behaviour. So the dingo, for example, is identified as belonging to the genus of all wolves and dogs, *Canis*, the species of all domestic dogs, *familiaris*, and because of its long purebred isolation, the subspecies *dingo*.

Groups of related genera (the plural of genus) are called **families**. Family names end in –idae. They can be used adjectivally with –id endings and are often converted to nouns. From Aphididae, for example, we get aphids, and from Corvidae we get corvids. Families are grouped in **orders** such as the order Hymenoptera, which embraces wasps, bees and ants. Orders are in turn grouped in **classes** — all birds, for example, belong to the class Aves.

Where the name of a genus alone is used in *The Australian Wildlife Year,* it means that the characteristics discussed are common to several species. In picture captions it may be for the sake of brevity or because the species could not be determined without examining the subject.

Other technical terms have been kept to a minimum, and where possible used in an explanatory context. Here are some for which further definition may prove helpful in wider reading:

aestivation: the spending of a period of hot weather in a dormant state, with the rate of metabolism slowed down, and energy and water conserved; the summer counterpart of hibernation.

canopy: the topmost layer of vegetation in dense forest, particularly rainforest, through which only some of the largest trees protrude.

desiccation: the drying out of, for example, the body of an animal, or a fallen leaf.

diapause: a period during which development is suspended, or greatly slowed down. The time and stage at which a diapause occurs is usually characteristic of the species in the area in which it lives; for example, the winter diapause of the larva of a certain moth.

endemic: 1) in plant and animal geography an endemic species is one which at present occurs naturally only in a specific area, though it may have been introduced elsewhere; for example, the platypus is endemic to Australia. 2) in epidemiology, a disease is said to be endemic when it is always present in an area, but rarely at epidemic levels; for example, tuberculosis was once endemic to Australia.

metamorphosis: a change in body form (usually associated with physiological and behavioural changes) during the development of an organism; for example, a caterpillar metamorphoses into a pupa and then into a moth.

phase: when an animal can exist in several different forms, it is said to have different phases; these are often distinguished by colour. In many locust species, for example, crowded specimens develop into the migratory phase, which is browner than the greenish solitary phase, and is differently proportioned in wing and limb .

race: a non-obligatory level in the classification of animals, below the subspecies level. An island, for example, might have its own distinct race of a species of butterfly, which would differ from other races in a permanent way.

understorey: the level of vegetation in a forest consisting of the smaller trees growing beneath the canopy (see **canopy**).

BIBLIOGRAPHY

The following publications have been consulted in the preparation of this book, and are recommended for further reading:

Arid Australia ed. H.G. Cogger and E.E. Cameron (Aust. Museum)
Australia, a Geography: The Natural Environment ed. D.N. Jeans (Sydney University)
The Australian Climatic Environment E. Linacre and J. Hobbs (Wiley)
Australian Encyclopedia ed. John Shaw (Collins)
The Australian Fisherman Harold Vaughan (Landsdowne)
Australian Freshwater Fishes John Merrick and Gunther Schmida (Merrick)
Australian Geographic magazine
Australian Insect Wonders Harry Frauca (Rigby)
Australian Museum Complete Book of Australian Mammals ed. Ronald Strahan (Angus & Robertson)
Australian Native Plants A.M. Blombery (Angus & Robertson)
Australian Natural History magazine (Aust. Museum)
Australian Seashores W.J. Dakin/Isobel Bennett (Angus & Robertson)

Australian Weather A.J. Shields (Jacaranda)
Australia's Butterflies Peter Wilson (Kangaroo)
Beetles of Australia Trevor Hawkeswood (Angus & Robertson)
Bird Wonders of Australia Alec Chisholm (Angus & Robertson)
The Cold-blooded Australians Gunther Schmida (Doubleday)
A Field Companion to Australian Fungi Bruce Fuhrer (Five Mile)
A Field Companion to the Butterflies of Australia and New Zealand Bernard D'Abrera (Five Mile)
A Field Guide to Australian Native Shrubs Ivan Holliday and Geoffrey Watton (Rigby)
A Field Guide to Australian Trees Ivan Holliday and Ron Hill (Rigby)
A Field Guide to Australian Wildflowers Margaret Hodgson and Roland Paine (Rigby)
Fishing Australia Martin Bowerman (Child & Henry)
Freshwater Fishes and Rivers of Australia John S. Lake (Nelson)
The Insects of Australia CSIRO (Melbourne University)

Kakadu: A World Heritage of Unsurpassed Beauty Derrick Ovington (Aust. Govt Publishing Service)
The Koala Anthony Lee and Roger Martin (University of NSW)
Learning About Australian Birds Rosemary Balmford (Collins)
Life in Inland Waters W.D. Williams (Blackwell)
The Living Australia magazine (Bay)
Nightwatchmen of Bush and Plain David Fleay (Jacaranda)
Plants of the Tropical Woodland Mike Clark and Stuart Traynor (Conservation Commission of the NT)
The Platypus Tom Grant (University of NSW)
Reptiles and Amphibians of Australia Harold G. Cogger (Reed)
Sea Snakes Harold Heatwole (University of NSW)
South Australia's Mound Springs ed. John Greenslade, Leo Joseph and Anne Reeves (Nature Conservation Soc. of SA)
Spiders Barbara York Main (Collins)
Toxic Plants and Animals ed. Jeanette Covacevich, Peter Davie and John Pearn (Queensland Museum)

INDEX OF SCIENTIFIC NAMES

GENERAL INDEX

Page references to illustrations are given in *italic* type.

ACKNOWLEDGMENTS

The publishers, editors and author of *The Australian Wildlife Year* are grateful for advice and assistance from staff members of the Australian Museum, the Commonwealth Scientific and Industrial Research Organisation, state and Australian national parks and wildlife services, the Conservation Commission of the Northern Territory, state departments of agriculture and fisheries, the University of Sydney, the James Cook University of North Queensland and the Australian Institute of Marine Science.

The publishers give particular thanks to Auscape International (Auscape) and Australasian Nature Transparencies (ANT), also to the National Photographic Index of Australian Wildlife (NPIAW). Position of photographs on the page: t top, c centre, b bottom, l left, r right. Cover The Photo Library; inset, I R McCann/ANT. Endpapers Kathie Atkinson. 1 Esther Beaton/Auscape. 2-3 J-P Ferrero/Auscape. 4-5 Jiri Lochman/ Auscape. 8-9 Peter Jarver/Auscape. 10 c, Ken Griffiths; b, Reg Morrison/Auscape. 12-13 Peter Jarver/Auscape. 13 Robin Morrison/Reader's Digest. 14 t, D H Harding/Auscape; b, Gunther Deichmann/ Auscape. 15 t, Hans & Judy Beste/ Auscape; c and b, Len Zell. 16 J-P Ferrero/ Auscape. 16-17 The Photo Library. 17 t, Anita Rowney; b, J-P Ferrero/Auscape. 18 tc, A Young/NPIAW; tr, Esther Beaton/ Auscape; c, J-P Ferrero/Auscape; b, Michael Jensen/Auscape. 19 both Hans & Judy Beste/Auscape. 20 t, J-P Ferrero/ Auscape; b, C A Henley/Auscape. 20-1 C A Henley/Auscape. 22-3 Graeme Chapman/ Auscape. 24 c, Kathie Atkinson/Auscape; b, Hans & Judy Beste/Auscape. 24-5 J-P Ferrero/Auscape. 25 t, Graham Robertson/Auscape; c, M W Gillam/ Auscape; b, M P Kahl/Auscape. 26 tl, Reg Morrison/Auscape; tr, C A Henley/ Auscape; b, A Fox/Auscape. 27 t, Gunther Deichmann/Auscape; b, Peter Solness. 28 t, C A Henley/Auscape; b, J-P Ferrero/ Auscape. 29 tc, Graeme Chapman/ Auscape; tr, Hans & Judy Beste/Auscape; b, Michael Jensen/Auscape. 30 t, Graeme Chapman/Auscape; b, M P Kahl/Auscape. 31 t, W G Gillam/Auscape; c, Graeme Chapman; b, Graeme Chapman/Auscape. 32 Reg Morrison/Auscape. 33 tl & tr, G E Schmida; c, J-P Ferrero/Auscape; b, J White/NPIAW. 34 t, G E Schmida; c, G Shea/NPIAW; b, J C Wombey/Auscape. 35 t, G E Schmida; c & b, Bob Mossel. 36 tl & tr, G E Schmida; c & br, David P Maitland/ Auscape; bl, Bob Mossel.37 t, David P Maitland/Auscape; b, Reg Morrison/

Auscape. 38-9 Graham Robertson/ Auscape. 40 t, J-P Ferrero/Auscape; b, M Seyfort/NPIAW. 41 t & br, J-P Ferrero/ Auscape; bl, Hans & Judy Beste/Auscape. 42 t, J-P Ferrero/Auscape; c, Graeme Chapman/Auscape; b, F Woerle/Auscape. 43 tl, Gunther Deichmann/Auscape; tr, cl & cr, Hans & Judy Beste/Auscape; b, J-P Ferrero/Auscape. 44-5 J-P Ferrero/ Auscape. 46-7 C C Pollitt/ANT. 48 J Weigel/ANT. 48-9 J-P Ferrero/Auscape. 49 G E Schmida. 50 Tom & Pam Gardner/ ANT. 51 t, M P Kahl/Auscape; b, J-P Ferrero/Auscape. 52 Esther Beaton/ Auscape. 52-3 J-P Ferrero/Auscape. 53 t & c, J-P Ferrero/Auscape; bl, Grant Dixon/ ANT; br, Ralph & Daphne Keller/ANT. 54 both G E Schmida. 55 t, Robin Morrison/ Reader's Digest; b, G E Schmida. 56 Dave Watts/ANT. 57 J-P Ferrero/Auscape. 58 t, Tony Howard/ANT; b, J-P Ferrero/ Auscape. 59 t & bl, J-P Ferrero/Auscape; br, Esther Beaton/Auscape. 60 G E Schmida. 61 t, D & V Blagden/ANT; b, Klaus Uhlenhut/ANT. 62 t, Otto Rogge/ ANT; b, J-P Ferrero/Auscape. 63 t, Ken Griffiths; b, John Cann/ANT. 64 Ferrero-Labat/Auscape. 65 J Weigel/ANT. 66 t, Hans & Judy Beste/Auscape; b, Ken Griffiths. 67 t, Ken Griffiths; b, I.R. McCann/ANT. 68-9 Otto Rogge/ANT. 70 Ben Cropp/Auscape. 71 E Parer-Cook/ ANT. 72 t, Kathie Atkinson/Auscape; c, Lynn Cropp/Auscape; b, Klaus Uhlenhut/ ANT. 73 t, Kathie Atkinson/Auscape; b, John Cann/ANT. 74 Hans & Judy Beste/ Auscape. 74-5 J-P Ferrero/Auscape. 75 John Cancalosi/Auscape. 76 t, J-P Ferrero/ Auscape; b, Esther Beaton/Auscape. 77 both J-P Ferrero/Auscape. 78 tr, Stuart Chilcott; tl & bl, & 79, Kathie Atkinson. 80 J-P Ferrero/Auscape. 81 Graeme Chapman. 82-3 all Kathie Atkinson. 84 t, Kathie Atkinson; b, David P Maitland. 85 Otto Rogge/ANT. 86-7 C & S Pollitt/ANT. 88 both C A Henley/Auscape. 89 Jim Frazier/ANT. 90 Ralph & Daphne Keller/ ANT. 91 t, M P Kahl/Auscape; b, I R McCann/ANT. 92-3 c, Bruce Fuhrer; rest,

Kathie Atkinson. 94 Kathie Atkinson. 95 Frithfoto/ANT. 96 tl & b, C & S Pollitt/ ANT. 96-7 R Russell/ANT. 97 J-P Ferrero/ Auscape. 98 t, D & V Blagden/ANT; b, Y A Bertrand/Auscape. 99 J-P Ferrero/ Auscape. 100 t, Frithfoto/ANT; bl, D & V Blagden/ANT; br, Brian Chudleigh/ANT. 101 t, Klaus Uhlenhut/ANT; b, A Visage/ Auscape. 102-3 Kathie Atkinson. 104 Otto Rogge/ANT. 105 t, Densey Clyne/ Mantis Wildlife Films; b, J-P Ferrero/ Auscape. 106 t, Otto Rogge/ANT; b, Cyril Webster/ANT. 107 both Klaus Uhlenhut/ ANT. 108 bl, Dave Watts; br, Len Robinson/NPIAW. 108-9 Hans & Judy Beste/Auscape. 109 Glen Threlfo/ Auscape. 110 t, R Roberts/NPIAW; b, F Woerle/Auscape. 110-11 Michael Jensen/ Auscape. 112 t, Ron & Valerie Taylor; b, G E Schmida/ANT. 113 t, Rudie Kuiter/ANT; b, Australasian Marine Photographic Index. 114-15 all Kathie Atkinson. 116 Hans & Judy Beste/Auscape. 116-17 J-P Ferrero/Auscape. 117 Hans & Judy Beste/ Auscape. 118-19 Kathie Atkinson. 120 J-P Ferrero/Auscape. 121 A G Wells/NPIAW. 122 t, J-P Ferrero/Auscape; b, Klaus Uhlenhut/ANT. 123 Kathie Atkinson. 124-5 all Winston Ponder except isopod, inset, Kate Lowe/Australian Museum; goby, G E Schmida; perch, Bob Mossel. 126 Tom & Pam Gardner/ANT. 128 t, Hans & Judy Beste/Auscape; b, Bill Bachman/ANT. 129 t, M P Kahl/Auscape; b, C & S Pollitt/ANT. 130 t, Graeme Chapman/Auscape; b, G D Anderson/ANT. 131 t, M R Gray; b, Densey Clyne/Mantis Wildlife Films. 132-3 J-P Ferrero/Auscape. 134 courtesy Alan Jones Pty Ltd. 135 t, Frank Park/ANT; b, Hans & Judy Beste/ Auscape. 136 J-P Ferrero/Auscape. 137 Frithfoto/ANT. 138 t, F Woerle/Auscape; b, Graham Robertson/Auscape. 139 Otto Rogge/ANT. 140 t, J-P Ferrero/Auscape; b, M F Soper/NPIAW. 140-1 A Eames/ NPIAW. 141 J-P Ferrero/Auscape. 142 Ron & Valerie Taylor/ANT. 143 t, Howard Hall; b, Kevin Williams. 144 Ron & Valerie Taylor/ANT. 145 Dave Watts/ANT. 146

C A Henley/NPIAW. 147 t, John Cancalosi/ Auscape; b, Andrew Dennis/ANT. 148-9 C A Henley/Auscape. 150 D Parer & E Parer-Cook/Auscape. 150-1 G E Schmida. 152 Kathie Atkinson. 153 t, C & S Pollitt/ANT; b, Dave Watts/ANT. 154 t, J-P Ferrero/ Auscape; b, D Whitford/ANT. 155 G E Schmida. 156 t, Dave Watts/ANT; bl, Pavel German/ANT; br, Frithfoto/ANT. 157 t, Bill Bachman/ANT; bl, Dave Watts/ ANT; br, J C Wombey/Auscape. 158 Frithfoto/ANT. 159 t, D Whitford/ANT; b, G Weber/NPIAW. 160 t, J-P Ferrero/ Auscape; b, Hans & Judy Beste/Auscape. 161 t, Frank Park/ANT; b, Cyril Webster/ ANT. 162 t, Hans & Judy Beste/Auscape; b, Graeme Chapman/Auscape. 164 both Hans & Judy Beste/Auscape. 165 t, Kathie Atkinson/ Auscape; b, D & V Blagden/ANT. 166-7 Hans & Judy Beste/Auscape. 168 J & P Olson/Auscape. 169 D Hollands/ANT. 170 J & L Cupper/Auscape. 171 J-P Ferrero/ Auscape. 172 Tom & Pam Gardner/ANT. 173 t, M P Kahl/Auscape; b, Tom & Pam Gardner/ANT. 174 Cyril Webster/ANT. 175 t, N Chaffer/NPIAW; b, M P Kahl/ Auscape. 176 t, D & V Blagden/ANT; b, Michael Jensen/ANT. 177 t, I.R. McCann/ANT; b, Kathie Atkinson. 178 l, M P Kahl/Auscape; r, Graham Robertson/ Auscape. 179 t, Hans & Judy Beste/ Auscape; b, R Drummond/NPIAW. 180 tc, J-P Ferrero/Auscape; tr, Tom & Pam Gardner/NPIAW. 180-1 Reg Morrison/ Auscape. 181 tl & br, C A Henley/ Auscape; tr, M Seyfort/NPIAW; cl, Esther Beaton/Auscape; cr, Hans & Judy Beste/ Auscape; bl, Otto Rogge/ANT. 182 Ralph & Daphne Keller/ANT. 183 t, I R McCann/ ANT; b, F Woerle/Auscape. 184 t, D Whitford/ANT; b, D Parer & E Parer-Cook/ Auscape. 185 t, Esther Beaton/Auscape; b, Ralph & Daphne Keller/ANT. 186 Reg Morrison/Auscape. 187 Kevin Deacon/ Auscape. 188-9 R J Allingham/ANT. 190 G E Schmida. 191 t, G E Schmida; b, J-P Ferrero/Auscape. 192 t, G E Schmida; b, G E Schmida/ANT. 193 t, G E Schmida/ ANT; b, J-P Ferrero/Auscape. 194 t, Esther Beaton/Auscape; b, C A Henley/ Auscape. 195 t, G D Anderson/ANT; b, Hans & Judy Beste/Auscape. 196 t, Peter Krauss/ANT; b, Hans & Judy Beste/ Auscape. 197 t, Mike Tinsley/Auscape; b, G E Schmida/ANT. 198 t, D Parer & E Parer-Cook/Auscape; c, Robert W G Jenkins/ANT; b, Hans & Judy Beste/ Auscape. 199 t, S Wilson/ANT; c, M P Kahl/Auscape. 200 t, David P Maitland; b, Otto Rogge/ANT. 201 Tom & Pam Gardner/ANT. 202 t, Glen Threlfo/ Auscape; b, Ralph & Daphne Keller/ANT.

203 t, Glen Threlfo/Auscape; b, Hans & Judy Beste/Auscape. 204 t, Tom & Pam Gardner/NPIAW; b, T Howard/NPIAW. 205 t, R E Viljoen/NPIAW; b, Hans & Judy Beste/Auscape. 206 t, Dave Watts/ANT; b, I R McCann/ANT. 207 t, Keith K Vagg/ ANT; b, R J Allingham/ANT. 208 Jim Frazier/ANT. 209 t, Glen Threlfo/ Auscape; b, J & L Cupper/Auscape. 210 & 210-11 all G E Schmida. 211 c & bc, Kathie Atkinson. 212 M P Kahl/Auscape. 213 t, J-P Ferrero/Auscape; bl, M P Kahl/ Auscape; br, Tom & Pam Gardner/ANT. 214 t, J-P Ferrero/Auscape; b, J-M Labat/ Auscape. 215 t, Hans & Judy Beste/ Auscape; b, J-P Ferrero/Auscape. 216 l, D Parer & E Parer-Cook; r, Dave Watts/ANT. 217 t, Tony Howard/ANT; b, Francois Gohier/Auscape. 218 t, Graham Robertson/Auscape; b, Brian Chudleigh/ ANT. 219 t, Brian Chudleigh/ANT; bl, Tom & Pam Gardner/ANT; br, Brett Gregory/Auscape. 220-1 Graeme Chapman/Auscape. 222 Densey Clyne/ ANT. 223 Densey Clyne/Mantis Wildlife Films. 224 tl, C A Henley/Auscape; tr & bl, Densey Clyne/Mantis Wildlife Films; br, David Maitland/Auscape. 225 t, Densey Clyne/Mantis Wildlife Films; b, A & J Six/ Auscape. 226 Densey Clyne/Mantis Wildlife Films. 226-7 C A Henley/ Auscape. 227 Densey Clyne/Mantis Wildlife Films. 228-9 all Densey Clyne/ Mantis Wildlife Films. 230-1 all Densey Clyne/Mantis Wildlife Films. 232 both C A Henley/Larus Natural History Photographs. 233 t, Densey Clyne/Mantis Wildlife Films; b, Brett Gregory/Auscape. 234 t, C A Henley/Larus Natural History Photographs; b, Densey Clyne/Mantis Wildlife Films. 235 D & V Blagden/ANT. 236 tl, M P Kahl/Auscape; c, Hans & Judy Beste/Auscape; b, Kathie Atkinson/ Auscape. 236-7 T G Lowe. 237 tr, M P Kahl/Auscape; c, Hans & Judy Beste/ Auscape; b, Graeme Chapman/Auscape. 238 K Ireland/NPIAW. 239 t, Glen Threlfo/Auscape; bl, Graeme Chapman/ Auscape; br, J-P Ferrero/Auscape. 240 J Warham/NPIAW. 241 t, Hans & Judy Beste/Auscape; b, J Purnell/NPIAW. 242 t, Graeme Chapman/NPIAW; b, Hans & Judy Beste/Auscape. 243 A J Olney/NPIAW. 244 C A Henley/Auscape. 245 c & b, J-P Ferrero/Auscape; tr, Hans & Judy Beste/ Auscape. 246 t & br, C A Henley/Larus Natural History Photographs; bl, C A Henley/Auscape. 247 Kathie Atkinson. 248 J-P Ferrero/Auscape. 249 t, Kevin Deacon/Auscape; b, Ben Cropp/Auscape. 250-1, 252 G E Schmida. 253 t & c, J-P Ferrero/Auscape; b, G E Schmida. 254-5

G E Schmida. 256 J-P Ferrero/Auscape. 256-7 Kathie Atkinson/Auscape. 258-9 all J-P Ferrero/Auscape. 260 C A Henley/ NPIAW. 261 Hans & Judy Beste/Auscape. 262 Hans & Judy Beste/Auscape. 262-3 Esther Beaton/Auscape. 263 J-P Ferrero/ Auscape. 264-5 J-P Ferrero/Auscape. 266 t, J-P Ferrero/Auscape; bl, G A & M M Hoye/NPIAW; br, G B Baker/NPIAW. 267 t, J-P Ferrero/Auscape; b, Ken Griffiths. 268 J-P Ferrero/Auscape. 269 t, Klaus Uhlenhut/ANT; b, Graham Wood. 270 t, Hans & Judy Beste/Auscape; b, Graeme Chapman. 271 J-P Ferrero/Auscape. 272-3 tl, R Slater/NPIAW; rest, G E Schmida. 274 Kerrie Ruth/Auscape. 276 t, Hans & Judy Beste/Auscape; bl & br, Densey Clyne/Mantis Wildlife Films. 277 tl, C A Henley/Auscape; cl & br, David P Maitland/Auscape; tr, Hans & Judy Beste/ Auscape; bl, Densey Clyne/Mantis Wildlife Films. 278-9 all Densey Clyne/Mantis Wildlife Films. 280-1 all G E Schmida. 282-3 F Woerle/Auscape. 284-5 both Peter Fell. 286 Peter Fell. 287 C & S Pollitt/ANT. 288 G D Anderson/ANT. 289 G B Baker/ANT. 290 t, Graeme Chapman; b, C A Henley/NPIAW. 291 t, Graeme Chapman/Auscape; b, E E Zillmann/ NPIAW. 292 tl, J A Bailey-Ardea/NPIAW; tr, J-P Ferrero/Auscape; b, Graeme Chapman/Auscape. 293 t, Graeme Chapman; b, Tom & Pam Gardner/ NPIAW. 294 D B Carter/ANT. 296 tl, Gunther Deichmann/Auscape; tr, Kevin Deacon/Auscape; c & b, J-P Ferrero/ Auscape. 297 t, C A Henley/Auscape; b, Gunther Deichmann/Auscape. 298 Hans & Judy Beste/Auscape. 299 t, T J Hawkeswood/ANT; b, Ivan Polunin/ANT. 300 tl & br, Kathie Atkinson; tr, C A Henley/Auscape; bc, Ken Griffiths. 301 c, I R McCann/ANT; tr, Cyril Webster/ANT; b, David P. Maitland/Auscape. 302 Kathie Atkinson. 303 Densey Clyne/Mantis Wildlife Films. 304 Robin Morrison/ Reader's Digest. 306-7 David P. Maitland/ Auscape. 308-9 Peter Harrison. 310 Bette Willis. 311 Peter Harrison. 312-13 Kathie Atkinson. 314 Esther Beaton/Auscape. 316 both Kathie Atkinson. 317 tl, Sarah Wing/Auscape; tr & br, Kathie Atkinson; bl, Harry Frauca/Auscape. 318-19 all Kathie Atkinson. 320 J-M Labat/Auscape. 319 all C A Henley/Auscape. 322-3 all J-P Ferrero/Auscape. 324 tr, Brett Gregory/ Auscape; l & b, Esther Beaton/Auscape. 324-5 background, Kathie Atkinson. 325 tl, Esther Beaton/Auscape; tr, J-P Ferrero/ Auscape; bl, Kathie Atkinson; br, David P Maitland/Auscape.

Typesetting by Keyset Phototype Pty Ltd, Sydney
Colour separation by Curman Lithographics Pty Ltd, Sydney
Printed and bound by Dai Nippon Printing Co. (H.K.) Ltd, Hong Kong